Conflict Transformation and Reconciliation

This book examines approaches to reconciliation and peacebuilding in settler colonial, post-conflict, and divided societies.

In contrast to current literature, this book provides a broader assessment of reconciliation and conflict transformation by applying a distinctive 'multi-level' approach. The analysis provides a unique intervention in the field, one that significantly complicates received notions of reconciliation and transitional justice, and considers conflict transformation across the constitutional, institutional, and relational levels of society. Drawing on extensive fieldwork in South Africa, Northern Ireland, Australia, and Guatemala, the work presents an interdisciplinary study of the complex political challenges facing societies attempting to transition either from violence and authoritarianism to peace and democracy, or from colonialism to post-colonialism. Informed by theories of agonistic democracy, the book conceives of reconciliation as a process that is deeply political, and that prioritizes the capacity to retain and develop democratic political contest in societies that have, in other ways, been able to resolve their conflicts. The cases considered suggest that reconciliation is more likely an open-ended process rather than a goal—a process that requires divided societies to pay ongoing attention to reconciliatory efforts at all levels, long after the eyes of the world have moved on from countries where the work of reconciliation is thought to be finished.

This book will be of great interest to students of reconciliation, conflict transformation, peacebuilding, transitional justice, and IR in general.

Sarah Maddison is Associate Professor in the School of Social and Political Sciences at the University of Melbourne. Recent publications include *Beyond White Guilt* (2011) and *Unsettling the Settler State* (with Morgan Brigg, 2011).

Routledge Studies in Peace and Conflict Resolution
Series Editors: Tom Woodhouse and Oliver Ramsbotham
University of Bradford

Conflict Transformation and Reconciliation

Multi-level challenges in deeply divided societies

Sarah Maddison

Routledge
Taylor & Francis Group

LONDON AND NEW YORK

First published 2016 by Routledge

2 Park Square, Milton Park, Abingdon, Oxon OX14 4RN
711 Third Avenue, New York, NY 10017, USA

Routledge is an imprint of the Taylor & Francis Group, an informa business

First issued in paperback 2017

British Library Cataloguing-in-Publication Data
A catalogue record for this book is available from the British Library

Library of Congress Cataloging-in-Publication Data
Maddison, Sarah.
Conflict transformation and reconciliation : multi-level challenges in
deeply divided societies / Sarah Maddison.
   pages cm. – (Routledge studies in peace and conflict resolution)
   Includes bibliographical references and index.
   1. Postwar reconstruction. 2. Peace-building. 3. Reconciliation.
   I. Title.
   HV639.M34 2016
   363.34'988–dc23   2015002975

ISBN: 978-0-415-71159-3 (hbk)
ISBN: 978-1-138-07137-7 (pbk)

Typeset in Baskerville
by Wearset Ltd, Boldon, Tyne and Wear

Maddison perceptively and convincingly argues against the view of reconciliation as a utopian state where conflict is absent, and instead emphasizes the role of agonistic relationship in constructing a shared polity where disagreements and tension remain part of democracies and post conflict societies. The book is essential to scholars and practitioners who search for a more realistic understanding of conflict resolution and reconciliation.

Elazar Barkan, *Columbia University, USA*

Maddison writes that she hopes that this book will facilitate a deeper understanding of reconciliation in countries scarred by histories of violence and oppression. Maddison eloquently achieves this aim by presenting a complex understanding of reconciliation at the constitutional, institutional and relational levels. Through rich and original comparative material primarily focusing on South Africa, Australia, Guatemala and Northern Ireland, Maddison leaves the reader with a profound sense of the complexity of what it takes to build meaningful conflict transformation and reconciliation. Through in-depth interview work with a range of stakeholders, Maddison charts a way forward, both at the micro and macro levels, for those grappling with the challenges of coming out of conflict. The insights contained in *Conflict Transformation and Reconciliation* means it should be a key reference point for practitioners, academics and policy makers working in and with societies transitioning from a legacy of political violence.

Brandon Hamber, *Ulster University, Northern Ireland*

Contents

Abbreviations

AECG	Aboriginal Education Consultative Group
ANC	African National Congress
ANTaR	(formerly) Australians for Native Title and Reconciliation
ASC	*Asamblea de la Sociedad Civil* (Assembly of Civil Society)
ATSIC	Aboriginal and Torres Strait Islander Commission
BEE	Black Economic Empowerment
CACIF	*Comité de Asociaciones Agricolas, Comerciales, Industriales y Financieras* (The Committee of Agricultural, Commercial, Industrial, and Financial Associations)
CAR	Council for Aboriginal Reconciliation
CBI	Northern Ireland Confederation of British Industry
CEH	*Comisión para el Esclarecimiento Histórico* (the Commission for Historical Clarification)
CI	Controlled Integrated (schools)
CNR	National Reconciliation Commission Guatemala
CODESA	Convention for a Democratic South Africa
CONAVIGUA	*Comité Nacional de Viudas de Guatemala* (the National Committee of Widows of Guatemala)
CRC	Community Relations Council
DIGEBI	*Dirección General de Educación Bilingüe Intercultural* (The General Directorate of Intercultural Bilingual Education)
EMU	Education for Mutual Understanding
FRG	*Frente Republicano Guatamalteco* (Guatemalan Republican Front)
GEAR	The policy of Growth, Employment and Redistribution
GMI	Grant Maintained Integrated (schools)
HET	Historical Enquiries Team
IJR	Institute for Justice and Reconciliation
ILO	International Labour Organization
ILUA	Indigenous Land Use Agreement
IMF	International Monetary Fund
MINUGUA	*Misión de Verificación de las Naciones Unidas de Guatemala* (the UN Verification Mission in Guatemala)

NDR	National Democratic Revolution
NGOs	Non-Government Organisations
NIHE	Northern Ireland Housing Executive
NIWC	Northern Ireland Women's Coalition
OAS	The Organization of American States
OBE	Outcomes Based Education
PAC	*Patrullas de Autodefensa Civil* (the Civil Defense Patrols)
PAN	*Partido de Avanzada Nacional* (the National Progress Party)
PDMU	Personal Development and Mutual Understanding
PN	*Policía Nacional* (National Police)
PNC	*Policía Nacional Civil* (National Civilian Police)
PRONADE	*Programa Nacional de Autogestión para el Desarrollo Educativo* (The National Programme for Educational Development)
PSNI	Police Service of Northern Ireland
RA	Reconciliation Australia
RAP	Reconciliation Action Plans
RCIADIC	Royal Commission into Aboriginal Deaths in Custody
RDP	Reconstruction and Development Programme
REMHI	*Proyecto Interdiocesano Recuperación de la Memoria Histórica* (Recovery of Historical Memory Project)
RUC	Royal Ulster Constabulary
SACC	South African Council of Churches
TRC	South African Truth and Reconciliation Commission
UN	United Nations
UNDP	United Nations Development Programme
URNG	*Unidad Revolucionaria Nacional Guatemalteca* (Guatemalan National Revolutionary Unity)

List of interviewees

Northern Ireland

Eamonn Baker is Training Director with Towards Understanding and Healing.

Shona Bell is Programme Manager at the Corrymeela Community and previously Assistant Director at TIDES Training.

Sara Cook works as the Director of Compass, with East Belfast Mission, and is the former Coordinator of Towards Understanding and Healing.

Michael Culbert is a former IRA prisoner and later a member of the Victim's Forum. He is now a director of Coiste na nIarchimí, an organization working with the political ex prisoner community in Ireland.

Owen Donnelly has worked in the community sector since 1997, focusing primarily on community development and community relations. He is currently Training Development Officer at the Peace and Reconciliation Group.

Brian Dougherty is the Director of St Columb's Park House Centre for Reconciliation.

Barry Fennell is the Project Manager of the Family and Community Engagement Project at Co-operation Ireland.

Gerry Foster is a former INLA (republican) prisoner now involved in the From Prison to Peace Partnership.

Paul Hutchinson is the former Centre Director of Corrymeela.

Neil Jarman (PhD) is the director of the Institute for Conflict Research.

Alan Largey (PhD) is the New Technologies Manager in the Family and Community Engagement Project at Co-operation Ireland.

Mary Lynch is the director of Mediation Northern Ireland.

Brendan McAllister is a Senior Associate at mediatEUr. He was Victims Commissioner between 2008 and 2012 and prior to that was the director of Mediation Northern Ireland.

Roisin McGlone is Chief Executive Officer of InterAction Belfast.

Martin McMullan is Assistant Director at YouthAction Northern Ireland.

Ray Mullan is Director of Communications at the Community Relations Council.

Pádraig Ó Tuama is an Irish poet and theologian. In 2014, he was appointed as Leader of the Corrymeela Community.

Jim O'Neill is the Dialogue Development worker Community Dialogue and co-chair of Towards Understanding and Healing.

Katy Radford (PhD) MBE is Project Manager and Senior Researcher at the Institute for Conflict Research.

Jayme Reaves worked as Project Coordinator and Consultant for Healing Through Remembering from 2006 to 2014. She current works as a Community Advisor for Dorset Community Action in England.

Bill Shaw is the director of the 174 Trust, an organization involved in conflict resolution and social justice advocacy.

Trevor Temple is the historical researcher at the Diamond War Memorial Project, based in the Holywell Trust.

Kate Turner is the Director of Healing Through Remembering.

Wilhelm Verwoerd, originally from South Africa where he was a researcher in the Truth and Reconciliation Commission, was interviewed in his former role as facilitator within the Glencree Survivors and Former Combatants programme. He has since returned to South Africa and is currently a Director of Beyond Walls Ltd.

Séanna Walsh (Breathnach) is a former IRA prisoner and now works with *Coiste na nIarchimí*, an organization working with the political ex prisoner community in Ireland.

Michelle Wilson works in the Communities and Policing in Transition Project at Intercomm Belfast.

Derick Wilson is Reader Emeritus in Education (Restorative Practices) at University of Ulster. Derick helped establish Future Ways (1985–2006) and has been a member of the Corrymeela Community since 1965.

Australia

Leah Armstrong is a Torres Strait Islander, former Chief Executive Officer of Reconciliation Australia and currently on the Prime Minister's Indigenous Advisory Council.

Linda Burney was a Member of the Council for Aboriginal Reconciliation. She is the first Aboriginal person elected to the New South Wales Parliament (in 2003). She is of Wiradjuri descent.

Fred Chaney was Minister for Aboriginal Affairs from 1978 to1980. He is a former deputy president of the Australian Native Title Tribunal and on the Board of Directors of Reconciliation Australia.

Tim Gartrell is Joint Campaign Director for Recognise, former Chief Executive Officer of the Indigenous employment advocacy group GenerationOne, and a former National Secretary of the Australian Labor Party.

Jason Glanville was Chief Executive Officer of the National Centre of Indigenous Excellence and former Director of Programs and Strategy at Reconciliation Australia. He is of the Wiradjuri peoples from southwestern New South Wales.

Mick Gooda is the Aboriginal and Torres Strait Islander Social Justice Commissioner at the Australian Human Rights Commission, and a descendent of the Gangulu people of central Queensland.

Gary Highland is a former National Director of ANTaR (formerly Australians for Native Title and Reconciliation).

Janet Hunt is Deputy Director at the Centre for Aboriginal Economic Policy Research at the Australian National University ANU and is a past National President of ANTaR (formerly Australians for Native Title and Reconciliation).

Cheryl Kernot was a Member of the Council for Aboriginal Reconciliation. She is a former Leader of the Australian Democrats and a Labor shadow minister from 1998–2001. She currently works in the Centre for Social Impact at the University of New South Wales.

Peter Lewis (PhD) is the Aboriginal and Torres Strait Islander Peoples' Rights Advocacy Lead for Oxfam Australia and National President of ANTaR (formerly Australians for Native Title and Reconciliation).

Les Malezer is Co-Chair of the National Congress of Australia's First Peoples and former Chair of the Foundation for Aboriginal and Islander Research Action (FAIRA). He is of the Butchulla/Gubbi Gubbi peoples in southeast Queensland.

Florence Onus is former chairperson of the Aboriginal and Torres Strait Islander Healing Foundation and is a descendent of the Birri-Gubba and Kairi/Bidjara peoples.

Jacqueline Phillips was the National Director of Australians for Native Title and Reconciliation (ANTaR) from 2010 to 2013. She is currently Director of Policy at the Australian Council of Social Service (ACOSS).

Sharona Torrens is the Group Manager, Programs and Partnerships at Reconciliation Australia.

Leanne Townsend is Chief Executive Officer of the National Aboriginal Sporting Chance Academy and is the former Chief Executive Officer of the New South Wales Reconciliation Council. She is a descendant of the Aniwan people of northern New South Wales.

Guatemala

Miguel Ángel Balcárcel is Director of the National Dialogue System and director of the Multiparty Dialogue project with the UNDP. He was previously the General Secretary of the National Reconstruction Committee.

Julio Arnoldo Balconi Turcios is a former general in the Guatemalan armed forces, with 34 years service. He was National Defence Minister and a member of the Peace Commission of the Government from 1991 to 1996. He currently serves as Specific Advisor of the Executive Secretary of the Coordinator for Reduction Disaster.

María Rosenda Camey Huz is Founder of *El Grupo de Mujeres Mayas Kaqla* (Mayan Women's Kaqla Group) and is the Executive Director of the *Centro de Documentación e Investigación Maya* (CEDIM).

Gustavo Porras Castejón was President of the Peace Commission of the Government of the Republic during the last phase of negotiations and is now Chairman to the Economic and Social Council of Guatemala.

Otilia Lux De Cotí is the Executive Director of *Foro Internacional de Mujeres Indígenas* (International Indigenous Women's Forum) (FIMI). She is a former Commissioner for Historical Clarification and a former member of Congress of the Republic of Guatemala. She served as Vice President of the United Nations Permanent Forum on Indigenous Issues from 2001 to 2007. She is a Maya Quiche indigenous woman.

Doris Cruz is the Program Director for the Guatemala programme of the Netherlands Institute for Multiparty Democracy (NIMD).

Irma Alicia Velásquez Nimatuj (PhD) is Executive Director of the *Mecanismo de Apoyo a los Pueblos Indígenas* (Support Mechanism for Indigenous Peoples). She is a Maya K'iche woman from Quetzaltenango.

Arnoldo Noriega was a negotiator of the Guatemalan Peace Accords, founder and coordinator of the *Comisión de Acompañamiento de los Acuerdos de Paz* and founder of the National System for Permanent Dialogue of the Presidency of the Republic.

Elena Díez Pinto (PhD) led the Democratic Dialogue Regional Project of UNDP for Latin America and the Caribbean. From 1997 to 2000 she headed the multi-stakeholder dialogue process Visión Guatemala.

Alvaro Pop is founder and president of *Organismo Naleb*, was head of the Indigenous Electoral Observation Mission in Guatemala in 1999, 2003, 2007 and 2011, and is an Independent Expert and vice president of the UN Permanent Forum on Indigenous Issues. He is Maya Q'eqchi.

Mariel Aguilar Sanchez is an expert in intersectoral dialogue practice and a conflict resolution consultant for Interpeace in Guatemala.

Daniel Saquec is principal Technical Advisor of *El Programa Maya*, part of the United Nations Development Programme (UNDP).

Carlos Sarti is Executive Director of *Fundación Popaz*.

Julio Solórzano-Foppa is Chair of the Concord Memorial Project for the victims of Armed Internal Conflict in Guatemala (1960–1996) and established *ONG Arte y Cultura para el Desarrollo* (Art and Culture for Development NGO) in Guatemala.

Ana Glenda Tager Rosado is the Director of the Interpeace Regional Office for Latin America.

Catalina Soberanis has held a number of roles relevant to Guatemala's peace process, including as the coordinator of the *Comisión de Acompañamiento de los Acuerdos de Paz*. She spent nine years in Congress, including as Minister of Work and Social Prevention, and Presidential Secretary for Peace.

José Suasnavar is the Deputy Director of *the Fundación de Antropología Forense de Guatemala*, where he investigates and documents civil War human rights violations.

Rosalina Tuyuc Velásquez is one of the co-founders of the *Coordinadora Nacional de Viudas de Guatemala* (National Association of Guatemalan Widows – CONAVIGUA). She is also a former congressional deputy and former Senior Vice President of the Guatemalan Congress and former President of the *Comisión Nacional de Resarcimiento*. She is a Maya Kaqchikel.

Adrian Zapata is professor in the Faculty of Agronomy, USAC in the Area of Social Sciences and Rural Development. He has participated in multistakeholder dialogue processes including *Visión Guatemala* and was the Cabinet Executive Secretary for Rural Development.

Raquel Zelaya is the Executive Director of the think tank *Asociación de Investigación y Estudios Sociales* (Association of Investigation and Social Studies) and is a former Secretary of Peace and Minister of Finance.

South Africa

Rebecca Freeth is a dialogue facilitator and writer. She runs Just Facilitation, is a senior associate with Reos Social Innovation and teaches at the Sustainability Institute.

Steven Friedman (PhD) is Professor and Director of the Centre for the Study of Democracy at the University of Johannesburg and Rhodes University.

Shirley Gunn is Executive Director of the Human Rights Media Centre and a board member on the Khulumani Support Group.

Verne Harris is Director of Research and Archive at the Nelson Mandela Foundation, former Deputy Director of the National Archives and participant in the Truth and Reconciliation Commission.

Sello Hatang is Chief Executive of the Nelson Mandela Centre of Memory, former senior manager at South Africa's Human Rights Commission, and provided archival support for the Truth and Reconciliation Commission.

Stan Henkeman is head of the Building an Inclusive Society Programme at the Institute for Justice and Reconciliation and former Programme Manager: Western Cape at Operation HOPE.

Lucy Holborn is the former Research Manager at the South African Institute of Race Relations.

Haniff Hoosen is a Member of Parliament where he is the Democratic Alliance's Shadow Minister for Home Affairs. He was a participant in the Dinokeng Scenario Project.

Adam Kahane is Chairman, North America of Reos Partners, and was the lead facilitator of the Mont Fleur and Dinokeng scenario projects.

Catherine Kennedy is the director of the South African History Archive an independent activist archive based at Constitution Hill in Johannesburg.

Kallie Kriel is the Chief Executive Officer of AfriForum and was a participant in the Dinokeng Scenario Project.

Fr Michael Lapsley is the director of the Institute for Healing of Memories and former Chaplain of the Trauma Centre for Victims of Violence and Torture.

Kate Lefko-Everett is a Senior Researcher and Consultant at Mthente Research and Consulting Services and was formerly the Senior Project Leader for the Reconciliation Barometer at the Institute for Justice and Reconciliation.

Kenneth Lukuko is Senior Project Leader for the Building an Inclusive Society Programme's Community Healing Project at the Institute for Justice and Reconciliation.

Thabane Vincent Maphai (PhD) is a businessman, independent political analyst and former academic who has worked in a range of South African companies including South African Breweries. He was a convenor for the Dinokeng Scenario Project.

Rick Menell has over 35 years experience in the mining industry and is Founding Co-Chairman of the City Year SA Youth Service Organisation. He was a convenor the Dinokeng Scenario Project.

Namhla Mniki-Mangaliso is the Director of African Monitor, an organization that monitors development commitments across Africa. She was a participant in the Dinokeng Scenario Project.

Tim Murithi (PhD) heads the Justice and Reconciliation in Africa Programme at the Institute for Justice and Reconciliation.

Ollen Mwalubunju is formerly a Senior Manager in the Conflict Intervention and Peacebuilding Support Project at the Centre for Conflict Resolution in South Africa. He is now the Director of the National Initiative for Civic Education in Malawi.

Kindiza Ngubeni is a Senior Community Facilitator at the Centre for the Study of Violence and Reconciliation.

Ayanda Nyoka is the Project Leader of Inclusive Economies at Institute for Justice and Reconciliation.

Oscar Siwali is a former senior project officer in the Mediation and Training Services project at Centre for Conflict Resolution.

Raenette Taljaard is a Senior Lecturer in the Political Studies Department of the University of Cape Town. She is a former Member of the South African Parliament and former Director of the Helen Suzman Foundation.

Hanif Vally is Deputy Director at the Foundation for Human Rights.

Hugo van der Merwe (PhD) is the Head of Research at the Centre for the Study of Violence and Reconciliation.

Undine Whande was a Senior Specialist for Conflict Transformation and Organisational Learning for the Centre for the Study of Violence and Reconciliation and now works as a senior leadership coach.

Acknowledgements

The research for this book has been an extraordinary adventure, involving fieldwork in four countries over four years, and interviews with over 80 individuals and organizations. During this time I have relied on support and assistance from many, many people, all of who deserve my most sincere thanks.

First, however, I would like to acknowledge the traditional owners of the land on which I lived and worked for all but the last six months of this project: the Gadigal people of the Eora nation whose lands now form part of the Sydney area. I pay my sincere respects to the elders and ancestors of the Eora nation.

I offer my deepest thanks to the many reconciliation actors, working in challenging contexts in each of the four countries in this study, who agreed to share their time and their irreplaceable insight in interviews with me. Every effort was made to provide each interviewee with the opportunity to review their interview transcript and/or drafts of the book itself. In a few cases this has not been possible. While I am certain that all quotes are an accurate reflection of our conversations, any errors in interpretation are my own.

I am grateful to the Australian Research Council for making this research possible through their mid-career focused Future Fellowships scheme (grant number FT100100253).

During the period of research for this book I spent time at the Wits Institute for Social and Economic Research (WiSER) at the University of Witwatersrand in Johannesburg, at the International Conflict Research Institute (INCORE) at the University of ULSTER in Derry/Londonderry, and finally as a visiting scholar at the Institute for the Study of Human Rights at Columbia University in New York, where the bulk of this manuscript was written. I would like to thank colleagues at each of these institutions for their interest and engagement in my work. As it developed, parts of this work were also presented in seminars at Columbia University and the Australian National University, and at conferences including the International Political Science Association Congresses in 2012 and 2014, at the Australian Political Science Association conferences in 2012 and 2013, and at a European Political Science Association Consortium joint session on transitional justice in 2013. I thank all fellow presenters and participants for their comments and questions, which have helped to strengthen this work immensely. I am also grateful for critical commentary received from colleagues who read earlier drafts of this work, notably Elazar Barkan, Tom Clark, and Adrian Little.

I would like to thank the editors of the Routledge Series Studies in Peace and Conflict Resolution, Tom Woodhouse and Oliver Ramsbotham, for their enthusiasm for this book when it was proposed to them, and also Andrew Humphreys and Hannah Ferguson at Routledge for steering the manuscript so carefully through to publication.

Other individuals have also been essential to completing this work. In Guatemala, Sonia González was instrumental in providing introductions to key people and in ensuring that the necessary interpreting services were in place when I needed them. I cannot thank her enough. In Australia, Nick Apoifis provided outstanding research assistance during the final year of the project.

Finally, to my family: my adult children Sam and Eliza have again put up with a preoccupied mother, and even shown some interest in the research. Sam accompanied me during my time in Guatemala, which made a challenging trip immeasurably better. Most significantly, however, my beloved partner Emma Partridge (again) read every word before anyone else, and is still my biggest fan. For her, my deepest gratitude and biggest love always.

Introduction

Truce or transformation?

10 May 1994:

Nelson Rolihlahla Mandela is sworn in as the first black president of South Africa after centuries of white oppression and decades of struggle for freedom. In front of the jubilant crowd filling the Union Buildings amphitheatre in Pretoria Mandela declares that 'Never, never and never again shall it be that this beautiful land will again experience the oppression of one by another'. Across the nation, throngs of South Africans dance and celebrate in the streets, black and white together.

29 December 1996:

Crowds fill the Central Plaza outside Guatemala City's Presidential Palace, guerilla commanders standing next to army officers in unprecedented and previously unimaginable scenes celebrating the signing of the long-anticipated Peace Accords. The Accords, brokered by the United Nations, finally brought Latin America's bloodiest Cold War civil war to an end after four decades of violence. The final, overarching accord promises a commitment to 'a Firm and Lasting Peace', stating that 'Compliance with these Agreements is an historic, unavoidable commitment'.

10 April 1998:

After years of talks, and months of intense negotiations, the leaders of Great Britain, the Republic of Ireland and the political parties in Northern Ireland sign the Belfast Agreement, bringing direct British rule of Northern Ireland to an end and creating a new Northern Ireland Assembly. Just over a month later, on 22 May, a record turnout sees over 70 per cent of voters in Northern Ireland support the Agreement in a referendum, bringing an end to over thirty years violence that characterized 'the Troubles'.

28 May 2000:

> An estimated 250,000 people walk across the Sydney Harbour Bridge
> to demonstrate their support for reconciliation between black and
> white Australia. Over five-and-a-half hours, indigenous[1] and non-
> indigenous Australians stream towards the Sydney Opera House,
> where the event Corroboree 2000 is being held to mark the end of the
> formal Decade of Reconciliation. The Declaration Towards Reconcili-
> ation, presented at this event, asks all Australians to 'make a commit-
> ment to go on together in a spirit of reconciliation'.

***

Four deeply divided societies across one optimistic decade. Four seemingly
transformative moments promising new beginnings in the relationships
between groups torn apart by histories of colonization, violence, and
oppression; histories marked by resistance, struggle, and persistent efforts
to find ways to live together democratically and without violence. Yet
although each of these moments was a symbolic turning point in these
struggles, representing above all else a desire to break with the past, in
none of these cases has the promise of these moments come to pass. In
the years since, these momentous events have been all but swamped by the
challenges that have followed. The aspirations and beliefs that animated
the celebration of these events have been overtaken by the significant
social and political conflicts that have continued to mark the relationships
between these divided groups.

   The clues to the challenges that would follow were evident even amid
the euphoria of these events. In South Africa, much celebrating took place
amidst the abject poverty of the townships and informal settlements that
were the product of colonization and apartheid. In Guatemala, even as
exiles from around the world returned to share in the jubilation of the
moment, there was scepticism that the army, which had given itself a gen-
erous amnesty, would actually follow through on its support for peace
(Nelson 2009: 39–40, Jonas 2000: 9–10). In Northern Ireland, dissenters
from the Ulster Unionist Party joined forces with the Democratic Unionist
Party to campaign against the referendum. And in Australia, division was
evident even as marchers left the Harbour Bridge and walked towards the
Opera House, where they were greeted by Aboriginal and Torres Strait
Islander groups protesting against the limitations of a reconciliation
process that they saw as providing no redress for colonial injustice, holding
placards that stated 'No Reconciliation Without Justice', 'Restore Land
Rights Now' and 'Recognize Aboriginal Sovereignty' (Short 2008: 7).

   In a sense, it is these conflicts rumbling beneath the surface of celebration that are the concern of this book. Around the world, there is an
evident desire to draw a line under violent conflict and social division.

Moments such as those described above—often considered to be 'turning points' in a nation's history—signal that it is time to 'move on' from conflict and find peace. In the belief that the job is done, international attention turns to the next conflict in need of 'resolution', leaving notionally 'post'-conflict nations to rebuild themselves. Certainly, the 1990s represented a decade in which such hopes and expectations were high. In the wake of the end of the Cold War there was a flourishing sense of optimism that democratization had become an 'unstoppable wave', and a conviction that liberal interventions to support democratic transitions were 'working with the tide of history' (Ryan 2013: 27). The emerging field of transitional justice provided a so-called 'toolkit' of strategies, and suggested there would be an end point to struggles for justice.

In the twenty-first century, however, this optimism about transition, transformation and reconciliation has dissipated (Little 2014: 57). Indeed, what has become clear in the intervening years is that these hopes were unrealistic. Histories of violence and oppression can permanently scar a society. Conflicts once expressed through violence and bloodshed live on in segregation, hostility and inequality. And memories of violence create anxiety about continuing conflict, which is often 'managed' or repressed rather than engaged through democratic contestation. Together these dynamics form a potent, and poisonous, political context—a context that in no way allows a society to 'move on' from its violent past.

This book suggests a different approach, one that both highlights the necessity of conflict to democracy and political reconciliation and that draws attention to the multi-level complexity of reconciliation and conflict transformation. On the first point, the approach of this book draws on theories of agonistic democracy to conceive of reconciliation as a process that is deeply political, and that prioritizes the capacity to retain and develop democratic political contest in societies that have, in other ways, been able to resolve their conflicts. This approach is developed in the first three chapters of the book. On the second point, the book considers the demands of reconciliation across three porous, overlapping and interlinked socio-political levels: the constitutional, the institutional, and the relational. Each of these levels comprises a section in the book. The multi-level conflict transformation approach developed here suggests that reconciliation and conflict transformation are far more complex and open-ended processes than is sometimes acknowledged. This approach also drives an understanding of the Janus-faced requirements of political reconciliation, paying attention to social structures as well as psychologies, and encouraging the development of a shared vision that is broad enough to achieve change without demanding either agreement about the past or a singular, shared identity (Daly and Sarkin 2007: 187).

The approach developed in this book is informed by four years of research in the countries that form the base of this study—South Africa, Northern Ireland, Guatemala, and Australia. During this time, I interviewed over 80 reconciliation actors from all sides of these deep divisions, all of whom are struggling to transform the conflicts that still define their societies. Throughout this book you will find the voices of these actors, expressing their hopes, fear, disappointments and ambitions for the transformations they desire. They speak from vastly different contexts, out of different histories of violence and oppression, and yet they share many commonalities of both experience and aspiration.

At the same time there are significant differences in their experiences. Much of this book is concerned with scale, in the sense that the multi-level framework I am outlining maps onto ideas of macro, meso, and micro social scale. There is, however, another aspect to the idea of scale that shapes the cases in this book; specifically demographic scale, or how the relationship between minority and majority populations may influence reconciliation and conflict transformation efforts.

In Australia, for example, Aboriginal and Torres Strait Islander people make up only 2.5 per cent of the total population, meaning that the attitudes of the non-indigenous majority to indigenous claims is a hugely significant political factor that effectively determines the 'limits of electoral tolerance' that constrain government policy-making (Mulgan 1998: 180). Indigenous claims tend to be portrayed as less consequential 'minority' complaints requiring recognition from the state, rather than a radical restructuring of the framework of the state as happened in South Africa where the black majority ensured that such transformation (eventually) occurred (Short 2005: 270–1). The majority of the non-indigenous population in Australia does not know or have relationships with indigenous people, which, as Leanne Townsend suggests in our interview, leaves many people making 'an educated guess' about 'what the issues are within the Aboriginal community'. Les Malezer points out that such a small population does 'not pose any threat' to the wider Australian population, which leaves Aboriginal and Torres Strait Islander people with little in the way of political influence or leverage. Fred Chaney agrees, suggesting that if there was a sizeable Aboriginal majority in Australia the country would have had to consider more seriously indigenous demands for secession or independence. Without this majority such claims become 'theoretical and interesting' rather than politically pressing.

In South Africa the demographic scale is reversed, with around 80 per cent of the population belonging to one of several Black African ethnic groups, and the remaining 20 per cent comprised of White, 'Coloured', Indian and other populations. This inversion of demographic scale was 'a big problem for white supremacy', but also essential to the South African economy, shaping both the regimes of colonialism and apartheid, and the struggle against them (MacDonald 2006: 49). These demographics also mean that while most white South Africans have some contact with black South Africans, most black South Africans have no contact at all with white South Africans. Catherine Kennedy describes the 'minority-majority dynamic' in her country as 'really in your face', making the fact of continuing socioeconomic injustice impossible to escape. White South Africans have also had to accept that, as Steven Friedman points out, 'this is always going to be a majority-ruled place'. Yet the white population is still of sufficient size and influence that at the time of the transition to democracy, there was a concern that white South Africans might set out to 'wreck this place', something Friedman considers to have led to a constrained period of official reconciliation as the ANC government was eager to move from the 'reconciliation phase' to the 'governing phase' as a means of reassuring white capital.

Guatemala tells a different story again. There, it is estimated that around 60 per cent of the population belong to one of the groups of (predominantly Maya) indigenous peoples: Achi', Akateco, Awakateco, Chalchiteco, Ch'orti', Chuj, Itza', Ixil, Jacalteco, Kaqchikel, K'iche', Mam, Mopan, Poqomam, Poqomchi', Q'anjob'al, Q'eqchi', Sakapulteco, Sipakapense, Tektiteko, Tz'utujil, Uspanteko, Xinka and Garífuna. However, even this figure is debated, with the army and some political leaders maintaining that the indigenous proportion of the population is considerably lower. Yet, whatever its size, the indigenous population in Guatemala, and the revolutionary movements it has spawned, has meant that counterinsurgent forces, which were 'strong enough to prevent a popular or revolutionary victory' were unable to 'triumph definitively over the carriers of revolt, or to control the social forces unleashed by chronic crisis' (Jonas 2000: 17).

Finally Northern Ireland, where the demographic division is more equal between the Protestant and Catholic communities, each of which make up just under 50 per cent of the population (with the remainder claiming no or neither main religion). This creates a different kind of complexity, because neither major group would countenance leaving the territory, but nor can either group attain complete control (Mac Ginty *et al.* 2007: 8). The small size of the overall population has also shaped the form of 'post'-conflict work, effectively constraining the possibilities for reconciliation and transformation efforts. As Maureen Hetherington (2008: 49) suggests, for example, a truth and reconciliation process would be deeply painful in a 'small community with a large social network' like Northern Ireland, potentially causing 'irreparable damage' to the 'interwoven fabric of society'.

Thus in all these cases, it is evident that demographic scale is a significant influence on both the shape of historical conflict, and the nature and extent of the reconciliation and transformation efforts that follow. Equally significant is each country's pathway to the 'end' of conflict and the beginning of the reconciliation efforts that follow.

Histories of reconciliation

In 1994, the 'new' South Africa was born, ending centuries of colonial oppression that eventually produced the horrors of four decades of apartheid. Like both Northern Ireland and Guatemala, the violent struggle in South Africa did not end with a victory of one side over the other, but rather a stalemate that both sides recognized as unsustainable. After many behind the scenes talks facilitated by international actors, the National Party government led by F.W. de Klerk finally released Nelson Mandela from prison in 1990 and 'unbanned' political organizations such as the African National Congress (ANC). Over the following four years, the ANC and the government negotiated a peaceful transition to democratic rule, culminating in the election of Mandela as president. At his inauguration in May 1994, Mandela proclaimed:

> The time for healing the wounds has come. The moment to bridge the chasm that divides us has come {...}. We have triumphed in our effort to implant hope in the breasts of the millions of our people. We enter into a covenant that we shall build a society in which all South Africans, both black and white, will be able to walk tall {...} a rainbow nation at peace with itself and the world.
>
> (Quoted in Segal and Cort 2011: 130)

The transition to democracy was considered by many to be 'miraculous', creating an overwhelming sense of relief and optimism among the majority of South Africans. The rest of the world applauded what appeared a remarkable success story, 'captured by the rapture of a nation that seemed to achieve the global aspiration of reconciliation, multicultural diversity, and interracial harmony' (Irlam 2004: 697). Indeed, the South African transition from apartheid to democracy became fundamental to the emergence of the global reconciliation agenda (Little 2014: 56).

Key among the initiatives embarked upon in the newly democratic South Africa was its famous Truth and Reconciliation Commission (TRC), held between 1996 and 1998 (discussed further in Chapter 10). The approach of the TRC recognized that it would be impossible for a nation like South Africa to achieve its ambitions for a new society without first coming to terms with its past. Over time, however, the apparent success of the TRC came to both define the reconciliation process in South Africa, and to constitute a template for reconciliation efforts in other parts of the world. Indeed, as Gibson (2004: 2) suggests, much of the successful transition to democracy is attributed almost solely to the work of the TRC. But while the Commission was certainly important in laying 'building blocks' for reconciliation in South Africa (Boraine 2000: 154), it is both simplistic and overly-optimistic to suggest that its contribution was greater than this. As the TRC's chairman, Archbishop Desmond Tutu points out, the

Commission was meant to *promote* rather than *achieve* national unity and reconciliation, and should today be seen as 'only a contribution to a process that was envisaged as being a national project' (Tutu 1999: 165). Yet, as Catherine Kennedy suggests, the way the TRC has been portrayed has contributed to 'that sense that the reconciliation work is over, and we're back to business'. Haniff Hoosen agrees, acknowledging that while the TRC was 'an excellent event' it was '*only* an event, one that should have been the *start* of a process'. Namhla Mniki-Mangaliso makes a similar point, describing the TRC as 'brilliant' but suggesting that 'reducing our reconciliation strategy to the TRC was a ridiculous mistake, in the sense that really the TRC should have been the 1 per cent that we do as part of a more meaningful effort to have long-term reconciliation'.

Indeed, the scale of the hoped-for transformation in South Africa—including the need for simultaneous social, political and economic transformation at all levels (Ramphele 2008: 13)—was far beyond what any one institution could achieve. There was no aspect of South African society that had not been scarred by its history, and the work of healing these scars became a national ambition. There has certainly been significant progress, as Steven Friedman observes, telling me 'You look around this society and you see human beings who, when I was a kid, were totally crushed, were totally cowed, and who are now human beings with voices.' Yet despite such evident progress, early optimism has given way to disappointment and frustration. Demands for justice now compete with 'new' conflicts centred on economic inequality and corruption, reminding many South Africans of the fragility of their new democratic institutions (du Toit 2009: 233–4). Indeed, the process of reconciliation in South Africa could at best be described as 'ongoing' (Villa-Vicencio and Ngesi 2003: 295), although many of my interviewees used far stronger language to describe the 'mess' that their country has become. Indeed, Raenette Taljaard maintains that most South Africans understand that they are 'sitting on top of a fundamentally unsustainable situation'. Yet, as Tim Murithi suggests, elite resistance from 'the beneficiaries and the bystanders' sees issues of ongoing inequality and structural violence 'pushed under the carpet'. Mniki-Mangaliso suggests that where South Africans have 'failed' is in 'not striving hard enough to have the conversations that need to be had'. Many have been 'more comfortable just moving along and not dealing with the issues'. Today, Kate Lefko-Everett observes that South Africans are 'tired of talking about reconciliation', instead asking 'At what point does this end? At what point are we a functional democracy?'

Like South Africa, Guatemala has also emerged from a period of extreme violence and repression. The civil war, waged between a revolutionary guerrilla movement and the counterinsurgency state, is thought to have been far more violent and repressive than the Cold War civil wars in other countries in the region, killing or disappearing some 200,000 civilians and virtually eliminating the Guatemalan human rights movement

(Jonas 2000: 17; Sikkink 2011: 81). Indeed, the military counterinsurgency of the 1980s waged a scorched earth war that 'went beyond all conceivable horror and extinguished any hopes for change' (Recovery of Historical Memory Project (REMHI) 1999: xxxii), including wholesale massacres of Mayan villagers suspected of sympathizing with the guerillas (Sieder 2003: 213). Yet despite this destruction, the guerrilla movement—the *Unidad Revolucionaria Nacional Guatemalteca* (URNG, Guatemalan National Revolutionary Unity)—maintained enough resistance that a chronic state of social crisis prevailed, and both sides began to recognize the need to end the violence. The URNG accepted that they would not be able to take state power militarily and that continuing the violence would create ongoing suffering for the civilian population. After the return to civilian rule in 1986, the guerrillas began pursuing political means to end the war, pressing for political negotiations with the government and the army (Jonas 2000: 31).

In light of this history, the 1996 Peace Accords, ultimately brokered by the United Nations, were an extraordinary achievement, going far beyond merely ending the violence to establish a set of ambitious reforms intended to truly transform the country. As Susanne Jonas (2000: 37) has suggested, the Accords appeared to be 'a truly negotiated settlement; rather than victors imposing terms upon vanquished, they represented a splitting of differences between radically opposed forces, with major concessions from both sides'. And following the signing of the Accords, political actors in Guatemala—both inside and outside the state—expended enormous energy in their efforts to implement the reforms contained in the agreement. Social movements including the Mayan and women's movements began to play a new role in Guatemalan democratization, an achievement made all the more remarkable given the devastation that the war had wreaked upon these sectors of the community in particular (Nelson 2009: 48).

Yet almost two decades after the signing of the Accords it seems that for many Guatemalans, poverty, insecurity and human rights abuses may be as bad as—if not worse than—they were in 1996 (Nelson 2009: 45). Unlike South Africa, there was no democratic victory for the majority indigenous population in Guatemala, many of whom remain socially and politically marginalized (Sanford 2003: 259). Democratization in Guatemala has been 'an attenuated and problematic process' (Sieder 2003: 211) that has left many political actors exhausted and confused. Overall, the country remains quite extraordinarily divided, split along lines of ethnicity and poverty that maintain widespread social exclusion. The distribution of wealth in Guatemala remains amongst the most unequal in the hemisphere and the country's political and economic elites have shown themselves to be deeply resistant to change (Reilly 2009: 17). As Rosenda Camey tells me, in her opinion the war in Guatemala 'hasn't finished. It continues because in their hearts people continue to cry for all of the violations of their rights in the communities.' Alvaro Pop also points to the need for deeper transformation in Guatemala and specifically for 'strong institutions' pertaining to citizenship and political recognition, the absence of which, Pop suggests, explains 'everything else' that challenges the country. Yet the stagnation of reconciliation efforts leads Glenda Tager to fear that Guatemala will have to 'go even more deeply into the bad situation in the country until we really realize that we need to do something'.

As in the other countries in this study, the conflict in Northern Ireland also revolved around a central division, in this case between two mutually exclusive orientations towards constitutional nationalism—one with the ambition of a unified Ireland, and the other in favour of a United Kingdom that continues to include Northern Ireland (Mac Ginty *et al.* 2007: 7). Although it was one of the longest running violent conflicts in the world, the death toll in Northern Ireland was relatively low by the standards of other civil wars (a little under 3,500 people were killed between 1969 and 1998). Nevertheless, the relative impact on Northern Ireland's small population (of 1.68 million) and small geographical area was substantial, with a disproportionate number of deaths among young working class men (Mac Ginty *et al.* 2007: 4).

The end of the violent conflict in Northern Ireland also came as a result of stalemate rather than the defeat of one side by the other. And, like South Africa and Guatemala, the international community was deeply involved in facilitating talks—including secret talks between the British government and the IRA—that would eventually lead to the paramilitary ceasefires in 1994 and the signing of the Belfast Agreement in 1998. Since the signing of the Agreement, and the stabilzation of power sharing arrangements in the Northern Ireland Assembly in 2007 (following the St Andrews Agreement of 2006) Northern Ireland has achieved something of a 'sea-change' in political relationships (Kelly 2012: 11). Indeed, life in Northern Ireland has become relatively peaceful, and its political institutions now seem to be secure, with all five main parties working within an agreed political framework—an arrangement that public opinion polling suggests is preferred by the majority of citizens (Nolan 2012: 7).

Yet despite these advances, Northern Ireland also remains a deeply divided society. There is a persistent 'nexus of hostility and separateness around politics' that is generally described as 'sectarianism' (Community Relations Council 2011: 11). Social and political divides remain embodied in the 'peace walls' and multitudinous other 'interfaces', that carve up urban and rural areas across the region. While there has been an increase in intercommunal interactions in many workplaces, deep segregation still determines where people live, what sport they play, and where they shop, socialize, and go to school (Aiken 2010: 175; Kelly 2012). There seems remarkably little in the way of social or political will to address this fact; sectarianism and segregation have been normalized over the years and the population still seems happy enough to pay the approximately £1.5 billion it costs each year to maintain their separate spaces (Deloitte 2007). As Gerry Foster suggests, people in Northern Ireland do not refer to a 'peace process' but rather to a 'political process', because, he maintains 'This isn't peace. This is just an absence of violence.'

Indeed, while the Northern Ireland peace process has achieved many successes that deserve celebration, there remain significant structural and psychological barriers to attaining a vibrant and cooperative democracy in the region (Smithey 2011: 10). In a culture where public expressions of pain and grief (such as characterized South Africa's TRC) are frowned upon, there is a perceived sense of 'safety in saying nothing', and silence has become 'a powerful protector for those who feel threatened or vulnerable' (Hetherington 2008: 48). Wilhelm Verwoerd observes that there is a 'much greater sense of stability' in Northern Ireland because the conflict there has taken place within a politically stable region, unlike that of his home country of South Africa, where he observes 'a fundamental sense of insecurity and instability'. The consequence of this perceived stability in Northern Ireland, however, is the lack of a sense of urgency, which discourages the belief that actors 'need to step out of their comfort zones and figure it out'. Indeed, in a conversation with a youth worker in Belfast I asked how people lived their lives when looking out their windows they were confronted by imposing concrete peace walls. His reply was telling; he simply said 'Curtains.' At the same time as people are happy to draw their curtains, however, periodic outbreaks of low level violence, including the 2012 riots that broke out in response to the Belfast City Council decision to limit the number of days the Union Flag is flown from Belfast City Hall, prompt continuous debate about the stability of peace in Northern Ireland.

The Australian case presents a somewhat different example of efforts towards reconciliation and conflict transformation, one that underscores the expanded timescale in which we might think about this work. Australia differs from the other cases considered in this book in some key ways. First, unlike South Africa, Guatemala, and Northern Ireland, although the British did not declare war against Aboriginal and Torres Strait Islander people upon their arrival, the indigenous peoples of the continent were, in effect, defeated militarily after ongoing frontier combat waged between the 1790s and the 1920s. There was no stalemate, and no two parties prepared to negotiate an agreement. Rather, the indigenous population in Australia was violently decimated and subsequently contained and oppressed through decades of brutal colonial policy. As a result, the political claims of Aboriginal and Torres Strait Islander peoples, like indigenous peoples in other settler colonies, have never been adequately addressed.

Second, because the number of indigenous people is small relative to the wider Australian population, the reconciliation process that was eventually undertaken in Australia did not occur in the shadow of the threat of widespread violence. This meant that the majority non-indigenous population had to be persuaded of the merits of participating through other means. Third, rather than a case of transition from authoritarianism to democracy, Australia represents an example of the politics of reconciliation 'migrating' to an established democracy as a framework for addressing historical injustice (Bashir and Kymlicka 2008: 4). In this sense, Erin Daly and Jeremy Sarkin (2007: 146) contend that Australia presented:

> the best possible conditions for the promotion of reconciliation—a generally liberal public, a tiny minority of people in the (therefore non-threatening) victim class, few perpetrators still alive to be punished or shamed (and therefore few people with a large stake in resisting the dissemination of the truth) and a prevalent morality that soundly rejects legalized racial oppression. Almost no one in Australia now maintains that the policies of the past were good, and few would argue publicly that they were justified even at the time they were promulgated and enforced.

Yet even in these apparently favourable circumstances, reconciliation has proven more challenging and complex than many people anticipated.

The formal Australian reconciliation process originally developed out of a recommendation in the Royal Commission Into Aboriginal Deaths in Custody Report (RCIADIC).[2] The government of the day created the Council for Aboriginal Reconciliation (CAR) and set out the timeline for the formal process, to conclude in 2001. The Minister for Aboriginal Affairs at this time, Robert Tickner, has since outlined what he saw as the three objectives for reconciliation in Australia. First, the need to educate non-indigenous Australians about Aboriginal and Torres Strait Islander culture and the extent of disadvantage still experienced by indigenous people. Second, the process needed to get onto the public agenda what Tickner—in an attempt to get away from the apparently polarizing language of 'treaty' —described as a 'document of reconciliation'. Through the formal reconciliation process Tickner hoped there could be some agreement on the terms of such a document and a further agreement on how it might be achieved. Finally, Tickner envisaged that the reconciliation process would build a social movement that would drive the nation to 'address indigenous aspirations, human rights and social justice' (Tickner 2001).

A change of government in 1996, however, saw a significant change in government attitudes towards the aspirations of the reconciliation process, with the rejection of anything thought to be merely 'symbolic' and a new focus on the need to adopt 'practical measures' to address indigenous disadvantage. The prime minister rebutted renewed calls for a treaty, contending that 'an undivided nation does not make a treaty with itself' (Howard quoted in Sanders 2005: 156). Founding member of the CAR Linda Burney describes the early years of the 1990s as 'an extraordinary time where this country was on the move', recalling the honour and excitement of 'being involved in the organization that was leading a conversation and being part of seeing a country coming to terms with itself'. Yet, like others, she felt that movement stall in the latter part of the decade. Fellow CAR member Cheryl Kernot believes that from the election of John Howard as prime minister in 1996 the Australian reconciliation movement 'started to die a very slow death'.

As noted above, many Aboriginal and Torres Strait Islander people were ambivalent about the formal reconciliation process from the outset, seeing it as an attempt to avoid a political settlement. The response from the non-indigenous population was also mixed. After ten years of effort focused in large part on an educative strategy directed at non-indigenous Australia, public opinion data suggested that little had changed. Focus groups undertaken at the end of 1999 and the start of 2000 found universal agreement that the position of Aboriginal people in Australia was a 'tragedy', and widespread agreement that Aboriginal people had been 'badly treated by the early white settlers'. However, many people found it 'hard to face up to this', with the more defensive participants in the research arguing that 'there was bad behaviour on both sides'. Few were 'inclined to see one side as the invader and the other as the invaded', nor did many 'accept any responsibility for what happened in what most see as far-off days' (Newspoll *et al.* 2000: 37). Further, the focus group data suggested that most people 'had given little thought to reconciliation' and knew very little about the process, with only 'one or two' even registering the existence of a document of reconciliation (Newspoll *et al.* 2000: 40). Today, Jacqueline Phillips believes that Australia has 'lost its way' with regard to what she describes as 'reconciliation consciousness'. Phillips sees the root of these problems in the process itself, suggesting that Australia never really 'tried' reconciliation but instead 'spent a decade inquiring into what it might mean'.

Indeed, as Angela Pratt has argued, while the formal reconciliation process in Australia did introduce a new and broad 'moral language' with which to speak about issues of Indigenous social justice, it did not 'help to resolve any of the questions these issues raised' (Pratt 2005: 157). There were no significant improvements in socio-economic inequality between indigenous and non-indigenous people, and no treaty or 'document of reconciliation' that addressed the political grievances of Aboriginal and Torres Strait Islander peoples (Gunstone 2009: 47). Like some others, Mick Gooda is more optimistic, pointing to the 'continuum' of changes over the twentieth century in Australia, including the 1967 referendum, the 1993 *Native Title Act*, and the 2008 apology to the Stolen Generations, all of which he believes have led the country 'in the right direction'. But, for many critics, including many indigenous people, the process was little more than an exercise in colonial obfuscation of ongoing dispossession, assimilation, and the persistence of settler colonial structures (Short 2008: 8).

The diversity of these examples underscores the importance of understanding reconciliation efforts through deeply contextualized analyses of political conflicts (Little 2014: 51). High profile reconciliation policies and practice have tended towards rapid international diffusion, based more on a hoped-for imitation of 'success' than on domestic political circumstances (Sikkink 2011: 22). What is needed instead is an understanding of the complexities and challenges of reconciliation across multiple socio-political levels.

Mapping multi-level conflict transformation and the realities of reconciliation

In much of the literature pertaining to reconciliation and conflict transformation there is a tendency to oversimplify what is at stake, to establish and then contest a set of binaries: reconciliation requires truth or justice, vengeance or forgiveness, it is about unity or difference, race or class, recognition or redistribution. Of course, it is about all of these things, and all the messy, complicated, exasperating ways in which they overlap, compliment, contest and discredit other points of view. While the scholarly debates have done a great deal to further conceptual clarity, and even to refine the application of these ideas, they also tend to narrow the horizons of the observer, distracting and obscuring the view of the full picture.

In contrast to these approaches, this book attempts to engage with the full complexity of reconciliation and conflict transformation. As noted at the outset, the approach in this book understands reconciliation efforts as a mode of political engagement and agonistic struggle across these three porous, overlapping and interlinked socio-political domains: the constitutional, the institutional, and the relational. This multi-level approach conceptualizes reconciliation as the need to reshape the *whole* of a society, taking a broader perspective on a range of structural, institutional and interpersonal transformations that promote democratic values and contestations. This approach recognizes that there are different requirements, different norms and imperatives, that affect the dynamics of reconciliation at different socio-political levels (Verdeja 2009: 3–4). This is also a dynamic view, acknowledging tensions between short-term stability and compromise on the one hand, and long-term aspirations towards economic justice, political equality, and the redress of structural violence on the other. Such an approach allows actors to resist the desire for 'closure' in favour of broad and deep social and political reforms that are unlikely to proceed smoothly and harmoniously, but instead progress in ways that are disjunctured and uneven (Leebaw 2008: 118; Verdeja 2009: 21). It also recognizes the enormity of the challenge of asking 'whole societies wrapped in histories of violence that date back generations, to move toward a newly defined horizon' (Lederach 2005: 31).

Further, the approach outlined here recognizes that narrower conceptions of reconciliation and conflict transformation can, as Zinaida Miller
(2008: 267) argues, become

> a definitional project, explaining who has been silenced by delineat-
> ing who may now speak, describing past violence by deciding what and
> who will be punished and radically differentiating a new regime in
> relation to what actions were taken by its predecessor.

Efforts that focus only on dealing with the pain of the past are likely to
sublimate the need for contemporary redress. Focusing attention on
soothing tensions rather than engaging conflicts between historical
enemies is likely to promote collective social amnesia and assimilative resolution (Hirsch 2012: 79). In any deeply divided society, what emerges as
'the problem'—whether, for example, that be 'race' in South Africa or
ethno-national conflict in Northern Ireland—becomes a filter for understanding both conflicts and their solutions, subsuming discussion of other
forms of structural inequality and division (Little 2014: 13). Further, to
narrowly define what is available for transformation in this way inevitably
serves the interests of political and economic elites and others concerned
to preserve the status quo. More limited approaches to reconciliation tend
to avoid underlying structural conflicts, with unknowable consequences
for future relationships and the resurgence of violence.

The levels mapped out in this book are all equally important to reconciliation efforts. At the constitutional level, societies emerging from civil
war, engaged in a transition from authoritarianism to democracy, or still
grappling with colonial and historical dispossession and injustice must all,
in their own ways, confront the question of how they are constituted and
in what ways they need to *re*-constitute themselves. The process of political
reconciliation is driven by 'the hope of establishing a new beginning' that
is 'self-consciously enacted in the gap between past and future' (Schaap
2005: 91). In contrast to a view of reconciliation that sees such a process
initiated by a public acknowledgment of past wrongs, this view of political
reconciliation sees it initiated in the act of constitution itself, in which that
public, the 'we' of the society, is in fact instantiated. As Schaap argues, 'the
constitution of a space for politics makes possible a future collective
remembrance' (Schaap 2007: 15). Thus, the work of constitutionalism, in
both its political and legal senses, provides a founding moment, a space
for politics, which is inevitably a space for conflict and contestation. In the
framework outlined here, the constitutional space for political reconciliation involves three elements: citizenship (discussed in Chapter 4), settlements and agreements (Chapter 5), and constitutional design and reform
(Chapter 6).

The institutional level of the multi-level framework for conflict transformation recognizes that overcoming structural injustice will open spaces

in which further transformation can occur (Ramsbotham *et al.* 2011: 246). Beyond the space of political institutions reshaped by constitutional trans- formation, such as parliaments and electoral systems, there are a number of institutional domains in which transformation is imperative if politics is to flourish. In the analysis that follows I focus on land reform and eco- nomic redistribution (Chapter 7), education, policing and justice (Chapter 8), and the roles of civil society and religious institutions (Chapter 9). (I have had to exclude an analysis of other crucial institu- tions, such as those associated with public health, not because they are not important but purely due to limitations of space.) These chapters suggest that sustaining reconciliation efforts requires visible, tangible progress in spaces of social transformation and reconstruction; processes in which states must invest resources over the long term, ensuring that government departments and civil society organizations are well-funded and endorsed by the central government (Daly and Sarkin 2007: 115). Crucially, however, the chapters analysing institutional transformation also reveal the extent of elite resistance to many reconciliation efforts.

The last level of analysis in this framework is the relational level, which concerns the transformation of relationships among people. This level is perhaps closest to more popular understanding of reconciliation, pointing to the ways in which reconciliation addresses both historical wounds and their contemporary, relational manifestations. Indeed, the very concept of reconciliation is based on the idea that a stable future order, of the kind initiated in political reconciliation, is only possible if the psychological sources of conflict—'the residues of violence and death that linger long after open hostilities have ceased' (Hutchison and Bleiker 2013: 81)—are engaged alongside broader efforts at constitutional and institutional trans- formation. Scholars from a range of disciplines have stressed the import- ance of focusing on the underlying psychological and sociological needs that animate conflictual relations, including needs for recognition, accept- ance, respect, security, and justice (Tropp 2012: 4). It is in practices of relational engagement that attempt to address these needs that we can most clearly see the requirements for agonistic processes able to support difficult, ongoing conversations about the past (Chapter 10), about sharing space (Chapter 11), and about maintaining dialogue with one another (Chapter 12). Through transformative relational processes, citizens may begin to understand that their individual experiences are also collective experiences, in one way or another opening up a space in which to speak of a shared history and a shared future (Daly and Sarkin 2007: 112). Indeed, in the terms of this book, the goal of relational transforma- tion is to create the conditions in which an enemy to whom you might want to do physical harm can become an adversary—someone with whom you instead engage in a democratic contest of values and ideas.

So to what ends are these multi-level efforts directed? The question of how to conceptualize reconciliation is addressed in depth in Chapter 2. In many contexts, reconciliation has become a dirty word associated with meaningless platitudes rather than transformation. In contrast, the broad understanding that informs this book is one that sees reconciliation as an endless, agonistic process centred on the creation of political space in which divergent views can be engaged without fear of violence or reprisal. The ambition is explicitly *not* one of pursuing communitarian social harmony, or of assimilating difference—approaches that would 'threaten the very fabric of democratic participation' (Villa-Vicencio 2009: 55). Instead, as Andrew Schaap (2005: 84) contends, 'Agreement on moral norms is not required in order to initiate a process of reconciliation. Rather, political reconciliation presupposes only the will to live together in the mode of acting and speaking.' Understood in this way, political reconciliation is a process of revolution rather than restoration; it is not the return to some prelapsarian state of harmony but rather the constitution of a space for politics that would allow a society to grapple with the many and complex transformative challenges it will inevitably confront (Schaap 2005: 87).

The ways in which these levels are mapped out in the structure of the book may lead some readers to interpret them as discrete, perhaps sequential tasks. This is far from the case. The levels point more to complexity than simplification, recognizing that the tasks of reconciliation are multitudinous, overlapping and interdependent. Reconciliation cannot only be about rights, but nor can it focus solely on psychological questions or attitudinal factors to the neglect of material (re)distribution and structural transformation. Change at one level may be dependent on change at the other levels. Each of the levels is important to reconciliation efforts, and it is equally important to consider how they connect to, support or disrupt each other.

Challenge and complexity, struggle and effort

What is common to most thinking about reconciliation is that it requires ongoing effort and hard work. Engaging in reconciliation efforts after violent struggle is an 'acute challenge' (Ramsbotham *et al.* 2011: 248), it 'is not intuitive and it is not easy' (Villa-Vicencio and Doxtader 2004: viii), and it requires 'restraint, generosity of spirit, empathy and perseverance' (Villa-Vicencio 2004: 4). Many practitioners have become aware of these challenges through their efforts. At the end of the decade of reconciliation in Australia, for example, the CAR described the process as 'a long, winding and corrugated road, not a broad, paved highway' (Council for Aboriginal Reconciliation 2000: 101). More recently, the Community Relations Council (2011: 9) in Northern Ireland described the need for 'systematic partnership {…} care and attention'. And in our interview, Adam Kahane, who has worked as a dialogue facilitator in many countries, including both South Africa and Guatemala, concedes that many people working on reconciliation efforts, himself included, 'thought this was all easier than it really is'.

But as the cases in this book make clear, no matter how challenging and difficult, there is really no alternative to these struggles. Ignoring conflict will only drive it underground where, like a cancer, it will eat away at social structures and human relationships, inevitably erupting again in painful, unpredictable and violent ways. Brought into the light, however, conflict can be engaged in the kind of agonistic contestation that is the basis of a healthy democracy, creating new opportunities for reconciliation and conflict transformation efforts across all levels of society. My hope is that this book will facilitate a deeper understanding of reconciliation in all its complexity, not as a line to be drawn, but as an ongoing process that may be the only way forward for countries scarred by histories of violence and oppression.

Notes

1 Broadly speaking, indigenous people are the original inhabitants of a territory that has been conquered by ethnically or culturally different groups and who have subsequently been incorporated into states that consider them inferior 'outsiders' (Maybury-Lewis 2003: 324). Throughout this book the terms 'indigenous people' or 'indigenous peoples' are used to refer to all such groups including the combined groups of Aboriginal people and Torres Strait Islanders who make up Australia's indigenous population, as well as the Mayan populations of Guatemala.

2 The Royal Commission into Aboriginal Deaths in Custody (RCIADIC) (1987–1991) was appointed to study and report upon the underlying social, cultural and legal issues behind the high number of deaths in custody of Aboriginal people and Torres Strait Islander people. The Commission found that the immediate causes of the deaths investigated (99 in total) did not involve the deliberate killing of indigenous prisoners by police or prison officers, however it did find gross deficiencies in the standard of care afforded to many of the deceased.

Part I

Conceptualizing reconciliation and conflict transformation

1 Understanding divided societies

The starting point for developing an interpretive framework for reconciliation and multi-level conflict transformation is to understand the ways in which conflict shapes societies over time. Conflict is frequently described as conforming to a cycle, which begins with the development of a latent tension within a society that later emerges into the public domain. The conflict subsequently escalates before arriving at an often 'hurting stalemate', which in turn leads to de-escalation and the resolution or settlement of the conflict. The cycle is thought to be completed by a period of 'post-conflict' reconciliation (Brahm 2003).

But while the idea of such a cycle may be a useful heuristic device, in reality conflict is a far more complex social phenomenon that remains embedded in social and political relationships, causing periodic ruptures, contributing to physical and structural violence, and framing and constraining political relationships. These dynamics are present to greater or lesser degrees in all societies, but they have particular force in countries emerging from periods of violence and civil war, or that have other significant cleavages resulting from historical violence. These societies are often referred to as *deeply divided societies* (Guelke 2012), and in this chapter I explore some of the dynamics present in the deeply divided societies that were the focus of this study.

Actors engaged in reconciliation efforts in deeply divided societies face many challenges. The violent conflict, repression, and injustice that make up the history of such societies are multilayered and multifaceted, making it virtually impossible to determine which wrongs can feasibly be addressed, what this process might entail, and how to prioritize such efforts. For example, as the ANC recently recalled, at the start of South Africa's transition to democracy in 1994, the imperatives confronting the incoming regime included 'crafting a new political dispensation and polity; ensuring political stability, reconciliation, deracialization, gender-equality and nation-building; and tackling the all-pervasive socio-economic legacy of apartheid-colonialism and patriarchy' (African National Congress 2012: 6). At the time, just knowing where to begin must have seemed overwhelming. Similarly, in Guatemala Daniel Saquec, advisor to the

UNDP's Maya programme, acknowledges that even today in his country 'there are so many problems with no easy solutions that we can't see what direction we need to go {...}. It's like a labyrinth. You're in it, but you don't know exactly where you're going to end up.' And even in periods described as 'post'-conflict there are significant philosophical divisions, historical memories and emotional attachments that, as in the case of South Africa, prevent the many critics of the now twenty-year old democracy 'from finding common cause, let alone political unity. There is too much embedded in the fibres of existence to allow this to happen in the immediate future' (Villa-Vicencio and Soko 2012: 15).

Alongside this complexity, reconciliation actors must also confront a widespread sense of insecurity that can impede conflict transformation efforts. The fear of returning to a situation of violent conflict can produce a kind of political paralysis. Where less divided or more stable democracies are at least partly defined by their capacity to accommodate political conflict between citizens without the eruption of violence, in deeply divided societies political conflicts are often suppressed or avoided in order to preserve peace (Mitchell 2011: 207). In Northern Ireland, for example, Kate Clifford expresses the widely held fear that peace is still 'fragile', 'precious', and 'precarious'. She observes that, rather than opening political space, this sense of insecurity can impede political engagement; society is still 'on a knife-edge'; people are 'afraid to be in opposition to peace' and are 'frightened of upsetting peace', to the 'detriment of so much other activity'. Like many others, Clifford does not see Northern Ireland as a 'peaceful' society, merely one that is enjoying 'an absence of violence', and she observes that 'The hatred is still there, the intolerance is still there, and people are happy because the bombing has stopped {...}. But we're just post-conflict, we're no further forward than that.'

While Clifford's meaning is clear, the approach of this book in fact contests the view that an absence of war, or a formalized agreement for 'peace', constitutes a situation that can be described as 'post-conflict' in any meaningful sense. While 'post-violence' may be a more accurate description even this is contestable, as will be discussed later in this chapter. In a political sense, no society is, or should aspire to be 'post'-conflict. Conflict is ubiquitous (Ryan 2013: 28) and enduring (Little 2014). It is a 'universal feature of human society' that originates in 'economic differentiation, social change, cultural formation, psychological development and political organization—all of which are inherently conflictual', finding expression in opposing political parties with seemingly incompatible goals (Ramsbotham *et al.* 2011: 7), as well as in the contentious actions of social movements and other forms of political dissent. Rather than suggesting that conflict and division should be disregarded or avoided, this book is oriented towards the challenges involved in *engaging* conflict in deeply divided societies. Understanding the dynamics of such conflict is an important first step towards this goal.

The dynamics of conflict and division

In the deeply divided societies that are the focus of this book, and indeed many others, sources of division can be multiple and may include class, caste, religion, language, race, ethnicity, and clan. To these can be added significant binary divisions such as settler versus native, immigrant versus indigenous population, peasant versus land owner, urban versus rural and so on (Guelke 2012: 14). In the main, these divisions tend to pit one group against another, as, according to Adrian Guelke (2012: 13) the existence of more than two groups tends to work against such polarisation. Nevertheless, Adrian Little (2014: 78) reminds us that even where societies *are* divided between two groups, these groups are likely to be 'internally diverse and indeed divided vis-à-vis other structuring factors in society', adding to the complex dynamics in these cases.

A view of their society as polarized along a binary division was common among my interviewees. In Guatemala, for example, Irma Alicia Velásquez describes 'two Guatemalas': the 'beautiful Guatemala' where 'everything is perfect' and people have security, contrasted with the rural areas, which she describes as 'another country'. Carlos Sarti also describes 'two Guatemalas', referring both to the differences in development and opportunities for people living in the countryside and in the city, and also to the differences that are evident between different urban neighborhoods. Rosalina Tuyuc suggests that the high profile genocide trial against General Efraín Ríos Montt also proved that there are 'two Guatemalas' evident in the starkly divergent views on whether there had or had not been a genocide in the country. For Elena Díez, the root of Guatemala's binary division is colonization (discussed further in Chapter 3) and the historical failure to recognize indigenous rights, which today can trigger conflict over mining, water, or land (discussed further in Chapter 7).

The divisions in Guatemala are evident in extraordinary and deepening socioeconomic inequality that is the result of uneven economic development, and reluctance by the Guatemalan economic elite to relinquish any share of their wealth. Violence of various kinds has become commonplace and insecurity characterizes the daily life of many citizens. Indeed, the 'postwar' has hardly been peaceful. From the 1998 murder of the head of the Catholic truth commission, Bishop Juan Gerardi, to present-day gang violence, drug trafficking, kidnapping rings and the lynchings of suspected criminals, along with the risk of assassination that plagues any critic of Guatemala's power structure, including peasants pursuing land claims, Guatemala now exhibits 'a profound sense of insecurity' (W.E. Little 2009: 2). Despite years of struggle to create change, it is not clear that these efforts have transformed much about people's everyday lives, and Guatemala today remains 'a deeply wounded society' (Arriaza and Roht-Arriaza 2010: 205–6). Almost all my interviewees expressed a sense of despair and confusion about why their efforts had not been more transformative of

Guatemalan society, a condition that Susanne Jonas describes as 'Guate-phrenia'; a condition 'caught between hope for a better future (*la Guate-mala posible*) and exasperation, even horror, at how slowly things change here' (Jonas 2000: 10).

Northern Ireland also exhibits a distinctive pattern of continuing division, notable for a polarized political system that mirrors the central cleavage in society. Well over a decade after the signing of the Belfast Agreement formally ended 'the Troubles', Northern Ireland is remarkable for its high levels of communal segregation and a persistent sense of inter-communal mistrust and resentment. The stability in the region is considered a result of an 'equilibrium' that has been achieved through political power-sharing arrangements, rather than any deeper reconciliation between the two communities (Nolan 2012: 10). Indeed, the Community Relations Council (2011: 36) describes a situation of 'antagonism and parallel development' that remain 'serious obstacles to a normal, open and peaceful society'. The fragility of the peace is evident in the tension and sporadic violence that characterize the annual summer marching season, and in disruptions such as the 2012 rioting mentioned in the introduction to this book. Belfast continues to be shaped by so-called 'peace walls', and despite being applauded internationally as a 'success story' the region is still perceived as vulnerable to a return of wider sectarian violence and disorder with the potential to stall the peace process altogether (Byrne 2012: 14–15). Indeed, Ray Mullan observes a 'wariness' among the 'hard core elements' in both communities about taking Northern Ireland's transformation 'beyond a comfortable separa-tion', suggesting that 'as long as there's equal treatment' the communities are mostly 'happy to be separate'.

South Africa's post-apartheid reality is also markedly different from the 'much eulogized' success story that has been told around the world. Despite undeniable successes in its political transition, South Africa remains divided by a range of 'social pathologies' manifest in a high crime rate, violence, corruption, and a huge burden of disease in the form of HIV/AIDS and tuberculosis, all of which are underpinned by enormous socioeconomic inequality. Neville Alexander (2013: 24) describes the growing gap between rich and poor in South Africa as 'like the elephant in the room, an overwhelming presence that everyone tries to ignore' that risks wrecking 'the entire edifice'. Continued social division also persists, as the 'discouragingly consistent' findings of the South African Reconciliation Barometer survey have shown since it began in 2003 (Lefko-Everett *et al.* 2011: 7). Indeed, in June 2011, the South African National Planning Commission's diagnostic overview found that 'South Africa remains a divided society, and the major dividing line is still race' (cited in Lefko-Everett *et al.* 2011: 7). Oscar Siwali observes the maintenance of these divisions in housing, where a few black people may move in to a new, mostly white neighbourhood, but 'once it's 40 or 50 per cent black, the white people move out and then it becomes black'. These divisions lead Pieter Meiring (2000: 199) to conclude that, despite having stepped out of 'the wreckage of the past', as a nation South Africa remains 'in many respects a spiritual wasteland' that requires 'healing in every sense of the word'.

Australia presents a slightly different example of a divided society, but one that rounds out an understanding of these contexts. Despite Australia's general prosperity and quality of life, Aboriginal and Torres Strait Islander people experience dramatically shorter life expectancy, higher death rates, higher rates of substance abuse, and high levels of individual and community poverty. Recent years have seen some improvement in areas such as infant mortality and educational attainment, but incarceration rates and hospitalizations for intentional self-harm have worsened (Steering Committee for the Review of Government Service Provision 2014). Political discourse in Australia is dominated by stories of dysfunctional communities, welfare dependency, child abuse, alcohol, and violence, which tend to focus on regional and remote Indigenous communities. Yet over two-thirds of Aboriginal people live in urban areas in 'geographically integrated, culturally separate Aboriginal communities' (Behrendt 1995: 75–6), which provide an appearance of integration while masking persistent, deep divisions.

Across these cases we can observe a number of similar characteristics. Guelke (2012: 30) suggests that in deeply divided societies, unlike more stable societies, conflict tends to exist along a 'well-entrenched fault line' that contains the potential for a recurrence of violence. There is often a strong desire to reduce complex political histories into simplified binaries that both describe and contain social reality, as John Paul Lederach (2005: 35) explains:

> People, communities, and most specifically choices about ways they will respond to situations and express views of the conflict are forced into either-or categories: We are right. They are wrong. We were violated. They are the violators. We are the liberators. They are oppressors. Our intentions are good. Theirs are bad. History and the truth of history is most fully comprehended by our view. Their view of history is biased, incomplete, maliciously untruthful, and ideologically driven. You are with us or against us.

Further, the characteristics of these divisions give rise to forms of violence other than physical violence. Johan Galtung (1990: 292) has defined violence as 'avoidable insults to basic human needs', and has famously distinguished between 'direct' violence and 'structural' violence (1969), later introducing the idea of 'cultural' violence that moves from a social 'process' to a 'permanence' (1990: 294). As Oliver Ramsbotham (2010: 53) explains, there are 'complex interconnections' between these forms of violence: 'Structural violence (injustice, exclusion, inequality) and cultural violence (prejudice, ignorance, discrimination) lead to direct violence; direct violence reinforces and perpetuates structural and cultural violence; and so on'. Structural or symbolic violence often appears 'reasonable', thereby disguising the interests that benefit from it and the force that is required to impose it on particular social groups (Woolford 2010: 144). In a settler colonial society such as Australia, for example, where colonizers have used force to dominate and intimidate indigenous peoples, the settler state rarely considers its actions to be violence 'either morally or under the law' (Atkinson 2002: 12). The forms of 'everyday violence that keeps groups in a state of subjection' contribute to a sense of there being 'two (or more) different worlds' in which direct, structural and cultural violence overlap:

> In the first, there is low infant mortality, high literacy, economic security, and more opportunities for people to live their lives in a manner of their choosing. In the second, endemic poverty may be responsible for needless deaths of children, famine, displacement, shortened life spans, and a condition in which people's freedom to make choices in their lives is severely curtailed – if it exists at all.
>
> (Arthur 2011: 10)

Understanding the complex nature of violence in this way also helps to reveal the enduring nature of the conflicts violence serves to perpetuate.

The nature of conflict

The premise of this book—and one increasingly shared by others in the field—is that conflict cannot, and indeed should not, be overcome or 'resolved'. Conflict is an essential democratic dynamic that may enable political actors to contest unjust situations, suggesting that there may need to be more rather than less conflict in order for political goals to be achieved. The aim of reconciliation efforts, according to Ramsbotham (2010: 53) is 'to transform actually or potentially violent conflict into non-violent forms of social struggle'.

This is a view of conflict advanced by Little (2014) who contends that what he describes as 'enduring conflict' is a feature of both stable democracies and divided societies. Little argues that enduring conflict is 'written into the social and political fabric of all societies' in ways that influence contemporary structures, institutions, and relationships, forming a 'background condition' that has become part of the 'everyday operation' of social and political life (2014: 5). And while conflict may be a more obvious structuring factor in the divided societies that are the focus of this book, this does not mean that less overtly conflictual societies are in fact more harmonious. Little reframes conflict as 'a standard element of the political' (2014: 14) and cautions that the ambition to 'overcome' conflict may in fact neglect the potentially positive role it plays in political struggle, simultaneously causing us to 'avert our eyes' from the ways in which conflict endures in many contemporary societies and instead producing narratives of conflict triumphantly overcome and resolved (Little 2014: 13). As the cases in this study make clear, such narratives are rarely accurate.

Little (2014: 14) also warns that focusing on various forms of political violence risks neglecting the crucial ways in which everyday social and cultural practices may in fact reinforce violent discourses and behaviours (Little 2014: 26). This neglect is inherently dangerous, as it drives enduring social and political conflict underground from where it will inevitably surface in unpredictable and violent ways. As Brendan McAllister, the then Victims and Survivors Commissioner in Northern Ireland, contends:

> Conflict is a natural phenomenon, and like any natural phenomenon, it has to find expression. So, if you dam up water in one place, it will look for the next weakest place to get out.

In Northern Ireland, McAllister suggests, conflict 'has found expression around big communal issues' including civil rights, housing, unemployment, educational access, policing and so on.

None of this is to suggest that an approach to conflict in divided societies should disregard the particular risks that inhere to these contexts. As discussed above, these divisions tend to polarize groups, meaning that the conflict in divided societies is likely to be intergroup conflict. This in turn affects the types of reconciliation and conflict transformation efforts that are possible in these contexts. Intergroup conflict often involves direct violence that may result in death and/or serious injury on a mass scale. Direct violence in these contexts is also likely to be further compounded by structural and cultural violence in the form of marginalization, repression, and discrimination (Nadler 2012: 293). A society's vulnerability to violence may be the result of a lack of consensus on the legitimacy of the political process and outcomes produced by the state or other decision-making framework (Guelke 2012: 32). This lack of legitimacy is likely to be further entrenched by contested historical memories that continue to fuel the intergroup conflict (Nadler 2012: 293).

In most divided societies conflict has deep historical roots. According to the Recovery of Historical Memory Project in Guatemala, for example, the roots of that conflict 'are found in a tradition of social exclusion, ethnic discrimination, and social injustice that permeates the state structure' (Recovery of Historical Memory Project (REMHI) 1999: xxxii). In South Africa, Kindiza Ngubeni points out that, since 1994, the emphasis on divisions 'only between white and black' has been problematic as this has neglected that 'going deep, communities were also divided' and that these many divisions were actually 'created by the system many, many years ago'. For Michael Lapsley, these deep conflicts play out in 'the relationship of the nation to the individual', in which each person wrestles with questions: 'What do I carry in me as a consequence of the context in which I've lived? How has the national story impacted on me? How has what happened to my parents or grandparents and great grandparents impacted on me?' These questions point to the specific legacies of past violence in maintaining division and fomenting the challenging social dynamics that typify deeply divided societies.

The legacy of violence

Most societies hold concerns about violence, usually the individual violence associated with crime. In deeply divided societies, however, the threat of violence has a particular potency, 'looming large' in the concerns of citizens who know that security is not something to be taken for granted (Guelke 2012: 33). In each of the countries that form the focus of this book, a history of violence has been a defining feature, whether it is the colonial violence of Australia's frontier wars, or the more recent violence of Northern Ireland's Troubles, South Africa's struggle against apartheid, or *la violencia* of Guatemala's 36-year civil war. In these contexts, the memories, insecurities, and intergenerational traumas that are the direct legacy of violence continue to shape and constrain contemporary social dynamics and political possibilities. For example, *la violencia* 'has become a touchstone for measuring and evaluating an ordinary sense of things'. Things are 'better' because the totalizing violence of the civil war, although vividly remembered, is now considered to be a thing of the past (Benson and Fischer 2009: 151). And there are tangible ways in which the end of mass violence *has* greatly improved life in deeply divided societies. The decline in violence in the decade following Northern Ireland's initial ceasefires means that there are several hundred mostly young working-class men, who are 'alive and well who might otherwise be prematurely in their graves' (Coulter and Murray 2008: 14).

For survivors, however, the past remains very much a part of the present. A history of violent conflict can defeat the capacity to reason and produce individual experiences of emotional dislocation that translate into collective memories, that shape contemporary political formations and frame capacities for reconciliation and conflict transformation (Hutchison and Bleiker 2013: 82–3). These emotional legacies 'plant a time bomb in the depth of the human psyche' with the capacity to blow apart present and future relations (Shriver 2002a: 155–6). And although often concealed by formal political settlements and peace agreements, these experiences of unresolved victimization can take on a structural character over time, contributing to cyclical patterns of violence that may well play out along different lines of division to the original political conflict (Simpson 2000: 17), as in the 2008 outbreak of xenophobic violence in South Africa discussed further below.

The Australian case provides evidence of the enduring nature of the legacies of past violence and trauma. Many Australian indigenous scholars and commentators point to the forms of lateral violence and abuse that today disrupt life in some Aboriginal communities. Indigenous Trauma expert Judy Atkinson (2002: 8) points to the 'despair and rage' that she sees 'being re-enacted by our people on ourselves in diverse and damaging ways' that have the effect of perpetuating the cycle. These impacts are the result of both direct violence and structural and cultural violence. As Atkinson (2002: 53–4) argues, collective trauma

> seeps slowly and insidiously into the fabric and soul of relations and beliefs of people as a community. The shock of loss of self and community comes gradually. People, feeling bereaved, grieve for their loss of cultural surrounds, as well as for family and friends. Feeling victimized, the same people may also carry a deep rage at what has happened to them, but may be unable to express their anger at those they perceive to have violated their world.

This pain and rage is often turned inwards, expressed through binge-drinking and shocking rates of suicide, or it is externalized and expressed through abusive behaviours directed towards family and community. This experience 'cascades down the generations', over time growing more entrenched and complex (Atkinson 2002: 80), becoming what Patrick Dodson (2008: 31) has described as 'a festering cancer on the nation's soul'.

Guatemala's more recent history of violence tells a similar story. In the wake of the scorched earth practices that characterized *la violencia*, terror has become a 'filter' through which to 'understand the past and interpret the present'. Victoria Sanford (2003: 13–14) argues that this legacy will continue to constrain all efforts to construct a more democratic society until the nation develops an understanding of how the majority rural Maya experienced and internalized state and insurgent structures of terror as part of their individual and collective identities. This is made more difficult by the lingering fear of continued violence that contributes to a silence about past traumas, including sometimes within families, and is thought to have produced 'myriad types of social dysfunctionality, from lynchings to somatic illnesses' (Arriaza and Roht-Arriaza 2010: 209). Thus, *la violencia* represents both the actual violence and its effects, leaving the experience of genocide 'resting fitfully' in Guatemala's collective unconscious as 'an officially silenced national trauma reverberating throughout the society' (Sanford 2003: 212).

South Africa is also attempting to emerge from a past that was often defined by violent struggle. In our interview, Namhla Mniki-Mangaliso spoke of her sadness that some of the forms of violence learned in the course of the struggle against apartheid—such as necklacing—continue to manifest themselves in the wake of the transition to democracy. She sees this as South African society 'turning inward' and 'acting out the anger towards the nearest, closest perceived enemy'. For Mniki-Mangaliso a response to this legacy must involve a recognition of the 'level of damage that happens in people's identity' under a regime like apartheid, damage that is done to both black and white South Africans. But, as Oscar Siwali reminds us, apartheid was intended to 'cripple the mind'. The legacy is that people have been 'dispossessed' of 'the right to be able to think, to be able to make a living for themselves, to be able to see themselves becoming a people'. When combined with the enormous structural divisions that also continue to cripple divided societies, discussed in the next section, these psycho-social legacies of violence undoubtedly constrain the capacity for transformation.

Structural divisions

The emotional legacy of violence discussed above is often fuelled by the deep inequalities that produce endemic poverty and deepen people's despair. The depth of these structural divisions can prevent societies from engaging in important political conflicts, even about these same inequalities, because of what Charles Villa-Vicencio (2009: 81) describes as 'the unending inner roar of pain, anger, and fear' that can drown out other dialogue.

Each of the countries that are the focus of this book manifests persistent structural divisions. Julio Solórzano-Foppa, who is working on developing a *Memorial para la Concordia* in Guatemala, maintains that the inequality, malnutrition, and racism there today are much the same as the conditions that 'generated the war in the first place'. Irma Alicia Velásquez agrees, suggesting that the elite in Guatemala maintain 'almost total power', meaning that Guatemala maintains structural divisions that are 'like South Africa'. And Jose Suasnavar maintains that 'since colonial times' there has been a concerted effort 'to maintain this very same structure' of segregation and division, which when combined with racism makes it 'difficult for us to co-exist'. For Suasnavar conditions in Guatemala today seem 'pre-conflict' rather than 'post-conflict', and he expresses great frustration that the country's 'fanatics' have not learned the lesson to be learnt from 'so many dead'.

South Africa is little changed in this regard either, with the gap between rich and poor still creating the biggest divide in the country (Lefko-Everett *et al.* 2011: 8). Despite South Africa's transitional aspiration towards being a 'rainbow nation', today the divide between rich and poor is still defined in terms of indigenous African and European populations, very much the 'two nations'—one rich and mostly white, the other poor and almost entirely black—that the then deputy president Thabo Mbeki described in a 1998 speech (cited in Fairweather 2006: 160). The lack of change in these structural divides belies the 'international media fantasy of the New South Africa', with waves of so-called 'service delivery protests' and violence between police and miners continually forcing the issue of socio-economic equality onto the national agenda (Biko 2013: 28). Although a small business and political elite among black South Africans has made economic advances, the period since the transition to democracy in 1994 has essentially seen the hopes and dreams of the majority of ordinary South Africans betrayed:

> Many say that freedom was supposed to mean houses, jobs, land, and food for everyone. That freedom meant a life free from the stranglehold of patriarchy and violence. But for many none of this has materialized and for many more things are getting worse.
>
> (Essof and Moshenberg 2011: 2)

Australia's structural divisions are less obvious. While the majority of Aboriginal and Torres Strait Islander people endure greater poverty than the non-Indigenous population, as noted above, over two-thirds of the Indigenous population live in urban areas. Urban ghettoes are certainly present, but have come under increasing pressure from property development. The most intensive policy focus in Australia centres on the extreme poverty in many remote communities, and on debate about so-called 'welfare dependency' that tends to be abstracted from the historical factors that have structured this dependency. Indeed, as I have argued elsewhere (Maddison 2009), it is evident around the world that colonization *creates* dependency, which manifests itself in ways that have proven to be profoundly damaging to indigenous peoples' lives. Even advances in Australia such as land rights legislation have not successfully addressed these historical legacies. While it was assumed that land restoration would lead to economic development, in fact the land that has been returned to indigenous people has generally been remote, arid and of low commercial value (Altman *et al.* 2005: 3). And the economic elite in Australia has worked to ensure that this is the case, with mining companies, farmers, and conservative politicians waging a major public relations campaign against the native title reforms of the 1990s (Short 2008: 128, discussed further in Chapter 7).

Northern Ireland is another complex case of structural division. Although the Troubles developed out of the civil rights movement advanced by the Catholic/nationalist/republican[1] community, which itself rested on different constitutional views (as will be discussed further in Chapter 6) today the picture is less clear. Northern Ireland remains polarized along key structural divisions including housing, education, and social and religious life (Kelly 2012: 3). Efforts to break down the separation between communities, have been stymied by a complex range of interrelated factors including historic patterns of division; entrenched institutional practices; a lack of political and community leadership; fear and mistrust of the 'other'; a widespread sense of insecurity; and limited resources available to make the systemic changes required to create 'new patterns of interaction and integration' (Kelly 2012: 110–11).

In each of these cases, state capacity for the reform of structural divisions seems a significant factor hampering transformation. It is a common challenge for post-violent conflict societies to confront the reality of fragile or non-existent state institutions at precisely the moment that citizens are making unprecedented calls for effective state intervention. Certainly this was true in Guatemala where it is widely held that the state did not, and still *does* not, have the capacity to implement policies aimed at structural reform as it is comprised of weak or non-existent governance institutions. Arnoldo Noriega recalls a colleague declaring that, when the Peace Accords were signed, he realized that 'there wasn't a state' in Guatemala, 'we just had an army'. A lack of state capacity is further undermined by the intense self-interest maintained by the Guatemalan elites who were, it must be remembered, 'willing to commit genocide to maintain their position'. These elite blocs ensured that the Accords relating to the role of the military and the socioeconomic structure were the most contested (Nelson 2009: 49). The resulting stagnation in the transformation of structural divisions in Guatemala has produced a 'half-relieved, half-despairing sentiment' that the country is 'no longer a special postwar case, but just another third world country' (Nelson 2009: 307).

South Africa also inherited a degree of state incapacity with regard to transforming structural division, based less on a problem of fragile state institutions, and more on the fact that the existing civil service was 'racially constituted' and the state itself 'badly fragmented' (Powell 2010: 243). South Africa has proven itself unable to match its vision for social transformation with the institutional capacity required to implement change, which has doubtless contributed to frustrated expectations across the country (Simpson 2000: 11). And as these frustrations spill over into protest and visible discontent they also contribute to the widespread sense of insecurity that characterizes deeply divided societies, further challenging efforts at reconciliation and conflict transformation.

Peace and quiet, noise and riot

In divided societies with a recent history of violence there is a great desire to preserve the peace and avoid a return to violent conflict. And yet in each of the countries in this study, including Australia where the central conflict ended long ago, violence remains a defining feature of the social and structural division. Both South Africa and Guatemala are considered to be amongst the most violent countries in the world, with high rates of violent crime including kidnapping. South Africa's violence exploded in a tragic fashion during the 2008 wave of xenophobic attacks against migrants and refugees from other parts of Africa (Gobodo-Madikizela 2010: 135). Northern Ireland can move quickly from what Martin McMullan describes as 'this most peaceful and beautiful place' to one where a tension emerges and quickly becomes 'the catalyst to riot and full-on confrontation'. For Kate Turner this is evidence that a generation of violence has left Northern Ireland with 'a very damaged way of looking at things', where violence is the 'default' response to conflict. Australia too has had its share of explosive violence, for example the Palm Island[2] and Redfern[3] riots, both in 2004. The latter has been described as 'the worst race riot in Australian history', which 'peeled back the thin veneer of an undercurrent of racial tension' (Ridgeway 2004: 1).

Certainly it seems evident that efforts at reconciliation and conflict transformation in deeply divided societies must come to terms with the changing nature of conflict and violence in the society, rather than expecting the simple end to such confrontation (Simpson 2000: 3). Opening up political spaces in the wake of violent conflict or civil war may often create new channels through which violence can be instigated. This may be more opportunistic, localized violence than the violence that characterized the period of conflict, and can be understood as both a continuation of the national struggle and as an exploitation of the fluidity that exists during periods of transition. This suggests a need to problematize the distinction between 'political violence' and 'crime', as it is often difficult to observe a straightforward delineation between political violence and the kinds of violence that seem compatible with 'peace'. This means that the ways in which post-conflict violence is discussed can and should play an important role in the way reconciliation and conflict transformation efforts are approached (Schuld 2013: 62).

Certainly the way in which violence is spoken about changes once a violent conflict is thought to be formally concluded, despite the fact that there are often considerable 'continuities of violence' between the brutality of the war and the 'postwar' (Schuld 2013: 69). In Guatemala, for example there is now a 'lexicon of adjectives' used to describe the high rates of violence that persist there, including 'state-sponsored', institutional, structural, ethnic, organized, and 'criminal violence', which may include gang activity and mob justice such as lynchings (Reilly 2009: 39). In South Africa the militarism learned during the anti-apartheid struggle continues to manifest through individual gun ownership, vigilantism, and sometimes extreme private security arrangements (Hamber 2010: 80). But where the media in post-conflict societies tends to refer to these forms of violence as new phenomena, often in an effort to discredit the new regime, generally there is considerable continuity with earlier periods of violence. Understanding these continuities requires that we 'look beyond the label of crime' to observe that these same modes of violence were also typical of periods of armed conflict, suggesting direct links between the two phenomena (Schuld 2013: 66).

Of the countries in this study South Africa and Guatemala most clearly represent these continuities, and both are considered to have skyrocketing postwar crime rates. South Africa today is widely considered to be one of the most 'criminally violent' societies in the world (Powell 2010: 246–7). Hlumelo Biko (2013: 95) suggests that some South Africans have responded to the sense of injustice perpetuated by the structural inequalities discussed above by turning to 'populism, xenophobia, corruption and crime', each problematic on their own, but particularly dangerous when operating in parallel. Crime, in particular, is seen as 'an individual protest mechanism' against the injustices of the South African status quo (Biko 2013: 206), with 'highly militarized' segments of South African society using violent crime and 'private justice' to express frustration at continued inequality and marginalization (Simpson 2000: 2).

Despite a view of crime as racially divisive, however, most South African crime in fact occurs in poorer areas, and is referred to as 'black on black', although 'black on white' crime attracts far more media attention. Lucy Holborn tells me that white South Africans 'feel' that violent crime has got 'terribly worse', when in fact that is not borne out in statistics that show an increase in robberies, but a decrease in sexual assault, murder, and other gun crime. What has changed is the locations in which crime is occurring, as Holborn explains:

> There was the same if not more crime pre-1994, but most of it was confined within black communities because if you were a black person walking along a white suburban street someone could stop you and ask what were you doing {...}. Suddenly whites are opened up to the potential that they can be equally a victim of crime. It's almost like crime has been democratized, as it were, but the effect has been that white people feel like there's a political and racial motive behind all of this and they're being targeted, which I don't think is the case at all.

In Guatemala, gang culture, and gang violence, have become the 'most visible and brutal' forms of violence since the signing of the Peace Accords, spreading from the city into rural areas including villages that were previously free of violent crime (Burrell 2009: 99–100). Gang violence is also fostering generational conflict in Guatemala, and is itself met with increasingly violent forms of resistance and repression, including curfews, attempted lynchings, murders, and the creation of village 'security committees' that 'closely resemble' the civil patrols of *la violencia* (Burrell 2009: 98, 101). The growth of gang activity is thought to be connected to the number of ex-combatants left jobless due to military downsizing, and is increasingly connected to organized crime and drug trafficking. Guatemala is also increasingly becoming a site for both the transit and primary production of illegal drugs, including marijuana in the department of Petén, and opiate poppies in the San Marcos region. Former Minister of

National Defence, Julio Balconi, tells me that 25 years ago, when police discovered the first poppy fields in San Marcos, they found around 200,000 plants. In 2012 they found 70 million plants. Balconi observed that these operations have moved into the 'empty spaces' where there 'was no presence of military or the police'. Many of these spaces are now controlled by members of the formerly state sanctioned death squads, which have maintained close connections to the Guatemalan elite and now have 'de facto control' over many communities, using 'intimidation, violence, and terror' to maintain their power (Suarez and Jordan 2007: 2). Indeed, Alvaro Pop describes Guatemala as 'a society that is permeated by violence all the way through {...} because of organized crime and drug trafficking'.

Another form of violence that is common to deeply divided societies is what Karl von Holdt (2011) describes as 'insurgent citizenship', evident in South Africa's so-called 'service delivery protests' and similar protest activity. Violence was a central component of civil society mobilizations against apartheid in the 1980s, and the insurgent citizenship that von Holdt observes uses similar repertoires to contest contemporary claims. In 2008 South Africa's insurgent citizenship was expressed in a fortnight of xenophobic violence directed at foreign Africans resulting in the deaths of at least 61 people, with over 100,000 people displaced (von Holdt 2011: 5). These attacks, which again demonstrated characteristics of struggle-era violence, were motivated by the tensions between South Africans and foreign nationals who found themselves living in shared poverty, in competition for jobs and services. Oscar Siwali recognizes aspects of the xenophobic violence as belonging to the struggle against apartheid, and argues that 'If you raise a generation of people with the mentality of making things fall down', as the struggle veterans did in the quest to make the apartheid state 'ungovernable', then there needs to be a point at which people understand that it is time to stop the destruction. For Siwali, this point has not yet been reached across South Africa. In fact Hugo Van der Merwe suggests that the South African transition 'didn't really redefine the role of violence' in South African society:

> There's an assumption that, with democracy, there is no need for violence, but, at the same time, the language of violence is still fundamental in terms of how we deal with differences. We haven't transformed how we engage with conflict {...}. Okay, we're not torturing political people anymore {...} we're killing Zimbabweans {...}. What we've got now is a sense of nationalism where it's not okay to kill a South African, but it's still okay to kill someone else. There's a certain value system that hasn't been redefined sufficiently.

Indeed, it seems not uncommon that violence in deeply divided societies is directed towards groups that fall outside of the main social cleavage. In Northern Ireland, for example, alongside the seasonal rioting associated with parades, the violence that has previously been targeted on a sectarian basis is now finding what the Community Relations Council (2011: 14) calls 'brutal parallels' in attacks on other marginalized groups based on minority ethnic background or sexual orientation. Paul Hutchinson acknowledges that these sentiments derive from persistent feelings of social exclusion, particularly among working class people, but he nevertheless laments that Northern Ireland has 'proved to be as racist as we have been sectarian'. Indeed, following violent attacks in 2003–2004 directed against members of the Chinese community living in Belfast, and later attacks against Polish and Roma people, Northern Ireland was dubbed the 'race hate capital of Europe', apparently 'unable to cope with multiculturalism' (Knox 2011: 387–8).

As has been noted above, a key factor underpinning the violence in divided societies is a view that the state is lacking in legitimacy, or that state legitimacy has not 'fully stabilized' (von Holdt 2011: 28). State violence against civilians has the effect of negating the meaning of authority as a force for serving and protecting the community. In contexts such as this violence against the state, or in protest against state (in)action, may seem both justified and necessary.

There are, however, other motivations also in play. In Guatemala, for example, there is suspicion that some forms of political violence—such as assassinations and 'mob violence'—may have been deliberately orchestrated in order to produce an electoral climate favourable to a 'strongman' promising citizen security (Reilly 2009: 38). The spike in crime in Guatemala following the signing of the Accords became a challenge to their successful implementation, particularly with regard to the role of the army. One of the more hotly contested provisions in the Accords called for the army to relinquish its internal security role to the new civilian police force, but the slow pace of constituting this new force left a 'security vacuum' that lead successive presidents to deploy the army to help combat violent crime (Stolper and Hammond 2010: 162; Jonas 2000: 148). Several of my interviewees joked about the ineptitude of the Guatemalan police, suggesting that an army officer had to follow along behind to ensure the safety of police officers patrolling the streets. Today many Guatemalans still turn to the military for the restoration of order, providing further justification for their continuing domestic security role. The national security ideology that underpins the role of the military 'casts social peace and justice as counterplots', with stability perceived to have higher moral standing than justice (Sanford 2003: 252).

One further dimension to the role of the state with regard to continuities of violence pertains to the corruption, or perceived corruption, that seems to afflict some states emerging from periods of internal violent conflict. In South Africa there is a common view that those in power justify the provision of favours to family and friends through the expression that it is their 'turn to eat', an attitude that overrides their commitment to community welfare (Mbeki 2010: 5), and has produced a culture of 'cronyism, clientelism, and corruption' (Mbembe 2008: 6). Tim Murithi suggests that many white South Africans see a 'corrupt black elite {...} hell bent on self enrichment to the exclusion of everything else' essentially 'running the country into the ground'. More insidious still is the view that an elite few have profited from the transition to democracy at the expense of greater equality, with many of those who were a part of the first democratic government now occupying board positions in the same corporations that benefited from the abuses of the apartheid economy (Barnard-Naudé 2008: 195). The relationship between the Guatemalan economic elite, which essentially forms a power oligarchy within the country, is seen in similar terms, with Velásquez expressing the view that Guatemalan political parties are profoundly dysfunctional because they only respond to particular families and their businesses. Impunity is also a part of this messy equation, with Suasnavar suggesting that there is little reason for citizens to have confidence that the state can either provide security or address underlying social conflict. As he put it in our interview, if you live in a state where 200,000 people were killed and 'disappeared' with impunity then it is easier to assume that 'the way to solve a problem now is just to kill the person' because 'nobody is going to investigate or punish the perpetrator'.

All of these dynamics—from crime to violent protest and perceived state corruption—have a profound effect on efforts towards reconciliation and conflict transformation. Crime produces new victims and perpetrators, perpetuates trauma, increases insecurity, and may further entrench both social divides and state illegitimacy (Daly and Sarkin 2007: 219). Violence also remains a direct challenge to the goal of nonrepetition of past conflict. As the Northern Ireland Community Relations Council (2011: 14) argues, any form of social apartheid that is 'rooted in exclusion and supremacy' can never be seen as benign or accidental, as it 'always conceals exclusion based on violence and threat'. The resulting spread of insecurity may also result in increased electoral support for right-wing politicians and contradictory expectation about the advancement of human rights (Sieder 2008: 76). This has been the case in Guatemala where Ríos Montt has remained a force in domestic politics, even receiving electoral support from many Maya who have seemingly transformed the man responsible for genocide and gross human rights violations into 'a defender of law and order' (Stolper and Hammond 2010: 189). Ultimately, the continuation of direct violence in deeply divided societies is both a reflection of, and a distraction from, other forms of structural and cultural violence that continue to stymie efforts at more profound conflict transformation in those societies.

Transforming enduring conflict

In each of the countries in this study, various forms of deep division persist that make it difficult for opposing communities to begin to know one another. Trust is in short supply. Divisions between communities are maintained in a variety of subtle and not-so-subtle ways. In Northern Ireland, for example, where the communities are physically indistinguishable, there is a practice known as 'telling', whereby a range of clues is used to interpret an individual's community of origin. Clues include the sport a person plays or the team they support, the school they attended, the pronunciation of certain letters, and the presence of cultural symbols such as jewellery, badges, or brands of clothing. Upon making a new acquaintance it is usual to ask a series of question that will make it possible to 'tell' which community a person comes from, and until that is established a conversation will be limited to 'safe' topics. Neil Jarman tells me that this process happens 'very quickly, very intuitively', and is a key practice that maintains social segregation. Words and phrases are understood to indicate political or religious affiliation in ways that produce invisible barriers to communication between the two communities (Kelly 2012: 12).

It is in light of such practices that Little (2014: 7) contends that 'the aspiration to peace and the absence of conflict as the normal state of affairs is fundamentally at odds with the experience of both divided and seemingly harmonious societies'. In some fundamental ways this is an entirely accurate observation. As this chapter has observed, conflict in divided societies endures in deep and complex social phenomena, in structures, institutions and relationships, and in the hearts, minds and memories of all those affected by violence. This point is acknowledged by some of my interviewees. Jarman, for example, agrees that conflict does not 'come to a neat, shuddering end' but instead 'takes a long time to work itself out'. In a society such as Northern Ireland, historical division and a framework that aspires to nothing more than 'coexistence' have entrenched separate development and perpetual division.

Yet, as this chapter has shown, there are some very good reasons why people living in divided societies may seek to transform the nature of the conflicts that divides them. While the approach of this book rests on an understanding that conflict is an important and potentially productive political dynamic, it is also true that the experience of intractable conflict and the maintenance of segregation is exhausting and oppressive. As Shirley Gunn, a long term struggle veteran from South Africa suggests, the endless focus on conflict can be 'so demoralizing that it can render one completely and utterly useless' such that at times she feels she needs to 'relinquish responsibility' in order to 'maintain sanity'. Susanne Jonas observes that Guatemalans have 'had to train themselves in mental gymnastics' in order to 'keep their eyes on the prize of the *imaginario*'—the Guatemala 'that they dream of creating or inventing' (Jonas 2000: 232–3).

These personal challenges are immense, and can translate into deeper chill factors that affect social and political efforts to transform conflict. The persistent sense of insecurity, and the structural violence of racism and inequality all flag the potential fragility of the settlement that ended the violence. In these contexts, most people desire a future where they can 'find each other' across profound differences and, to whatever limited extent, perhaps even agree on elements of a common future agenda (Kollapen 2010: 25). With this in mind, in the following chapter I will begin to conceptualize what a process of 'reconciliation' and conflict transformation might realistically entail.

Notes

1 Throughout this book, the terms 'Protestant' and 'Catholic' to refer to the two main ethnic communities in Northern Ireland. These terms are often used in conjunction with the political designations of unionist/loyalist or nationalist/republican. Unionism refers to the belief, held mainly by Protestants, that Northern Ireland should remain part of the United Kingdom, while nationalism refers to the belief, held mainly by Catholics, that Northern Ireland should unite with the Republic of Ireland. The more extreme version of unionism, often associated with support for paramilitary violence, is loyalism; its nationalist counterpart is republicanism.

2 The riot in the Aboriginal community of Palm Island followed the violent death in custody of an indigenous man arrested on a public nuisance charge. When the severity of the deceased man's injuries was revealed, the community on Palm Island erupted into violence that saw its police station and barracks burnt to the ground. The police officer charged over the man's death was subsequently acquitted of the charges, despite the state anti-corruption agency finding that the police service had colluded to protect the officer and taint the available evidence.

3 The riot in Redfern (a central Sydney suburb that has long been a hub for Aboriginal community and activism) was sparked by the death of a young Aboriginal man who was impaled on a fence while evading police he believed were chasing him. Aboriginal people from across Sydney gathered to protest the death, with the resulting violence injuring 40 police officers.

2 Conceptualizing reconciliation

As the previous chapter makes clear, the challenges facing deeply divided societies are complex, multiple, and immense. In each of the countries in this study, and indeed in many more around the world, many thousands of actors are working to create change in their societies, pursuing goals such as 'peace', 'justice', 'democracy', and 'reconciliation'. Yet none of these concepts are simple or straightforward, and the definitional complexity that characterizes this field can further complicate their efforts. This book is particularly concerned with the framing of this kind of work as efforts towards 'reconciliation'. Despite its complexities, I am interested in retaining the rhetorical power of the concept of reconciliation, while also broadening its use to become an umbrella term that incorporates aspects of transition, peacebuilding and transformation. I see value in the particular role that Paul Muldoon (2008: 125) suggests reconciliation can play, that is, in 'constituting a space for democratic politics out of a condition of violence'. Thus, unlike some of the common approaches to reconciliation that conceive it primarily as a relational practice, in what follows I will outline a conceptual approach to reconciliation that can be applied to the multiple demands of divided societies, with a view to enabling the development of sustainable democracy and non violent conflict.

This chapter proceeds to map the conceptual terrain that contributes to work on reconciliation. Although it draws from analyses of related fields such as transitional justice and peacebuilding I distinguish reconciliation from these approaches. Transitional justice (the limitations of which are discussed further in Chapter 3) has been criticized for its aspiration to convert 'the constitutive and agonistic quality of reconciliation' into a more limited, adversarial application of the rule of law (Doxtader 2012: 29). Peacebuilding, particularly in the mode of the 'liberal peace' agenda (discussed further in Chapter 9), has been similarly criticized for seeking to impose Western liberal institutions in conflict-affected countries, fuelling concerns that the specifically liberal character of these interventions has caused, or at least perpetuated, many of the pathologies and divisions they still endure (Zaum 2013: 109). The approach here instead advances an argument for reconciliation as a complex, agonistic and transformative process. Counter to the view of reconciliation as concerned with harmony, consensus, and closure, this view values a politics of reconciliation that foregrounds conflict, plurality, and openness. As Andrew Schaap (2005: 9) suggests, 'If we are to understand reconciliation as a political concept, then we must consider not only how politics might be conciliatory but how reconciliation might be politicized'. Thus, the reconciliation conceived here is one that pursues the opening of political space in which divided societies may continue to engage in vibrant clashes of passion and identity, without resorting to violence.

Conceptual confusion

In recent decades, reconciliation has become a commonplace term expressing a regulative ideal in political discourse (Christodoulidis and Veitch 2007: 3). Developing first in relation to 'transitional' societies emerging from periods of authoritarian rule or civil war, the politics of reconciliation has since expanded to include the efforts of established democracies, notably settler colonial societies still grappling with historical wrongs such as Australia and Canada (Bashir and Kymlicka 2008: 3–4). Over time the term has become increasingly used in the political arena, moving from 'the seminary and the academy into public policy' (Hamber and Kelly 2009: 286). In response to this expansion of reconciliation discourse and practice, scholars of political science have engaged with reconciliation in both theory and empirical study. Despite their commitment however, there remains a significant lack of agreement about the meaning, content, staging, timing, and measurement of reconciliation efforts involving a range of political actors (Daly and Sarkin 2007: xiii). As Adrian Little (2012: 84) suggests, many advocates of reconciliation realize that the term is complex and used in many different ways, while commentators on transformational politics in fact say 'widely divergent things in the name of reconciliation'. Indeed, the meaning of reconciliation will vary from context to context, and although the proliferation of terms used to describe reconciliation efforts may not be inherently problematic, it may contribute to a general inability to communicate clearly about the significance and implications of this work.

High profile processes such as the South African Truth and Reconciliation Commission (TRC) have tended to narrow and dominate the field (Renner 2012: 51), receiving an unwarranted level of investigation in relation to other conflict transformation efforts. As Eric Doxtader (2012: 28) has suggested, while the TRC was indeed 'quite important', reconciliation in South Africa neither began nor ended there, and the institution itself displayed little in the way of 'philosophical flair' in considering either the practice of reconciliation or critical inquiry into the concept itself. The 'sloppy' use of the term during the TRC process coloured debate in South

Africa, leaving people confused about what reconciliation could achieve, with wide ranging consequences (Borer 2004: 23). Nevertheless, high profile processes like the TRC have fostered the idea of reconciliation as a normative good, deployed by a range of activists and civil society organizations to support their claims, although leaving such actors poorly equipped in terms of analytical capacity to understand the performance of these policies and processes (Little 2014: 92, Renner 2012: 51).

Much research has attempted to further narrow and define the concept of reconciliation in an effort to 'boil it down' to an agreed policy framework (Renner 2012: 55). As Daly and Sarkin suggest (2007: 4), however, despite the huge political and economic capital being expended on reconciliation-promoting projects, there remains a broad inability to either understand reconciliation or 'confront its multitudinous and sometimes contradictory relationships'. Further, as some of the promise of post-conflict efforts in South Africa and elsewhere has faded in light of ongoing struggles and challenges, a more critical perspective on the meaning and possibility of reconciliation has emerged (Little 2014: 92). These debates continue, offering divergent and contradictory understandings of the concept.

Yet this is not intrinsically problematic. As Schaap (2005: 13) contends, there are advantages to this conceptual ambiguity, as by 'accommodating multiple meanings' the idea of reconciliation 'provides a common vocabulary within which citizens may contest the terms and possibilities of their political association'. The alternative—pursuing a definitional consensus—would have the effect of containing reconciliation discourse, effectively limiting how it might be communicated and understood. Instead, it seems important to focus on the ways in which the language of reconciliation can open up and frame the spaces in which to debate about the multiple demands of conflict transformation (Little 2012a: 84).

Context is certainly important to understanding the different ways in which the concept of reconciliation is used, heard, and understood. In Northern Ireland for example, the Community Relations Council (2011: 20) notes the 'enormous efforts' that have gone into the pursuit of 'real and meaningful reconciliation', and the risks that were taken in these efforts 'even when reconciliation was dismissed as naïve'. Considerable financial resources have been invested in efforts towards 'peace', 'reconciliation', 'equality' and 'good relations' and yet the region continues to wrestle with both the meanings of these terms and how these goals might be effectively supported and achieved (Kelly 2012: 11). Partly this is the result of the complex, often-pejorative undertones that accompanied ideas of reconciliation in the Northern Ireland context, which made it difficult to operationalize in ways that did not in fact exacerbate political conflict (Little 2012b: 73). There has been a persistent level of anxiety in Northern Ireland that 'genuine reconciliation' would require an unacceptable compromise involving the 'rehumanization of old enemies'

(Hamber and Kelly 2005: 11). While many unionists in Northern Ireland considered reconciliation to be 'little more than a rather poorly concealed republican Trojan Horse', republicans were also sceptical, with Sinn Féin regarding it as 'a rather vague, middle class concept' that was intended to facilitate a '"shaking hands and moving on" approach that failed to deal adequately with the past' (Little 2012b: 73). Thus, a term that, in South Africa, had facilitated a degree of healthy political contestation, in Northern Ireland became more likely to close down space for political engagement (Little 2012b: 68). As a result, other terms such as 'parity of esteem' or 'good relations' have come to be used in place of reconciliation.

The other countries in this study have also struggled in their attempts to determine what reconciliation means in their particular contexts. In South Africa, the idea of reconciliation, 'never quite defined but always passionately advanced', became central to the rhetoric of how the nation would manage the transition to democracy and shape the new nation (Kollapen 2010: 18). Today South Africa remains closely associated with the concept, most notably through the fame of the TRC, but has faced high levels of internal criticism about the role that reconciliation has played in the country's transition. Hugo Van der Merwe tells me that in many ways reconciliation has become 'a dirty word', at least in part because of the conceptual confusion associated with it. For many South Africans 'there isn't a clear sense of what are the priorities, what is the national debate that needs to be had, what are the kinds of values that need to be introduced amongst kids'. It has become 'exhausting' to talk about reconciliation, even as it 'still dominates' public discourse. Tim Murithi speaks of a sense that reconciliation in South Africa has only been 'artificial' or 'superficial', never really addressing the depth of the damage done by apartheid to 'the psyche of the individuals' in ways that affected 'everything, from politics to economics to society to culture, even religion'. Others question whether reconciliation may even have facilitated the perpetuation of violence in South Africa, distracting the nation from attending to structural divisions and acting as 'opium' that has obscured the all-encompassing nature of apartheid by focusing on individual victims and violations (Hovland 2003: 7–12). As Eric Doxtader and Fanie du Toit (2010: ix) contend, sometimes South Africans think of reconciliation as 'our most prized idea, the next moment as cheap deception'. Pumla Gobodo-Madikizela (2010: 135–6) suggests that these perceptions 'may be at the heart of deep, unnamed fears' that beset South Africans as they 'struggle to deal with the changes that have come with the democratic process'. Many South Africans felt a sense of pressure to ensure that the reconciliation project succeeded, a challenge made infinitely more difficult, however, by the fact that there was no agreed understanding of the 'content' of reconciliation, which remained 'vague and fuzzy', thereby allowing dominant political forces to ascribe 'limited, inappropriate and incomplete meanings' to a concept that was 'central to our growth as a people' (Kollapen 2010: 19).

Reconciliation in Australia has confronted similar definitional dilemmas. At the end of the formal ten-year reconciliation period (1991–2000) the Council for Aboriginal Reconciliation asserted that if the strategies outlined in their final report to parliament were acted upon, then Australia would have 'a solid claim to asserting itself as a reconciled nation' (Council for Aboriginal Reconciliation 2000: ix). Yet this goal today remains as opaque and remote as it has ever been. Many indigenous people have been openly hostile to the concept, conscious that the ten-year process of reconciliation was offered as compensation for the Hawke government's failure to deliver on their promise of national land rights and a treaty (Gunstone 2009: 45). As Kevin Gilbert expressed with force:

> What are we to reconcile ourselves to? To a holocaust, to massacre, to the removal of us from our land, from the taking of our land? The reconciliation process can achieve nothing because it does not at the end of the day promise justice.
>
> (quoted in Mudrooroo 1995: 228)

Irene Watson (2007: 20) has asked similar questions more recently, wondering

> what does reconciliation really mean? Will it provide homes for the homeless, food for the hungry, land for the dispossessed, language and culture for those hungry to revive from stolen and dispossessed spaces? How can you become reconciled with a state and its citizens who have not yet acknowledged your humanity, let alone your status as the first peoples of this conquered land?

Indeed, the formal Australian reconciliation process was widely criticised for its 'intense resistance' to any decolonizing action, meaning that '"education" for the non-indigenous rather than "justice" for the indigenous emerged as the dominant focus of the process' (Short 2008: 7, 36). As Janet Hunt suggests in our interview, despite the efforts of historians and many Aboriginal people, there is still no 'really deep understanding that there has been a conflict' in Australia, which could drive the need for more wide-reaching conflict transformation. While Hunt accepts that the focus on building relationships is 'helpful', she maintains that, as a nation, Australia still needs to acknowledge the 'huge violations of people's human rights' that are the foundation of the settler state. In the absence of such acknowledgement, as Damien Short (2008: 162) argues, the discourse of the Australian reconciliation process placed a 'colonial ceiling' on indigenous aspirations by emphasising nation-building and national unity above all else. Indeed, the Australian reconciliation process remained extremely tightly controlled and managed within politically acceptable boundaries, thereby shutting down political space for a deeper process of transformation. Today, the concept has to some extent fallen from what Jacqueline Phillips calls 'public consciousness', lamenting that reconciliation is no longer 'a dominant frame within political dialogue in Australia'.

Guatemala has also faced challenges associated with the concept and practice of reconciliation, not least because of elite manipulation and control of the process. The Peace Accords there make no specific mention of reconciliation, an omission that Helen Mack (2011: 450) describes as 'clearly deliberate', because the social, political, and institutional transformations required by the term were 'something for which Guatemalan society is not prepared, especially those who still hold power'. Despite two truth commissions, and the signing of a broad set of accords that should have institutionalized much of the country's hoped-for transformation, today reconciliation actors are bewildered by the lack of change they observe. Daniel Domingo Lopez observes that while reconciliation in his country requires the 'reconstruction of the state for there to be peace', instead the concept has been used as 'a strategy to delay things' and elicit wide social complacency. This runs counter to Domingo's idea of reconciliation, as he sees the lack of reconciliation and transformation in Guatemala as in fact producing more political conflict due to 'the lack of recognition, and the lack of respect for rights'.

It is clear that these different countries provide different contexts in which the concept of reconciliation has taken root—or not—and grown in different directions. It is also clear that the prospect of seeking reconciliation in the context of any divided society is not a 'small tinkering enterprise' but instead one that proposes 'a new "normal"' (Community Relations Council 2011: 26), whatever that may involve. Complicating these aspirations further are the endless debates about the component pieces and priorities that make up the field of reconciliation.

The pieces of reconciliation

The approach of this book rests on the idea that reconciliation is concerned with the political challenges involved in finding ways for people in deeply divided societies to live together democratically and non-violently, *with radical differences* (Ramsbotham *et al.* 2011: 246). The countries in the study have all had some sort of institutionalized process of reconciliation (although not always named as such), and in each case the pursuit of reconciliation has both announced and constituted 'an exceptional political moment' (Muldoon 2008: 124–5). But in each case this moment has been decidedly different in content, focus, and aspiration. None of these approaches is necessarily more right than any other. Their differences do, however, reveal the debates and decisions about what properly constitutes reconciliation that have swirled around these and many other cases.

The goals of reconciliation are expressed in a vast body of literature from both scholars and practitioners, much of which emphasizes ideas of unity and shared aspirations. For example, reconciliation is thought to involve: 'a setting aside of past animosities and the possibility of former enemies working together in the future' (Hamber and Kelly 2009: 287); it 'promises regeneration and transformation' (Phillips 2005: 119); suggests 'a desire for the movement towards unification' (Bhandar 2007: 94); pursues 'a commitment to a shared future' (Chapman 2002: 265); by increasing the capacity for people to 'understand, accept, and even appreciate differences in groups other than their own' (Gibson 2004: 118); seeking 'an improved, morally more accountable relationship' (Krüger 2006: 34); and 'an acknowledgement and practical bridging of the fractures caused by colonialism and apartheid {...} thus overturning the oppressive inclusions and exclusions of those systems' (van der Westhuizen 2010: 103). Villa-Vicencio (2010: 164–5) draws together many of these aspirations, suggesting that reconciliation is

> a slow, multi-faceted process. It takes time. It is both *process* and *goal*. As process it is inevitably uneven, lapsing into counter-productive, even violent, ways of redressing conflict. It requires restraint, generosity of spirit, empathy and perseverance. It is about exploring ways of gaining a deeper and more inclusive understanding of the problems that are the root cause of conflict. It is about opening the way to better understanding, respect and trust-building. Above all, it is about finding ways to connect people across what are often historical and entrenched barriers of suspicion, prejudice and inequality. The goal is a change of values, a willingness to venture beyond the promotion of rigid identities that result in war and cultivate a new attitude towards others—as the basis for addressing the major material and structural challenges that so often cause post-conflict societies to slide back into war. Reconciliation is an art rather than a science {...}. Reconciliation is about risk and the ability to imagine a different set of relations with one's adversaries and enemies.

Some approaches to reconciliation emphasize the importance of nation-building and the creation of national unity. This was evident in the South African discourse of a unified 'rainbow nation', and also very strongly dominant in Australian reconciliation discourse. As noted above, this denied Aboriginal and Torres Strait Islander peoples the opportunity to properly pursue their claims regarding colonial injustice, providing them with 'a right to be incorporated into the Australian nation but not a right to refuse' (Short 2005: 274). Leah Armstrong suggests that this use of 'nation-building language' in Australia has allowed the country to become 'too small minded'.

Other approaches emphasize the need for justice, although, as evident in the Australian case, these may only apply a limited notion of what actually constitutes justice for victims. Although Daly and Sarkin (2007: 15) point out that there should be no inconsistency between justice and reconciliation if an understanding of justice includes its restorative dimensions, Elizabeth Kiss (2000: 82) suggests that reconciliation requires political actors to juggle both demands for accountability and the desire to reconcile fractured relationships—issues that are explored further in Chapter 10. There is certainly tension between the exacting requirements of perfect justice, in a legal sense, and the transformative potential of reconciliation, which aspires to transcend purely legalistic demands (Phillips 2005: 119).

Underlying this particular debate about the relationship between reconciliation and justice lies a perceived tension between reconciliation and the protection of human rights. While human rights and reconciliation advocates share the goal of attaining and sustaining peace and transforming relationships within a divided society, in practice these advocates have often been at odds in their views of how these goals might best be achieved. Human rights actors strive for 'a principled outcome', in which justice and the rule of law are seen as an essential foundation for peaceful coexistence. Reconciliation advocates, by contrast, emphasize the 'process of dialogue that generates a culture of human rights', seeing the development of greater mutual understanding and the capacity to live together as essential for justice and the development of the rule of law (Holkeboer and Villa-Vincencio 2004: 108–9). Where the former see investigations of past wrongs that do not result in legal sanctions as a means of 'institutionalizing impunity', the latter are concerned that pursuing trials may in fact place democratic transition and future reconciliation efforts at risk (Sieder 2003: 209).

Despite these tensions, however, the concepts of human rights and reconciliation remain intrinsically linked. Stephanus du Toit (2009: 255) suggests that the paradigm of reconciliation provides an 'interpretative framework' that may facilitate the implementation of human rights. Further, Mieke Holkeboer and Charles Villa-Vincencio (2004: 108) contend that human rights and reconciliation are in fact deeply interdependent. They insist that developing a culture of human rights in the aftermath of conflict is not possible 'without the active and engaging work of reconciliation', nor is reconciliation possible 'among human beings who disregard one another's humanity and continue to commit human rights abuses'. As Desmond Tutu (1999: 23) argued in defence of the work of the TRC, any process of conflict transformation must 'balance the requirements of justice, accountability, stability, peace, and reconciliation'. In South Africa, he maintains, a decision to pursue only retributive justice in response to gross violations of human rights could have left the country 'lying in ashes—a truly Phyrric victory if ever there was one'.

Like many others in the field, however, Martha Minow (2000: 254) emphasizes the need to 'attend to those who were victimized' insisting that reconciliation must 'invigorate remembrance of what happened and prevent any future dehumanization of the victimized'. Minow's approach to reconciliation falls into one of two common ways of classifying reconciliation, described as either 'thick' and 'thin', or 'maximalist' and 'minimalist'. The maximalist approach focuses on interpersonal reconciliation, drawing on either a religious (confessional) or medical (therapeutic) paradigm, and is associated with language such as healing, forgiveness and apology. Maximalists assert that reconciliation takes place in those occasions when perpetrators are able to acknowledge responsibility, repent, and are subsequently forgiven by their victims (Verdeja 2009: 14). Indeed, much of the reconciliation literature has focused on a vision of 'communitarian social harmony' achieved through collective acts of public apology and forgiveness that attempt to substitute the conflict of the past with the '"overlapping consensus" of community' (Hirsch 2012: 1–2). This approach has been criticized for its 'illiberal' aim of 'expecting an entire society to subscribe to a single comprehensive moral perspective' (Gutman and Thompson 2000: 32). In contrast, the minimalist approach draws more from a political paradigm and is associated with the transformation of sociopolitical institutions and processes (Borer 2004: 25). Where the first approach envisages harmony and the overcoming of social division, the second accepts that conflict is intrinsic to politics and can be understood as a sign of a healthy society. As Tristan Anne Borer puts it, 'one approach to reconciliation requires people to get along; the other assumes they won't' (Borer 2004: 31).

As should be evident by now, this book advances a view of reconciliation more in line with the so-called 'minimalist' approach, although I can see nothing minimal about the type of multilevel political engagement and effort that I am proposing. I understand the 'maximalist' or 'thick' versions of reconciliation as problematic for both practical and moral reasons, not least of which is the burden placed on victims who are expected to forgive the perpetrators of mass atrocity in order for reconciliation to be achieved (Crocker 2000: 108; Verdeja 2009: 16). The maximalist version of reconciliation remains imbued with religious connotations, particularly due to the focus on forgiveness, which is seen to undermine victims' justifiable anger or desire for justice (Hamber and Kelly 2009: 287). And although the minimalist approach is often criticized for failing to sufficiently engage with the past, or for being too 'legalistic' to the neglect of relational efforts (Verdeja 2009: 20), that is a somewhat limited notion of what is required for political reconciliation, and again is at odds with the approach advanced here. Any truly political reconciliation must engage with the past, not only for the sake of acknowledging the harm done to victims, but also in order to address current injustices arising from the institutions that perpetuate the uneven distribution of power and resources that continue to benefit past perpetrators (Verdeja 2009: 14), an argument that will be further pursued in subsequent chapters.

The role of the past in contemporary reconciliation efforts is not, however, a simple matter. There are, for example, concerns with regard to the relationship between present-day efforts at reconciliation, and the history of the nation in which these efforts are engaged. The roots of the concept in biblical language and texts suggest restoration and wholeness in political relationships (Philpott 2006: 12). Many critics of reconciliation note that the word itself—*re*-conciliation—implies a desirable, prelapsarian state to which a nation might return, through a narrative of 'harmony, rupture, and eventual reunion' that risks ignoring ineradicable differences and discouraging political dissent (Verdeja 2009: 17). Such an approach also tends to obfuscate or erase the 'messy history' of the nation's contemporary conflict (Hirsch 2012: 3), as will be discussed further in Chapter 3. As those involved in reconciliation efforts point out, however, in many (if not all) cases, this previous condition of harmony is mere myth, as in South Africa where it has been observed that 'there is nothing to go back to, no previous state or relationship one would wish to restore' (Krog 1998: 143). Adrian Zapata in Guatemala expressed a similar sentiment, telling me that in his country 'the word reconciliation is not being correctly used', because 'this society hasn't been conciliated, so you can't reconciliate what hasn't been conciliated before'.

A further concern relates to the role of 'truth seeking' in reconciliation efforts. Both religious and secular observers have emphasized the need to 'come to terms with the past' rather than attempting to forget or repress past wrongs. Through commissions and other truth recovery processes, establishing a shared truth about past collective violence and human rights abuses is seen as 'a prerequisite for achieving accountability, meaningful reconciliation, and a foundation for a common future' (Chapman 2002: 260–1). As a result of high profile institutions such as the South African TRC, the linking of truth and reconciliation has become something of a truism, although evidence of any causal link has proved difficult to discern. This is not to suggest that the recovery of truth and historical memory does not play an important role in reconciliation and conflict transformation processes—as will be discussed further in Chapter 10 it is clear that their contribution is essential. However the now commonplace reductionist approach to *truthandreconciliation* is profoundly unhelpful to understanding the far more complex requirements of conflict transformation in deeply divided societies.

More helpful are the approaches to reconciliation that are explicit about its inherent complexity. Both scholars and practitioners have developed various schema for analysing the component parts of these efforts. Hamber and Kelly (2005: 7), for example, suggest that reconciliation involves 'five interwoven strands': the development of a shared vision of an interdependent and fair society; a means of acknowledging and dealing with the past; the building of positive relationships; significant cultural and attitudinal change; and substantial social, economic and political change. Similarly, the South African Reconciliation Barometer has developed 'six complex hypotheses and indicators' for measuring the progress of reconciliation, namely: political culture, human security, cross-cutting political relationships, dialogue, race relations, and historical confrontation' (Lefko-Everett *et al.* 2011: 8). The Australian CAR also defined 'eight key issues' as essential to assessing the process of reconciliation:

- a greater understanding of the importance of *land and sea* in Aboriginal and Torres Strait Islander societies;
- *better relationships* between Aboriginal and Torres Strait Islander peoples and the wider community;
- recognition that Aboriginal and Torres Strait Islander *culture and heritage* are a valued part of the Australian heritage;
- a sense for all Australians of a shared ownership of our *history*;
- a greater awareness of the causes of *disadvantage* that prevent Aboriginal and Torres Strait Islander peoples from achieving fair and proper standards in health, housing, employment and education;
- a greater community response to addressing the underlying causes of the unacceptably high *levels of custody* for Aboriginal and Torres Strait Islander peoples;
- greater opportunities for Aboriginal and Torres Strait Islander peoples to *control their destinies*;
- agreement on whether the process of reconciliation would be advanced by a *document or documents* of reconciliation.

(Council for Aboriginal Reconciliation 2000: 13, emphasis in the original)

Schema like these emphasize both the complexity and the pragmatic nature of reconciliation work, even as the goals may remain somewhat utopian. Reconciliation can be seen in these schema as both goal and process, balancing the tension between any number of important aspirations that open the space for political contestation about the nature of conflict transformation. Reconciliation seeks to anticipate the future while acknowledging and memorializing the past; it seeks to be politically inclusive while focusing on the needs and rights of victims (du Toit 2009: 256); it is both discursive and normative (Renner 2012: 55); and 'at once political, legal, cultural, moral, psychological, and spiritual' (Kiss 2000: 80); it incorporates 'psychological, structural and political elements' (Wale 2013: 8); it is concerned with both institutional transformation and the restoration of trust (Mack 2011: 450–1); and it operates at multiple levels, including the personal and the political (Quinn 2009: 4). Reconciliation is emphatically not a process of conflict resolution of the kind that delegitimizes or represses important forms of political resistance and struggle (Schirch 2008: 3). Indeed, such struggles are essential to political reconciliation, which, as Schaap (2007: 9) contends, 'will not get off the ground' if a society must first establish 'a shared moral account of the nature of past wrongs'. Fundamentally, reconciliation is fuelled by the belief that 'things could have been otherwise' (Hirsch 2012: 80), and the conviction that it is still possible to transform the relations and structures that continue to divide societies, causing violence and insecurity.

Agonism, reconciliation, and conflict transformation

As noted above, much of the reconciliation literature continues to focus on the normative ambition of achieving social harmony. In contrast, a fully political understanding of reconciliation recognizes the futility of attempting to transcend conflict in this way, instead framing reconciliation as 'a potentially agonistic clash of worldviews within the context of a community that is "not yet"' (Schaap 2005: 4). In Schaap's (2005: 21–2) view, a 'politically adequate conception of reconciliation' would be alive to the inherent risk of politics, that is,

> that community is not inevitable and that conflict may turn out to be irreconcilable {…} if the ideal of reconciliation is to open up a space for politics between former enemies rather than cover over the conflicts that threaten their political association, reconciliation should be kept in view for being a potentiality of action in the present, which depends upon accepting the risk of politics (and the opportunity it presents) rather than eliding it.

This is a profoundly pragmatic approach to conflict, which contests a normative aspiration to 'peace.' It instead recognizes that a more realistic normative context, in which conflict is managed and potentially transformed, 'is one where there is a disorderly mixture of peace and conflict and where democratic politics co-exists with other forms of political expression' (Little 2014: 138). Further, such an approach foregrounds the fact that in assuming that conflict is reconcilable, in the sense of achieving harmony and consensus, the politics of reconciliation become obscured (Schaap 2004: 524). An agonistic approach, by contrast, holds out hope that in spaces of irresolvable conflict divided societies will expand their political capacities, embrace conflict without violence, and find new ways of respecting old adversaries.

A conflictual approach to reconciliation recognizes that in many deeply divided societies, the capacity to 'disagree respectfully' may be the most that can be expected from conflict transformation efforts (Daly and Sarkin 2007: 238). More significantly, it recognizes that democracy *thrives* on conflict, and is at its best when citizens and groups are able to disagree with one another. It follows, then, that when reconciliation generates pressure towards consensus it does not serve democracy (Gibson 2004: 345). Thus, while the desire to end or resolve conflict is common to many views of reconciliation and peacebuilding, the approach in this book instead contends that this is both unrealistic and undesirable. Instead, non-violent conflict is here conceived as a social good, or at least as *potentially* a social good, but one that requires institutional interventions if it is to harness its democratic potential rather than devolve into violence. The challenge, according to Charles Villa-Vicencio (2009: 62) is 'to develop ways of engagement that allow for nonconformity, dissent, open debate, and orderly political change when necessary'.

This approach to social and political conflict takes seriously the insights of agonistic democracy theory, drawing particularly on the work of theorists such as Andrew Schaap (2005) and Adrian Little (2014), *inter alia*. These approaches suggest the need to rethink the intrinsic and potentially productive role of non-violent conflict in reconciliation and conflict transformation work. Agonism can be understood as 'a technique for managing conflict' that recognizes the fluid nature of political conflict and the resulting need for political responses that are context specific rather than attempts at a universal model (Little 2014: 7). Agonistic democrats affirm the central place of conflict in any democratic politics, a view that reflects their concern that anything resembling consensus 'too often become a way of co-opting radical challenges to the dominant interests within a society' (Schaap 2006: 257). Agonists instead foreground the inherent struggles that are constitutive of political life, promoting an ideal of democracy that is marked by an 'epistemic openness' to difference and conflicting points of view (Chakravarti 2012: 11). This understanding of political life has particular resonance for societies engaged in a politics of reconciliation, where the need to open—and to keep open—political spaces in which divided and opposing groups can engage is crucial. Conflict is thus understood not as a negative dynamic in reconciliation processes, but as an essential and ever-present political dynamic that allows opposing groups in divided societies to engage in passionate democratic contestation about their future ways of living together. Indeed, Muldoon and Schaap (2012: 182) contend that reconciliation processes are *inevitably* agonistic in nature precisely because they 'open up a space of contestation and disagreement' between opposing groups focused on claims and counter-claims about past wrongs. Thus, rather than bracketing or avoiding conflict, the aim in an agonistic reconciliatory engagement is to 'transform actually or potentially violent conflict into non-violent forms of social struggle and social change' (Ramsbotham 2010: 53). As Ed Wingenbach (2011: 61) has suggested, agonistic engagements provide 'an outlet for passion and dissent' that may in fact make the eruption of violent, antagonistic relations less likely.

Schaap (2006: 258) has argued that an agonistic approach to reconciliation and conflict transformation is important because it foregrounds what is at stake in the *politics* of these processes. He contends that less critical accounts of reconciliation that emphasize ideas of 'settling accounts', 'healing nations' and 'restoring community' start from the presumption that unity is an unquestioned social good, thereby depoliticizing the terms in which the unity of the polity is constructed and represented. Counter to this approach, an agonistic perspective makes it possible to conceive of reconciliation as something other than a state-sanctioned project of nation building, instead creating space for a more radical democratic politics. Indeed, as Muldoon (2008: 127) has suggested, an agonistic perspective makes it possible to understand how reconciliation makes it onto the political agenda—not because there is sudden agreement about past wrongs, but because marginalized groups politicize those past actions by renaming them as injustices.

One well-known formulation of agonism, advanced by leading theorist Chantal Mouffe (2007, 2005, 2000), asserts that the primary task of democracy is to convert antagonism into agonism and enemies into adversaries or, as William Connolly (1991: x) puts it, to 'cultivate agonistic respect between interlocking and contending constituencies'. This, as Mouffe suggests, has consequences for how we imagine politics and the nature of the public sphere. Rather than eliminating passions, or attempting to contain them in the private sphere to better support a national consensus, these passions can be 'mobilized' towards 'the promotion of democratic designs'. In this way, consensus can be seen as a result of a temporary stabilization of power—the kind of stabilization often pursued in divided societies—that inevitably entails some form of exclusion (Mouffe 2007: 43). In an agonistic mode of reconciliation, such stabilizations of power may be acknowledged as sometimes necessary, but always to be resisted. Democracy is envisioned as a 'continual contest among incompatible visions, identities, and projects' in which no view can dominate or assume hegemonic status for very long (Wingenbach 2011: 21).

Little (2014: 75) points to the normative dimension in these formulations of agonism, suggesting that theorists such as Mouffe attempt to 'domesticate' political conflict by 'broadening the spectrum of acceptability in the analytical framing of particular issues'. In this view, although agonists resist the reconciliatory drive to fabricate social and political consensus, and emphatically do not want to delegitimize disagreement, they do see the potential for politics to more effectively accommodate difference by improving the nature of the interaction between conflictual actors. In my view, this normative agonistic desire to foreground and yet domesticate conflict is no bad thing. An approach to reconciliation that recognizes the central place of conflict is not without risks, suggesting that some degree of institutional intervention or 'domestication' may be of political benefit. As Villa-Vicencio (2009: 43) contends:

The complexities and dangers inherent to this process are huge. On the one hand this could result in a clash of interests that, if left unmanaged, might undermine the political climate needed to build a new political dispensation. On the other hand, the essence of the demands made by the different sectors of society could be so restrained and diluted that the political process would be undermined to the point that in the interests of compromise and consensus, critique would be closed down. The outcome would be a society built on soft mediocrity and compliance that would fail to provide the space and social structures through which people could give expression to their needs and promote their interests.

The challenge, according to Villa-Vicencio (2009: 43) is to 'build a national consensus' while still encouraging debate about longer-term ideals. From an agonistic perspective, however, this recourse to 'national consensus' as the pathway through this challenging terrain is inadequate. A looser agreement, enough only for disparate groups to agree to be governed in common while still contesting the terms of their association (as discussed further in Chapter 4), may allow former enemies to envision themselves as part of a shared, if contested, order (Wingenbach 2011: 34). This more open structure to political cohesion can provide enough space for an agonistic politics of reconciliation to develop.

An agonistic politics of reconciliation also supports the exercise of what Lederach (2005: 5) describes as the 'moral imagination', which requires (among other things) the capacity for citizens to imagine themselves in a 'web of relationships' that includes their enemies, embracing complexity and risking the unknown. Freedom arrives not only through resistance to the status quo, but also through the development of social and political capacity to shape power in democratic and inclusive ways (Wingenbach 2011: 34). Rather that pursuing a static consensus, agonism allows complexity, dynamism, dissent and challenge enough to genuinely *transform* the political order without recourse to direct violence. These attributes have the capacity to counter the 'consensual drift' that tends to close down spaces for political engagement rather than opening them up to transformative ideas (Little 2007: 154, 158). A focus on transformation also takes us away from the idea of 'transition', encouraging a long-term focus on the development of sustainable processes for democratic engagement and contestation, and the transformation of social, economic and political structures across multiple social levels. The temporal aspect of this is significant. Agonistic conflict transformation will require opportunities for the continued recognition and articulation of conflict over time (Little 2014: 8).

In spite of what I see as the transformative potential of agonistic political reconciliation, I note Audra Mitchell's important critique of the conflict transformation framework. As Mitchell (2011: 32–3) argues, conflict transformation efforts are based in the view that direct violence has deep roots in the 'collective history, memory, culture and practices of conflicting groups', informed by collectively held social values and beliefs and structural social and economic divisions. Conflict transformation strategies view conflict over these inherent differences as a central cause of violence, and so seek to change the ways and means by which people engage in conflict in order to convert conflict into non-violent forms. However, Mitchell suggests that, in an attempt to eliminate or alter the threat that conflict appears to present, transformation efforts may in fact 'enact radical violence' against conflicting groups. As a result, she argues that the form of peace that is pursued in these efforts may work to perpetuate forms of structural, cultural and symbolic violence upon many constituent groups (Mitchell 2011: 25).

These threats are doubtless real. As noted in the previous chapter, the persistent insecurity in many divided societies leads many to pursue a peace that does indeed perpetuate forms of indirect violence, not least through efforts to shut down protest and dissent. Thus, while transformation can be understood as a 'powerful ideal' that 'evokes images of total and complete change, even emancipation', it can also become a tool for a hegemonic and destructive mode of intervention and social control that has the effect of disciplining 'the political' (Mitchell 2011: 93–4). This has been observed for example in South Africa where Achille Mbembe (2008: 16) notes that when used as an 'expediency' transformation 'risks codifying within the law and within the psyche of its beneficiaries the very powerlessness it aims to redress'. As with any framework for engaging with the challenges facing deeply divided societies, the idea of transforming conflict through reconciliation efforts requires great care and constant vigilance, particularly with regard to the exercise of power, to ensure that it does not merely replicate and reinscribe these relations.

Transformative possibilities

Reconciliation is a complex field. It is riddled with questions and contradictions that fuel intense debate amongst scholars and practitioners. Yet when the desire to pursue an endpoint to reconciliation can be avoided, and it can instead be maintained as an 'open horizon', reconciliation has the capacity to *sustain* politics in divided societies (Schaap 2005: 84). This is a crucial dynamic. As Alvaro Pop in Guatemala tells me, despite extraordinary levels of violence, mistreatment, racism and segregation, his society 'never loses hope'. For Pop, and many other reconciliation actors, the goal is not the restoration of some imagined past community, but the possibility of opening a moment in which 'to weave the fabric of society' (Doxtader 2012: 36). Reconciliation in this sense is not a romantic or utopian ideal. Pursuing the type of open-ended, conflictual, *political* reconciliation articulated here, stretching the limits of what seems possible at the time, may in fact be the only alternative to persistent and escalating violence. This mode of reconciliation promises only a contingent response not an unconditional outcome, suggesting a sense of movement in spaces that 'remain both open and closed, infinite and finite' but avoiding a normative prescription for how 'to do' reconciliation (Christodoulidis and Veitch 2008: 9; McGregor 2007: 112). As Florence Onus tells me, the work of reconciliation is 'going to be continuous journey. I don't think there's really an end to it'. The prevailing condition for this journey will most likely be disorderly and complex, in which democratic politics and other forms of political expression tussle and tangle over historic challenges and contemporary divides.

No one approaching this kind of work can know all the answers, nor assume a common vision about what remains to be created. This lack of certainty, while often challenging on the ground, leaves societies open to new possibilities, new ways of reimagining social life. But any active engagement in reconciliation work must take account of the necessity for multi-level, long-term, multi-generation work. Thus, in the next chapter I consider the question of time and the ways in which the temporal dimension of conflict in deeply divided societies shapes contemporary reconciliation and conflict transformation efforts.

3 The problem of time

The dynamics of time shape the contours of both conflict and division and the reconciliatory and transformative responses that may follow. It is well understood that the temporal dimensions of reconciliation and conflict transformation efforts are significant. Indeed, Christodoulidis and Veitch (2007: 2) suggest that reconciliation is 'all about time'. Contemporary conflict and injustice are 'temporally multilayered', arising out of previous regimes and systems of injustice that continue to manifest in the present (Daly and Sarkin 2007: 170). Actors in reconciliation processes do not ever begin with a blank slate, but must instead craft their efforts within a context that is laden with problematic historical events that remain alive in contemporary consciousness and demand attention and recognition (Little 2014: 56; Lederach 2005: 140). However, Christodoulidis and Veitch (2008: 20) also note that the temporality of reconciliation remains under-theorized, arguing that reconciliation tends to overdetermine the past, projecting into it 'the origin of a common future' while often missing the fact that this future is only possible if the conflict of the past is seen as something that can be overcome. The politics of reconciliation, they contend, requires an engagement with the problems of establishing responsibility through time.

Little (2014: 62–6) suggests five ways in which the temporal complexity of reconciliation needs to be considered in conflict transformation efforts. First, he suggests that in both transitional and post/settler colonial contexts there is a tendency to believe that contemporary institutions can somehow 'draw a line' under unjust past practices through acts such as apologies or truth commissions. It is an error, Little believes, to consider such efforts as 'any kind of conclusive step in grappling with the temporality of conflict'. Rather, and this is Little's second point, historical events not only affect human responses to conflict (as discussed in Chapter 1), they also contribute to the ways in which contemporary practices and institutions are established and reproduced, foreclosing policy options in often unpredictable ways. Third, Little suggests it is important to reconsider the often well-meaning efforts by governments and international actors to deal with past wrongs in light of these complexities. Fourth, he emphasizes that, unlike straightforward narratives of historical conflicts, it is rare for conflict to either escalate in a linear fashion or conclude with a defined 'peace process' that produces a set of 'reconciliatory institutions'. Finally, Little cautions against the elision of the end of conflict and the emergence of less overtly violent social relationships because this leads to an emphasis on containing violence rather than wider efforts at conflict transformation. Little (2014: 68–9) concludes that

> complex temporality is a residual factor in conflictual societies because the full ramifications of conflict are never wholly played out. There isn't an end point at which we can say that historical events or practices have run their course and no longer influence evolving social and political relations. Because conflicts are alive, they are constantly being reiterated, renegotiated and reconstituted and thus their impact on social and political structures is continual.

This chapter examines several aspects of this complex temporality, from the idea of 'transition', to the continued impacts of colonialism, and contemporary intergenerational relations, all of which frame and constrain efforts at reconciliation and conflict transformation.

Transitions and established democracies

Reconciliation is often associated with periods of regime change and democratic transition. In recent years this work has increasingly come under the banner of 'transitional justice'. Understood as 'both practical tools and discursive project', transitional justice mechanisms are both constituted by and construct new regimes directed towards enforcing new liberal norms and doing justice for past wrongs, with the aim of creating a more peaceful future (Miller 2008: 166). As practice, transitional justice deploys a range of 'tools' including trials, truth commissions, apologies, reparations, and institutional reform. As a concept, transition implies a beginning and an end, as societies move from war to peace or from authoritarianism to democracy, while attending to questions of justice in the present for victims of the previous regime (Quinn 2009: 3). Justice may be pursued both with regard to specific and defined crimes, but is also thought to be imperative as a means for dealing with the past.

As previous chapters have suggested, however, the process of conflict transformation is more layered and complex than a 'transition' might suggest. South Africa, Guatemala, and Northern Ireland all experienced such transitions, undergoing episodes of rapid political and/or regime change. Australia, however, has experienced no such transition, and yet it, too, has utilized several 'tools' from the transitional justice 'toolbox' in its efforts to reconcile its colonial past. This would suggest that the complex temporality of reconciliation may be partially obscured by the dominance of transitional justice as a means for understanding the demands of trans-formation. In fact, if we look again at those nations more recently 'in transition', we can see that there too there are far longer histories of colonization, dispossession, and oppression that have continued to fuel conflict up until the present day.

The *politics* of transitional justice seems inclined towards an unhelpful simplification of history, time, and past injustice. The idea of transition allows complex histories to be reduced to the most recent past conflict, and contest over the future delimited by the promise of a more civilized form of democratic society (Hinton 2010: 7). Dirk Venema (2012: 74–5) contends that transitions are 'not historical in the chronological sense, but in the political sense', meaning that it is politics that uses a range of tech-niques to 'create, mediate, symbolize, sustain and consolidate' an histor-ical political discontinuity. Transitional institutions become definitional, both delineating past and future and delimiting the range of past viola-tions, victims and perpetrators (Miller 2008: 291). An emphasis on 'trans-ition' as 'a moment of discontinuity and rupture' allows newly created transitional institutions to in fact set the 'chronological parameters' for the conflict and its transformation, generally limiting the focus to specific forms of direct violence thought to have ended with the old regime (Miller 2008: 270). Thus, although the field of transitional justice is intended to ensure that political choices do not come at the expense of accountability for past wrongs, this accountability—and indeed the wrongs themselves—tend to be limited in scope.

These limits have recently been acknowledged by some practitioners, who have suggested that the scope of transitional justice should be widened to include the socioeconomic injustices that fuel and sustain con-flict, and which often survive the end of direct violence. Derek Powell (2010: 235) contends that without the inclusion of socioeconomic injus-tice in its conception of justice, transitional justice cannot explain either injustice or transition in South Africa. Highlighting the limits of the South African TRC, Powell points out that:

> A black woman in South Africa who was tortured by the apartheid state is {...} covered by TJ's remit. The fact that the state willfully stripped her of political rights, denied her a proper education and basic social services and dispossessed her family of its land to further its policies of racial exploitation is not. The fact that these systemic abuses were designed to serve and preserve white privilege is not. Nor are her expectations that the postconflict state will take positive steps to redress the inequalities forced upon her by virtue of her skin colour and ethnicity.

Powell insists that there is much at stake in these debates about the scope of transitional justice given the influence of these practices, and the outcomes they seek during transition, precisely when 'things are the most precarious, dangerous and fraught' (Powell 2010: 247). That historically-rooted socio-economic inequality both fell outside the remit of transitional justice in South Africa and yet remains an enormous threat to continued stability in the country today seems compelling enough reason to question the temporal simplification that transition implies. Some of the conclusions reached by proponents of transitional justice may in fact perpetuate the injustices they intended to repair, encouraging the closure of the transformative window through an exhortation to 'move on' once the transitional measure has been applied (Hirsch 2012: 3). Indeed, this is a problem with all approaches that insist on focusing on the future by drawing a line under the past, a rhetorical strategy that does little more than evade the claims of indigenous peoples (among others) who point out that they are still suffering the effects of colonialism—'a structure of oppression that is for them a current reality rather than a historical artifact' (Woolford 2010: 147).

To counter these tendencies two approaches are suggested. Paige Arthur urges caution, suggesting that transitional justice measures should not be 'burdened' with 'expectations that they cannot possibly meet', particularly with regard to the transformation of entrenched social structures (Arthur 2011: 11). Conversely, Louise Arbour (2007: 3) contends that transitional justice should be more ambitious in its scope, and ought to 'reach to—but also beyond—the crimes and abuses committed during the conflict that led to the transition' in order to address the violations that 'pre-dated the conflict and caused or contributed to it'. While this latter view has been contested on the grounds that the challenges in settler societies are 'temporally distinct' from those in societies engaged in a current transition to democracy, therefore requiring a deeper investigation of historical violence and injustice and their impacts on contemporary society (Verdeja 2009: 7), in fact there has been a growing application of 'transitional' mechanisms in supposedly peaceful, settled democracies such as many settler colonial societies. As Courtney Jung (2011: 231) asserts, the scope of transitional justice 'has the potential to be contested temporally', broadening the concept of transition and drawing in a wider range of historical wrongs as still in need of contemporary justice. Indeed, recent years have seen a focus on transition not just from war to peace or authoritarianism to democracy, but also as a means by which settler societies may 'transition' from their colonial past to a more democratic and inclusive present.

The reality, however, is that transitional justice has been no more successful than other approaches to transforming the deep divisions that characterize settler societies. In part this has been because of what Andrew Woolford (2010: 137) describes as 'transitional symbolic violence', evident through the failure or refusal to adequately recognize past harms. Long histories of oppression and domination leave 'a deep wound' that goes to the core of group identity (Bashir 2012: 129). A commitment to a Westphalian framework that locates transition within the confines of the nation-state profoundly limits the capacity of settler states to address historical injustice and heal these wounds (Woolford 2010: 138). Indeed the very notion of transitional justice emphasizes the importance of establishing a legitimate political order 'from the ashes of an illegitimate former regime' (Short 2005: 269). These constraints have the effect of derailing the transformational capacity of transitional justice measures such as apologies or truth commissions, instead serving to legitimate the settler colonial status quo (Jung 2011: 217).

It is also apparent that settler states and indigenous peoples may pursue transitional measures for quite different ends. While indigenous people may, for example, seek to use public discourse surrounding a government apology for a specific harm to generate a wider debate about contested sovereignty and collective rights, governments may use these same measures in an effort to draw a line under the past, locating injustices and human rights abuses firmly in history and allowing the settler society a sense that such issues have been resolved. The 'transition' in the government view is to what the state might consider a level playing field, where present day governments can no longer be held accountable for past injustice. This is markedly different to the desires of indigenous leaders, who may see transitional justice as building 'not a wall but a bridge', using transitional justice measures to 'draw history into the present' and highlight the complex ways in which contemporary policy regimes reinscribe historical injustices (Jung 2011: 231).

The Australian case reveals much about the temporal dimension of the transitional justice ideal in a settler colonial context. Some may date the start of Australia's 'transition' to federation in 1901, others may consider a more recent temporal frame, perhaps beginning with the constitutional referendum in 1967.[1] Whatever the specific timeframe, however, it is evident that Australia has been engaging with transitional justice mechanisms over several decades yet, like other settler colonial states, has also demonstrated considerable resistance to addressing the more complex social divisions that have resulted from colonial injustice. Thus, although Australia has deployed transitional measures at various times in its history, including some minimal constitutional reform in the 1960s, landmark legal judgments in the 1990s, and, more recently, a form of truth commission followed (eventually) by an apology, these measures have all strenuously rejected calls for more radical forms of political transformation, thereby entrenching the structural violence of colonization (for more see Maddison and Shepherd 2014). The temporal dimension provides insight to what Short (2008: 160) describes as 'the cosmetic display of reconciliation' in which the acknowledgement of '*past* colonial racism and the promise of *future* reconciliation effectively re-imagined Australia as *currently* post-colonial'. Locating colonialism in the past has the effect of 'periodizing' the problem and legitimating contemporary settler colonialism, creating Australian reconciliation as little more than 'an exercise in discursive legitimization' where 'substantive change is always coming but never here' (Short 2008: 160–1). At the heart of this resistance to more substantive change is a reluctance to genuinely engage with the fact that the 'long ago' harms of colonialism are still causing trauma and division in the present.

Long colonial history

Each of the countries in this study has at one time been colonized, and in each case this colonial history both frames and constrains the capacity for reconciliation and conflict transformation in the present. The Australian case has been briefly considered above, but it is worth noting here some of the ways in which a history of colonization affects contemporary conflict and division more broadly.

Northern Ireland has perhaps the longest history of colonization in this study, having endured twelve centuries of invasion, colonialism and conflict, leading to the incursion by English and Scottish settlers from the beginning of the seventeenth century and the subsequent oppression of the Gaelic Irish population. This history set the stage for centuries of conflict over the merits and injustice of British rule that continue to divide the society today (Smithey 2011: 9). The Plantation of Ulster created an ethnic differentiation between the colonists and the dispossessed Irish that has been core to the conflict ever since. Indeed, the Good Friday Agreement is based on a recognition of the 'two communities' that populate contemporary Northern Ireland (Nolan 2012: 19).

Nicholas Frayling (2009: 27) lists the reasons that he, as an Englishman, has become troubled by the 'bitter legacy' that his country has bestowed on the island of Ireland:

1   We invaded Ireland, and we fought our own battles there.
2   We robbed the Irish people of their language and their literature, and we attempted to rob them of their church.
3   We colonized Ireland with foreigners and persecuted the Irish people when they would not conform to our religion.
4   We drove the Roman Catholics into exile and killed thousands of women, men, and children; and we invoked God as our justification.
5   We failed to feed a starving people whose country was politically part of our own, leaving millions to die or emigrate without hope.
6   We degraded the Irish people by caricaturing them in the British press and media.
7   When they protested, we met violence with violence.
8   These atrocities were not confined to the native Irish. When it suited our purpose, we 'planted' the land with Protestants, took advantage of their loyalty (especially allowing them to die in unparalleled numbers

in two world wars), enriched ourselves from their industry, and then told them we no longer needed them.

These combined impacts allowed the Ulster Protestants to use their majority to deny the Catholic nationalist community their civil rights (Wells 2006: 190), a key factor prompting the civil rights movement of the 1960s that in turn gave way to the violence of the Troubles. Michael Culbert points out that part of the struggle for Irish republicans has concerned the widespread failure to recognize the history of Northern Ireland 'as a colonial situation' that gave rise to 'an international conflict between indigenous Irish and either the colonial power or local representatives of the colonial power'. He insists that the framing of the conflict as centering on the Catholic-Protestant division is an effort to obscure this history in contemporary political debate. Today the tensions surrounding this history remain at the centre of social divisions in Northern Ireland, 'literally circulating in the streets' during the parading season each year, when direct violence is still likely to erupt around who has 'the right to remember what date in history, in which way, and on whose geography' (Lederach 2005: 134).

The roots of the conflict in Guatemala, culminating in the 36-year civil war that ended in 1996, also reach back through several centuries characterized by the violence and ethnic exclusion of colonialism. The Spanish conquest of Guatemala saw the ancient socio-economic order of the Maya replaced with a brutal plantation economy. As in other colonized societies, indigenous peoples' ways of life were profoundly disrupted, their access to land severely limited, while they were also forced into slave labour and seasonal migration. Even after gaining independence in 1821, Guatemala continued to be ruled by a series of military dictators funded by, and aligned with, a small landed oligarchy whose primary concern was the preservation of elite Ladino interests (Crosby and Lykes 2011: 460). This history, combined with more recent U.S. foreign policy (notably the U.S. financed and trained counterinsurgency forces, for which former President Bill Clinton apologized in 1999), and the neoliberal economic reforms of the post-Accord period, have produced the social and political conditions of Guatemala today (W.E. Little 2009: 3). Yet, as in Northern Ireland and South Africa, the focus in reconciliation efforts is on the most recent experience of violence and oppression, in Guatemala's case the '"holocaust" period' from 1978 to 1983 when around 200,000 people were killed under the directions of generals Luca Garcia and Ríos Montt (Reilly 2009: 45). A culture of 'historical forgetting' supports a system of structural violence that maintains the country's deep divisions, not least between Mayas and Ladinos (Benson and Fischer 2009: 156).

Despite this, the Mayan movement continues to emphasize a longer temporal frame, citing 500 years of colonial murder and dispossession (Nelson 2009: 107), a past that 'continues to hang like a diaphanous pall over the country' (Philpot-Munson 2009: 42). Irma Alicia Velásquez insists that the long ago past cannot be separated from the present, no matter how much the government and others may wish it. She tells me that:

> The indigenous people have two memories: long memory and short memory. Both work together. The overlapping is permanent {...}. It's difficult for the Ladino people to understand here. The majority of the news or opinions in the newspaper you read say, 'Please stop it. You don't need to talk about 500 years ago, about colonisation, about what happened there. We are in another time. We need to move on.' But for indigenous people it's impossible because our history is full of injustices that continue to determine the lives of indigenous people and communities.

Daniel Domingo López tells me that Mayan activists in Guatemala are 'not just speaking about reparations of recent events in the armed confrontation' when they demand reparations because 'all of it has a historical origin. The violations of rights have a historical origin. The country was invaded and a way of living was imposed on the people'. Domingo also makes a link between colonial oppression and the more recent conflict, arguing that 'when the time came that people realized that they were subordinated and they struggled against that, that was when they started to claim for justice. But on the other hand that was when repression started as well, so that was the conflict.'

The more recent horrors of apartheid have similarly obscured the longer colonial history of injustice in South Africa. Racism and oppression were a feature of South African society from the earliest days of colonialism, developed over time as both the British and the Afrikaners advanced policy rooted in a shared belief in the total separation of black and white South Africans (Villa-Vicencio and Ngesi 2003: 279). Apartheid was merely the successor regime to colonialism, which over centuries had constructed an unjust political system in South Africa specifically intended to foster racial economic exploitation (Powell 2010: 237). The transition to democracy did not undo this longer history or erase the residue of colonialism. Indeed, Melissa Steyn (2001: xxiv) has suggested that the violence of apartheid, the process of reconciliation, and the crime that characterizes contemporary South Africa are all concerned with 'the working through of dynamics set in place by the colonial nature of the initial contact between the racial groups'. In the wake of apartheid some argued that the period under consideration by the TRC should go as far back as the arrival of the first white settlers in 1652, or at the very least to the creation of South Africa's first constitution in 1910. Instead, however, the decision was made to focus only on the period from March 1960 (the date of the Sharpeville massacre and the banning of political organizations) to December 1993 (when the amnesty provision in the Interim Constitution was agreed, later extended to May 1994) (Boraine 2000: 141). This focus on more recent wrongs means that there has been no redress for colonial wrongdoing, a point underscored by the 1913 cut off date for land restitution claims (Roux 2008: 157, discussed further in Chapter 7). Lungisile Ntsebeza (2011: 301) points out that the history of colonial conquest and land dispossession 'lies at the heart of the land question in South Africa', making it hard to imagine that any process of land redistribution that 'submerged this history' could have legitimacy in the eyes of those whose land was stolen.

In comparison to these other colonial invasions, the colonization of *terra australis* was relatively recent, beginning only with the arrival of the First Fleet in January 1788. But despite the common characterization of the years that followed as involving a relatively peaceful 'settlement', in fact there was violent conflict and war there too, which broke out within weeks of the invading settlers' arrival and continued on multiple frontiers for the next 140 years (Reynolds 2013: 49). The denial of this history allowed the settler 'bushman' to emerge as an heroic national icon, ensuring that no one would notice 'his bloodied hands or the notches on his rifle butt' (Reynolds 2013: 89). But as Reynolds (2013) points out, the frontier wars cannot simply be removed from Australian history. They were not only ever present, they also influenced the shape of the settler colonial order that followed, which saw Aboriginal and Torres Strait Islander people pushed to the margins of Australian society both literally and figuratively. Decades of assimilation policy followed federation in 1901, promising to provide to Aboriginal people 'the best things of civilization and spirituality coming from a Christian tradition', but with no regard for 'the existing sophisticated, complex, erudite and wonderfully woven spirituality that existed and still exists' (Dodson 1997: 145). The replacement of the direct violence of colonization, with the structural and cultural violence of the settler colony have combined to produce profound and lasting effects that Kevin Gilbert describes as leaving 'the Aboriginal psyche shattered, ripped, tattered' (Gilbert 2002: 6).

The neglect of these long colonial histories, and their contemporary legacies, points to the inadequacy of reconciliation efforts that concentrate only on a restricted temporal frame. While non-indigenous people may perceive past wrongs as belonging in a long ago history that has no place in the present, and for which they bear no responsibility, it is common for indigenous people to still experience the trauma of historical abuses suffered by their ancestors, which live on in both memory and oral tradition (International Center for Transitional Justice 2012: 4). Restrictions on the temporal frame of reconciliation reveal this underlying tension. The attempt to 'transition' from a colonial society to a post-colonial nation requires the repression or erasure of an ugly past. While the process may also be accompanied by a genuine desire to do justice and restore dignity to the victims of historical injustice, this is almost always dominated by the desire for legitimacy and the requirement to disavow wrongs of the past. As Muldoon and Schaap (2012: 183) suggest:

> Viewed in a more antagonistic light, claims for the recognition of suffering present a challenge to existing social relations, not because their satisfaction requires the postcolonial state to engage in extraordinary acts of supplication, but because they draw attention to the deeper sources of misrecognition in the desire for sovereign unity.

The urge to secure legitimacy and unity also drives a sense of impatience in reconciliation and conflict transformation efforts.

Immediacy, impatience, and unfinished business

The evident need for a more expansive temporal frame to reconciliation work sits in tension with the fact that strategic gains often rest on a sense of urgency or 'ripeness'. In each of the countries in this study there have been periods in which there was a perceived need for conflict transformation efforts that could capitalize on changes in political opportunities. In South Africa, Northern Ireland and Guatemala, for example, the 'hurting stalemate' that was eventually reached in the violent conflict provided opportunities to open new dialogue towards the kinds of political settlements to be discussed in Chapter 5. Similarly, truth commissions are thought to have more 'emotional relevance' if they occur close in time to the injustices under investigation, 'before a consensus about moral context can be constructed' (Zachar 2006: 76).

The long histories of many of these conflicts, as discussed above, make progress towards transformation slow and difficult. Yet reconciliation and conflict transformation efforts are often imbued with impatience, which can become another source of conflict if it is not addressed. Neil Jarman suggests that the impatience to move on from Northern Ireland's deep segregation is 'naïve' even 15 years after the signing of the Belfast Agreement, 'considering segregation was there for 150 years before the conflict began'. In South Africa, Oscar Siwali tells me that as the country made its historic transition to democracy there was a feeling that lives would change rapidly, that everyone 'would have a house in some lovely white neighbourhood' that would embody their freedom. The fact that these dreams have not been realized in the 20 years since the transition has created 'an anger that remains in the hearts of millions of South Africans'. Rebecca Freeth also observes this dynamic, noting that while Nelson Mandela's release from prison 'opened up this really big space for people to be in conversation' in a way that they had not been before, this appetite for engagement quickly burnt itself out as people realized the enormity of the transformational challenge their country faced.

These conflicting temporal frames are at the heart of a sense of 'unfinished business' in many reconciliation efforts. The long, colonial history of many conflicts leads both to impatience for change and an insistence on recognition and redress for long ago wrongs. Urgency for resolution sits alongside the reality that conflict will continue to erupt as long as this past remains inadequately addressed.

As discussed earlier in this chapter, each of the countries in this study was, at different times in history, the subject of colonization, with their resulting division into 'settlers and natives' provided the basis for the subsequent polarization of society (Guelke 2012: 22). Acknowledging the basis of present day division in a nation's colonial history calls into question the legitimacy of continued settler rule—a key component of the unfinished political business that feeds abiding conflict in deeply divided societies. In the South African context, for example Joan Fairweather (2006: 175) suggests that 'there will be no stability or social justice until the legitimate demands of the dispossessed have been met'. Alex Boraine also maintains that until the social and economic legacy of apartheid is dealt with it will be 'impossible to sustain the miracle, consolidate democracy, and ensure a peaceful future' (2000: 142). Or as Jaco Barnard-Naudé contends, for a country like South Africa, 'Moving on to a future that reproduces the past is in fact no moving on' (2008: 203).

Australia provides an interesting case in this regard, as despite the fact that the direct violence of Australia's 'forgotten war' was concluded long ago, the unfinished business of colonization still looms large in the nation's psyche; what Larissa Behrendt (2003: 20) describes as 'the pervasiveness of Australia's psychological *terra nullius*'. Aboriginal people have found that struggling for indigenous justice is an isolating, disheartening, and frustrating experience, confronting seemingly insurmountable barriers of 'ignorance and disinterest' while the majority remains inclined to 'paper over the darker aspects of its history' (Cooper 2005: 15). Irene Watson (2007: 29), among other indigenous scholars, insists that the nation must move beyond debate about 'the Aboriginal problem' to a conversation about the problem of colonialism. Yet as Aboriginal and Torres Strait Islander activists have long understood, without a change in the legal and political relationship between indigenous peoples and the state, indigenous people remain stranded in a political no man's land. As the late Kevin Gilbert once asked, 'Where can blacks turn? To whom can they appeal? Where do you appeal, after all, when you know that the thief is the judge? (Gilbert 2002: 208). Nevertheless, if the stated goal of those who refuse to contemplate a meaningful change in the relationship is to maintain national 'unity' and stability, this approach will continue to be self-defeating (Bradfield 2004: 171). Florence Onus is convinced that Australia remains divided because the nation avoids the important issues for Aboriginal people, which she names as 'sovereignty, justice, and compensation'.

These dynamics are not restricted to Australia. In Guatemala the economic and military elite still advocate forgiving and forgetting, urging that the country move on and focus on democracy and development rather than the unfinished business of the country's colonial and wartime past. Yet Guatemalan activists understand the difficulty of opening spaces for political reconciliation without changes to the historical structure of power, which continues to privilege the few and exclude the majority (Isaacs 2009: 141). Persistent historical denial further entrenches these challenges. Many of my interviewees maintained that Guatemalans living in the capital go so far as to insist that there was no war. Gustavo Porras recalls that people would ask, 'Why are they signing peace accords if there wasn't any war?' Mariel Aguilar also suggests that urban Guatemalans will maintain that the stories revealed in the nation's two truth commissions are 'a lie made by the guerrilla'.

Northern Ireland also has its own version of unfinished business, reinforced by the flying of flags and the displaying of emblems that reveal differences in both historical understanding and political aspiration. Terence McCaughey (2003: 294) contends that the Troubles in Northern Ireland, which only began in 1969, was just the most recent outbreak of violence in a conflict that has spanned 'at least 350 years', and which recurs because 'people on all sides have repeatedly supposed that there was unfinished business to be done'. There is what Kate Clifford describes in our interview as a 'seething resentment' that continues to manifest around these historical issues. Martin McMullan from YouthAction shares his belief that the Protestant 'celebrations' each July 11 and 12 are profoundly 'anti-Catholic', based on 'celebrating a victory of one over another'. For McMullan this is a fundamental aspect of Northern Ireland's unfinished business: attempting to resolve how a 'shared society' can enable the celebration of conflictual histories and cultures, when such celebrations are about 'opposing' and 'intimidating' another culture, which for him is 'not acceptable'. Yet in each of these cases, the temporal framing of reconciliation tends to nudge conflict transformation efforts towards some kind of premature closure that insists that historical 'business' has in some way in fact been concluded.

John Paul Lederach remembers a moment in which an impatience for resolution collided with an entirely different temporal frame. Lederach recalls that in negotiations during the 1990 Oka Crisis, which centred on a land dispute between the town of Oka and the Mohawk community of Kanesatake near Montreal, a point was reached when the emphasis on the urgency of the situation was tempered by an elder who reminded everyone of Mohawk time. '"Decisions made seven generations ago affect us today," he said, "and decisions we make today will affect the next seven generations."' Lederach appreciated that this understanding of time was directly concerned with responsibility and relationships in a way that framed the Mohawk approach to the negotiations:

> For the Mohawk, the past was alive. It accompanied every step of the journey. The very nature of who they were in that crisis and how they

were in relationship with the other peoples and nations arose from a historical context that was alive in their physical and social geography. Most important, the past was alive in the responsibility they felt for the well-being of the lands and the lives of their great-grandchildren. For the Mohawk, it was as if the negotiation table was an expansive space of time that connected the voices of a distance but very much alive past with a distant but very much present future. The active present was fourteen generations.

(Lederach 2005: 133)

In contrast, to this sense of inter-generational responsibility, Lederach (2005: 133) observed that the government representatives were driven by a 'pragmatic politics' that allowed space only for a view of recent events, 'demanding immediate decisions in order to secure political stability in an equally short-term future'. By contrast, the Mohawk had a keen sense of inter-generational responsibility that drove a longer-term vision. This case is illustrative of the vastly different temporal perspectives that proponents may bring to reconciliation efforts—perspectives that can also vary across the different generations that engage with conflict and transformation.

Generations

Societies entering a period of so-called 'post conflict' tend towards the belief that the end of wide-scale direct violence has guaranteed a better future for children and future generations. In many ways this is true. But in more complex ways, inter-generational relationships suggest another avenue of agonistic engagement, which directly encounters different experiences of conflict and violence over time. Violence and struggle leave deep scars on the people who are directly engaged in fighting, and on their families and communities, who all endure a range of complex emotional burdens. Furthermore, as discussed in Chapter 1, it is now well understood that trauma is transmitted through the generations, with debilitating effects (Staub and Pearlman 2002: 225). The feelings that most often accompany traumatic memories of historical violence—fear, hostility, and anger—can be passed down through generations influencing present and future perceptions of the other community, and fueling the kinds of volatile political environments found in divided societies (Hutchison and Bleiker 2013: 84). Guilt and responsibility for past wrongs may also be transmitted across generations, although in this regard the 'generational question is anything but straightforward' (Barkan 2000: 344; see also Maddison 2011). Long periods of violence also disrupt social processes of intergenerational cultural transmission. In South Africa, for example, the struggle against apartheid was primarily a burden borne by young people, creating something of a role reversal between parents and children, which had the effect of fracturing the intergenerational transfer of knowledge, and creating mistrust between the generations (Ramphele 2008: 24). For some reconciliation actors, this intergenerational complexity adds a sense of urgency to their work. Brendan McAllister expressed his view that in Northern Ireland there was an urgent need to create as much change as possible while 'the generation that fought and was divided' was still living, to ensure that they were 'handing on something better'.

The most overriding emotion with regard to younger generations, however, is one of hope—a sentiment expressed by many of my interviewees. In South Africa, the fact that children and young people of the 'Born Free' generation, particularly those in the middle class, are now beginning to interact and engage is seen by many as a sign of hope for a better future (Alexander 2013: 40). This generation of South Africans has spent some or all of their high school years being educated in the country's new pro-democracy curriculum (discussed further in Chapter 8), rather than the apartheid era system of segregated education systems that reinforced a racist ideology. The Born Frees 'confront a totally different world than that of their parents', in which they have freedom of movement, residence, association, and relationship, and have experienced several peaceful democratic elections (Mattes 2012: 139). They have not, however always taken up the new opportunities for democratic participation that are available to them, in part because, as Robert Mattes (2012: 151) argues, many of the cleavages of the apartheid era have been replicated within the Born Free generation. As a result, 'whatever advantages might accrue from the new experience of political freedom and a regular, peaceful electoral process {...} are diminished by frustrating encounters with the political process, victimization by corrupt officials, and enduring levels of unemployment and poverty'. Kenneth Lukoko suggests that the resulting disillusionment has contributed to the rise of new leaders, such as the controversial former head of the ANC youth wing, Julius Malema:

> The Mandela generation was the freedom charter generation of 1955. Then you've got the 1960 generation and the 1976 generation. So as people {...} slowly disappear from the scene, the next generation of leaders that come are not necessarily going to articulate the need for reconciliation in the same way. They might say, 'Yes, it was fine to talk of this freedom charter and everything, but now we articulate this whole argument for transformation and the future South Africa differently.' So for example, the whole youth generation of the present, the Malemas and others, the way they talk of the same problems that leaders who came before them is quite different.

Undine Whande is sympathetic to the generation of Born Frees, who she suggests are 'not quite born free', and who have inherited what she describes as 'the heavy rainbow' of expectations around reconciliation. Whande suggests that this generation exists in a complex 'emotional matrix' of hope and expectation for reconciliation, which does not truly gel with their lived experiences of frustration and disappointment. For Tim Murithi this situation requires active intervention that specifically targets young people. On the one hand he says that he can regularly observe the way in which racist sentiments are still being passed between generations, particularly among white South Africans. On the other hand he remains optimistic that with targeted efforts it will be possible to ensure that 'future generations do not repeat the atrocities of the past and can find ways to work through what has happened and build a more stable society'.

The situation in Guatemala is strikingly similar. For most Guatemalan children today, *la violencia* is an artefact of their parents' generation, rather than part of their own lived reality. But the war has also 'shaped that reality', disrupting family structures, changing gender relations, limiting the speaking of Mayan languages, and relocating entire families to new communities (Maxwell 2009: 92). Jennifer Burrell (2009: 102) describes a situation in which:

> Traditional civil-religious hierarchies have broken down in many places, contributing to fuzziness in terms of age or grade and what one ought to be doing at a particular point in life, roles that were sharply defined. Instead, current generations are defined by the historical moments that have shaped their lives: war and counterinsurgency for parents and postwar and post-Peace Accords for their sons and daughters.

These ruptures have contributed to the rise in post-conflict violence discussed in Chapter 1, which has in large part been driven by the gangs or *mara*. The generation of young adults to which the *mareros* belong is the first generation to come of age since the end of *la violencia*, a fact that has led to a great deal of intergenerational conflict, further fuelled by ongoing inequality and structural violence (Burrell 2009: 98). Rosenda Camey shares her concerns about the ways in which former members of the *Patrullas de Defensa Civil* (PAC)—essentially the Guatemalan paramilitary, recruited (often by force) and trained by the military—are today passing on their learned violence to their children. Camey maintains that PAC members had their minds and spirits 'manipulated' during training, which has left them damaged and dominating. Today, even though there are only a few former paramilitaries left, Camey observes that they are 'multiplying that way of behaving' because 'the children in these families have grown up and they are now violent in their own families as well'.

Intergenerational tensions are also evident in Northern Ireland, where children as young as ten have participated in so-called 'sectarian rioting', leading many to question how the 'peace process generation' could be involved in behavior that was thought to belong to a previous era. It is evident that the persistent sectarianism and segregation that characterize Northern Ireland society directly contribute to this replication, with almost all young people exposed to the competing flags, cultural symbols, parades and murals, and the associated historical justifications that support them (Bell *et al.* 2010: 11). Survey research indicates that young people, and particularly Protestant youth, tend to be less in favour of integration than adults (Smithey 2011: 15). Children in Northern Ireland are also keenly aware of the legacy of violence, and continue to have their sense of identity shaped by historical factors. Research also shows that young Protestants are more likely to refer to themselves as 'British' and young Catholics more likely to refer to themselves as 'Irish', with only around a quarter of all young people (most of them Protestant) describing themselves as 'Northern Irish' (Bell *et al.* 2010: 48).

Several of my interviewees noted the extent to which these sectarian identities are perpetuated within families where, as Derick Wilson tells me, there is great store in teaching children 'to put your flag out, or wear your cultural symbol, at certain times of year, to march or demonstrate whenever you have to {...} [all] as part of your culture'. Wilson is concerned with the way these views sometimes translate into threats of further violence, having heard young people express the view that they would 'take up arms and finish the job' that was 'not finished' by older generations. Gerry Foster shares this concern, and, as an ex-prisoner now involved in community education, suggests that those who were involved directly in the violence of the Troubles need to take some responsibility for glamourizing their actions. Foster was one of several people who told me of the expressed desire among some young people to 'grow up to be an ex-prisoner', based on a feeling that they had missed out on the excitement of the conflict. Foster suggests that many people involved in the fighting painted a picture of the time full of images of adventure, 'the near misses, the near captures, the near being shot'. It was this realization that prompted him to focus his work in schools on talking about 'friends who were killed, the horrors of conflict, the down side of prison, you know, the impact it has on you, the impact it has on your family, the isolation of prison' in an effort 'to try and counter that adventure story'. However several interviewees also wanted to point to signs of hope with regard to intergenerational transformation. Katy Radford suggests that there are many young people who are 'written out of the equation' of Northern Ireland's deep divisions, but who are 'quite happily getting on across the interfaces'. Wilson also believes that an important aspect of the intergenerational complexity in Northern Ireland is the extent to which young people are breaking down barriers, transgressing the traditional generational model where 'parents go into spaces first and make them safe for children and young people'. In Northern Ireland, he suggests, 'we've had a lot of young people go into spaces where their parents have never been'.

In Guatemala, too, despite the depth of frustration and disappointment to be found there, the younger generation provides some hope. Catalina Soberanis expresses the view that young people are 'cleaner' than the older generation, less 'permeated by conflict', and carry fewer stereotypes and prejudices. This she sees as an opportunity for interventions that may 'contribute to generating among young people this willingness to look at the world in a different way'. Daniel Saquec agrees, noting among Mayan young people, in particular, a new preparedness to participate in political processes, citing the example of a recent evaluation of Guatemala's engagement with the United Nations Declaration on the Rights of Indigenous Peoples, at which every forum had a majority of young participants. Julio Balconi believes that, because of this interest in improving the country that he likewise observes among young people in Guatemala, when the next generation come into leadership positions, 'change will start to occur'. And, in South Africa, Michael Lapsley notes that there are many people 'of integrity who have a hope for society, who have moral vision and who give leadership' who he describes as 'the signs of hope'. He celebrates the young people he sees 'just flowering in their commitment to issues of justice and wanting to change their world'.

But while in other cases there is genuine hope that it will be the younger generation that creates impetus for continuing reconciliation efforts, this is not the case in Australia, where it has been a cause for concern for some time that the reconciliation 'movement' is ageing. For Jacqueline Phillips, then the national director of ANTaR, her experience of that organization's membership leads her to conclude that reconciliation has 'not captured the imagination of younger Australians at all'. She suggests that while young people would be aware of the paradigm of 'Closing the Gap', they 'would not even know what reconciliation means'. ANTaR's membership has been in a steady decline since the early 2000s, and Phillips feels that the organization has struggled to 'cut through' or 'excite and engage people' in the way that their high profile Sea of Hands actions did in the late 1990s.[2] Leanne Townsend, then the director of the NSW Reconciliation Council agrees, noting that the average age of members in that organization is around 65, and that many members of the local reconciliation groups that form the grassroots base of the Australian movement are the same members that started these groups over 20 years ago. The fact that these groups have not grown or changed in this time suggests to Townsend that the movement has not been inclusive, tending to meet in people's homes rather than reaching out to the wider community, and has been characterized by what she describes as a 'mission lady approach' in that the groups are made up of mostly middle class white women whose concern is to 'help these poor black people out of their terrible existence'. Jason Glanville observes a similar dynamic, suggesting that many reconciliation groups he has encountered still want Aboriginal people to 'cleanse them of their baggage', suggesting that even though they are 'great people' they still tend to 'bring a whole bunch of other stuff into this movement that distracts them from the true purpose'. Glanville suggests that the movement needs to be revitalized by 'making some decisions around who's in and who's out' and politely asking some people to leave by saying, 'Look, you've been of enormous service, we love and respect you deeply, but you're actually not making a contribution and you're getting in the way of progress'.

Evident in these various analyses of the level of intergenerational momentum for transformative change are the complex relationships between different groups of citizens. It is to these complex relationships, and the ways in which they constitute deeply divided societies, that I turn in the next chapter.

Notes

1 In 1967 Australians voted in support of modest changes to the Australian Constitution that gave the Commonwealth Government the power to make laws in relation to (although not necessarily for the benefit of) Aboriginal and Torres Strait Islander people, and to allow Aboriginal and Torres Strait Islander people to be counted in the national census. This referendum remains widely misunderstood as giving indigenous people citizenship and/or the franchise.

2 ANTaR's Sea of Hands project created a powerful, physical representation of the Citizen's Statement on Native Title – a petition circulated by ANTaR to mobilize non-indigenous support for native title and reconciliation. The first event, in October 1997, saw plastic hands in the colours of the Aboriginal and Torres Strait Islander flags, each carrying a signature from the Citizen's Statement, installed in front of Parliament House in Canberra what was then the largest public art installation in Australia. In subsequent years the Sea of Hands became a symbol of the People's Movement for Reconciliation.

Part II
Constitutional challenges

Part II

Constitutional challenges

4   Who needs to reconcile?

The long histories of conflict that were examined in the previous chapter have given rise to a range of complex, hybrid identities that are often the focus of a society's continued divisions. As discussed in Chapter 2, political reconciliation does not presuppose a prior, peaceful community that requires restoration, but instead recognizes the possibilities that may be revealed in political interactions between identity categories that are invoked and contested in the wake of violence (Schaap 2005: 84). These conflicts are not just a matter of incompatible personal preferences, but concern the conflict of identities that have been constituted through violent political struggle (Schaap 2006: 266). Agonism is centrally concerned with identity as a feature of politics (Wingenbach 2011: 26), a fact that is highlighted when considering the identity conflicts that animate political reconciliation. An agonistic view of reconciliation is not concerned with overcoming divisions in order to create a unified national identity. Rather, this chapter contends that a central task of reconciliation is the (re)constitution of deeply divided societies through the creation and expansion of political spaces in which the full range of views and perspectives can be heard. The challenge is for conflict transformation processes to engage identity conflicts in ways that enable the contestation of ideas of belonging and citizenship without resort to violence.

This chapter also begins to focus on the constitutional level of reconciliation as part of the multi-level framework of conflict transformation proposed in this volume. The first aspect of constitutional transformation is a consideration of the efforts required to (re)constitute the category of 'citizen'—that is, who does or does not constitute the nation, and who does or does not belong in the post-violent conflict state. The kind of political reconciliation advocated here is one in which citizens must hold a commitment to sharing a polity with their historical enemies or oppressors, not transcending former enmity but transforming it into a relation of civic friendship (Schaap 2007: 15).

Each of the countries in this study displays deep, often binary, divisions that are a source of tension in the society. In Northern Ireland, for example, this is labelled 'sectarianism', and has resulted from the parallels between the historical religious divides between Catholics and Protestants and the associated political contentions over sovereignty and equality. The two main traditions continue to define themselves and construct their collective identity in relation to one another, as 'victims of their enemy' (Hetherington 2008: 40). In South Africa, Melissa Steyn (2001: xxi) describes the nation as 'engaged in one of the most profound collective psychological readjustments happening in the contemporary world' as the different population groups attempt a significant political realignment of their relationships to one another. The fact that these relationships continue to foment political contestation in post-apartheid South Africa reveals their deep and historical significance (Alexander 2013: 13). Indeed, none of these divisions between social groups are trivial. In Guatemala, Daniel Domingo describes the conflict between Maya and Ladino as occurring between 'two forms of being' with 'different concepts of life'. He quite rightly acknowledges that this 'makes reconciliation more complex'. Guatemalans of all ethnic backgrounds are struggling to know themselves and each other, in the wake of violence, and to live together in the 'postwar' (Nelson 2009: 160). And in Australia, although the era of violent struggle between settler and native is long past, the indigenous rights movement that emerged in the second half of the twentieth century saw more and more Aboriginal and Torres Strait Islander people come to see themselves less as an excluded minority seeking inclusion as Australian citizens, and more as colonized peoples seeking the recognition of their sovereignty (McGregor 2011: 164).

What these experiences suggest is that reconciliation efforts must engage with the complexities of (post)conflict identity, including conceptions of enemy, friend, neighbour, and fellow citizen. The democratic challenge in these contexts involves the need to balance the desire for community and a sense of national identity with the recognition that continuing conflict and contestation between identity groups is not only inevitable but is in fact a sign of democratic health.

The limits of community and citizenship

Political reconciliation has a central concern with the ways in which alienated and opposing groups in deeply divided societies learn to live together as victims and perpetrators of past violence. Many groups and individuals in deeply divided societies express a desire to 'heal' their relationships in order to form a more peaceful community. As Villa-Vicencio (2004: 4) suggests, reconciliation implies that 'people are incomplete to the extent that they are alienated from one another'. This aspiration towards community and social solidarity is widely understood as a requirement for avoiding a return to violence. The challenge is therefore to (re)constitute a political community without suppression, exclusion, or assimilation. Yet as Schaap

(2004: 538) contends, an agonistic reconciliation is 'predicated on an awareness that community is always not yet'. The goal is not some expansive common identity but the creation of space for politics that allows divided citizens to debate and contest the terms of their political association.

Key to enabling democratic coexistence in deeply divided societies are two important normative requirements. The first is that agonistic reconciliation should allow for the coexistence of multiple communities, without any community threatening to dominate any other (Daly and Sarkin 2007: 82). This type of coexistence ought to be *respectful*, in that it requires 'mutuality in paying attention, according regard and recognition {...} [and] {...} taking seriously what the other regards as important', and it ought to be *functional*, in that it rests on a degree of interaction that 'invokes the cultural worlds of the players' (Kwenda 2003: 69). An agonistic view of this type of coexistence insists on relations of 'adversarial respect' between 'interlocking and contending constituencies' rather than pursuit of communitarian ideas of consensus (Connolly 1991: x). It accepts the right of others to hold different views and values, which should be accepted as an important contribution to the debates that enliven democracy. This type of coexistence may be framed as 'accommodation' or as 'toleration', but it should emphatically avoid any form of assimilation, integration, absorption, or forced unification (Daly and Sarkin 2007: 205). Rather, the form of mutual tolerance that is required in agonistic reconciliation rests on respect for the other as a moral equal, allowing members of a community to see themselves as part of a shared community even though they continue to strongly disagree. Tolerance in this sense can act as 'an endorphin to the contentious body politic' that enables robust political debate (Gibson 2004: 214).

The second requirement for coexistence is a very cautious approach to developing a unified national identity. James Tully (2008: 255) points out that the assumption that political unity requires uniformity among citizens derives from an earlier period in which cultural differences were experienced as a threat, a view that 'has no place in the world of today'. Instead, agonistic reconciliation suggests a transformative view of citizen identification, implying vibrant contestation over belonging and identity, but acknowledging that these contests may only lead to democratic outcomes if there is some limited consensus that binds the diversity of citizens (Wingenbach 2011: 63). For Mouffe (2007: 44) the aim is a pluralism 'that valorizes diversity and dissensus' and recognizes the contests between diverse communities as 'the very condition of possibility for a striving democratic life'. This non-authoritarian version of national identification would not supplant the sense of loyalty that individuals feel for their own communities, but would *broaden* this localized loyalty to potentially *include* a sense of national identification (Daly and Sarkin 2007: 100). This view reverses the traditional idea of including diverse communities within a nation, to suggest instead that national identity is just one identity that people may embrace. These ideas challenge the more staid ideas of citizenship and national identity that often inform reconciliation efforts.

Struggles for citizenship have been a component of each of the major conflicts in this study, and these struggles should in no way be minimized. Conflicts that involve identities, which is almost universally the case, usually also involve different citizenship regimes that mandate the exclusion of particular groups from full participation in public life and deny them equal status (Fullard and Rousseau 2009: 4). Aboriginal and Torres Strait Islander people in Australia, Catholics in Northern Ireland, Mayans in Guatemala, and 'non-Whites' in South Africa have all fought for full inclusion in their nations. In many ways it is accurate to note that it is only through seeing each other as citizens with a stake in the shared body politic that it is possible to really talk about reconciliation or make progress in other areas of transformation (Verdeja 2009: 33). Indeed, as Susanne Jonas (2000: 234) contends, 'long-range peace processes are largely about constructing citizenship'. 'The people' of any polity cannot be understood as a pre-existing entity, but rather as another fundamental element of ongoing political contestation and construction (Wingenbach 2011: 29). Political reconciliation in this sense depends on citizens transcending their relation to their neighbour as enemy and instead transforming it into one of 'civic friendship' (Schaap 2007: 15). Yet in this view the commonality of citizenship can only ever be 'a difficult, fragile and contingent achievement of political action' (Schaap 2006: 258).

Struggles to transform citizenship vary greatly by context, and these variations also reveal the limitations of citizenship as a political institution. No political institution alone can (or should) transform a divided society. In Northern Ireland, for example, where around half the population see themselves as British subjects and the other half as Irish citizens, the continued dependence on sectarian narratives of identity has hindered the development of a 'functional commonality' within the region (Houston 2012: 34). The sorts of structural divisions in Northern Irish society outlined in Chapter 1 are almost entirely dependent on the maintenance of sectarianism, and even though, as Little notes (2009: 192), there are 'few acknowledged sectarians', there remains a tangible 'nexus of hostility and separateness around politics and religion' that defines the limits of Northern Irish politics. Although progress has certainly been made through the functioning of devolved political institutions, it is also evident that the creation of new democratic institutions did not erase deeply ingrained differences in Northern Irish society. The Community Relations Council (2011: 11) observes the ways in which sectarianism has left 'a deep imprint' on Northern Irish identity, such that 'social worlds were often built on the basis of the "them and us" shaped by exclusion, fear and bitter experience'. Sectarianism remains part of life in Northern Ireland, shaping both political relations and daily life.

Reconciliation in South Africa also required a radical reconceptualization of citizenship. The anti-apartheid movement was, at its base, a struggle for black citizenship (von Holdt 2011: 22). Apartheid had created a racialized hierarchy of social identity that relied on a form of citizenship that 'forged whites into a club', and which in turn required black South Africans to defeat an entire political system in their aspiration for citizenship (MacDonald 2006: 64). The transition to democracy in 1994 'disentangled citizenship from race' but it did not undo the immense structural divisions that the apartheid system had created (MacDonald 2006: 126). Mamphele Ramphele (2008: 126) contends that this means all South Africans are now 'newcomers to citizenship of an inclusive democracy in their own country', with all the challenges that such novelty implies. In our interview Raenette Taljaard questions whether South Africa has even yet developed true citizenship, and highlights the widespread and continuing distrust in the state as a reason to ask this question. Without a strong sense of citizenship and an accompanying sense of trust in the state that provides a 'kind of forward cover of goodwill', Taljaard is concerned that it is hard for governments to introduce policies that will be 'more aggressively redistributive'.

Mayans in Guatemala have also endured extraordinary struggles for citizenship, although here too the political and economic elites have been reluctant to give up the privileges that have come with their historical citizenship. The form of 'memory politics' that emerged through the two truth commissions in Guatemala (discussed further in Chapter 10) has assisted the development of a more inclusive citizenship by strengthening rights claims among many highly marginalized sectors of the population, contributing to 'the construction of citizenship "from the bottom up"' (Sieder 2003: 222, 226). Daniel Saquec maintains that in this development of inclusive citizenship, people in Guatemala 'are transformed' and are then more able to transform the political system. For Saquec the transformation of former enemies into civic friends is the key to the broader changes needed in Guatemalan society. Despite Saquec's optimism, however, it seems evident that theories of inclusive citizenship are not able to satisfactorily address historic injustices, and nor do many approaches to reconciliation properly address ethnic, racial, and religious diversity (Bashir and Kymlicka 2008: 17). This is especially the case for indigenous peoples, for whom the links between citizenship, nation building, and reconciliation remain an inadequate response to their challenge to the legitimacy of an imposed settler state, and the desirability of citizenship in such a state (Short 2008: 20).

Indigenous peoples, 'race', and non-racialism

Around the world, indigenous peoples maintain a unique relationship with the ideas and institutions of citizenship and reconciliation. Indigenous peoples resist being classified as 'minorities', instead emphasizing their distinctive relationship with the settler state, which rests on the issue of consent. Unlike voluntary immigrant communities, members of which have willingly chosen to become citizens of the settler nation, indigenous peoples have been forcibly deprived of their political autonomy, producing distinct moral and political claims as dispossessed first nations (Short 2008: 19). Many of the people I interviewed, particularly in Australia and Guatemala, discussed the specific struggles they had engaged in as indigenous peoples. Otilia Lux points out that the Mayan movement has been highly active since at least the 1970s, demanding the recognition of indigenous rights in Guatemala. And while she feels they have been 'heard' at different times, she also observes that indigenous claims were 'never taken on as a real agenda in order to really make a difference in Guatemala'. Saquec also expresses disappointment that the protection of indigenous rights is not more of a priority in Guatemala, despite the 'persistent efforts' of Maya, Xinca and Garifuna peoples directed towards 'opening spaces' and pursing the goal of a 'more democratic, pluralistic state'. Rosalina Tuyuc makes a similar argument, pointing out that despite 'over 90 consultations' with indigenous peoples in Guatemala that 'have reflected that Mayan groups want self-determination', successive Guatemalan governments have failed to observe the requirements of ILO Convention 169. In Australia, Mick Gooda also points to the international arena, describing the UN Declaration on the Rights of Indigenous People as a 'key document', but one that is continually resisted by Australian governments who fail to enact domestic legislation that would codify the Declaration articles in Australian law.

As the previous chapter made clear, reconciliation can have the effect of placing a 'colonial ceiling' on indigenous aspirations. Citizenship can function in a similar way, essentially requiring that indigenous people give up their claim to sovereignty in order to be accepted as citizens of the settler colonial state. From an indigenous perspective, reconciliation should not mean that one national identity becomes dominant while others are excluded or absorbed (International Center for Transitional Justice 2012: 3). Although attaining citizenship rights can be a significant step towards equality, such rights are also understood to emanate from an illegitimate settler state, and therefore as failing to do justice to the unique status that abides in *indigeneity* (Short 2008: 21). In Australia, for example, assimilation policies insisted that Aboriginal and Torres Strait Islander people give up their cultural distinctiveness to be absorbed into the Australian polity. Assimilation became the condition on which Aboriginal people could become citizens (Peterson and Sanders 1998: 5). And while the Australian indigenous civil rights movement saw many Aboriginal and Torres Strait Islander people pursue the chance for equality, substantive citizenship rights came 'at a heavy price' according to Michael Mansell (2003: 7) who argues that the cost was 'the abandonment of indigenous sovereignty, and with it the loss of self-determination'. The dominance of this political logic has had the effect of blunting the impact of various reconciliatory initiatives, such as the apology to the Stolen Generations in 2008, which saw its potential to transform the relationship between Aboriginal and non-Aboriginal people 'diminished by the presumption of a certain unity of the polity' (Muldoon and Schaap 2012: 188).

The drive behind this framing of reconciliation and citizenship is primarily a nation-building approach to these institutions. A nation-building model of reconciliation is focused on achieving 'a harmonious and integrated society' by converting diverse people(s) into 'non-racial citizens of a "rainbow nation."' As Bashir and Kymlicka (2008: 15) note, this model of reconciliation implies that it is only the artificial divisions created by earlier oppressive policies that keep groups in society divided. Without these policies the expectation is that divided groups should 'feel that they belong together in a unified political community', moving away from their older, divisive identities towards a new, shared, national identity. Critics, of course, point out that it was precisely in the name of building unitary nations that indigenous peoples were oppressed and victimized, stripped of land, denied cultural practices, and marginalized politically.

The Australian formal reconciliation process certainly pursued this strongly nationalist approach, committed to a framework that encouraged a notion of 'final settlement' through an emphasis on the importance of indigenous-non-indigenous relationships and partnerships rather than on the need to explore the moral issues relating to the contemporary repercussions of colonization and dispossession (Gunstone 2009: 153). Damian Short (2008: 161) points to the vision statement from the Australian Council for Aboriginal Reconciliation annual report for 1994–1995, which aspired to 'A united Australia which respects this land of ours; values the Aboriginal and Torres Strait Islander heritage; and provides justice and equity for all.' Short observes that this statement highlights two central tenets of Australian reconciliation that were profoundly problematic. First the 'united Australia' theme that directed the nation building agenda by embracing the colonial assumption that indigenous groups were not, and are not, distinct nations in their own right. Second, Short points to the inclusivity suggested by the focus on 'justice and equity for all' rather than on justice for the *victims* of the colonial regime. And although the last few decades, including the decade of formal reconciliation, have presented multiple opportunities for the Australian state to move away from this homogenous view of civic identity and explore creative options for a more differentiated indigenous citizenship—'"separate" from the state, while also being aligned with the state'—the nation has in fact chosen to rein-scribe earlier cycles of domination-resistance that see indigenous demands repressed but never fully eliminated (Bradfield 2006: 97).

Aboriginal and Torres Strait Islander peoples in Australia are consistently ambivalent, if not hostile, to nation-building forms of reconciliation that focus on inclusion in the settler state. Mick Dodson (2003: 31) argues that the right to control one's identity is at the heart of the right to self-determination. Invasion and colonization saw the desecration of this right, along with the denial of indigenous sovereignty. In the face of this onslaught, justice is intimately bound up with the right to self-definition, the ability to 'be free from the control and manipulation of an alien people' and 'the freedom to live outside the cage created by other peoples' images and projections'. Les Malezer suggests that a lot of Aboriginal people are 'being sold the middle class option' of pursuing a form of assimilation or integration into Australian culture, prepared to identify as being of Aboriginal descent, but 'not prepared to say that they want to have a future *as Aboriginal people*'. Yet Leah Armstrong, then the CEO at Reconciliation Australia (RA), tells me that even though many Aboriginal and Torres Strait Islander people shy away from the language of 'reconciliation', they are responsive to the framing of the concept around 'relationships, respect and opportunities'. Her organization still struggles, however, to extend these ideas to a notion of 'shared pride', as both indigenous and non-indigenous Australians are uncomfortable with the idea of shared culture. More successful for RA has been the use of the concept of 'national pride', which encourages all Australians to feel a sense of pride in a nation that has 'a unique culture and history'.

Indigenous peoples in Guatemala face similar challenges. Guatemala has one of the highest percentages of indigenous population in the Americas, but despite decades of indigenous political organizing, it was only in the late 1980s that organizations specifically demanding collective rights *as indigenous peoples* began to emerge (Sieder 2011: 252). Nevertheless, the impact of these organizations was significant, most notably during the peace process when the *Acuerdo de Identidad y Derechos de los Pueblos Indígenas* (the Accord on Identity and Rights of Indigenous Peoples) was negotiated, which proposed to formally define Guatemala as a multiethnic, multicultural, and multilingual nation and recognize that the identities of the indigenous peoples (Maya, Xinca, and Garifuna—including diversity among the Maya groupings) 'are fundamental to the construction of national unity' (Jonas 2000: 75). In a society like Guatemala, where overt and covert discrimination against indigenous people was completely the norm, this inclusion of indigenous rights during the peace negotiations was truly radical (Reilly 2009: 48). It was, as Irma Alicia Velásquez points out 'the first document in the history of this country that recognizes that Guatemala has indigenous people'. The terms of the Accord were broad, including the protection of cultural rights and institutions; educational reforms; provisions relating to overcoming historic discrimination, exploitation and injustice; protecting the rights of indigenous women; ratifying ILO 169; constitutional recognition of languages; recognizing Mayan spirituality; incorporating customary law into national legislation; community determination of development priorities; guaranteeing indigenous political representation at all levels and in administrative units;

guarantees of community consultation; and the translation of court proceedings (Jonas 2000: 75–6). The May 1995 signing of this agreement—one of the most controversial accords negotiated during the peace process—by both the Guatemalan government and the guerillas of the *Unidad Revolucionaria Nacional Guatemalteca* (URNG) committed the Guatemalan state to a series of constitutional reforms that would recognize indigenous peoples' collective rights (Sieder 2011: 252). It was, then, perhaps predictable that business elites would campaign stridently against the constitutional acceptance of the reforms, claiming that they were 'divisive' and a threat to 'national unity' (Jonas 2000: 108). These campaigns, which contributed to the 1999 rejection of the constitutional reforms (to be discussed further in Chapter 6) masked the elite fear that they would give weight to indigenous land claims that would impact upon farming and resource extraction (Sieder 2011: 253).

In the wake of the failure of the constitutional reforms, the recognition of indigenous rights in Guatemala remains weak—what Susanne Jonas (2000: 108) describes as 'electoral democracy within the context of de facto apartheid'. Roddy Brett (2013: 237) concludes that the formal peace process in Guatemala denied Mayan peoples the experience of full emancipation by constituting only a partial and exclusionary multi-cultural state. Saquec tells me that although there has been some 'significant progress' in the last three decades, including since the signing of the Accords, the 'spaces for political participation' for indigenous people are 'still insufficient'. He describes the three greatest needs of indigenous peoples in Guatemala today as participation, quality education, and justice based on national and international law that enables the fulfilment of indigenous peoples' rights. Like others he looks to the realm of international law—specifically ILO Convention 169 and the UN Declaration on the Rights of Indigenous Peoples—to achieve self-determination and recognize the reality of 'interdependence {...} but under dignified conditions'. Or as Velásquez puts it, 'The indigenous people—we don't need donations you know? We need politics'.

Alongside the struggles of indigenous peoples are other ethnic and racial divisions that form the basis of conflicts in a range of contexts. The hope for many reconciliation efforts is that they will begin to make inter-racial cooperation possible through a recognition of commonality that will, in turn, lead to respect and the possibility of political coalitions (Gibson 2004: 345). In many cases, however, what reconciliation brings to situations of racial division is the imperative to 'move on' from categories of 'race' towards the kind of 'rainbow nation' to which South Africa aspired. Alexander and Mngxitama (2011: 60) suggest that this framing of post-apartheid race politics in South Africa 'functioned to make talk about blackness taboo' and 'precluded any focus on the black subject', seen as potentially destabilizing for reconciliation discourse. The effect was that the 'desire to be one people, with all colours standing shoulder to shoulder as a 'rainbow', displaced the discourse of blackness and whiteness without settling the basic historical conditions that brought about these categories'. Indeed, the 'new' South Africa of the post-apartheid era was quite explicitly constituted as 'non-racial' in the 1997 constitution.

In the early years following the transition to democracy it was evident that Nelson Mandela and his government saw non-racialism as central to answering 'the national question', and made tangible steps in this direction through the effective repeal of all racist legislation and the restructuring of public institutions on a 'non-racial' basis (Alexander 2013: 125). While intended to create tolerance of racial and cultural differences, in fact South African non-racialism has drifted towards a form of 'liberal colour-blindness', which has led both black and white, especially in the middle class, to express the view that drawing attention to issues of race is 'anachronistic and harmful', so that '[t]o name race is taken to be racist' (Steyn 2001: xxxi). As a result, South Africa 'began to create a fetish of race relations', with healing and reconciliation promised as a national cure for the sickness of racism and apartheid, 'paving the way to entry into "citizenship" as a guiltless member of the new South Africa' (Biko 2013: 56–7). Rather than developing any coherent strategy for engaging with race in post-apartheid South Africa, debate has become tangled up in suggestions that the nation needs to 'depoliticize' race, while simultaneously using race as a political tool in a range of ways (Hammet 2010: 250), including through a range of policies and programmes intended to transform the highly racialized socioeconomic inequalities that are one of apartheid's most pernicious legacies. These programmes, in the form of affirmative action and Black Economic Empowerment policies (discussed further in Chapter 7) have served not only to keep race on the political agenda, but also to reinforce the racial categorizations of an earlier era.

Not surprisingly, despite the hope that a non-racial 'rainbow' citizenry would emerge in South Africa, identities are still defined by apartheid-era racial markers, and 'race remains central to everyday life" (Hammet 2010: 247). Tim Murithi maintains that 'the racial prism is incredibly strong' in South Africa, and Kate Lefko-Everett observes that, from her research on the South African Reconciliation Barometer, it is evident that 'people are still really strongly attached to racial ethnic identities' which remain 'the major predictors for attitudes on different issues'.

The South African racial regime included elaborate constructions and definitions of what constituted 'white', 'black', and 'coloured' population groups that were codified in the 1950 *Population Registration Act*, and which remain in use both as bureaucratic identifiers and as newly politicized identities. The 'coloured' category remains particularly contentious, but persists in both government policy and popular usage. Namhla Mniki-Mangaliso suggests that at least part of this persistence has its roots in the apartheid era, when coloured sat above black in the hierarchy of races that the system had created. This sentiment, she suggests, still contaminates contemporary race relations, with some evident degree of resentment towards 'coloured' people who don't identify as 'black' because they don't want to be 'at the bottom of the food chain'. Conversely, as Claude van Wyk (2014) suggests, many coloured South Africans live an experience of 'inbetweenity', caught between the privilege of the white community on one side, and previously disadvantaged black community (now perceived to be favoured for economic restitution), on the other'. Stanley Henkeman tells me that the 'average, working class coloured person' is likely to say, 'First we weren't white enough and now we're not black enough', with the result that he often observes the coloured population to be 'a group of people who feel totally marginalized' in the new South Africa. Others, however, suggest that after nearly 50 years of using this 'violently coercive nomenclature' South Africans from all ethnic backgrounds are now engaged in a process of reclaiming shattered identities, and renaming themselves where they can, including members of the 'coloured' community who are now reclaiming their many pre-apartheid microcommunity identities (Irlam 2004: 699–700).

Whiteness also remains a problematic racial category in South Africa, although for different reasons. In pursuit of harmony in the 'non-racial' South Africa, the post-apartheid leadership was eager to assure the white population that they still had a role and a future in the country. While this aspiration is understandable, and in many ways laudable, it seemed to come at the expense of any significant level of understanding among the white population that post-apartheid reconstruction would require their effort and commitment to overcoming the legacy of inequality that the new regime had inherited (Kollapen 2010: 20). Mbembe (2008: 12) argues that it is one of the great ironies of the transition to democracy in South Africa that white people continue to both deride the project of socio-economic transformation and retain their own sense of entitlement and privilege, ignoring the 'accumulated atrocities' upon which their privilege rests. Stanley Henkeman suggests that while many South Africans still use race as a weapon as a 'fall-back position', in particular it is white South Africans who try to 'dominate the dialogue' by insisting that it is time for the country to 'move on' from discussions of race. Lucy Holborn is struck by the fact that the angriest people in South Africa are white people, rather than the black and coloured South Africans who suffered under apartheid. She points to the 'victim mentality' among white South Africans who feel that they have fewer opportunities than under the previous regime, despite all the evidence to the contrary. White South Africans also choose to maintain their ignorance about the lives of other South Africans, as Holborn tells me:

> The average white South African never sees the day-to-day life of many black South Africans. They may never have bothered to ask their

domestic worker 'What sort of place do you live in? How many people do you live with in your tiny little house?' They don't think to be interested in that sort of thing. There are probably many white South Africans who are vastly out of touch and assume that in black townships things have vastly improved.

Dialogue practitioner Rebecca Freeth, whose work has been explicitly focused around race and race relations for many years, suggests that these 'unresolved and unaddressed' issues are the 'biggest obstacle' to a more inclusive South African citizenship. Freeth observes that most South Africans 'still see each other as so different, as so separate' and she suspects that

> people are afraid that having not had the conversation for, let's say 300-odd years, what will be unleashed will be unmanageable. So whether that's a sense of anger or whether that's a sense of guilt and shame or whether that's a sense of fear of the other or of oneself—a fear of being exposed for one's own racism, for one's own hatreds—it just feels like it will be a tidal wave of emotion. We've held it back this long people can't imagine what it will be like to just to bring the wall down {...}. It's such a strain to keep the walls there, but the notion of those walls coming down is just horrifying, overwhelming.

Indeed, in each of the countries in this study it is evident that 'racial' divides still structure relationships and present significant challenges to progressing transformation across other socio-political levels. In part, this is due to the entanglement of race with identities constituted in histories of violence.

Victims, perpetrators, bystanders

A significant part of the resistance to engagement in conversations around deep race-based (and other) divisions, is the discomfort associated with understandings of right and wrong, which translate into new identity categories in the 'post'-conflict era—those of victim and perpetrator. During periods of violent conflict, many citizens also became 'combatants', perpetrating violence against others in the name of their cause, and creating the need for post-violence strategy to 'contend with the detritus' (Daly and Sarkin 2007: 9). Identity descriptors such as these are both politically powerful and deeply problematic. The dichotomy between victim and perpetrator is often understood as reductionist and counter-productive in political debate, over simplifying complex relationships and histories and encouraging zero-sum thinking (Beyers 2009: 51). This distinction is far from impenetrable, however, as in many situations of violence people may be both victim and perpetrator.

In some post-violence contexts, notably Australia, people reject the label of victim altogether, preferring to highlight their strength as 'survivors'. In Guatemala, Rosenda Camey is also careful to point out that they 'don't speak so much of victims, but survivors' because as a victim 'if you really internalize it, you believe it, and there's a process of internal repression that starts'. Hugo Van der Merwe tells me of a similar shift in terminology in South Africa, although he sees victim terminology coming back into usage as people highlight the fact that the label of 'survivor' suggests that people are being 'taken care of' when this is far from the case, and in many ways victims are 'not surviving'. In contrast, in East Belfast, dialogue practitioner Sara Cook tells me of the people she encounters who have been told that they are 'lucky' to have survived the conflict in Northern Ireland, and should just 'get on with it'. These people not only feel guilty about surviving, they 'feel guilty about feeling like they are carrying wounds with them, they feel like they should just be lucky that they're alive'; they are not allowed to be victims.

A central struggle in most deeply divided societies is for a form of public remembering and acknowledgment of harms, which legitimizes or delegitimizes the standing of victims. Expecting victims to forgo their claims to moral acknowledgement in favour of preserving the peace, thus eliminating their suffering from public consciousness, would involve a further moral injury against them (Verdeja 2009: 8–9). In South Africa, for example, the public hearings of the TRC conferred 'credibility and dignity' to scores of victims and their relatives, making it extremely difficult for white South Africans to deny the suffering caused by the apartheid regime (Chapman 2002: 272). But the 'victims' in the TRC process were also carefully defined, limited to those who had experienced gross violations of human rights, thereby excluding the structural abuses that were legal under apartheid. Also excluded were those who saw themselves not as victims but as 'unrepentant soldiers of a just struggle' (Leebaw 2008: 113; Kollapen 2010: 21). Tim Murithi highlights the huge impact of these distinctions, pointing out that the TRC only identified 21,000 'victims' of apartheid who were due some form of reparation, ignoring the other '43 million people who could not come to the TRC', a point made emphatically by organizations such as the Khulumani Victim Support Group. [1] The same process can be observed in Australia, where the 2008 apology to the Stolen Generations was addressed only to the victims of the specific harm of child removal, not the wider indigenous population who had been subjected to a range of other abuses. When the category of victim is narrowed in this way, it also closes down spaces for political engagement over further reparations.

Northern Ireland is also engaged in political contestation around the concept of victimhood, which is inextricably bound to the disputed history of the island. Over time, a 'hierarchy of suffering' has emerged that perpetuates a contest over who suffered more, and who are the real victims

(Hetherington 2008: 39–40). Adrian Little (2012: 89) maintains that debates over the status of victimhood have been much more divisive in Northern Ireland than they were in South Africa where, to some extent, the question of the rights and wrongs of the conflict have been settled. In Northern Ireland, any suggestion that there is a form of moral equivalence between members of paramilitary organizations and members of the security forces, let alone innocent civilians, is unacceptable to the unionist narrative of a 'just and fair society that was undermined by the actions of terrorists' (Little 2012b: 74). The refusal to open up this narrative to collective scrutiny through any formal process has radically constrained the Northern Irish capacity to transform relations between the two communities. Noel Large sees that the lack of consensus around 'who is a victim' as Northern Ireland's 'biggest problem', worsened by the difficulty in providing victims with 'a platform that's not hijacked by others'. Brendan McAllister, then the Victims and Survivors Commissioner in Northern Ireland, expresses his own discomfort with the 'concept of victim', suggesting that the experience of victimhood is 'more amorphous and complicated' than often assumed. The Victims and Survivors Forum in Northern Ireland is attempting to counter this politicization of victimhood. Derick Wilson sees it as a very positive move that the Forum is emphasizing the shared experience of trauma, and refusing to create a 'hierarchy of victims'.

The category of perpetrator is no less problematic, with Guatemala providing an extreme case of some of the complexities involved in even naming perpetrators, let along pursuing justice against them. During *la violencia*, the army created paramilitary units known as the *Patrullas de Autodefensa* (the Civil Defense Patrols or PAC), which included young Mayan boys and adult Mayan men, who were often abducted and forced to collaborate through warnings that, if they did not, they themselves would be killed as presumed sympathizers, or their families would be subjected to worse atrocity (Arriaza and Roht-Arriaza 2010: 209). The PAC system not only created an 'enemy within' (Crosby and Lykes 2011: 472), it also forced other villagers, and sometimes an entire village, to participate in killing or torturing their neighbours or desecrating their bodies, intentionally tearing apart community bonds through horrific experiences that continue to traumatize and divide communities today. At the peak of the civil war, around 800,000 men were involved in the PACs, effectively dividing the civilian population against itself (Sieder 2003: 213–14). These divisions are evident in the complexities surrounding what many see as the inexplicable support by some K'iche' people for Ríos Montt during his trial for genocide. As Catalina Soberanis explains, many of his supporters were forced into the PACs, essentially making them complicit in Ríos Montt's campaign. This has caused contemporary confrontations between those K'iche' who will say 'there was no genocide and people on the other side of the line who say, yes, there was genocide committed'. These complexities underscore the need for political space in which these challenging histories can be discussed, and which may allow perpetrators to also heal from the wounds they have inflicted on themselves through the infliction of great harm on others (Staub and Pearlman 2002: 208).

One of the groups most actively targeted during reconciliation efforts are those described as 'ex-combatants', groups that are a visible reminder of the threat of violence (Mitchell 2011: 117). In Guatemala this group—the guerrillas—were the subject of a specific accord focused on the integration of the URNG (the *Acuerdo sobre Bases para la Reincorporacidn de la URNG a la Legalida)*. This accord included provisions for a *National Reconciliation Act* that was intended to prevent revenge against the guerrilla, while also protecting and compensating victims, and particularly (through the Truth Commission), to uphold their right to know the truth about human rights abuses during the war (Jonas 2000: 90). In Northern Ireland, ex-combatants from paramilitaries on both sides have been the focus of intense efforts at reintegration, often through community organizations. Many are now themselves engaged in community education work in schools and other fora, having attained positions of power or influence within the new polity by taking an active role in promoting transformative processes. Audra Mitchell (2011: 122) suggests, however, that while the focus on the transformation of this group is considered a priority in efforts to avoid a resurgence of violence, is not unproblematic. She points out that in Northern Ireland many members of the paramilitary groupings associated with both communities resent the idea of 're-integration'—republicans because they dislike the suggestion they were not acting on the will of their community, and loyalists because they understood themselves to be acting in defence of the [British] state. Yet this view is countered by others who suggest that, in a conflict transformation process, the onus is on the ex-combatants, who are often already looked up to as community role models, to 'provide leadership' in conflict transformation efforts (Beyers 2009: 57). And these individual transformations are not easy. For example, Gerry Foster describes his 'sense of betraying who you are and what you were, betraying your dead friends' when engaged in relational work with members of the Protestant community. In eventually finding compassion for the families of British soldiers and unionists who had died during the Troubles, Foster was able to accept that this did not mean he had 'lost his politics', but it did mean he was able to accept that 'there is a human cost to conflict'.

Despite these complexities, in any conflict, groups of victims, perpetrators and combatants—however contested these terms may be—make up a relatively small part of the overall population. So how do we describe the rest? In many cases the majority of the population are thought of as 'bystanders', a generally pejorative term, particularly with regard to those who are perceived to have benefited from either the conflict or the previous regime. Like the categories discussed above, the distinction between perpetrator and beneficiaries is less than stable (Barnard-Naudé 2008: 186), however bystanders are generally seen to have helped abusive governments to retain their power through passive inaction rather than active collaboration. It is often the case, however, that just as processes such as truth commissions create particular types of victims, they also draw attention away from a sense of wider social accountability for the structures and institutions that supported past wrongs (Miller 2008: 285). Yet as a moral category of persons in the conflict transformation landscape, bystanders are thought to carry a particular form of responsibility, one that cannot translate into guilt in the judicial sense but whose existence allows both elites and other citizens to distance themselves from their moral obligations (Verdeja 2009: 152). Thus, bystanders often attract considerable hostility. In Northern Ireland, for example, members of the Rural Communities Network describe the people who 'never got their hands dirty' and are seen to have 'walked away with their image intact, and their conscience intact' while others have struggled in the aftermath of violence.

Certainly it is evident that the majority of white South Africans are still thought of by non-whites as 'silent accomplices' who enjoyed economic and political benefits during the apartheid era, and have done little since to acknowledge their political and moral responsibility (Chapman 2002: 272). As Villa-Vicencio (2003: 247) insists, any South African who did not 'actively oppose the prevailing system' can 'scarcely insist on having clean hands'. Ramphele (2008: 130) describes this group as 'free-riders', happy to be 'passive beneficiaries of a system that protected their material interests, while pleading powerlessness to influence the direction society was taking'. In the absence of any public accountability for these (in)actions, many ordinary South Africans have struggled to recognize what Villa-Vicencio (2003: 242) describes as a 'little perpetrator' in everyone, and therefore do not see the need to contribute to the material restoration of those who suffered most, or even to become active to ensure that the evils of the apartheid era are never repeated. Many white South Africans complain that they are ' "sick and tired" of being reminded of their apartheid debt' even as this debt remains unpaid (Terreblanche 2012: 126). In fact, over time many white South Africans have come to see themselves as suffering under the new democratic dispensation, and opinion poll data suggests that many white South African see little difference between the violence committed on behalf of the liberation struggle, and that undertaken to suppress it (Chapman 2002: 274).

This is not to suggest that there are not beneficiaries engaged in more critical reflection of their roles. Antje Krog (1998: 125) notes that during the period of the TRC in South Africa there were 'hundreds of Afrikaaners' grappling with 'their own fears and shame and guilt {...} utterly sorry {...} deeply ashamed and gripped with remorse'. In Guatemala too there is guilt, not just among Ladinos, but among other survivors who struggle to live with the reality that they 'did not better protect murdered relatives and friends' (Isaacs 2009: 127–8). Elsewhere I have written of the guilt affecting Australians in the contemporary settler colonial state (Maddison 2011). The question—and the challenge—in these contexts is how to create spaces that will enable engagement and political debate across these often deeply entrenched divisions among citizens.

Gender

There is one remaining area of identity conflict to consider in the remainder of this chapter: that between men and women. Each of the divisions discussed in this chapter is also profoundly gendered, and each of the countries in this study includes histories of gendered violence, including sexual violence. So although major conflicts are rarely fought along explicit divisions of gender, these cannot be left out of any understanding of the requirements of conflict transformation efforts. Gendered divisions affect every single member of a divided society, including where gender intersects with other axes of identity, yet gender is often an add-on or an afterthought to reconciliation efforts, if indeed it is considered at all. While conflict and 'post'-conflict periods are well understood to throw accepted or traditional gender relations into disarray, often redefining traditional roles and reconfiguring gender relations, this opportunity to transform gender relations is frequently overlooked. In many cases the existing gendered hierarchies are not contested, but instead are further entrenched through conflict transformation processes that purport to be gender neutral (O'Reilly 2013: 58, 62).

Policy making in relation to reconciliation and conflict transformation has come late to these realizations, creating a slow but evident shift in the rhetoric concerning both the gender-specific consequences of violent conflict, and the need to integrate a gender perspective into reconciliation and conflict transformation efforts. Research has found that peace processes with significant participation by women are seen as more legitimate and are therefore more sustainable in comparison to those with little or no female participation (Thornton and Whitman 2013: 104). Women also tend to promote reconciliation and conflict transformation efforts that are specifically attentive to gender-based violence (Hammond-Callaghan 2011: 94). The United Nations has recognized the important contributions from women in conflict transformation processes, and has formalized this shift through the adoption of Security Council Resolution 1325, which entails a broad sweep of measures that prioritize women's participation in conflict transformation efforts and maintains that the full and equal participation of women is essential for a 'sustainable peace' (O'Reilly 2013: 57).

Yet despite these developments in policy and rhetoric, women still tend to be noticeably underrepresented within official peace processes, where important decisions about conflict transformation and new forms of governance are made (UN Women 2012: 2). The significant contributions that women have made to peace processes are still neglected in official accounts, rendering them largely invisible except as victims (Noma *et al.* 2012: 7). The issue of gender equality is rarely seen as a priority in the negotiation and implementation of peace agreements, and war crimes of gender violence tend to be addressed inadequately (if at all) in transitional justice processes. This situation leads some to question the ways in which peace and reconciliation processes may '(re)construct gendered forms of domination, injustice and insecurity in transitional societies, rather than empowering women (and marginalized men) to achieve political, economic and social transformation in the aftermath of war' (O'Reilly 2013: 57).

Despite these challenges, as often-marginalized citizens women have access to unique standpoints from which to understand and conceptualize the nature of conflict and division in their society, which often places them at the forefront of local reconciliation efforts (Thornton and Whitman 2013: 104). This is not to suggest some essentialized idea of women as 'peacemakers', rather it is to acknowledge the unique insights women can bring to conflict transformation work, which in turn suggest the need to prioritize their involvement at all stages, and across all levels, of these efforts. Underscoring this point is the experience of women in Northern Ireland, where it is recognized that women's participation in reconciliation extends beyond their inclusion (or otherwise) in official peace processes (Hammond-Callaghan 2011: 94–5). Following some decades of organizing in women's peace groups in Northern Ireland, women eventually secured a place in the 1997 peace negotiations through the formation of the cross-party political Northern Ireland Women's Coalition (NIWC), which 'built bridges' between women in the two main communities (UN Women 2012: 2). The NIWC is recognized as having played a key role in securing the Belfast Agreement, including through the contribution of several key elements concerning the principles of inclusion, equality and human rights (Hammond-Callaghan 2011: 103–4). Indeed, this agreement was the first political initiative in Northern Ireland to call for the greater political representation of women, and also committed the various political parties to pursuing the 'right of women to full and equal participation in political life' (Hayes and McAllister 2013: 125).

Yet women's involvement in the formal peace process has not been more widely transformative. The NIWC rapidly lost political influence and despite significant—if modest—early gains in terms of the number of women elected to the devolved parliament (14 out of 108 elected members in 1998), the Northern Ireland Assembly remains exclusionary and inhospitable. This is evident not least through the 'overwhelming and continuing male opposition' from all sides of politics to considering any extension of the 1967 *Abortion Act* to Northern Ireland (Hayes and McAllister 2013: 126, 129). Women remain invisible in most analyses of the Troubles, while the hegemonic masculinity that dominates 'post'-conflict politics in Northern Ireland remains unproblematized, including with regard to the poverty experienced by working class women from both communities (Rooney 2006). As a result, Katy Radford describes 'a sense of defeatism' among many women in Northern Ireland, who continue to carry a heavy burden of loss and community responsibility in the wake of the Troubles. Michelle Wilson points out that although women were deeply involved in the conflict by 'making things work' while the men in their community were in gaol, these same women tended to be 'pushed to the side' once the combatants were released. Mary Lynch echoes this view, suggesting that 'the last stories to come out are always women's stories'. The dominant interest in the post-conflict narrative, she argues, still revolves around 'who died', while nobody asks 'those other questions of who did anything else that held the society together, who earned a position by keeping a culture alive, or keeping a language alive or anything'.

A similar situation can be observed in both South Africa and Guatemala, where women have both been deeply involved in the conflicts within their countries, and have fought for a place in official negotiations towards peace. In neither context, however, has there been a resultant transformation in women's status or safety in their communities. During the negotiations in South Africa, for example, the ANC Women's League organized a diverse group of South African women to fight for women's inclusion (Segal and Cort 2011: 87), and the Women's National Commission insisted that 50 per cent of participants in the Multi-Party Negotiating Process be women. Around three million women participated in focus groups and discussions across the country, with the result that a 30 per cent female quota was adopted for the 1994 elections. Following the transition to democracy there have been numerous advances in South Africa intended to promote gender equality and reduce the level of violence against women, such as legislation including the *Domestic Violence Act*, the *Promotion of Equality and Prevention of Unfair Discrimination Act* and the *Employment Equity Act*, and the creation of the Commission for Gender Equality. Despite these advances, however, women's physical and economic security in South Africa remains notoriously perilous, with little suggestion that improvement is on the horizon (Hamber 2010: 75–6).

In Guatemala, although only two women were included in the government and URNG negotiating teams, women greatly influenced talks leading up to the Peace Accords, particularly through civil society participation that ensured the Accords eventually contained important provisions relating to gender equality (UN Women 2012: 2). Women in Guatemala have continued to struggle for representation and redress for the violence they experienced during the war. Otilia Lux describes the struggles of the women's movement in Guatemala, which had to fight both Catholicism and wider social conservatism in order to see women 'recognized as rights bearers'. The organization *Comité Nacional de Viudas de Guatemala* (CONAVIGUA, the National Committee of Widows of Guatemala), founded by Rosalina Tuyuc and other women in response to the deaths and disappearances of so many husbands, fathers, and sons, has become a significant organization focused on women's human rights in Guatemala. Tuyuc told me of the careful work the organization is doing to improve the mental health of women who have been left scarred by their experiences during the war. Tuyuc sees this work as 'reparation action' undertaken by a collective of women who understood that there was 'a need to work on gender and not just on ideologies focused on the different political parties'. Over time their work has also expanded to the legal domain in an effort to decrease violence against both women and indigenous peoples. In 2010 the Tribunal of Conscience for Women Survivors of Sexual Violence during the Armed Conflict in Guatemala, which was organized by several civil society organizations, was held with the specific intention of creating public space for women survivors to 'tell their truths and be heard by their fellow citizens and the state' in preparation for a legal case to be brought in the Guatemalan courts with regard to the use of sexual violence as a weapon of war (Crosby and Lykes 2011: 457).

These initiatives point to the continuing efforts required by women, for women, if there is to be any gendered analysis in conflict transformation efforts. A significant aspect of women's exclusion from reconciliation efforts is what Catherine Kennedy describes as women's 'exclusion from the telling of history'. Kennedy observes that in many of the community history projects that her organization undertakes in South Africa, women are simply 'invisible', with little community awareness of the fact that it was the 'behind the scenes work' undertaken by women that enabled men to engage in the armed struggle against apartheid. Undine Whande observes that continuing oppression of women within South African society is 'intimately connected to the systemic nature of the autocracy and the oppression that was happening' during the apartheid era, but that many women feel that their experiences of domestic violence or rape 'don't count' because they are personal rather than public. In Northern Ireland, Wilson also notes that women's experiences of interpersonal violence have been excluded from public debate 'for the greater political cause'.

Of course the gendered effects of violent struggle do not only concern women. There is a growing body of research on post-conflict masculinities that suggests that the impact of violence on men also requires serious consideration in conflict transformation efforts. A frequent suggestion is that men, and particularly young men, are 'emasculated' by the unemployment and poverty that often follows violent struggle, and seek to 'recover their masculinity' through behaviours associated with a more militarized masculinity through which they can confront authority (von Holdt 2011: 28). In Northern Ireland, Radford describes a kind of 'hyper-masculinity' that is, at the same time 'emasculated', which she sees turning men 'really vicious'. Similarly, in South Africa it is often argued that what is referred to as 'struggle masculinity' has evolved out of the violent masculinities of the past, and that some men report finding the changing status of women in their society 'profoundly destabilizing' (Hamber 2010: 78–80). Men may now find themselves vilified for behaving in the same ways that once saw them recognized as heroes, with a common outcome being the reassertion of a violent masculinity in private spaces where they are least likely to bear any legal consequences. However, Brandon Hamber (2010: 84) cautions against this narrative of male anomie, suggesting instead the need to 'recognize that male cries of insecurity are the product of social and political context in which gender is integrally linked with power relations in a myriad of ways'. Hamber contends that a more productive narrative might involve the recognition that South African gender relations have been in a state of turmoil since 1994, which has not created a crisis for men specifically, but instead implicates all members of the society through the collective construction of gender relations.

Hamber's analysis is a reminder that it is not enough to ensure that women are able to participate in peace negotiations. A wider view of the construction of gender both during and after violent conflict is needed, one that pays attention to the roles and lived experiences of women and men, that acknowledges the ongoing efforts made by women to ensure that their needs and experiences do not disappear from view, and that is fundamentally concerned with transforming the experience of conflict for women, men and everyone in between, of all races and ethnicities, who constitute the nation that is striving for reconciliation. In Alvaro Pop's view, a country like Guatemala, with all its immense challenges, does have a future, but he says:

> We have to start all over again and we have to establish a political and social pact in which indigenous people, for example, women and young people, can be recognized as the new actors. If we don't do that in the next 10 years these emerging actors will become again the fuel for new conflicts.

While starting all over again may not be an option, the pursuit of reconciliation that requires a recognition of the moral worth of others will enable citizens to acquire new, post-violence identities that cut across the fault lines that have sustained deep divisions (Verdeja 2009: 3). This conception of identity conflict takes a decisive step away from the pursuit of community harmony as a goal, instead prioritising the pursuit of *just enough* respect to allow democratic contestation without violence. One key arena for this contestation is within efforts to negotiate a peace settlement or agreement, the subject of the next chapter.

Note

1 The Khulumani Support Group is a South African advocacy organization made up of approximately 85,000 victims and survivors of Apartheid-related violations in South Africa.

5   Settlements and agreements

Peace agreements have a significant impact on reconciliation and conflict transformation efforts, particularly where they provide a framework for addressing the conflictual relationships that were the focus of the previous chapter. Settlements can resemble a kind of constitutional 'big bang' that enables a deeply divided society to radically overhaul its political institutions and create a space for political experimentation that can support efforts at democratic renewal (Bell and O'Rourke 2007: 295–6). Yet settlements and agreements rarely signal the end of conflict. Although they are often represented as a solution to an historic problem, in reality they are more likely to offer a compromise that parties to the conflict can agree to live with. Although research on peace agreements tends to focus only on elite political pacts, 'like icebergs' these agreements tend to hide much of the conflict that endures beneath the surface (Reilly 2009: 3), meaning that the underlying work of conflict transformation will remain substantial.

This chapter continues the examination of the constitutional level of conflict transformation through a consideration of various processes by which societies in conflict have pursued a political agreement to end violence. It argues, however, that while the architecture of an agreement or settlement is important, this alone will not predict the success of post-violent conflict transformation. Indeed, the ingrained nature of social and political conflict suggests that political agreements in isolation will rarely bring about substantive change (Little 2014). Instead, a promising settlement may help to (re)constitute a nation by recognising and bridging conflicting interests within a normative framework that represents the diversity of values to be found among the wider, conflictual society (Ramsbotham *et al.* 2011: 188). Ideally, a newly crafted settlement will open spaces in which common ground can be recognized while protecting from further oppression the identities, cultures, and interests of diverse citizens. What matters is the extent to which settlements and agreements are designed in ways that might transform or merely contain a conflict, how they might keep open or close off future political debate, and the wider cost to democratic participation when it is perceived that there is no viable political alternative to the agreement that is in place.

'Settling' a conflict

After decades of violent conflict there is an obvious desire to bring an end to direct violence and the associated physical and cultural trauma that violence produces. Through negotiation, it is hoped that peace settlements or agreements will 'translate' violent conflict into less violent political struggles that create space for further political efforts towards conflict transformation (Bell 2009: 25). Certainly it is true that in many cases, including South Africa, Northern Ireland, and Guatemala, achieving a peace agreement enabled the society to enter into dialogue while living with continuing disagreement (McCaughey 2003: 289), at least to some extent. However, many negotiated peace agreements remain fragile. An estimated 50 per cent of all peace agreements collapse within the first five years (Zelizer and Oliphant 2013: 5). In part this is because conflict transformation efforts at the other levels outlined here are generally untouched during the negotiation process, only becoming the focus of attention once an agreement has opened the space for dealing with other aspects of conflict transformation 'free from the sound of guns or the cut of the machete' (Brewer 2013: 164–5). However, many peace agreements simply collapse under the weight of expectations attached to them. There is increasing scepticism about what peace agreements can actually achieve, and in many cases it appears that a couple of decades on from a peace settlement, agreements have in fact produced new conflicts, displaced conflict across borders, or have been poorly implemented to the extent that countries remain in 'frozen conflicts', caught between war and peace (Bell 2013: 257).

Common among the expectations that weigh on these processes is the idea that an agreement can provide a 'solution' to a conflict, or that an agreement means a conflict has ended (Lederach 2005: 44). This is rarely the case. As Mac Ginty *et al.* (2007: 1) put it, 'Reaching a peace deal is not the same as reaching peace'. On their own, political agreements rarely bring about substantive change (Little 2014: 2), although they may allow the *expression* of the conflict to change and provide new spaces for (re)defining relationships (Lederach 2005: 46). Indeed, an agonistic approach suggests that the aim of a settlement or agreement should be to 'transform actually or potentially violent conflict into non-violent forms of ongoing political struggle', accepting that conflict remains central to any serious politics (Ramsbotham 2010: 211). While agonistic theories of democracy do not yet offer an adequate or explicit account of the institutions that are needed to produce collective decisions, including through negotiation, there is acknowledgement that institutions are needed to provide some form of 'provisional stability' that can allow citizens to engage in agonistic contestations in a context of adversarial respect (Wingenbach 2011: xii). Peace agreements may be one such institution, provided they are thought of in such provisional and contingent terms.

More frequently, however, the reverse is true. As political institutions, peace agreements tend to reinscribe the conflict that they are intended to contain, including by (re)constructing existing social divisions and fuelling different manifestations of the same contentious issues (Little 2014: 21–2, 35). The Belfast Agreement in Northern Ireland, for example (and discussed further below), only looks the way it does because the conflict between 'two communities' has been reinscribed through the consociational power sharing arrangement established in the Agreement. As Little (2014: 21) suggests, examples such as this imply that 'our conflicts are written into the very structure that we use to regulate non-conflictual social and political life'. In part this is due to the nature of peace negotiations, which for pragmatic reasons tend to focus on the most recent violence rather than on the deeper complexities of historical conflicts, which often remain untouched and unchanged. Nevertheless, many people expect more from agreements than they can possibly provide. As Villa-Vicencio (2009: 61) suggests, a peace agreement 'is only the first step toward sustainable peace', and what follows may be far more demanding. While negotiators and observers may believe that an agreement is equivalent to having fixed a broken machine, in reality they have done little more than open the door to the workshop, or at best provided an instruction manual.

None of this is to suggest that agreements are not an important component of conflict transformation efforts. A good agreement may create significant common ground among citizens, while ensuring that the identities, cultures and interests of vulnerable groups are protected from both the state and private interests (Daly and Sarkin 2007: 215). It may also represent a new set of norms and values that can guide the wider community in further conflict transformation efforts (Ramsbotham *et al.* 2011: 188). Too often, however, the process of creating an agreement can leave local communities feeling disconnected from what are often seen as 'elite pacts', negotiated by remote national and international actors (Mac Ginty *et al.* 2007: 2). While peace agreements need the consent of the leaders of the major groups involved to be effective, they can also test the strength of relationships between these leaders and their communities, with agreements often regarded as 'self-seeking' elite settlements that benefit those already privileged in the society (Villa-Vicencio 2009: 42). As was suggested in the previous chapter, core groups—notably women—are often denied a seat at the negotiating table, with significant consequences for the issues of most concern to them. Feminist scholarship has suggested that power sharing arrangements, such as those enshrined in the Belfast Agreement in Northern Ireland, may sacrifice claims for women's equality in the interests of 'communal unity' (Hayes and McAllister 2013: 124). Conversely, there is also a strong correlation between the organized participation of women's groups and greater gender-sensitivity in the text of the agreements (UN Women 2012: 3–4). Nevertheless, 'gender-blind' peace agreements still tend to be the norm, with only infrequent mention of the specific measures needed to undo women's exclusion and inequality (UN Women 2012: 17).

Also problematic is the fact that agreements are often shaped by the 'liberal peacebuilding' agenda, which focuses on establishing liberal institutions such as democracy, human rights, and the rule of law, as a key condition for the development of a 'sustainable peace' (Zaum 2013: 107–8). Although most peace processes occur in the global south, they are often designed, funded, and led by organizations and actors from the global north, creating a sense that 'peace' has been 'imposed' by elites, no matter how well intentioned these processes may be (Mac Ginty 2013: 3). International institutions, including the World Trade Organization, the International Monetary Fund, and the World Bank, have become important actors in peace negotiations, often imposing demands for economic liberalisation as a condition for future participation in global trade. This was a key factor in both the South African and Guatemalan agreements, as will be discussed further below. As a result, as Ismael Muvingi (2009: 171) argues, external pressure to create conditions conducive to international investment is often prioritized over a concern for local socioeconomic equity, meaning that negotiated settlements 'have as much to do with the outside world as they do with internal factors'. These liberal peace interventions not only deny local autonomy, they may also cause many of the subsequent 'pathologies' that continue to divide the country (Zaum 2013: 109). Often these feelings of disconnection or resentment towards the eventual terms of a peace agreement are the result of the compromises made to appease both adversaries and international allies.

Ambition and compromise

It is common for the drive to 'settle' a conflict and bring an end to violence and repression to result in consensus-based compromises that enable an agreement to be signed. These compromises may be required to achieve pragmatic and immediate ends, but it is also the case that they can close down political space, with problematic long-term implications.

The South African example illustrates this concern. The violent struggle against apartheid in South Africa was brought to an eventual end through the negotiation of an historic agreement, intended to stop an escalating conflict that threatened to tear the country apart completely, destroying the 'identity, infrastructure, and promise of a nation yet to be born' (Villa-Vicencio 2009: 42). It took two years for the leaders of the white establishment and the black resistance to get to know each other well enough, and develop enough mutual trust, to be able to agree on the form and content of the substantive negotiation, eventually agreeing on the framework for a new political and constitutional order (Thompson 2001: 247). Spikes in violence followed the progress of the negotiations, and the threat of election boycotts or military takeover were considered very real. Ultimately, however, these threats had the effect of driving the negotiating parties closer together by underscoring the urgency of finding a workable settlement (Powell 2010: 240). To move the negotiations forward, agreements between the African National Congress and the National Party came to rely on what was termed 'sufficient consensus' on the key issues of concern to both parties. The historic settlement is recognized as having pulled the country back from outright civil war, and is thought possible only because both sides recognized that there was no real alternative to the compromises that a settlement would require.

It was the eventual success of these negotiations without the outbreak of civil war that have led some to view the South African transition to democracy as the 'miracle' that Archbishop Desmond Tutu (1999: 21) considers it to be. In the context of the extreme violence of the preceding years, this success may well be understood as miraculous. Certainly the negotiations gave ordinary South Africans the opportunity to see their leaders relating to one another in a civil and non-violent manner, and images of opposing leaders embracing became a regular feature of the daily television coverage of the Convention for a Democratic South Africa (CODESA) talks that produced the interim constitution. These new images of cordiality assisted other South Africans not involved in the negotiation process to accept the eventual settlement. Indeed, beyond the settlement itself, the process is thought to have 'inspired a new culture of democratic engagement' in South Africa, which also gave further popular legitimacy to the constitution that emerged (Powell 2010: 240). Villa-Vicencio (2009: 45) argues that the politicized nature of South African society, along with the social organizations that mobilized participation, 'drew people into the political process' with the result that 'they felt it was their settlement, at least to the extent of having shared in the buildup to it and in the celebration of its implementation'.

However, Villa-Vicencio and Ngesi (2003: 267–8) also caution that an overly idealistic perception of the transition can 'underestimate the levels of resentment, alienation, disappointment and compromise' that are also the result of political compromise on the scale involved in the South African settlement. They suggest that the settlement is more usefully understood as a 'contested process—driven as much by pragmatic needs and rugged compromise as by high ideals and moral intent'. The formation of the short-lived Government of National Unity in 1994, which limited majoritarian rule and allowed a form of power sharing between the parties, was certainly one such compromise (Muthien *et al.* 2000: 8). Another so-called 'Faustian bargain' involved the ANC allegedly 'trading amnesty for peace', rather than pursuing a more retributive form of justice against the apartheid regime in order to secure majority rule (Gibson 2004: 259). These and other such compromises were thought crucial to the nation's future stability, as the ANC's chief negotiator Cyril Ramaphosa has acknowledged:

The interim constitution was a document which, for all its admirable aspects and historic provisions, was formulated in an effort to accommodate those forces whose cooperation was necessary to ensure a smooth transition {...}. The failure to accommodate a single organization could have seriously threatened the success of those elections.

(quoted in Segal and Cort 2011: 126)

Over time, however, it has become clear that some of these compromises have had the effect of closing down spaces for further discussion—for example, about more radical economic restructuring. In subduing important conflicts in favour of a desired consensus, South Africa has perpetuated deep social divisions, meaning that in key ways the South African settlement has produced a political reordering of the society that left many of the apartheid era structures and institutions untouched (Little 2014: 35). While some see these economic compromises as little more than a cynical and calculated pact between two groups of political elites, Hlumelo Biko (2013: 56) suggests that the ANC was poorly prepared for 'the barrage of lobbying, corporate bullying, and sometimes outright bribery' that vested interests brought to the negotiating table in order to protect the economic spoils of apartheid. Hugo Van der Merwe considers that it is unclear 'how much was given away under pressure versus how much was a rethink and ideological shift on the part of the ANC'. Today he wonders what might have been possible had there not been 'such pushback from the apartheid government'.

Central to the inevitable compromises that had to be made for the settlement to succeed was a concession to the view that economic restructuring to provide redress for the gross socio-economic inequality experienced by the black majority population would be too great a risk to the 'delicate balance' on which the process rested (Ramphele 2008: 24). In the wake of the changed macro-economic context after 1989, it was argued that South Africa risked complete economic collapse if it pursued a programme of radical economic restructuring. Raenette Taljaard certainly agrees that this context was significant to the terms of the South African settlement. Specifically she points to 'the end of the Cold War and what that meant for newly emerging countries in terms of casting their macro-economic policy'. Taljaard says this context had huge implications 'in terms of how brave South African politicians could afford to be {...}. How much they would be given leeway to make radically redistributive decisions without having very significant consequences flowing from those decisions'. This compromise was certainly extremely difficult for the ANC, which had long articulated their vision of a National Democratic Revolution (NDR), a concept that 'captured far-reaching social transformation'. In opting instead for a 'limited NDR' it is considered that the ANC prioritized 'a close relationship to existing capital', believing this was required to 'finance the transition', even though this change in policy would merely reinforce existing economic power relations (African National Congress 2012: 8). For Biko (2013: 56), this compromise on key economic policy has produced 'one of the biggest frauds ever'.

More significant, however, is that rather than re-opening the terms of this settlement in light of considerable social unrest about persistent inequalities, South Africa seems intent on pursuing the neoliberal economic policies that underpinned it. Developments since 1994 suggest that another 'national conversation' that would prioritize material need and social diversity is now as important as the conversations that led to the 1994 agreement and the subsequent transition to democracy (Villa-Vicencio and Soko 2012: 35). To re-open the discussion about re/distribution in South Africa would, however, require a move away from the elite consensus that informed the settlement. A more agonistic approach, although necessary, would introduce uncertainty and require that South Africans embrace a more open ended, conflict-laden engagement.

The Guatemalan case involves some striking parallels with the South African settlement. As in South Africa, by the late 1980s it had become increasingly clear that there would not be a definitive victory by the Guatemalan military over the guerrillas, and neither did the isolated guerrillas stand any chance of taking power. Also like South Africa, it took some considerable period of dialogue between military, guerrillas, and politicians, led by international interlocutors and the Catholic Saint Egidio community, to help build *confianza* (trust) among the opposing sides (Reilly 2009: 23). By 1990 there was a developing national consensus that the civil war needed to end, and a growing recognition that Guatemala could not be truly democratized until a settlement was reached and the country was demilitarized, and until significant structural inequalities and persistent ethnic discrimination were addressed (Jonas 2000: 27).

In 1994, after several stalled attempts at advancing the negotiations, the UN stepped in to moderate the process at the request of both parties, which in turn opened the door for significantly increased involvement by the international community. Early in 1994 the parties signed the agenda-setting *Acuerdo Marco* (Framework Accord), which formalized the involvement of the 'Group of Friends' governments (primarily Mexico, Norway, Spain, and the United States and, to a lesser extent, Venezuela and Colombia) and also established the *Asamblea de la Sociedad Civil* (ASC), to structure the participation of organized sectors of Guatemalan civil society and enable them to put 'consensus proposals' to the negotiating parties and to endorse (or not endorse) accords once they were signed. Building on their experiences in an earlier multisectoral forum, the *Instancia Nacional de Consenso*, indigenous organizations and other sectors in civil society, which by this time had come to see the peace process as a legitimate arena for addressing issues that were being ignored elsewhere, joined with established political parties and other sectors to participate in the ASC (Jonas 2000: 43–4).

Rather than a single agreement, however, the Guatemalan peace process produced a wide-ranging set of *Acuerdos* (Accords), each addressing a specific area of contention. The list of accords was extraordinarily ambitious, including those clearly linked to an end of violent conflict (concerning ceasefire, demobilization, and repatriation), others linked to the causes of the conflict (including the highly contentious issues of land distribution, racism, and civil and military relations), and still others addressing specific policy questions (such as multilingual education). Broadly speaking, the peace settlement emphasized the historic exclusion of Guatemala's majority indigenous population as one of the central causes of the conflict, and in response advocated a range of measures of redress aimed at making state institutions more inclusive and less discriminatory (Sieder 2008: 76). Charles Reilly (2009: 26–7) notes that these were 'huge issues' that had gone unaddressed for centuries, meaning that, while expectations were high, few of the goals set out in the Accords were 'attainable in the short or middle term'.

Assessment of the process itself is also contested. On the one hand, by creating space for non-military and non-government actors to participate in the peace negotiations, the ASC is understood as offering Guatemalan civil society a unique opportunity to 'democratize an exclusionary system' and negotiate on issues that had been, and remained, 'taboo' in Guatemalan politics (Jonas 2000: 95–6). In a sense, this forum had the appearance of an agonistic institution at work, enabling the peace process to become 'the terrain on which competing agendas about the country's future were being played out' (Jonas 2000: 44). Daniel Saquec agrees that while the historical and contemporary political context in Guatemala 'has been a limitation to real active participation by indigenous people {…} the peace process did contribute to opening spaces for a large sector of the population'. Mariel Aguilar also believes that 'change has happened, especially for indigenous people and for women' who have 'conquered spaces in the society that wouldn't be possible without the peace accords'.

At the same time, however, this process was under attack from government and military elites, who according to Jonas (2000: 44–5) used 'psychological warfare' intended to intimidate both participants and the wider society. For example, just days after the Accord on human rights was signed in March 1994, Guatemala's 'peace resisters' sent a message of condemnation through the assassination of the head of the Constitutional Court. Adrian Zapata recalls the frustration of having the 'the army present a discussion agenda' during the peace process, an agenda 'which had certain limits and was restricted to ending the conflict and incorporating legal aspects'. Critics like Zapata insisted that they 'wanted to discuss the structural causes of the conflict, which are historical causes'. While the peace accords did eventually come to address these structural issues, Zapata sees that these gains have been lost and that the 'root causes' of the conflict still 'have not been touched'. Pressure from elites also ensured that despite efforts by civil society, negotiation of the more 'sensitive issues' on the table, specifically land distribution and socioeconomic inequality, was severely curtailed in order to maintain the stability of the process and minimize the impacts of 'spoilers'. In effect this meant that the limits of the peace process had been established before the public talks even began. As one former negotiator stated to Roddy Brett (2013: 230–1) in an anonymous interview, 'We knew that certain issues, such as land distribution and territorial autonomy would never be discussed or negotiated. These were untouchables'. Thus, although the balance of power definitely shifted toward the civilian population during the course of the negotiations, the military remained the most powerful political force in the country, and the resulting Accords are noticeably weak on the issue of demilitarization (Sieder 2003: 215). As Susanne Jonas (2000: 12) notes, the awareness of these restrictions have led some to ask whether the army and the peace resisters in Guatemala ever intended to implement the outcomes from the Accords, or whether they merely used the process to 'lay a trap' that would achieve their goal of demobilization by the guerillas 'without really conceding a thing'.

As in South Africa, Guatemalan cynicism about the agreement process is exacerbated by the observation that elite pressure to limit the focus of the peace negotiations bore the hallmarks of the liberal peace agenda. For some, the neoliberal climate reduced the negotiations to little more than a mechanism by which transnational elites were able to eliminate market obstacles (such as armed conflict), while the impoverished majority gained little or nothing (Jonas 2000: 222). This view, as outlined by Roddy Brett (2013: 223, 229) sees that the emancipatory potential of the process was 'severely constrained' by the 'wielding' of the liberal peace agenda and the imposition of elite interests, which in turn minimized the significance of 'local' concerns. While causal, structural issues were ostensibly on the negotiating table, and to some extent even addressed in the Accords, the negotiations were still devoid of any serious engagement with these issues. In sum, according to Brett (2013: 223),

> the content of the peace accords was undergirded by a vision that prioritized those individual rights deemed essential to liberal democracy, and which coincided with liberal peace parameters, through a package of rights agreed upon by triumphalist Guatemalan elites after severe cajoling from the international community. The positioning of collective rights, rights critical to the interests and claims of indigenous peoples, was limited in this vision {…}. Despite unprecedented formal participation of civil society actors in the negotiations {…} civil participation remained ancillary and served to legitimise a process imposed from above and outside by national and international, principally male, non-indigenous metropolitan elites.

A further, hugely significant problem concerning the Guatemalan Accords has been the country's almost complete incapacity to implement the changes to which the agreements aspire. In the years immediately following the signing of the Accords there was an unsuccessful campaign to achieve the necessary constitutional amendments (discussed further in Chapter 6). The Accords set a highly unrealistic, four-year timeframe for addressing an extensive list of issues that reached back centuries, creating hopes that the promised external investment that was the payoff for reaching 'peace' would help to 'quickly glue the country together' (Reilly 2009: 20–1). Yet Brett (2013: 230) maintains that the design of the process itself impeded possibilities for deeper conflict transformation, even before the Accords' limited implementation became obvious. He sees the combination of elite resistance and the imposition of 'one-size-fits-all policy prescriptions' as ringing the death knells for meaningful structural transformation. Glenda Tager agrees with this view, suggesting that the transition in Guatemala 'wasn't a real transition', it was merely 'something like a concession from the military', and the result 'wasn't a real democracy' of the kind the wider Guatemalan society wanted. Tager believes that while the work of the ASC 'was good on paper', allowing some of the more organized civil society groups to participate in the negotiations, this 'doesn't reflect a real engagement from the society'.

Carlos Sarti maintains that while there has been 'some progress' in Guatemala, all governments since the Peace Accords were signed have 'failed' because they have not addressed 'the structural problems underlying the conflict'. The current government he says 'is like the previous government and the previous one, and the one before that'. Governments remain 'dominated by the economic sectors, both traditional and emerging, meaning that the economic sectors decide what changes are going to be made and they do not agree with making important changes like tax reform or land reform'. Otilia Lux agrees with this assessment of Guatemala's political paralysis, and ascribes it to the sense of 'ownership' that political and economic elites feel towards the Accords, which has seen the hard won interventions from civil society lost amid a reassertion of elite control; a situation she describes as 'a very serious mistake for Guatemala'. Like many others, Lux is clear that elite obstruction of the Accords has left Guatemala in a precarious situation.

These factors have combined to reduce the Accords to a role 'more as north star than road map', as is evident from the poor performance of several post-accord administrations, which have 'dashed expectations' (Reilly 2009: 21). Many of my interviewees found it hard to sustain a positive view of their impact. Carlos Sarti agrees that the signing of the Accords 'created a positive context' and motivated many people 'to work strenuously to build peace'. However, Sarti now notes that 'this enthusiasm has diminished' as people have come to believe that 'problems are not being resolved, and violence is increasing'. As a result, according to

Sarti, some people now say, "You must not speak of the Peace Accords, but the memories of peace." Raquel Zelaya suggests that 'When the peace accords were signed the people's expectations were very high' but that public expectations about their impact were not realistic, particularly in light of Guatemala's weak state with its limited capacity for implementation. As in South Africa, widespread frustration and disappointment about the lack of transformation have functioned to maintain deep social divisions, fuelling 'spiralling and multifaceted post-conflict violence' (Brett 2013: 223) as discussed in Chapter 1. Indeed, many participants in the negotiations now realize the magnitude of the efforts that will be required for more meaningful conflict transformation in Guatemala, as one put it, 'the peace process will have to be reinvented over and over again' (quoted in Jonas 2000: 244).

Both the South African and Guatemalan cases suggest the possibilities inherent to peace negotiations in terms of opening political spaces for agonistic engagement across profound differences. In both cases, however, the decision to compromise with economic elites—undoubtedly seen as necessary at the time—had the effect of closing down these potentially transformative spaces, while also derailing agendas that were concerned with radical economic restructuring, as will be discussed further in Chapter 7.

Sharing power

The Northern Ireland peace process shares some similar characteristics to the processes of reaching agreement in South Africa and Guatemala, but produced some markedly different outcomes. The central focus in Northern Ireland was on developing institutional designs that could allow the two main communities to share power in government. The sorts of internal power-sharing arrangements advanced in Northern Ireland, known as consociationalism (see Lijphart 1969), have become the dominant institutional approach to 'settling' conflicts on the international stage. Rather than the more conventional government-and-opposition political arrangement, consociation instead sees all political parties sit in one coalition, where seats are won on electoral strength (Nolan 2012: 23). Proponents of consociationalism contend that this means of structuring deep ethno-national divisions into political institutions is the most effective way of regulating antagonism and conflict between groups (Hayes and McAllister 2013: 123). This was certainly the view in Northern Ireland, where many people viewed a consociational arrangement as the only possible means of ending the violence and creating a sustainable peace; an innovative response to the 'zero-sum equation' that had characterized the Troubles in Northern Ireland (Nolan 2012: 19), and the 'least worst option available' when the political context would permit few alternatives (Houston 2012: 23).

At its signing, the Belfast Agreement was celebrated as an 'historic compromise' that would allow the two communities to 'transcend' their differences and begin a new era of engagement and cooperation (Coulter and Murray 2008: 15). It is certainly the case that this agreement, and the follow up St Andrews Agreement, facilitated the eventual development of a functioning Northern Ireland Assembly and Executive when, in May 2007, the Democratic Unionist Party and Sinn Fein entered government together—an occasion that many in the British and Irish political classes viewed as the end of the conflict (Power 2011: 1). Certainly the new political arrangements have seen an indisputable 'sea-change' in relations between political leaders, which in turn has brought increased stability to the region (Kelly 2012: 11). And in the context of decades of violence, the signing of the Agreement was undoubtedly a remarkable achievement that required significant shifts among those involved. For example, Séanna Walsh, from *Coiste na nIarchimí*, a republican ex-prisoners organization, recalls the change in mindset and language that the ceasefires and peace negotiations required. He tells me that during the conflict the language of 'victory' was what 'gets you up out of bed in the morning to go and engage and struggle'. After the ceasefire, however, 'the first thing on the agenda is compromise', which is 'not easy' to accept.

And of course the Belfast Agreement did not deal only with institutional design. Rather it was 'comprehensive and clever', its content 'detailed, multi-faceted and wide-ranging' (Coulter and Murray 2008: 2, 4), dealing with a complex range of issues relating to both the causes and effects of the Troubles (Lundy and McGovern 2008: 34). The components of the Agreement on policing, paramilitary decommissioning, demilitarisation, and devolution of powers were all 'characterised by their historic ambition, their willingness to imagine a shared and better future, and by their determination to replace hostility and exclusion with a culture which promoted interdependence, full and equal citizenship for all, and respect for mutual rights and responsibilities' (Community Relations Council 2011: 22). The Community Relations Council (2011: 21) contends that the Agreement 'cemented the values of reconciliation and mutual respect in an international peace treaty'. Despite evident shortcomings, discussed further below, Gráinne Kelly (2012: 108) maintains that the Agreement 'also articulated a vision for deep and broad change, and promoted a commitment to equality, human rights, inclusion, and good relations'.

But not everyone agrees with the form that the Agreement took, creating two quite divergent assessments of the Northern Ireland peace process: one sees an innovative resolution to a centuries-old conflict, and the other considers the political architecture of the Agreement to be fatally flawed due to its foundation in sectarian communal identities (Nolan 2012: 13). Critics of the Agreement note the tendency of consociationalism to 'freeze' and 'reify' deep divisions, particularly along ethno-national lines, and suggest that the focus on providing an institutional fix to communal division also overwhelms other concerns about class or gender based inequalities. The elite-level political compromise allows little space for alternative political identities to develop (Power 2011: 3), and because the institutions of the new political system depend on self-identification by elites there is little incentive for politicians to seek to 'transcend the sectarian divide' (White 2011: 40). Alan Largey tells me that in Northern Ireland, the population has now 'settled for separateness'. Daly and Sarkin (2007: 225) maintain that 'consociation is to political systems what walls are to territory', that is, a way to 'divide up the goods to keep everyone happy'—at least for a time. But while these walls of consociation may ensure that there are safe political spaces for interests to be encouraged and expressed, over time these divisions become entrenched in ways that obstruct conflict transformation, removing incentives for coalition-building and intergroup communication. The Agreement is thought to have 'reinforced the essentialist politics of ethno-national solidarity' (Bean 2011: 162), institutionalizing rather than overcoming the political divisions it was intended to address.

Like the agreements in South Africa and Guatemala, consociational models such as the one in the Belfast Agreement are also criticized for their focus on accommodation among political elites, while having little impact on wider public attitudes (Hayes and McAllister 2013: 124). In Northern Ireland these elites have often been extremists who have captured the political imagination of their respective constituencies. Drawing these groups into dialogue that produced an historic compromise between sworn enemies had the effect of converting 'former terrorists' into acceptable politicians (Bean 2011: 155). To achieve this, and in an effort to 'square the circle' of the incompatible demands from nationalist and unionist communities, the Agreement advanced a 'constructive ambiguity' intended to signal that there were no 'losers' in the settlement (Coulter and Murray 2008: 8). In the wake of its positive reception, the British and Irish governments came to view the peace process as complete, fully expecting that the citizens of the region would simply follow the example set by political elites and overcome divisions (Power 2011: 1). Thus, despite the concession from some critics that Northern Ireland 'probably required a power-sharing system' there remains considerable debate about the 'democratic credentials' of the consociational arrangements (Little 2009: 180). The institutionalization of elite, power-sharing divisions has not fostered a culture of democracy in Northern Ireland that would support deeper levels of debate, discussion, disagreement, compromise, and cooperation (Etchart 2011: 131).

The Agreement also neglected the key areas of historical division in Northern Ireland, failing to include any measure focused on dealing with the past. These issues were not 'high on the agenda of any of the major actors' in either the conflict or the peace negotiations (Lundy and McGovern 2008: 34), despite the fact that they continue to be a major source of division. No agreement was ever reached with regard to the morality of violence during the Troubles as, in the interest of stability, it was thought preferable to leave these contentious issues unresolved in the 'fault neutral' framework of the Agreement, effectively ruling out any proposal for a truth commission intended to address the past (Aiken 2010: 175). Neil Jarman suggests that, in contrast to the South African transition, in Northern Ireland there is a 'much less clear understanding of what the end result was'. He likens the end of the Troubles to a draw in football, 'which went to extra time and penalties and still didn't produce an effective result'. In other words, Jarman says, there is 'no real consensus' about 'who won'. This uncertainty leads some to question whether the template provided by the Agreement can lead to 'a genuinely trans-formative trajectory away from Northern Ireland's sectarian legacy' (Houston 2012: 27).

A further effect of the power sharing arrangement in Northern Ireland is a lack of trust in political processes, because power sharing is seen to involve an undemocratic sharing out of interests and influence. Derick Wilson observes that while the power sharing arrangements are 'supposed to be a coalition', in practice this means the two main parties 'carve every-thing up', with detrimental effects on the delivery of policy and pro-grammes. Gerry Foster suggests that the vested interests at work in this 'carving up' of power mean that while politicians 'pay lip service to try and end sectarianism' in effect they are 'actually encouraging it because the divided society guarantees their vote and {...} maintains their power there'. Pádraig Ó Tuama agrees, but suggests that this is also the result of a lack of political sophistication, which produces 'a very immature capacity to cope with tensions on a governmental level'. Ó Tuama sees power sharing resting on an assumption that 'we can't cope if we disagree with each other', which broadly speaking, he says is 'correct'. The commonly used expression 'Whatever you say, say nothing', illustrates this resistance to political conflict, and suggests the cultural challenges in the way of a more agonistic engagement with these concerns.

And while the Agreement does go some way towards addressing the historical structural inequalities that were a driver of the conflict, it does not go nearly far enough. For this reason, the Agreement is seen as fairly ineffective in terms of 'charting a transformed future', leading Houston (2012: 23), among others, to argue that 'while power sharing might be a necessary *first* step towards a peaceful Northern Ireland, it is not sufficient in and of itself'. Thus, despite the growing level of political stability that is associated with the peace process, the development of a 'shared and better future' is still far from complete, with much effort still required in terms of institutional and relational transformation in particular (Kelly 2012: 11). As Ray Mullan from the Community Relations Council contends, although when the Belfast Agreement was signed many people said '"Right that's it, that's peace. We've got it now," the CRC was quick to remind people that 'This is a process {…}. A political settlement does not in itself transform divided communities. You need to tackle issues like policing, you need to tackle issues like segregated housing, segregated education, the use of public space, the use of symbols of parades and flags.' Gerry Foster, makes a similar point, stating that 'The issues of the conflict haven't been solved, haven't been spoken about. It's just an agreement to stop fighting, basically.' Foster maintains that when people voted for the Agreement 'what they were actually voting for was just peace and quiet'. Like many others, Jim O'Neill agrees that the situation in Northern Ireland is 'better' than it would have been without a peace process, conceding that 'Having people here at work cooperating together in government' is 'not a bad thing', but he maintains that 'there's still a lot left to be desired'. For Houston this leaves an 'awkward-if-obvious-question' namely 'What next? Is power-sharing the end point of political rapprochement? Is the fragile elite level accommodation combined with wider mutual indifference or even residual suspicion within Northern Irish society the best to be hoped for?' (Houston 2012: 24).

As the experience in Northern Ireland suggests, where reconciliation is understood in this relatively limited sense, the risk is that the first step of negotiating an end to the violence will be seen as the last step. Furthermore, the effort to reach agreement on ending violence can exhaust future efforts for more radical conflict transformation, and the signing of an agreement can close down political space that ought to be opened up in a context newly freed from violence.

When there is no settlement

Not all violent conflicts end with a peace process that may produce a negotiated settlement or agreement. Many other deeply divided societies are the result of the conquest of one group by another or, as in the case of Australia, the colonization, dispossession and marginalization of an indigenous minority. In Australia, the issue of a treaty or some other form of agreement between Aboriginal and Torres Strait Islander peoples and the Australian state has been a bone of political contention for many decades. Rather than being dealt with by way of a treaty or treaties as other indigenous peoples had been, indigenous peoples in Australia were both physically brutalized and legally ignored. Australia today remains the only former British colony that has not made a treaty with the original inhabitants of the territory. For Aboriginal and Torres Strait Islander people, a treaty or treaties would be a significant step towards resolving unfinished business, potentially allowing some form of redress for historic injustices and providing a new framework for the settler colonial political relationship. Larissa Behrendt (1995: 97–8) articulates the aspirations of many Aboriginal and Torres Strait Islander people when she writes:

In the heart of many Aboriginal people is the belief that we are a sovereign people. We believe that we never surrendered to the British. We never signed a treaty giving up our sovereignty or giving up our land. We believe that we are from the land, that we are born from the land. When we die we return to the land {…}. Land, in our culture, cannot be bought or sold. It always was Aboriginal land. It will always be Aboriginal land.

Many Aboriginal and Torres Strait Islander peoples continue to interpret the lack of a treaty to mean that there has been no settlement or agreement between their nations and the Australian settler state on these issues. Indeed, in our interview Les Malezer is emphatic in his view that Australia 'can't be in reconciliation mode' because the nation 'has not yet reached a settlement'. The problem, he says is that 'there hasn't been the first process' meaning that 'everyone's wishing for the coming together and the putting aside of guilt {…} without even knowing or thinking about a settlement, and what justice needs to be achieved'.

In this 'unsettled' context, debates about treaty-making have remained a feature of Australian politics over decades. Indigenous claims have taken various forms, some conciliatory, some secessionist. For example, Patrick Dodson (2000: 17) articulated the key principles that would need to be addressed in a more conciliatory agreement or treaty, specifically including political representation; reparations and compensation; regional agreements; indigenous regional self-government; cultural and intellectual property rights; recognition of customary law; and an economic base. In contrast, Kevin Gilbert (1988: 53) developed a draft treaty that called for the creation of a sovereign and autonomous Aboriginal State, which comprised a land base of 'not less than forty percent of the land mass of each "Australian State."' Gilbert's draft was a central component of the Treaty '88 campaign, which saw protests disrupt the Australian bicentennial celebrations in 1988. Also in that year, the then Prime Minister, Bob Hawke, was presented with the Barunga Statement,[1] and in response made a commitment to negotiate a national treaty with Aboriginal people. Indeed, both conservative and Labor governments entertained the proposition of a treaty in the 1980s, but by the 1990s the claim to Aboriginal sovereignty, which underwrote the demand for a treaty, had been deemed unreasonable by both major political parties. Hawke eventually reneged on his commitment, and during the debate about a treaty in 1988, John Howard (who would go on to be Australian prime minister from 1996 to 2007) declared it 'an absurd proposition that a nation should make a treaty with some if its own citizens' (cited in Schaap 2009: 209). The formal reconciliation process was proposed as an alternative, although the federal government minister responsible for legislating and steering the reconciliation process at its inception, Robert Tickner (2001: 29) still articulated the need for a treaty, claiming that a key objective of reconciliation was 'to put on the nation's public policy agenda the issue of some formal document or agreement as one of the outcomes of the reconciliation process'. However, Tickner also acknowledged the level of political discomfort with the term treaty, suggesting that the debate needed to move away from preoccupation with the concept to focus instead on the 'form and content' of such an agreement. Indeed, as Damien Short (2008: 36) has noted, Australian politicians have always shied away from the word 'treaty', fearing that it implied a negotiation between two sovereign nations, preferring instead to speak of the possibility of a 'compact' or 'agreement'.

However even this more cautious approach to the idea of negotiating a treaty was unsuccessful. Efforts by the now defunct Aboriginal and Torres Strait Islander Commission (ATSIC) to keep the issue alive during the 1990s (see Aboriginal and Torres Strait Islander Commission 1995) reinforced by the CAR at the Corroboree 2000 event, failed to engage mainstream politicians, particularly following the election of the Howard government in 1996. Indeed, the Howard government's formal response to the CAR final report vehemently rejected calls for a treaty, arguing that

> such a legally enforceable instrument, as between sovereign states, would be divisive, would undermine the concept of a single Australian nation, would create legal uncertainty and future disputation and would not best harness the positive environment that now exists in reconciliation. In fact, such a process could threaten that environment.
>
> (quoted in Gunstone 2009: 26)

In rejecting calls for a treaty in this way, the unity of the Australian state was defined in such a way that alternatives allowing for both domestic citizenship and some form of political independence became impossible (Bradfield 2006: 83). As discussed in the previous chapter, reconciliation in Australia was strongly inflected with the logic of nation building, by definition closing down space in which it might be possible to negotiate new possibilities of shared sovereignty (Muldoon and Schaap 2012: 192). A treaty was considered 'too divisive' for the Australian nation, with reconciliation instead offering to 'include' Aboriginal and Torres Strait Islander peoples in the Australian state (Short 2008: 7). In large part, as will be discussed further in Chapter 10, this resistance stems from the widespread failure to acknowledge that there is a conflict in Australia that still requires a formal settlement. Yet, despite a decade of attempting to educate the non-indigenous population about the realities of this history, the CAR chose to move away from contentious treaty discourse, and navigate a more moderate, middle ground. The final Document Towards Reconciliation from the CAR, originally intended to resemble the terms of a treaty, was reduced to an 'aspirational text' designed to have broad appeal, steering far away from any further consideration of a formal agreement (Short 2008: 143).

Yet even these repeated efforts by Australian governments have not succeeded in closing down the treaty debate, and have most certainly not addressed indigenous claims for justice. The current campaign to see Aboriginal and Torres Strait Islander people recognized in the Australian constitution, which will be discussed in the next chapter, has brought treaty talk back into public discourse, and such a future possibility does not seem impossible. Former federal government minister Fred Chaney advances the view that Australia still needs 'an overarching treaty' that would be a way to 'lay down some broad principles' that could 'provide an enabling framework' for relations between indigenous peoples and the Australian state. Unlike many of his former parliamentary colleagues, Chaney believes that 'It's not hard to imagine that that could be done'.

Indeed, as in cases where an agreement or settlement *has* been achieved, the rejection of any such 'conclusion' to political conflict, is not, and must not, be the end of politics. Ideally, an agreement will create enough stability that political space can open up, and more transformative challenges can be addressed with energy. And in situations where agreements have failed or where, as in the Australian case, the desire for such a settlement has been denied, there is a similarly pressing need to keep returning to the conversation, re-opening the terms of contestation, and pursuing a more agonistic engagement. This includes over the terms of a country's constitution itself, as the following chapter will explore.

Note

1 The Barunga Statement is a statement of national Aboriginal and Torres Strait Islander political claims, presented to the then prime minister, Bob Hawke, at the 1988 Barunga Festival. The statement from 'the Indigenous owners and occupiers of Australia' called for (among other things) self-determination, land rights, and the negotiation of a treaty. Prime Minister Hawke responded with a commitment to making such a treaty by 1990, a promise that was never fulfilled.

6 New constitutional frameworks

Beyond peace settlements, once an agreement is in place a country attempting to re-constitute itself must develop a new political 'container' in which to govern itself. Often this will take the form of a new or radically revised legal constitution that will allow former enemies to develop ways of governing together. A new constitution can form part of a new national narrative, reflecting the experiences of diverse citizens, protecting their individual and group rights, ensuring freedom from future oppression and, most importantly, contributing to reconciliation through the creation of legal institutions within which these ambitions may be realized by diminishing the gulf between the powerful and the powerless (Daly and Sarkin 2007: 216, 218).

But while Daly and Sarkin (2007: 217) contend that a new government 'needs the strong backing of an emphatic constitution' if it is to 'subdue the tensions that people may feel towards one another', an agonistic view of these constitutional requirements suggests that an 'emphatic constitution' should not seek to subdue social tensions at all, but instead to create political space in which such tensions can be engaged and contested. Indeed, as Schaap (2005: 91) has argued, in its political sense constitution 'refers to the founding act by which a space for politics is established', driven by the hope of establishing a new moment of beginning that engages both past and future. Indeed, constitutional transformation is often expressly focused on the future, as deeply divided societies work to establish the terms of a shared future through the creation of a new social and political covenant (Chapman 2002: 267). The challenge, as with the making of agreements, is to ensure that the process of (re)making a constitution creates enough stability to allow new political spaces to open up, while resisting the sense of closure or completion that such an endeavour may engender, which would effectively close such spaces down.

Constituting the 'post'-conflict nation

Deeply divided societies frequently see the (re)making of a national constitution as an important priority in their conflict transformation efforts.

Attending to the (re)constitution of the nation, through the creation of a constituent assembly or other group with responsibility for making a new constitution, is often one of the first tasks approached by a society in transition. Similarly, settler colonies may turn towards constitutional reform in order to address historical exclusions and injustices. Paul Muldoon suggests that this aspect of reconciliation efforts, whether they be in transitional regimes or colonial regimes, provides a moment in which 'questions of constitutional justice—those relating to the very foundations of the political order—take centre stage' (Muldoon 2008: 125). Constitutions can be an important starting point for redressing entrenched inequalities that have resulted from historical divisions, tying a range of human rights into the domestic legal system in ways that can contribute to addressing historical injustice and abuse (Arbour 2007: 21), and that establish the institutions needed to ensure the government's commitment to rule of law and human rights (Daly and Sarkin 2007: 216). Making or re-making a constitution during a political transition is thus typically associated with 'restoring' the rule of law and enabling the non-violent arbitration of political conflict in order to secure and protect the rights of citizens (Schaap 2007: 25). Further, a constitution can form part of a new national narrative, communicating a set of (potentially) shared ideals and values that give expression to the experiences and aspirations of the diverse peoples that constitute the nation (Daly and Sarkin 2007: 216).

But the promise of constitutionalism also has clear limits. The national focus of constitution making can also reinforce the nation building agenda of a reconciliation process with, as previous chapters have discussed, all the problems that may bring. Unless the national narrative expressed in a constitution can be opened up to conflict and contestation it will inevitably contain unjust exclusions. Schaap (2007: 26) argues that law may in fact frustrate political reconciliation by 'representing community as the given end of politics' rather than as a 'contingent historical possibility' in which we find the possibility of politics. Indeed, it is the very indeterminacy of community that creates a space for political reconciliation, a space that is closed down through the regulation required in a founding legal document. While the law may have a significant role in mandating the conditions necessary for reconciliation, Schaap contends that in the immediate wake of civil war or the end of a repressive regime, the 'we' that is imagined in a constitution can only belong in an imagined (and contested) democratic future (Schaap 2007: 26). It does not become real, and is not settled, by the creation of a legal founding. Instead, according to Schaap, 'a legal constitution forecloses the opportunity to contest the terms within which such a relationship is determined' (Schaap 2007: 28).

Indeed, legal concepts and the law itself clearly play a role in mediating social relations, evident in the arena of constitutional law, which is most often concerned with what is included and what is excluded from 'normal' political contestation. As it is largely in this domain that reconciliatory politics are contested, it is vital that divided societies do not foreclose this capacity to contest the terms of the relations, but instead open up the often hidden assumptions that may constrain or distort the terms of political debate that is intended to contribute to reconciliation (Christodoulidis and Veitch 2007: 4–5). In other words, where reconciliation discourse attempts to depoliticize the law by reducing it to 'an applicable tool', the challenge is instead to open up the possibilities inherent to the tasks of understanding, revising and reformulating a legal system that was likely an active participant in the previous regime (McGregor 2007: 115).

Thus, an agonistic view of democracy and democratic institutions suggests that the objective of constitution making cannot be to bring power under the control of citizens as it is not possible to conceive of a politics that is beyond power. Instead the ambition is to make structures of power more visible in ways that enable marginalized and oppressed groups to challenge the legal and political hegemony (Wingenbach 2011: 28). As Ed Wingenbach (2011: 33) argues,

> the agonistic project emphasizes the creation of a symbolic space or regime of cultural intelligibility enabling citizens to engage in contestation without destroying the conditions of association that make community possible {...}. Thus a democratic polity must propose terms of political association that permit antagonists to see themselves as part of the same community while fostering practices of critique and contestation in civil and political society.

This point is worth expanding as it goes to the heart of the challenges that inhere to this level of conflict transformation. As Wingenbach (2011: 55) explains, an agonistic view sees a constitution as capable of both enabling democratic contestation and as 'the *ongoing product of this activity*', meaning that a constitution's authority will always depend upon its capacity to sustain rather than constrain democratic activity. Constitutions are 'living codes' that derive their authority from the capacity to foster rather than foreclose democratic conflict over their own meanings. Many agonists do, however, recognize that this conflict must be bounded in some way if a constitution is to enable the emergence of non-violent political contest. While the terms of democratic engagement found in a constitution must always be open to contestation, contestation need not be perpetually present in order to maximize democratic outcomes (as some strands of agonistic theory may assert). The key point that Wingenbach (2011: 56) makes in this regard is that democracy

> can be considered free to the extent the rules negotiated to maintain the enterprise are subject to dissent, revision, and renegotiation, and that these rules make such agonistic engagement plausible and accessible rather than difficult and rare.

Thus, to the extent that a constitution is considered the final word in resolving important and inevitable political disputes, rather that opening a dispute to the next phase of contestation, it can be seen as dangerous to democracy (Wingenbach 2011: 56). Given the situated context of all democratic institutions, however, including constitutions, which tends to solidify the stability of institutions over time, ongoing effort is required to disrupt this tendency towards sedimentation (Wingenbach 2011: 97). This is most particularly the case in deeply divided and post-violent conflict societies, which experience strong forces driving *towards* stability, with understandable, although ultimately unhelpful, suspicion of disruption and contest.

These cautions about the political shortcomings inherent to the framing of a legal constitution can be applied to a range of settings, from a nation like South Africa, which famously embraced the opportunity to produce a new constitution, to a settler state such as Australia, which has struggled to reform its constitution to reflect its colonial past and the place of Aboriginal and Torres Strait Islander people within the nation. In South Africa, for example, where it is evident the new constitution and associated reforms of the judicial system have become perhaps the most important legacy of the transition to democracy, the question remains as to whether this model constitution has opened up agonistic space for political contestation, including over its own terms. And in Australia, current contestation over proposals to provide a very modest form of recognition for Aboriginal and Torres Strait Islander peoples is also raising questions about the role of constitutionalism in reconciliation efforts. The insistence by political leaders that Australia is constituted as a singular nation that cannot recognize the existence of indigenous nations within its borders, invokes a 'we' that clearly does not yet exist, underscoring Schaap's concerns in very real terms. In particular, this assertion of a unified nationhood—in both political discourse and in the constitution itself—ignores perpetual and unresolved questions about Australia's legitimacy and sovereignty.

Questions of sovereignty

At its base, a national constitution, whether written or composed of unwritten conventions, is intended to outline the body of laws, principles, institutions, and values by which a country is governed. Often this legal framework draws on the history of the country's founding or, in the case of countries undergoing a transition, its new aspirations. As such, a constitution is an expression of state sovereignty, including internal sovereignty or the authority of the state to make laws for its own citizens. The assertion of internal sovereignty without recourse to violence requires the popular acceptance of the state's legitimacy, usually expressed through electoral and other democratic means. It is often with a focus on shoring up this sovereign legitimacy that a nation-building approach to reconciliation will direct attention toward processes that are intended to overcome past divisions and replace them with a sense of shared nationhood (Bashir and Kymlicka 2008: 14).

Questions of sovereignty may thus create particular dilemmas in societies that are attempting to address historical injustices, particularly those against indigenous peoples, for whom an emphasis on reinscribing a common national identity and defending the moral authority of state sovereignty may be problematic and strongly contested (Jung 2011: 242). Reinforcing the sovereign authority of the state through the assertion of a common national narrative and identity may perpetuate the colonial harms experienced by indigenous peoples who continue to challenge the legitimacy of an imposed sovereignty. In spite of colonization, many indigenous peoples still claim their status as sovereign nations or peoples. This fact is central to an evaluation of reconciliation processes in settler states, intended (perhaps) to address the historic injustices of colonial dispossession and its contemporary legacies, as it can 'elucidate a benchmark by which to ascertain the authenticity of such a process' (Short 2005: 273). The loss of sovereignty is central to the historic injustices experienced by indigenous peoples whose own sovereignty over territory was not recognized by invading colonial powers, and the challenge to the sovereign authority of the state has become the defining claim of the international indigenous rights movement (Jung 2011: 241). Indeed, there seems little reason that indigenous peoples in Australia and elsewhere would feel a sense of allegiance to a legal and political system that has been imposed on them without their consent, and which perpetuates the structural violence of the settler colonial order (see Maddison 2013).

It is in light of these concerns that Australia is currently engaged in a new process of constitutional reform that is attempting to provide some modest recognition to Aboriginal and Torres Strait Islander peoples. Although Australia's constitutional and legal order is regarded as one of the world's most stable, adaptable, and popularly supported systems, it has long been pointed out that this stability rests on what Melissa Castan (2000: 202–3) describes as some 'inherent defects' that undermine its acceptance by indigenous people. Chief among these is the Australian constitution's neglect of historical dispossession of Aboriginal and Torres Strait Islander peoples. Castan maintains that until such defects are addressed 'reconciliation of our past history with our present aspirations for justice will remain unattainable'. Many Aboriginal people still contest Australia's sovereign legitimacy. Michael Mansell (2005: 83), for example, rejects 'the claims by Australia to having won the right to act on behalf of Aborigines, either through invasion or by Aboriginal consent'. And Larissa Behrendt (2003: 103), who contends that recognition of indigenous sovereignty would not threaten Australian sovereignty, still questions the legitimacy of Australian state authority on the basis of its historical exclusion of indigenous people. Today, she contends, the assertion of indigenous sovereignty 'seeks a fundamentally different relationship' with the Australian state. Unlike post-colonial states there has been no decolonization of the Australian settler state, 'no return of sovereignty, no final lowering of the imperial flag' (Reynolds 2013: 248).

These debates have been central to Australia's reconciliation efforts for several decades, including during the formal reconciliation process. In the 1990s, constitutional politics in Australia centred upon these differing interpretations of the founding of the state. As noted in earlier chapters, these interpretations still animate competing Australian narratives, with the indigenous narrative of invasion and survival undermining the legitimacy of mainstream heroic settler nationalism. Indigenous leaders have continued to call attention to the fact that Aboriginal and Torres Strait Islander peoples were omitted from the original constitution on which the federation of the Commonwealth of Australia was based. The failure to recognize indigenous Australians in the constitution is thought to perpetuate the original injustice of invasion, undermining the capacity for a more transformative dialogue between indigenous and non-indigenous Australians (Schaap 2007: 27–8).

In the early part of the campaign for constitutional recognition, which will be discussed further below, the loudest dissenting voices have come from Aboriginal people who insist that recognition within what they see as an illegitimate constitution does not address their claims upon the legitimacy of the nation. These groups instead seek a form of sovereignty or recognition through the making of a treaty or treaties between Aboriginal and Torres Strait Islander peoples and the Australian state, as discussed in the previous chapter. The 'we' that they constitute situates itself outside of the Australian nation-state. Indeed it is evident that the proposed constitutional reforms will not go nearly far enough. Courtney Jung (2011: 245–6) has argued that where transitional justice measures are directed either toward indigenous peoples or, more generally, in cases where there has been no regime transition, their success 'must be measured by their capacity to transform the playing field'. Indeed, to properly address colonial injustice, measures such as constitutional reform may be wholly inadequate, as their starting point is to assume the legitimacy of settler state sovereignty over indigenous peoples (Short 2005: 275). To meet the challenge raised by indigenous assertions of their abiding sovereignty, a decolonizing reconciliation process must find ways to recognize indigenous peoples as distinct political entities to be treated as 'nations *equal in status* to the settler state' (Short 2005: 276). Some, such as historian Henry Reynolds (1998: 212–13) hold out hope that this is possible, arguing that the division of Australian sovereignty between state and federal governments at federation in 1901 suggests that sovereignty could in fact be 'cut again' to allow Aboriginal and Torres Strait Islander communities to run their own internal affairs. However this would require a far more agonistic approach to Australian constitutionalism, while at present there seems to be little interest in discussing more creative ways of recognising indigenous sovereignty in Australia, including in the current proposals for constitutional recognition.

But at least the current proposals have opened some new space for contesting this hegemony. For example, in a question to the Australian television programme 'Q&A' in August 2014 (Australian Broadcasting Corporation 2014), one young indigenous woman, Jazlie Grugoruk, posed a question to the panel of indigenous leaders and politicians:

> The Australian constitution and the Australian state were founded on the myth of *terra nullius*: the assertion that Australia was uninhabited at the time of settlement. As an Indigenous person who has lost my language, my culture and identity under white colonialism, why should I assent to falsely established Australian law by asking to include my people within its founding document? A treaty is the only way to assert our original sovereignty and equality, so why are you, with respect, our Indigenous leaders, settling for a watered down attempt at recognition in the Australian Constitution?

The panel members responded with general sympathy for her point of view. For example, the indigenous Member of Parliament, Ken Wyatt, agreed that Aboriginal and Torres Strait Islander people

> were left out of the constitutional conventions. They were left out of the 1901 [constitution]. We live in this country and we deserve to be recognised within the constitution, but that doesn't negate aspirations for those who want treaty or sovereignty. When Australia is ready for that, that debate can occur in the future.

Tim Gartrell from the Recognise campaign acknowledges that there is 'quite a diversity' of indigenous views regarding the current proposals for constitutional recognition in Australia. These range from people who are 'concerned about issues of sovereignty and the fact that sovereignty was never ceded {...} who want those issues sorted out first' to those who argue that Australia should 'get the constitution sorted out so we can then move on to some sort of settlement of the issues around sovereignty and a treaty'. Gartrell thinks many indigenous people are 'pragmatic' in their response, taking the view that they 'mightn't like the way [the constitution] was formed' but agreeing there is a 'need to try and do something with it'. However he also acknowledges that those opposed to constitutional change on the basis that indigenous sovereignty was never ceded are expressing a view that 'actually comes from a solid base of historical fact—indigenous sovereignty *was* never ceded'. Gartrell notes, however, that this view needs to be weighed against the advice that none of the proposed reforms 'would negatively impact on future efforts to resolve issues around sovereignty or to negotiate a treaty'.

The Northern Ireland peace process has also centred on questions of sovereignty, although not in the context of a written constitutional document that might be amended. Adrian Little (2014: 112–13) points out that while the peace process in Northern Ireland had the effect of 'domesticating' key issues and drawing activists away from violence and into other forms of politics, this has not necessarily led to a change in political beliefs. For the republican movement in particular, the change has been primarily discursive rather than representing a break from the movement's political roots. And those roots are to be found deep in debates over the constitutional status of Northern Ireland as either a legitimate part of a sovereign United Kingdom, or as a colonized territory of a united Ireland. Indeed, the most contentious issue in the peace negotiations was always to do with the constitutional status of Northern Ireland. The Agreement itself did not resolve the thorny issue of sovereignty but rather deferred it, allowing for the status of Northern Ireland to be changed in the future if majorities in both the Irish Republic and Northern Ireland agreed (White 2011: 38). The text of the Belfast Agreement affirms that 'any change to the constitutional status of the region can happen only with the concurrent electoral consent of people living in both jurisdictions on the island' (Coulter and Murray 2008: 2–3). However, the understanding of this situation differs significantly between the two communities. Unionists understand the compromise to represent a final settlement of the constitutional issue, while republicans justify their acceptance of the 'consent principle' through the belief that the current framework is only temporary and will inevitably give way to a united Ireland over time. As Paul Nolan (2012: 15) puts it in a recent Peace Monitoring Report, 'Nationalists are still on a journey. Unionists think they have arrived at the terminus'.

And while some describe the republican 'inevitability thesis' as 'pure political fantasy', little more than a 'comforting mantra regularly rehearsed by the Sinn Féin leadership' (Coulter and Murray 2008: 5), it has certainly not been abandoned in political praxis. Republicans like Séanna Walsh remain philosophical about what will need to happen to see the constitutional status of Northern Ireland change in the future. In our interview Walsh acknowledged that it is only republicans who are going to 'drive anything forward because everybody else is comfortable':

The British are comfortable enough with the political situation as is. The unionists, they're quite happy with the way things are. The Dublin Government, they're shit-scared of political change and how any sort of major political change will affect their political landscape in the south. So everybody's sitting quite comfortable. The only people who are not are republicans, so we are the dynamic for change in all this.

Walsh also understands what needs to change in the political context for the constitutional question to regain political salience. He tells me that it is evident that 'there aren't enough republicans in the north' to achieve constitutional transformation, meaning that what republicans have to do is 'convince a section of those people who have up to now been unionist in their culture and their politics {…} that their best interests lie with the rest of the Irish nation and forging some sort of a new republic that can retain some sort of a cultural link with Britain'. He insists that republicans are 'not prescriptive about it' but maintains that the demographics make sense; it will be better for everyone in Northern Ireland to be part of a population of six million on the island of Ireland than being the one million Northern Irish among 50 million British citizens. For Walsh, 'That's our task. We have to convince a section of what are currently the unionist population to join us in our project for a new Ireland.'

At present there seems little momentum behind Walsh's aspiration. In our interview, Wilhelm Verwoerd notes the ability for people in Northern Ireland 'to live together with incompatible constitutional visions', a capacity he contrasts to other contexts such as South Africa. Polling in Northern Ireland indicates that 58 per cent of people believe the existing constitutional arrangement should be the long-term policy for Northern Ireland (Nolan 2012: 146). Paul Nolan suggests that anti-agreement unionists have now accepted that the Belfast Agreement has secured the constitutional position of Northern Ireland within the United Kingdom, although this has not stopped talk of a 'culture war', where the concern is no longer about Northern Ireland being taken out of Britain, but about 'Britishness' being taken out of Northern Ireland (Nolan 2014: 12). The leadership of Sinn Féin on the other hand, still holds ambitions for a referendum on the constitutional status of Northern Ireland by 2020, in the meantime working to secure a political foothold in both the Irish and Northern Irish administrations in order to build support for Irish reunification 'from a position of strength' (Byers 2013). The defeated 2014 referendum on Scotland's independence from Britain created some renewed interest in the Northern Irish constitutional question. Had the Scottish vote succeeded, many saw a referendum in Northern Ireland as an inevitable consequence, as Scottish independence would highlight the questions over Northern Irish sovereignty. In light of its failure, however, any further contestation over sovereignty in the region will be the domain of local political actors prepared to engage in new conversations.

The politics of constitutionalism

Issues of foundational legitimacy as they pertain to questions of sovereignty are one aspect of constitutionalism relevant to reconciliation efforts. Political legitimacy–concerning both the content and process of constitutional transformation—is another.

The South African constitution is widely regarded as one of the best in the world. It is comprehensive in its treatment of economic social and cultural rights, incorporating protections for rights relating to labour relations, environment, property, housing, healthcare, food, water, social security, education, and language and culture, violations of which had been widespread during the apartheid regime (Arbour 2007: 22). Indeed, the complete redrafting of the South African constitution was in large part a recognition that its future legitimacy would rest on its comprehensive rejection of the entrenched structures of social engineering and racial exploitation that apartheid had embedded into every level and every institution of South African society (Powell 2010: 237). The constitution established a set of complex institutions intended to support constitutional democracy and provide redress for past human rights violations. These included the Human Rights and Gender Commissions, the Public Protector and the Auditor General, the Commission for the Promotion and Protection of Cultural, Religious and Linguistic Communities, and the Independent Electoral Commission (Muthien *et al.* 2000: 11). In sum, the constitution is thought to reflect the 'delicate balance' struck by those involved in its creation between the demands of peace, democracy, human rights and social justice in what remains a highly divided society both racially and economically (Powell 2010: 241). Today the document remains 'written bold' within South African politics, encapsulating all the aspirations of the political settlement and providing 'an ethical high water mark' that cannot be easily dismissed (Villa-Vicencio and Soko 2012: 22).

But underpinning the content of the new constitution was an equally significant process of garnering the necessary support among South African citizens. Creating the new South African constitution was the second part of the two-stage transition from apartheid to democracy. The first stage involved the negotiation of the interim constitution, essentially a peace agreement, as discussed in the previous chapter. The second stage saw the newly elected parliament double as a constitutional assembly responsible for producing a final constitution that complied with the principles entrenched in the interim constitution (Segal and Cort 2011: 57). After the elections in 1994, the new Government of National Unity had a two-year mandate to produce the final constitution. Success in this endeavor would be seen to consolidate South Africa's transition to democracy, while failure would force a referendum on any unresolved issues, which both sides were eager to avoid. Political leaders understood that a constitution for a newly democratic society must have popular legitimacy and must stand the test of time in terms of rebuilding institutions and a democratic culture (Powell 2010: 242–3).

Cyril Ramaphosa highlighted the importance of popular legitimacy in the drafting of South Africa's new constitution, arguing that the final document must be a constitution that they [South Africans] own, a constitution that they know and feel belongs to them. We must therefore draft a constitution that will be fully legitimate, a constitution that will represent the aspirations of our people.

(quoted in Segal and Cort 2011: 142)

Developing this popular legitimacy relied on a strategy of broad public engagement in the drafting process. This included receiving an over-whelming 1,753,424 submissions during the first three months of the process, complemented by a 'constitutional road-show' targeting margin-alized rural and disadvantaged communities that were unlikely to access information through print or electronic media; public information made available through radio and other media; over one thousand workshops that reached approximately 95,000 people; and a broad constitutional education programme (Segal and Cort 2011: 148–55). Once a working draft of the new constitution was produced it was translated into all 11 offi-cial languages, and over five million copies were distributed throughout the country. Behind the scenes the process also focused on legitimacy. As the deadline approached some outstanding issues were addressed in private, bilateral negotiations, enabling protagonists to 'change their minds and positions gracefully' (Roelf Meyer quoted in Segal and Cort 2011: 163), culminating in a final all night negotiating session in April 1996 that saw agreement on the last areas of contention. In May 1996 the final constitution was adopted unanimously; 'The true birth certificate of the South African nation had finally been approved' (Segal and Cort 2011: 137). To further embed the popular legitimacy of the new constitution, following its eventual certification by the Constitutional Court in Decem-ber 1996, six million miniature copies in all 11 languages were distributed around the country. Ramaphosa expressed hope that the real legacy of the Constitutional Assembly was not just in these pages:

The real legacy {...} lies in the growing awareness of what a constitu-tion means. I appeal to you all to nurture, to claim the Constitution as your own. We have a constitution we can be proud of, now let's make it work. It must become a part of people's everyday lives.

(quoted in Segal and Cort 2011: 227)

In many ways, then, both the process and the content of the South African constitution are exemplary. And yet this is not the final step in ensuring the legitimacy of constitutional reform. The challenge for South Africa was to ensure that the 'skeleton' of democracy that was introduced in the constitution would actually lead to the growth of a healthy democratic society (Thompson 2001: 265), and it is here that the nation has stumbled. Stanley Henkeman observes 'a total, total disjuncture' between the consti-tution and 'the reality on the ground'. While the new constitution has been effective in framing the terms of South African reconciliation, the reality of the 'sluggish' realization of its ambitious values and principles has become a barrier to more transformative change (van der Westhuizen 2010: 103). Raenette Taljaard considers the constitutional settlement, and the constitution itself, to be 'under a review button' until South Africa experiences 'dramatic socio-economic change'. The South African system of constitutional democracy has not adequately held to account those who exercise power and privilege, and nor has it successfully built on the legitimacy of the system among South African citizens (Terreblanche 2012: 78). Transformation according to the principles in the constitution has been stymied by its own centralizing tendencies, which have been bolstered by the political culture of the ANC, which values 'hierarchy, secrecy, and unaccountability' and will likely remain the dominant party for the foreseeable future (MacDonald 2006: 131). There are also cultural incongruities. As Catherine Kennedy explained to me, in her organization's work in schools and communities she often hears that the human rights focus of the South African constitution 'undermines *ubuntu*'. The perception is that *ubuntu* centres on the idea of responsibility, while many see the individualistic approach of human rights as 'undermining community responsibility'.

More significant still, some have criticized South Africa's pursuit of constitutionalism as limiting the scope of democratic transformation, suggesting that the emphasis on constitutionalism and human rights has contributed to 'an absence of spaces for a politics of resistance to play out' (van Marle 2007: 225). Leon Wessels (2010: 12) has expressed his hope that it is 'within the safe spaces of the Constitution' that South Africans can revive a 'spirit of trust through dialogue'. Sello Hatang also recognizes the importance of maintaining—or re-opening—political space for debating the merits of the constitution. While he acknowledges that the South African constitution 'is held as one of the best constitutions in the world', he maintains that South Africa must be vigilant about 'ensuring that people benefit from it'. Hatang considers it crucial to open up difficult conversations: 'Was our constitution a negotiated sell out that does not ensure the progression of black people? {...}. We're now saying, let's have these difficult conversations about the constitution and what it does and doesn't do'. Oscar Siwali emphasizes this point, telling me that the struggle against apartheid was a struggle 'for freedom {...} there was nothing ever, ever, ever about democracy'. After 1994, however, democracy became 'the magic word' and more radical ideas of freedom were lost. These observations suggest that the high regard in which the constitution is held has actually had actually the effect of limiting its potential for agonistic transformation.

The South African achievement nevertheless seems remarkable when contrasted with the Guatemalan experience of constitutional reform. Following the celebrated signing of the Peace Accords in Guatemala in 1996 there was a period of intense debate and political maneuvering over the changes to the 1985 constitution required to legalize the most important elements of the Peace Accords and secure their popular legitimation. Although the existing constitution did contain a Bill of Rights, this was countered by its provisions relating to army powers that simultaneously put genuine democratization out of reach, particularly with regard to the recognition of indigenous rights. As a result, the most significant democratic gains from the peace process would not become reality unless the constitutional reforms proceeded (Jonas 2000: 98). In spite of this, the two most important conservative political parties in the Guatemalan Congress, the *Partido de Avanzada Nacional* (the National Progress Party, PAN) and former general Ríos Montt's party the *Frente Republicano Guatamalteco* (Guatemalan Republican Front, FRG), opposed the key reforms relating to the protection of indigenous and other human rights, eliminating clandestine security units, reducing the power of the army, and addressing socio-economic inequality. Although Congress finally approved the package of reforms in October 1998, these same parties did not support them in the national referendum that followed (Carmack 2008: 60–1).

The campaign in support of the reform saw considerable grassroots organizing throughout the country, particularly by indigenous organizations. However, opponents to the reforms were even more vocal, advancing racist claims that a successful referendum would force Ladinos to learn Mayan languages and would give indigenous people the right to claim whatever land they wanted by declaring it a sacred area (Nelson 2009: 49). Ultimately only 18.5 per cent of registered voters turned out to vote in the referendum, and the reforms were defeated by a margin of 55 to 45 (Jonas 2000: 10). The result was further evidence of Guatemala's deep divisions, with an overwhelming 'yes' vote in rural and indigenous areas, while Guatemala City and other Ladino areas were largely opposed (Carmack 2008: 60–1). Raquel Zelaya underscores the depth of these divisions, pointing out that there were areas in Guatemala with high indigenous participation that voted wholly in support of the reforms. In light of this she questions any assessment of the reforms as lacking popular support, asking, 'How can you think that nobody agrees with this just because in the capital city people don't agree with it?' Still, the result was heartbreaking for those who had worked for years in the peace negotiations, and was a devastating blow for the implementation of the accords (Nelson 2009: 50).

The defeat of the reforms came after two years of 'deterioration' following the signing of the Accords, during which Guatemala's 'stubborn resistance to change' was again reinforced (Jonas 2000: 10). The 'peace resisters' gained significant ground during this period, putting at risk the historical opportunity presented by the Peace Accords and contributing to a 'widespread erosion of faith in the potential of the peace process' (Jonas 2000: 138). The congressional debates on the reforms produced an enormously complex combination of measures, 'needlessly cluttered' by mixing significant reforms that were required to advance the peace process with more marginal proposals that served partisan processes (Reilly 2009: 14). Adrian Zapata agrees that there was a deliberate strategy by political elites 'directed towards avoiding the constitutional reform'. From the original proposals emanating from the accords, the 'main power sectors' in Guatemalan society worked to 'amplify these reforms to over 50'. Zapata recalls that

> There were so many reforms that were being proposed that, for example, I could agree with 15 and not with the others. So if you have a menu of 50 options [and] there's one option with which you don't agree, then you might not want to vote for the rest.

Adding to the confusion was the fact that there was only a little over two weeks available to educate the electorate about the content of the reforms. In the final month of the campaign those campaigning against the reforms 'left no stone unturned, no quetzal unspent, no distortion untold in the media, no fear unexploited' (Jonas 2000: 202). These factors led the majority of the population to abstain from voting entirely, indicating that although they clearly welcomed the peace agreed to in the Accords, they did not see their aspirations advanced by what Charles Reilly (2009: 30) describes as a 'congressional exercise in obfuscation'.

Alvaro Pop suggests that Guatemala's failure to create a popularly legitimate constitution 'based more or less on a consensus' is indicative of the country's weak political institutions and low levels of civic literacy. Pop argues that:

> the laws in Guatemala are not legitimate and the constitution itself has profound deficiency in relation to its legitimacy. Democracy in Guatemala was born and just remained there as a seed that wasn't propagated in the minds of many {...}. Democracy as a model of coexistence is not a cultural experience that Guatemalans are convinced of, for one simple reason; because the institutions haven't really created citizens. Guatemalans, the majority of us are not citizens {...} because we don't understand the political system.

Despite these serious concerns, some political actors in Guatemala retain an expectation that constitutionalism will provide some necessary spaces for wider public discussion on issues of reconciliation and conflict transformation. For example, Doris Cruz observes that politicians, who will point to the values in the constitution, often defer deeper debate about social values. Cruz acknowledges that to some extent the Guatemalan constitution does express some important values, but also suggests that 'the constitution is so far from the people' containing 'too many details', which means 'you don't leave any space to be able to have this discussion about our society'. This leaves the document fixed in time rather than an 'instrument' that can create space for discussion. Cruz maintains that the key purpose of any constitution should be to articulate the 'values of the country, that you have agreed upon, but that you have to constantly be revising and developing'.

Certainly many people in Guatemala remain dissatisfied with the level of reform that was achieved. For example, Arnoldo Noriega considers the failure to institute the constitutional reform intended to recognize Guatemala as a multiethnic, multicultural and multilingual country to be an 'embarrassment' because 'over 500 years after the Spanish invasion of Guatemala, and 200 years of independence, Guatemala is still not recognized for what it is'. Indigenous peoples in Guatemala are 'still punished by the worst poverty, health and education indicators, they are still excluded from decision-making', and Noriega insists these issues must be addressed. This conversation is far from over. After the defeat of the referendum in Guatemala, indigenous organizations continued to campaign for constitutional reform that would guarantee greater legal autonomy. The prospects of any such reform seemed remote until a case in 2010 saw the Constitutional Court of Guatemala adopt ILO Convention 169[1] (on indigenous and tribal peoples) into the country's constitution. Guatemala had ratified the convention in 1996 but it had not been instituted into domestic law. In 2010 the Court ruled that all the rights provided for in the Convention have constitutional status, although there has since been considerable debate—and further jurisprudence—concerning the legal status of consultation with indigenous peoples in Guatemala. Nevertheless, delayed reforms such as this, and a new push for constitutional transformation in Australia, suggest that the constitutional level of reconciliation effort can rarely be thought to have concluded.

A new constitutional conversation

Proposals for constitutional reform with regard to Aboriginal and Torres Strait Islander peoples in Australia are not new. The constitution that created a federation of the former Australian colonies in 1901, gave little thought to how indigenous peoples might be included in the new nation. In fact the only references to Aboriginal people were in Section 51 (xxvi), which empowered the federal parliament to make laws with respect to the 'people of any race, other than the aboriginal race', and Section 127, which excluded Aboriginal people from being counted in the national census. And while neither section actually excluded Aboriginal people from Australian citizenship, they both suggested that Aboriginal people were not a part of the Australian nation (McGregor 2011: xvii–xx).

In 1967, following a ten-year campaign, Australia passed a referendum intended to address these exclusions. The reforms in the 1967 referendum were quite modest, giving the Commonwealth government the power to make laws in relation to (although not necessarily for the benefit of) Aboriginal and Torres Strait Islander people, and allowing Aboriginal and Torres Strait Islander people to be counted in the census. The campaign for reform simply asked the Australian public to 'Vote yes for Aborigines', a request to which they responded with the highest majority (90.77 per cent) ever achieved in a referendum. In a country notoriously conservative when it comes to changing its Constitution (only eight out of 44 referenda have ever been passed) 1967 was a remarkable triumph. Many Australians believed that in voting 'yes' they were giving Aboriginal people citizenship, or the right to vote, or a conflation of the two. In fact, Aboriginal people had (at least technically) been citizens since 1948[2] and had had the right to vote (at federal elections) since 1962 with the passage of the *Common-wealth Electoral Act.* In retrospect, it is clear that the significance of the referendum lies not so much in the reality of the changes it brought about, but in the willingness of the wider Australian population to vote in support of a changed relationship.

But the issue did not end there—unsurprisingly given the persistent assertion of indigenous sovereignty as discussed above. For many Aboriginal and Torres Strait Islander people, the 1967 referendum was not as transformative as they had hoped. As Kevin Gilbert argued, 'Many blacks thought that at last a new deal for black people was imminent' and their disillusionment 'hit hard' (Gilbert 2002: 101). The referendum did little to change the Australian structures and institutions, let alone reverse the impacts of colonization and settler colonial policies (Behrendt 2003: 13). Following the referendum, the federal government 'sat on its hands', while the wider public seemed to feel that their 'duty was done' (McGregor 2011: 162). Thus, in 1983 a Senate Standing Committee returned to the issue, and recommended constitutional change that would permit the negotiation of a new relationship between Indigenous peoples and the Australian state (Senate Standing Committee on Constitutional and Legal Affairs 1983). Aboriginal people then had to wait until the 1992 *Mabo* judgment (discussed further in the next chapter) to have some degree of legal recognition for the fact that they had never relinquished their land or ceded their sovereignty. As discussed in the previous chapter, the focus on constitutional transformation during this period centred on calls for a treaty, which were ultimately deferred in favour of the much-criticized formal reconciliation process. Nevertheless, as Patrick Dodson has argued, many Aboriginal and Torres Strait Islander people continued to hope that government would one day engage in 'serious dialogue' about indigenous peoples' position in the Australia nation, ultimately leading to constitutional recognition 'as the first Australians, with our Indigenous rights, obligations, and responsibilities respected and recognized' (Dodson 2000: 13).

The contemporary conversation about indigenous constitutional recognition in Australia was prompted by a 2007 election promise by former prime minister, John Howard, who pledged to hold such a referendum if he were re-elected. In the years since then, a referendum on constitutional recognition has become the policy of both major parties and in 2010, the then prime minister, Julia Gillard, commissioned an 'Expert Panel' of indigenous and non-indigenous experts to undertake extensive, nation-wide consultation on the issue. The work of the panel did a great deal to enhance the popular legitimacy of any proposed reforms, including a spectrum of indigenous and non-indigenous political views among its membership, and reaching an extraordinary number of indigenous people around the country. There was a significant effort made to make the work of the panel accessible, including by translating documents into indigenous languages as well as producing plain English versions and a visual representation. The Expert Panel released its report in January 2012, recommending the repeal of two provisions in the constitution that allow racial discrimination (Section 25 and Section 51 xxvi), and the cre-ation of a new section recognizing that 'the continent and its islands now known as Australia were first occupied by Aboriginal and Torres Strait Islander peoples'; acknowledging their continuing cultures, languages, heritage, and relationship to their traditional lands and waters; and pro-posing that the federal parliament have powers to make laws for the 'advancement' of Aboriginal and Torres Strait Islander peoples. The Panel further proposed two additional sections expressly prohibiting racial dis-crimination and providing for the recognition of indigenous languages. Significantly, however, the Panel rejected the call from many Aboriginal and Torres Strait Islander people that a referendum should consider the 'constitutional recognition of the sovereign status of Aboriginal and Torres Strait Islander peoples' on the grounds that such a proposal 'would be highly contested by many Australians, and likely to jeopardize broad public support' for the reforms (Expert Panel on Constitutional Recogni-tion of Indigenous Australians 2012: xvi, xviii).

Many non-indigenous Australians engaged in reconciliation efforts acknowledge the significance of even these modest proposals for constitu-tional recognition. For example, Jacqui Phillips finds it 'extraordinary' that there is still 'complete silence in our nation's founding document about even the existence of Australia's First Peoples' and even 'more dis-turbing' is the fact that there are two provisions in the Australian Constitu-tion that 'potentially allow racial discrimination'. Similarly, Tim Gartrell sees the campaign in support of the referendum as built around two key elements: 'Firstly we've got a constitution that doesn't recognize Abori-ginal people and their contribution and their unique culture, and sec-ondly, the Constitution still has racist elements.' Gartrell tells me that once these two things are explained to people they are generally supportive, 'but the problem is a lot of people don't know either of those things so we're working from a very, very low base of information about the history of the Constitution and the history of exclusion'. Gary Highland says he was 'persuaded' during the year he spent working for the Expert Panel that constitutional recognition is 'really worth doing; it would mean a huge amount to a lot of people and would make a contribution to resetting that relationship'. He stresses that he is not saying that recognition would be a 'big silver bullet' that would mean 'suddenly we're reconciled', but he feels strongly that a referendum on this issue would be 'the biggest opportunity in our generation to make a real difference'. But Phillips is fearful that these aspirations will not come to pass, that the nation 'will be offered much less than that', which would 'fracture the Aboriginal and Torres Strait Islander leadership even more around this issue. We'll see key leaders walk away'. Whether the government would even proceed to a referendum on 'something that's very weak and symbolic', about which 'everyone would feel just very halfhearted' is not clear. This, for Phillips, would waste a 'historic opportunity to re-enliven the reconciliation movement' in Australia.

Polling shows that the majority of Aboriginal and Torres Strait Islander people are supportive of the proposals, but there is also a degree of ambivalence and—as discussed above—some outright opposition. Les Malezer from the National Congress of Australia's First Peoples argues that his organization was prepared to support the report of the Expert Panel 'on the basis that it's a quality report' and is 'the best that could be achieved under the terms of reference'. However, he does not accept that the proposed reforms are 'necessarily the best way to address the constitution, or the best way to address the needs of Aboriginal and Torres Strait Islander people'. For Congress, however, Malezer maintains that the key to meaningful reform for Aboriginal and Torres Strait Islander people is 'the prevention of racial discrimination in the Constitution. Because this has been our biggest problem all the way through'. And he is clear that even achieving this reform will not be the end of the conversation, proposing that Congress intends to develop a 'declaratory statement' expressing indigenous rights to self-determination that might lead to a Constitution of Aboriginal Peoples that could be read in combination with the Australian Constitution. Malezer admits that this is 'a bit of a dream' but retains some optimism that the momentum generated by the campaign for constitutional recognition could generate enough support for future reforms in the political relationship.

Beyond the content of the reforms, however, some acknowledge that there is reconciliatory potential in the debates that will precede any referendum. Aboriginal and Torres Strait Islander Social Justice Commissioner, Mick Gooda, suggests that the 'beauty of referendums' is that 'the people speak', rather than only politicians or judges. This is particularly important in the case of a referendum on a matter like this because, for Gooda, 'This goes to the soul of Australia {...} and it's so important that the population gets to have a say on that because it actually will determine the future of Australia in a lot of ways'. To date, however, the Australian soul has been unmoved. Despite an ongoing campaign to build awareness of the case for constitutional reform, the proposed referendum has been delayed twice in the face of community apathy. Tim Gartrell from the campaigning organization Recognise, says his organization is focused on 'cranking up the grassroots pressure' through a range of awareness-raising strategies, while also continuing a 'constant dialogue' with political leaders in order to maintain pressure on them to follow through on their commitment. Florence Onus points to the need to build popular legitimacy through a broad-based social movement involving unions, churches, educators, and the rest of civil society, as was the case in the campaign for the 1967 referendum. But Jacqueline Phillips feels that the lack of momentum around the referendum campaign is indicative of the state of the wider reconciliation movement in Australia. She maintains that if that movement was 'still strong and vital and active' then it would have picked up the recognition issue 'in a really strong way' and the Recognise campaign would not find that 'two or three years on [there is] still only 30 per cent of the population aware of the issue'. Janet Hunt agrees, pointing to the lack of political leadership toward a referendum. Hunt suggests it is evident that politicians from both of Australia's major parties have put this issue 'very low down the priorities' and that, as a result, 'we have a community that is pretty unaware that it's even happening, or on the agenda to happen'.

But Hunt also acknowledges that whatever happens with the proposed referendum, Australia is 'a long way from satisfying Aboriginal desires for what a new relationship might look like, that might actually recognize their sovereignty and do something about shared sovereignty, perhaps, in the future'. There is general recognition that although non-indigenous Australians will need to support the referendum in large numbers for it to succeed, the final propositions put to the vote must also have the support of Aboriginal and Torres Strait Islander people. Leah Armstrong maintains that if 'Aboriginal and Torres Islander people don't see it as an important stepping stone then the rest of the population aren't going to vote for it'. The political challenge is finding what would be 'acceptable' for indigenous people while still maintaining bipartisan political support, which will also be required for a referendum to succeed. For Gary Highland, like others, the biggest risk of the proposed referendum is that 'it will be put up and will fail', which will 'send a message, not just to Aboriginal people but around the world, that Australia has not moved ahead'. But a secondary risk for Highland is that a referendum will be put to the people that is 'so tepid that it won't mean anything' and he believes that a weak version would fail as well because people would wonder 'why am I bothering to do this?'

These dilemmas, both in Australia and in the other cases considered here, point to the inevitability of conflict, compromise, and contingency in reconciliation efforts, including at the constitutional level. But in Australia, as elsewhere, the effect of reconciliatory efforts such as constitutional reform may be to close down agonistic spaces. In the South African context, Zackie Achmat (2010: 117) has argued that even an exemplary constitution like theirs 'requires active citizens' if it is going to contribute to conflict transformation. A transformative constitution requires a living culture of citizens who exercise the power of popular legitimation to ensure that their society engages with, and adheres to, constitutional rules and values. And as the Guatemalan case suggests, constitutions also require institutions, including the kinds of politico-legal institutions that will take seriously their commitment to enforcing constitutional principles and mandates (Daly and Sarkin 2007: 217).

It is to the demands of institutional transformation that I turn in the next section of this book.

Notes

1 International Labor Organization Convention 169 recognizes tribal peoples' land rights and says they should be consulted prior to the approval of any projects on their lands.
2 In 1948 the *Nationality and Citizenship Act* created the category of Australian citizen, which included Aboriginal people by virtue of the fact that they had been born in Australia. In reality, however, citizenship for Aboriginal and Torres Strait Islander people remained a legal rather than a lived reality until at least the 1960s.

Part III

Institutional challenges

Part II

Institutional challenges

7 Equity and redistribution

Reconciliation and economic transformation are deeply interdependent. Continuing economic inequality is a persistent source of conflict likely to impede reconciliation efforts unless there is political space available through which to contest these inequities. Yet many divided and post-conflict societies remain marked by gross social and economic inequalities that continue to undermine peace and stability. Transforming economic structures and institutions in a divided society requires long-term work focused on building more equitable relations between former enemies. This may involve the redistribution of wealth, land reform, or the payment of reparations—the delivery of a 'peace dividend'—often resisted by those who have previously enjoyed great wealth. Often these efforts are also hampered by the kind of path dependency that has been established by previous economic policies. This chapter documents some of the challenges and compromises in economic reform that have underpinned—or undermined—reconciliation efforts. It argues that in many cases these conversations must be reopened in order to challenge an economic status quo that has failed to effect any meaningful material transformation for the most marginalized members of society.

This chapter also begins to analyse the institutional level of conflict transformation efforts as part of the multi-level framework outlined in this book. Institutions are ubiquitous and necessary, and when well-organized, transparent and fair, they can bring 'certainty, security and an orderly means for the distribution of public goods' (Mac Ginty 2013: 4). Effective state institutions must be accountable to citizens rather than an elite minority, being seen to promote social, economic, and cultural rights as a means of rebuilding trust between the state and society and among social groups (UN Women 2012: 4). But analysing the institutional level of reconciliation efforts brings with it a stark confrontation with the unevenness of power, and the struggles that are required to achieve change in the face of intense resistance from political and economic elites. In each of the next three chapters this dynamic is clearly in evidence. Spaces of material and institutional transformation are also spaces of conflict within which a great deal is at stake. Conflicts over institutional transformation are imbued with political power imbalances characterized by the resistance of those who have benefited from previously repressive regimes. This is particularly the case with regard to the transformation of economic structures and institutions, despite a growing consensus that reconciliation without economic justice is no reconciliation at all.

Transforming economies

In each of the cases in this study, and indeed in many other instances around the world, systematic discrimination and inequality of access to resources, employment, and land, have either been a direct cause of violent conflict, have perpetuated violence, or have exacerbated the social tensions underlying violent conflict (Arbour 2007: 8–9). The identity-based divisions discussed in previous chapters invariably rest upon or mask these socioeconomic deprivations. As Daly and Sarkin (2007: 228–9) contend, economic oppression

> conduces to exhaustion, frustration, and ultimately violence. Desperately poor people have neither the time, the energy, nor the hope to participate in programs designed to foster democracy, reconciliation, or justice.

In order to plan a future and contribute to the development of new relationships and more just institutions, citizens must be able to look beyond their immediate survival needs (Brown and Magilindane 2004: 115). Thus, the multi-generational work of reconciliation and conflict transformation requires public confidence that is built on evidence of progress in transforming socioeconomic inequality. In our interview Raenette Taljaard maintains that, in South Africa and elsewhere, the 'reconciliation debate {…} will always be a socio-economic debate underneath all the powerful philosophical, emotional, moral, human elements that there are to it'. Indeed, in reimagining a society without violent conflict, citizens must also be able to conceive of a society without structural violence and injustice (Miller 2008: 275).

In most cases, however—and certainly in the cases in this study—the reality of economic transformation and redistribution falls well short of these ideals, with persistent injustices fuelling ongoing discontent and unpredictable resurgences of violent conflict. While countries like South Africa have made a significant political transition to democracy, economic justice has proven more difficult (Villa-Vicencio 2009: 28). The persistent failure to achieve greater distributive justice and alleviate poverty and underdevelopment is often experienced as a continuation of the injustice and exploitation that characterized a previous, oppressive regime (Selim and Murithi 2011: 58). Impoverished groups, that remain economically and socially excluded find themselves locked into cycles of poverty that can only be broken through significant structural reforms. When other forms of exclusion based on ethnicity, culture, or religion are accentuated by economic exclusion, the result is a potent mix of anger, frustration and discontent that is likely to see violence intensify in often unpredictable ways (Villa-Vicencio 2009: 44). The vacuum created by a state's failure to meet the basic needs of its citizens is often filled by opposition groups and cartels, which are able to secure dependency and patronage through the provision of services, in the process destabilizing a fragile government (Daly and Sarkin 2007: 49–50). Guatemala is a paradigmatic example of this disruptive dynamic.

It is for these reasons that Kim Wale, in her work on the South African Reconciliation Barometer, has called for reconciliation itself to be rearticulated in more radical form. As Wale (2013: 9) argues,

> The word radical implies depth in the sense of 'root', as in going to the root of the issue. Radical also means revolutionary, or to create something new that is different from what has preceded it. On both counts [a radical] understanding of reconciliation departs from the ambiguous, soft uses of the term that have preceded it. The term grounds reconciliation in a new direction, which places the connection between economic justice and reconciliation at the centre.

Often, however, rather than situating socioeconomic redistribution as central to conflict transformation, as Wale suggests, economic development is left out of the transitional narrative, making it a story only about political rather than economic change (Miller 2008: 280). Too frequently, this need for more radical reconciliation has been subsumed under the paradigm of the 'liberal peace'. This 'minimalist' interpretation urges a focus on struggles for other freedoms (of speech, of movement) rather than demands for economic transformation (Muvingi 2009: 178). At the same time the need to address profound structural inequalities is subordinated to the imperative of economic growth intrinsic to the international development 'industry' focused on state building and long-term recovery (Powell 2010: 248).

Over time, however, it has become more evident that the economic orthodoxies of the liberal peace are in fact likely to generate new dimensions of conflicts. Market-based economic policies—often a prerequisite for international support for transitional justice efforts—tend to perpetuate and even extend socioeconomic inequality. The most extreme examples of this among the countries in this study are South Africa and Guatemala, both of which demonstrate punishing and persistent inequalities. It is evident that the assumptions upon which liberal models of economic development rest have proven profoundly unstable. Despite the arguments of neoliberal economists, it is evident that economic growth does not in fact 'trickle down' to the most impoverished members of society (Simpson 2000: 4). In fact, each of the countries in this study—all of which have pursued neoliberal economics to a greater or lesser degree—can also lay claim to being amongst the most unequal in their region. In light of the theoretical concerns of this book, it is also evident that these assumptions about the 'right' model for economic development have the effect of closing down political space in which future options for economic reform and redistribution may be discussed. This dynamic is exacerbated by elite dominance and resistance to economic transformation, discussed further below, particularly where there is no political will to challenge this resistance. In these ways an opportunity is often missed for important dialogue about socioeconomic goals and priorities with a view to long-term transformation rather than short-term profit.

In the framework of the liberal peace, economic transformation is often understood to mean the provision of various forms of material reparations to 'victims' of an unjust regime. There are many shortcomings to this approach. Firstly, reparations can never be adequate, meaning that the 'reparative gesture' is only ever partial (Doxtader 2004: 25), and often little more than tokenism. Reparations tend to be limited in scope and, where the reparation is direct payment, also limited in amount, offering little in terms of meaningful redistribution. As Daly and Sarkin (2007: 233) put it 'restitution works best where it is needed least as an economic reform'. Second, reparations tend to be directed only to members of officially sanctioned categories of victims. This approach neglects the fact that economic exploitation is likely to have been systemic and institutionalized, affecting all members of an oppressed group not just those who can prove specific violations. By 'individuating compensation' the payment of reparations may further obscure the need for more radical systemic change (Muvingi 2009: 180; Miller 2008: 278). This second concern gives rise to the third, specifically the question of whether it is morally justifiable for scarce government resources to be spent on reparations to individual victims rather than on programmes that address structural disadvantage, such as education, housing, health, and critical infrastructure. Finally, reparations generally fail to improve the lives of even the few who may receive them, as they are usually an insufficient amount to change the socioeconomic status of the recipient. Thus, as Daly and Sarkin (2007: 236) suggest, a woman in receipt of material reparations 'may get enough to buy a new refrigerator, but she still won't have enough to pay for electricity to run it'.

None of this is to suggest that reparations should never be paid. There is certainly a claim, as has been advanced in Guatemala and elsewhere, that the payment of reparations is an 'obligation of the state' to acknowledge and make amends for past wrongs (Nelson 2009: 303). Rather the argument here is that reparations alone will not achieve the kind of redistributive justice that will make a genuine contribution to reconciliation efforts. And neither will the pursuit of market-based economic reform. As the cases in this study make clear, these strategies in fact have little impact on the lives of the most marginalized and impoverished members of deeply divided societies.

Searching for the 'peace dividend'

In the wake of violent conflict there is much discussion of an anticipated 'peace dividend', that is, the individual and communal improvements in the quality of life that derive from the end of violence. The aspiration is that 'peace' will translate into improvements in economic prosperity and human security that will, in turn, provide a safeguard against a return to violence (Powell 2010: 250). The search for the elusive dividend often drives efforts towards institutional transformation in recognition of the fact that citizens whose lives remain unchanged by the end of violence will experience dashed hopes and frustrated expectations that will further entrench social division (Brewer 2013: 166).

Each of the countries in this study has pursued various approaches to addressing the demand for greater socioeconomic equality (a key feature of the peace dividend), with varying degrees of success. The Australian case—where the indigenous population is small and the direct violence ended long ago—suggests the extent of these transformative challenges. Australia has long recognized that reconciliation is not possible while there are significant differences in the outcomes and life chances for Aboriginal and Torres Strait Islander peoples compared with the rest of the population (Council for Aboriginal Reconciliation 2000: 72). Yet these differences remain pronounced. Indigenous people in Australia have significantly shorter life expectancy than non-indigenous people, higher death rates, higher rates of infant mortality, higher rates of incarceration, higher rates of substance abuse, poor educational attainment, and high levels of individual and community poverty. In spite of this, however, the original proposal for the establishment of a Council for Aboriginal Reconciliation *and Justice* did not survive the legislative process. The title was changed despite a recognition by the minister responsible that 'the reconciliation process will be substantially judged on whether or not the national government delivers on the social justice objectives of the process' (Tickner 2001: 34). Instead, from 1996 the Howard government advanced the far narrower conception of 'practical reconciliation', which was understood by many as being an attempt to avoid public debate on the need for more significant structural change (Gunstone 2009: 145). A more modest campaign, known as 'Closing the Gap',[1] divorced distributive injustice from both history and contemporary settler colonialism, thereby reproducing those same dynamics through a form of 'rights paternalism' (Muldoon and Schaap 2012: 189). Land reform has also been a crucial part of these redistributive struggles in Australia, as will be discussed in more depth below.

In Guatemala, the Peace Accords raised popular expectations for a 'peace dividend' and an improvement in people's quality of life. It soon became clear, however, that the state did not have, and nor was it developing, the capacity to realize these expectations (Jonas 2000: 184). Adrian Zapata points out that, although the rural population makes up 71 per cent of the population, this group is still living in 'extreme poverty and exclusion'. Indeed, for the majority of Guatemalans, the peace dividend 'has been very modest indeed' (Reilly 2009: 25). The economy remains dominated by wealthy landholders and various types of organized crime, including drug cultivation and trafficking (Arriaza and Roht-Arriaza 2010: 206), while also relying on remittances sent home by members of the Guatemalan diaspora, which have become a key source of income for the poor (helping support approximately 25 per cent of the population). Indeed, it is acknowledged that without remittances, poverty in Guatemala would be 'overwhelming' (Reilly 2009: 26). Rosalina Tuyuc describes these persistent inequities, telling me that 'people in the urban area are consuming the largest amount of the state budget' but continue to believe in the trickle down approach and that by having 'all the wealth in the country {...} they can help the people in the interior to get jobs, for example, as domestic help. They will never accept that this wealth needs to be shared with other communities'. And as a result of these economic divisions, Rosenda Camey describes life in Guatemala as 'like living on a big plantation, because there are a lot of us who have nothing and just a few who have a lot'. These economic elites, she says 'are the ones who decide public policy and decide what to do with the economy'.

In both South Africa and Northern Ireland economic concerns also remain high on the political agenda, and it is worth considering some of the strategies that have been pursued in these very different contexts in greater depth.

In 2011 the South African National Planning Commission (2011) released their diagnostic overview, which identified nine key socio-economic challenges facing the country, specifically: that too few people work; that black learners endure poor quality education; that infrastructure is poorly located and maintained; that spatial patterns exclude the poor from the benefits of development; that the economy is unsustainably resource-dependent; that the widespread disease burden is compounded by a failing health system; that public services are poor quality and unevenly distributed; that corruption is pervasive; and that South Africa remains a divided society. Today the growing inequality between South Africans means that 71,000 U.S. dollar millionaires live alongside over four million people subsisting on less than a dollar a day (Biko 2013: 203). And although 14 million people now receive old age and child grants on humanitarian grounds, service infrastructure barely functions in some parts of the country and almost 25 million people cannot make ends meet (Biko 2013: 204; Terreblanche 2012: 71). The vast majority of poor black

South Africans still live in the former urban townships and rural Bantustans, and many 'Born Frees' face extraordinary levels of youth unemployment (around 25 per cent), high levels of poverty, inequality and a deep sense of hopelessness (Mattes 2012: 140). Over 80 per cent of South African land is still held by white farmers, corporations and the state, and four white-owned conglomerates continue to control 80 per cent of the Johannesburg stock exchange (Alexander and Mngxitama 2011: 51). This lack of any evident peace dividend goes some way to explaining the rise in popularity of the populist youth leader Julius Malema and his Economic Freedom Fighters party, which captured around 30 per cent of the vote in 2014 (see Forde 2014).

In light of this dire situation there is an increasingly dominant view that, as discussed in Chapter 5, the negotiation process in the 1990s did not adequately grapple with the country's gross economic disparities, which today are returning to threaten the settlement. The thinking at the time of the negotiated settlement was that the most effective way to draw white South Africans (who controlled the economy) into the new political dispensation was by providing them with a vested interest in the future of the nation (Villa-Vicencio 2009: 58). Indeed, the interests of white capital are thought to have prevailed throughout the negotiation process, as Patrick Bond (2005: 265) bluntly puts it,

> The deal represented, simply, this: black nationalists got the state, and white people and corporations got to keep their apartheid loot, and indeed move much of it out of the country. For those who remained, there were yet more privileges through economic liberalization, ranging from a wider range of luxury imports to higher executive salaries to deregulatory opportunities across a variety of fields.

In other words, the deeply racialized forms of economic exploitation that had characterized the apartheid era were allowed to survive the transition, with subsequent responsibility for economic transformation 'hived off to the market' and at least partially depoliticized (Christodoulidis and Veitch 2008: 18). The opportunity to create more radical economic transformation was wasted, and today many blame the economic compromise at the heart of the negotiated settlement for the country's continued inequality, which in turn has retarded reconciliation efforts. Verne Harris is of the view that, as a result of South Africa's 'embrace' of neoliberalism, 'the reconciliation project is in trouble because we have not fundamentally restructured the state and the economy to benefit the great majority of South Africans'. Raenette Taljaard shares this view, suggesting that it is impossible to 'divorce any debate on reconciliation from socio-economic conditions in South Africa until such time as there's a material change in socio-economic living conditions'. Indeed, Oscar Siwali wonders if his country is ever going to get out of this dark area that we find ourselves {...}. If we're looking at the issue of reconciliation, we're looking at the livelihood of people {...}. Where people don't have land and they don't have jobs and there's no food, there isn't going to be reconciliation.

As the party in government since the 1994 transition the ANC acknowledges these shortcomings, noting that despite significant achievements in terms of 'political liberation and democratization' there is a 'lack of commensurate progress in liberation from socioeconomic bondage' (African National Congress 2012: 8). The ANC now proposes what it terms 'a second transition' for two central reasons. First, they recognize that the consensus framework that supported the political transition 'has proven inadequate for a social and economic transformation phase'. Second, they acknowledge that the 1994 transition required 'an implicit bargain, involving the ANC committing to macroeconomic stability and international openness, and white business agreeing to participate in capital reform to modify the racial structure of asset ownership and invest in national priorities'. Two decades later, however,

> There is agreement that although we have liberalized and integrated into the global economy and we have macroeconomic stability, the structure of the apartheid colonial economy has remained the same, and that in this form, it is incapable of fostering either higher or inclusive growth.
>
> (African National Congress 2012: 34)

Yet despite this acknowledgment, the ANC seems unable to effect economic transformation, which has been fundamentally constrained by the three key approaches to economic policy in South Africa since 1994. The first concerns the role of the TRC in narrating the types of injustice that required transformation in the transition to democracy. As a discursive tool, a truth commission has great power to frame the dimensions of a conflict. In South Africa's case this meant that apartheid became a story of specific human rights violations rather than one about 'long-term, systemic abuses born of a colonial project with economic objectives' (Miller 2008: 280). In choosing a narrow interpretation of both its mandate and its key terms, including 'violations', 'abuses', and 'participation', the Commission provided only a thin conception of justice, which ignored economic and structural violence (Selim and Murithi 2011: 61–2; Chapman 2002: 273).

The second approach concerns the institutionalization of neoliberal economic policy evident in the transition from the Reconstruction and Development Programme (RDP) to the policy of Growth, Employment and Redistribution (GEAR). RDP began as a radical social democratic policy document based on the ANC Freedom Charter. It contained five transformative objectives: democratizing the state and society, meeting basic needs, deracializing the economy, developing human resources, and nation building (Powell 2010: 243). RDP was a key pillar of ANC policy between 1994 and 1996 when it was suddenly abandoned in favour of GEAR, a policy reorientation thought to have been 'forced' by the IMF and other international actors in order to co-opt South Africa into adapting to the 'realities' the global economy (Essof, Moshenberg 2011: 1). GEAR was overtly neoliberal from the start, combining austerity measures with liberalization, privatization, and labour market 'flexibility'. It quickly became 'one of the most controversial and divisive South African government policies' since the transition (Powell 2010: 244–5). As Hlumelo Biko (2013: 66) argues, 'If RDP represented watered-down concessions to the left, then GEAR represented the free-market centric view of how economic policy over the next ten years was to look'.

The third approach, known as Black Economic Empowerment (BEE), was an attempt to correct the economic imbalances of the past by enabling greater black ownership, management and control of South African financial and economic assets. By broadening the ownership of shares, assets, businesses and property, BEE aimed to enable participation in the economy by black South Africans who had been previously excluded (Brown and Magilindane 2004: 118). Essentially, BEE attempted to redistribute wealth through a pseudo-market (government-regulated) scheme that would 'appeal to the black aspirational community while remaining palatable to business' (Biko 2013: 72). But while the scheme has succeeded in creating a small black business elite it has failed to generate economic empowerment or employment for the majority of South Africans, and nor has it transformed the economic structures that were 'created by colonialism and apartheid' (Brown and Magilindane 2004: 118; Alexander and Mngxitama 2011: 52). This view is not shared by everyone. While Vincent Maphai believes that no single intervention can reverse the apartheid heritage, he defends the BEE legislation as 'one of the most effective ways of redressing racial imbalances'. But others contend that this approach has not aided reconciliation efforts at all. Indeed, Namhla Mniki-Mangaliso believes that many black South Africans are angry about two main things: 'One is just the injustice of an economic situation that has not changed in any significant way. The other is the rise of the new black elite who just seem much more concerned about acquiring their own personal wealth.'

Today, although there are calls for the country to 'press the reset button on redistribution' and explore alternative options for more effective redistribution (Biko 2013: 8), the reality is that there is no longer the sense of political urgency that characterized the period of the transition (Villa-Vicencio 2009: 58), meaning that until the level of social discontent becomes politically unmanageable there will be little will to open up a newly agonistic engagement on the need for more radical redistribution.

The economic situation in Northern Ireland was in many ways far less challenging that the situation confronting South Africa at the time of the transition to democracy there. Nevertheless, Northern Ireland has also focused on the economic dimensions of the much-desired peace dividend, with similarly disappointing (although less extreme) results. Northern Ireland remains one of the most unequal regions in Europe (Acheson *et al.* 2011: 18), and the global recession of 2008 further retarded progress on the 'equality agenda'. Catholics still trail Protestants across key socioeconomic indicators associated with unemployment and social deprivation (Nolan 2012: 9). Further, since the ceasefires and the signing of the Belfast Agreement, there has been 'little discernible peace dividend' for working-class people in either community, a fact thought to contribute to the reproduction of ethno-political conflict and division (Coulter and Murray 2008: 17). Almost all Belfast's 'peace walls' are located in the most socially deprived neighbourhoods in the region, where high levels of unemployment and low levels of educational attainment remain common (Byrne 2012: 14). Persistent outbreaks of violence at the interfaces are 'intrinsically intertwined' with the issues that arise from the poverty and deprivation experienced on both sides of the divide (Hancock 2012: 115) and yet few efforts have been made to link the poverty of the working classes in both communities. And, as with the South African settlement, the Belfast Agreement also institutionalized neoliberal economic policies that marginalize the most vulnerable members of society who often do not thrive in a competitive economy (White 2011: 39).

In contrast to South Africa, however, the dominant position of the state in Northern Ireland's political economy paved the way for an ambitious economic and social reform strategy. The neighbourhood renewal programmes in the region drew heavily on British policies that attempted to rebuild and regenerate fractured post-industrial cities and communities there. These programmes were further supported by considerable British subvention that maintained high levels of public sector employment (unusual given the extreme neoliberal policies being advanced by Britain at this time), which in turn produced a new middle class among the Catholic/nationalist community. This changing class formation is thought to have contributed to political de-mobilization and a 'deepening rapprochement between a new nationalist elite and the state' (Bean 2011: 164). The neighbourhood renewal approach has been supported by initiatives funded through the EU Peace Programmes (discussed further in Chapter 9), which distributed funds intended to 'incentivize the development of the economy' and which set specific targets for the levels of development that funded projects were expected to attain (Mitchell 2011: 81). Hamber and Kelly (2005: 53) compare this approach favourably to the South African approach to reconciliation, which some criticize for overly focusing on relationships at the expense of socio-economic reform. In contrast, they suggest that the approach in Northern Ireland, particularly through the Peace Programmes, has had a stronger socio-economic focus.

Despite these positives, however, over time it has become apparent that the neighbourhood renewal approach has had little or no impact on community disadvantage or inequality. Colin Knox (2014: 14–15) suggests that, despite a decade of relative political stability, 'quality of life indicators have barely shifted or got worse between disadvantaged areas and the rest of Northern Ireland', leaving young people in particular feeling little sense of engagement and vulnerable to paramilitary influence. For them, Knox argues, 'there has been no peace dividend'. The global financial crisis in 2008 also hit Northern Ireland hard, and a short-lived period of relative prosperity came to an abrupt end that, according to Brian Dougherty, felt 'like the rug has been pulled out from under our feet again'. Dougherty points out that some of the working class housing estates in Derry and Belfast remain 'amongst the most deprived in the whole of Europe', leading many in Northern Ireland to the view that 'there was no peace dividend really'.

These failures of the neighbourhood renewal approach are certainly recognized among the political elite, and in 2012 the First Minister launched a new initiative known as 'Delivering Social Change', intended to improve 'the quality of life of the most disadvantaged with a specific focus on breaking the long-term cycle of multi-generational poverty'. But for some community workers, such as Mary Lynch, it remains difficult to ask questions about economic inequality in Northern Ireland. Lynch suggests that the emphasis on peace has in fact 'done a massive injustice to the wider society' because by demanding that 'peace should come at all costs' struggling communities were in fact being told to 'put up with things'.

The lack of progress in addressing socioeconomic inequality in Northern Ireland has led to criticism of reconciliation efforts that focus on community relations rather than economic redistribution, because they allow governments to avoid addressing structural issues. There is a view among community activists that while improving community relations is helpful and necessary, development needs are more important (Hancock 2012: 120). However the Community Relations Council (2011: 13) counters such critiques by pointing to the overlap between the sociopolitical levels articulated here, arguing that it is 'ethically questionable and potentially dishonest' to suggest that equality can be achieved while inter-communal hostility remains (Community Relations Council 2011: 15). Certainly the extent of the division in Northern Ireland means that economic decision-making remains politically contentious, particularly given the history of policy designed to favour one community over another (Little 2014: 85). This has led to widespread cynicism that communal loyalty still determines economic policy-making. For example, Sara Cook suggests that while many politicians in Northern Ireland are 'still giving lip service to the working class so that they'll get them to the polls' in reality 'they're not actually doing anything for the working class'. Again, it seems that the political compromises deemed necessary to end the violent conflict have had the effect of shutting down political space in which important transformative debates might now take place.

Struggles for land

Given the argument made in Chapter 3 concerning the colonial-historical basis to the deep divisions in the countries in this study, it follows that land remains a central domain of contestation, with deep socioeconomic implications. Key among the many persistent impacts of dispossession is the loss of an economic base for dispossessed groups, who in each case— regardless of their demographic scale in relation to the dominant group— have found themselves oppressed and marginalized. Continued settler control over indigenous-owned land remains an 'unresolved contradiction and constant provocation' at the heart of these settler colonial relationships (Tully 2000: 39–40). As Paige Arthur (2011: 13) notes, questions of what to do about historically unjust property regimes seem to go beyond any remedy that the transitional justice framework can supply, and yet they remain among the key issues affecting efforts at reconciliation and conflict transformation. The challenge, Arthur suggests, is to develop greater sensitivity to 'the pernicious—and very contemporary and real—effects of these patterns', while also considering what strategies might address them and provide material relief.

Australia provides an interesting case of some limited progress in this area. Struggles over land have been a permanent feature of the relationship between Aboriginal and Torres Strait Islander peoples and the state ever since indigenous lands were first invaded in 1788. Like many indigenous peoples around the world, Aboriginal and Torres Strait Islander peoples' relationship with land goes beyond a western conception of property and ownership, instead underpinning their cosmology. As Larissa Behrendt (1995: 15) explains it, 'Aboriginal people believe the land gives life. The attachment of Aboriginal people to their land and the importance of land in Aboriginal life cannot be overemphasized'. In light of this, the mass appropriation of Aboriginal and Torres Strait Islander lands has been extremely traumatic for the traditional owners. Henry Reynolds describes colonization in Australia as 'one of the greatest appropriations of land in world history' (Reynolds 2013: 248) arguing that the British declaration of *terra nullius* set the stage for more than two centuries of land struggles, including the long frontier wars that Reynolds claims were inevitable in the face of these 'legal fantasies' (Reynolds 2013: 163–4).

Yet it was not until the second half of the twentieth century that struggles for the recognition of the prior and distinct nature of indigenous landholding began to gain ground. A landmark 1971 legal judgment accepted that indigenous peoples did indeed have a system of land ownership, but determined that the communal nature of that ownership, which bore little resemblance to Western property law, meant it could not be recognized in law. This view was maintained until the 1992 *Mabo* case, when the High Court of Australia determined that the communal owner-ship of land by Aboriginal people in fact constituted a unique form of title that had existed prior to colonization. The 1993 *Native Title Act*, the legis-lative response to the *Mabo* decision, created collective rights to land in the Australian legal system. During these same decades, demands for land rights had been fought in the courts and on the streets, eventually result-ing in state/territory-based land rights legislation around the country. Yet although land rights legislation has produced greater certainty for many indigenous groups, it has not been a radically redistributive tool. The terms of land ownership under the *Northern Territory Land Rights Act* (1976), for example, specify that the federal government retains owner-ship of subsurface minerals in Aboriginal land, meaning that Aboriginal and Torres Strait Islander people have not benefited a great deal from Australia's export-oriented resources boom, despite the fact that this wealth is extracted from lands over which indigenous people still assert their sovereignty.

The native title regime introduced in 1993 has also produced mixed results. In many ways, this response to the *Mabo* decision, coming as it did so early in the formal reconciliation process, saw the federal government approach the legislative process as a kind of 'reconciliatory settlement' that again asserted their colonial dominance (Short 2008: 42). One of the tests for native title is proof of continuous association with the land over which a group is claiming title, meaning that for those indigenous peoples whose dispossession was effected early and most completely—notably groups in the southeast of the continent—native title is placed cruelly out of reach. And although native title provides the crucial 'right to negotiate' that has enabled some indigenous groups to develop viable economic pro-jects, including with the mining industry, it is still often the case that even when native title rights are recognized, they are rarely economically pro-ductive. As will be discussed further in Chapter 10, the fundamental failure to see the Australian case as a conflict still requiring settlement has effectively placed land- and resources-based economic empowerment off limits to many Aboriginal and Torres Strait Islander people.

Nevertheless, despite these evident shortcomings in Australia's land reform processes, there is an emerging view that land rights and native title regimes *have* contributed to reconciliation in other ways. Russell McGregor (2011: 173) argues that struggles for the recognition of land rights promoted a diagnosis of indigenous disadvantage that emphasized 'dispossession over discrimination' and the notion of 'Aboriginal distinc-tiveness', and by translating these claims into title deeds, 'land rights pro-moted attentiveness to the deep past of Aboriginal societies and the recovery of traditional culture'. Florence Onus agrees, suggesting that the native title process 'has had a big part in reconnecting people back to country, land, the essence of who they are, their identity and their language'. Janet Hunt also points to successes in this domain, particularly the growing use of Indigenous Land Use Agreements (ILUAs) through which she suggests the recognition of native title can be understood as 'the beginning of a form of shared sovereignty'. Over time, it seems the issue of indigenous land ownership has become somewhat less divisive in Australia. Although neither land rights nor native title have provided the kind of economic redistribution that Aboriginal and Torres Strait Islander people need, it does seem that they are contributing to reconciliation efforts in other ways.

The same cannot be said for either Guatemala or South Africa, where the issue of land reform remains fraught and dangerous. In Guatemala, the Peace Accords attempted to grapple with this issue, but with very limited success. The REHMI report pointed to the 'historically unjust systems' of land ownership in Guatemala that had been exacerbated by 'war induced displacement' and the concentration of property ownership among a few families and corporations (Recovery of Historical Memory Project (REMHI) 1999: 323). Yet the drive to transform these unjust patterns of landholding was stymied by the terms of Guatemala's liberal peace, which denied indigenous people the capacity to frame their land rights claims as either economic rights or collective cultural rights (Brett 2013: 232). While the *Acuerdo sobre Identidad y Derechos de los Pueblos Indígenas* (the Accord on the Identity and Rights of Indigenous Peoples) did propose to recognize communal land and collective land ownership, and the *Acuerdo sobre Aspectos Socioeconómicos y Situación Agraria* (the Accord on Social and Economic Aspects and Agrarian Situation) proposed 'agrarian modernization', through a market-based programme of land redistribution intended to promote land ownership among peasants (Jonas 2000: 76, 79), neither proposed reform went nearly far enough. The poor implementation of the Accords in fact saw an increase in the level of violence associated with land conflicts after the end of the civil war—a problem exacerbated by government evictions of peasants involved in land occupations, particularly in indigenous areas (Jonas 2000: 182). More significantly, critics of the Accords suggest that the approaches to dealing with this deeply entrenched problem were inherently inadequate. Roddy Brett (2013: 231) argues that the indigenous accord imposed individual rights 'over and above any reference to collective land rights' while the agrarian accord entrenched a neoliberal policy approach to land redistribution that was 'dramatically inadequate as a means of addressing the causes of armed conflict'.

Today the issue of land reform in Guatemala remains fraught. Arnoldo Noriega describes land reform as a 'taboo subject' and points to ongoing resistance from the private sector. According to Noriega, this resistance and obstruction from the private sector (discussed further below), saw the 'window of opportunity' opened by the Peace Accords rapidly closed.

Adrian Zapata also refers to land reform in Guatemala as a 'taboo topic'. While working as the presidential commissioner for rural development, Zapata was involved in developing a political framework designed to regulate private investment in rural areas that focused broadly on environmental sustainability, wealth redistribution, employment, taxation, respect for indigenous rights, and the maintenance of market competition. Yet despite the balance in these proposals, Zapata tells me there is ongoing pressure from the private sector for this framework 'to be just abandoned or ignored'.

In response to this ongoing resistance, frustration among indigenous activists is high. Rosalina Tuyuc describes mining and resources developments by transnational corporations as a 'new invasion' of indigenous territories, which is supported by the corporate sector and the government. Tuyuc maintains that the Maya 'need to defend our land, and we need to defend the dignity of our communities'. Otilia Lux perceives mining in Guatemala to be 'a huge problem that will destroy the social fabric in any community' and argues that if Guatemala 'wants to see peace' then it needs to 'stop providing mining licenses to these corporations'. Alvaro Pop repeats a narrative I heard often in Guatemala, of resource companies buying up land, creating environmental destruction through their industry, failing to deliver on commitments for housing or health care for local communities, and then leaving a 'big hole' in the ground, with the poverty in those communities remaining 'worse than before'. As a result of these negative experiences, Pop describes himself as 'against mining completely', a position he says is 'non-negotiable'. He points to more successful endeavours, where local communities have been made 'shareholders' in a project such as a hydroelectricity plant, where participants both contribute to the project and benefit from the electricity that is generated. He contrasts this to the Chixoy plant, which has seen the 400 communities around the development continue to subsist without electricity, which is instead sent to distributors over 200 kilometres away. An approach like this, he tells me, is just 'stupid. How can you think that these people are going to applaud when they see that their children are dying of hunger, there are no hospitals and they have nothing?' Carlos Sarti finds the tensions between the corporations and the movement very worrying, telling me of his concern that the conflicts around Guatemala may one day connect, meaning that 'different conflicts in different places would become a single conflict and explode'.

South African attempts at land reform have not fared much better. As in Australia, most land in South Africa was taken from various African populations using the *terra nullius* principle (Biko 2013: 5). In 1913, the *Land Act* effectively ratified 'the colonial land grab of the previous two and a half centuries' (Roux 2008: 156), making 87 per cent of South Africa a 'white man's country' where Africans were allowed only under very strict conditions (Magubane 2000: 26). Today, while land inequality is far from the only measure of socioeconomic inequality, land remains central to struggles for both livelihoods and social inclusion (Ntsebeza 2010: 85). South African land reform policies have, however, proven inadequate for addressing these needs. As in Guatemala it seems that land reform in South Africa has been stymied by political compromise and the constraints of the liberal peace agenda. As Joan Fairweather (2006: 119) suggests, 'As in every area of administration in the new South Africa, apartheid has left a distinctive stamp on the land claim process.'

Land restitution was a highly contentious aspect of the transitional deal, which produced an overarching commitment to the protection of property rights that was entrenched in the new South African constitution (Roux 2008: 155). The property clause in the constitution recorded the need for land reform while at the same time ensuring that those who owned property would not be 'arbitrarily deprived of their assets' (Segal and Cort 2011: 182). This demand both shaped the land claims process itself (restricting it to a market-based mechanism as discussed below) and placed strict limitations on those who were eligible to make land claims. Specifically, the land restitution process would not deal with claims prior to 19 June 1913 (the date on which the *Natives Land Act* was promulgated). In a striking parallel with the Australian native title process, as Theunis Roux (2008: 156) notes, 'The oft-forgotten significance of the 1913 cut-off-date {…} is that it restricted the land restitution process to claims by people who had lost their land *after* the main period of colonial conquest was already over'. Further, the constitutional provisions pertaining to land reform are fundamentally contradictory in that they undertake to both protect existing property rights *and* enable the redistribution of land to the dispossessed majority. These two objectives cannot easily coexist given that the vast proportion of land that might be pursued as restitution is today under private ownership and therefore protected by the constitution (Ntsebeza 2011: 298). And white landowners still defend their rights to the land. As Kallie Kriel from Afroforum tells me, while his organization is 'not trying to say the previous land policy is something that we can be proud of' he also rejects any 'sweeping statement' that says 'this land was stolen'.

The market-based approach to land restitution has proved to be equally problematic. Land reform policy in South Africa is based on what is known as the 'willing seller, willing buyer' principle, and although there is an expropriation clause (with compensation) for situations where a seller is not willing, the constitutional protections of existing property rights make it extremely difficult for the government to exercise this clause in order to obtain land for redistribution. Where land *is* available, white farmers tend to charge exorbitant prices, which the government cannot usually afford to pay, leading some to suggest that the lack of commitment on the part of white farmers has caused land reform in South Africa to move 'at a snail's pace' (Ntsebeza 2010: 88). And while joint ventures (including contract farming, sharecropping and arrangements with white farmers to farm land now owned by an African community without resources) are becoming more common, these arrangements are not without risk. The major players in these ventures tend to be corporations and businesses, with all the power imbalances that implies with regard to the potential to disadvantage the African partner. Indeed, although the emergence of joint ventures may be seen as an 'encouraging sign' of a new willingness to cooperate over land, to date the primary beneficiaries have been white commercial farmers and corporations, and such ventures have done little to address the long-term problem of economic redistribution (Fairweather 2006: 172–3).

Over time it has become clear that a market-based approach to land reform is not suited to a situation of extreme inequality, as even when land is redistributed, it is unlikely that the new landholders will be able to compete with large-scale owners and agricultural producers, increasingly giant agri-business (Alexander and Mngxitama 2011: 53). For Lungisile Ntsebeza (2010: 89),

> This raises the question whether there can be any reconciliation in South Africa under current conditions where the bulk of the land remains in the hands of a white minority, with the majority of black Africans living under conditions of squalor and without land either in the rural of the urban areas.

As in Australia and Guatemala, land ownership in South Africa remains distinctly settler colonial in character. Land reform has fundamentally failed to either provide redress for victims of apartheid forced removals or attend to the urgent need for more radical socioeconomic redistribution. These concerns have raised significant doubt about the capacity of the current policies to contribute to South Africa's reconciliation efforts (Roux 2008: 145). Indeed, in each of these cases, the transformative capacity of policies aimed at land reform and socioeconomic redistribution has been thwarted by those intent on maintaining an unjust status quo.

Economic elites and resistance to transformation

As this chapter makes clear, continued socioeconomic inequalities pose a considerable risk to reconciliation efforts, perpetuating deep divisions and closing down spaces for democratic engagement. Too often, however, efforts at more radical redistributive transformation are resisted by economic elites intent on maintaining their wealth and privilege. These same economic elites also tend to be beneficiaries of a previous regime or earlier unjust or colonial policies that dispossessed indigenous peoples and other marginalized groups from land and other resources. Indeed, many—if not all—conflicts that appear to divide a society along the lines of ethnicity or political ideology have at their base a concern with the exploitation of natural resources, the maintenance of a cheap supply of labour, or the ownership of land, meaning that many companies and private interests have a direct stake in fomenting or abetting violent conflict. And while some claim that the short-term, profit-driven interests of the corporate and private sector are incompatible with the goals of reconciliation, it is also evident that multi-level conflict transformation will be more effective when business is involved in reconciliation efforts (Daly and Sarkin 2007: 237; Prandi 2013: 53). And this has at times been the case. In Northern Ireland, South Africa, and Guatemala, recognition of the financial costs of continuing violent conflict, including in terms of global economic participation and competition, has been a motivating factor for bringing the violence to an end. In Northern Ireland, for example, the Northern Ireland Confederation of British Industry (CBI) 'changed the terms of the political debate' about the Troubles by introducing the term 'peace dividend', and demonstrating that the desire for regional economic improvement was an area of agreement between the conflicting parties (Prandi 2013: 60).

More commonly, however, elite resistance in this domain remains considerable. The significant, if still minimal, changes to Australian land tenure discussed above reflect this resistance. The mining and pastoral industries are significant stakeholders in issues of land use and ownership in Australia and have been highly influential, often to the disadvantage of Aboriginal people. Indeed, the mining industry opposed the proposed *Native Title Act* during 1993 negotiations, and the compromises that were therefore made to ensure the passage of the legislation severely limited its transformative potential. Ultimately, rather than keeping open the political space created by activism and transformative legal judgments such as *Mabo*, the space of agonistic engagement was closed off by this compromise legislation, again driving enduring conflicts over land justice in Australia out of the public domain. These conflicts are not, however, 'resolved', and are guaranteed to surface again at some future time. In the meantime, however, the closing down of the nation's engagement over questions of land justice has further weakened relations of trust between Aboriginal and Torres Strait Islander peoples and non-indigenous Australians.

As a partial response to the history of exploitation and poor relationships between indigenous people and the corporate sector, Reconciliation Australia (RA) established what is now their flagship programme, focused on the development of Reconciliation Action Plans (RAPs). The RAP programme, launched in 2006, supports private and public organizations to make plans that 'identify clear actions with realistic targets that they can take to improve the relationship between Indigenous people and other Australians both within the organization and more widely'. Actions might include cultural awareness training or more directly redistributive goals relating to indigenous employment and training targets. As CEO at Reconciliation Australia until her departure in 2014, Leah Armstrong led an attempt to shift the focus of the RAP programme from the production of a document and the setting of targets towards 'the process and the relationships that are built along the way'. The director of the RAP programme at RA, Sharona Torrens, explains the shift in focus away from emphasis on employment targets towards an emphasis on relationship building, telling me

> [o]nce we've got those respectful relationships in place the opportunities will flow. The opportunity is a really important part of achieving or closing the gap or eliminating disadvantage but it, itself, shouldn't be the focus.

A 2012 evaluation of the programme, undertaken by RA, concluded that RAPs have had a generally positive impact on employees in organizations that have produced such a plan. For example, compared with only 46 per cent of respondents to RA's Reconciliation Barometer Survey, 75 per cent of employees in RAP organizations view the relationship between indigenous people and other Australians as very important for Australia as a nation (Auspoll 2012). Armstrong says RA takes great heart from these findings, particularly with regard to what they suggest about the capacity of the RAP programme to 'break down barriers of prejudice and perception', and she points to the 'multiplier effect' of participants who are able to take new thinking and attitudes home to their families or into their sporting clubs and so on. Fred Chaney is adamant that RAPs have contributed to some genuine changes in the culture of the Australian mining sector, beginning in the mid 1990s, and including cultural training for employees in order to change their behavior and funding philanthropic and educational initiatives. Chaney's personal observations of working with some of the biggest multinationals in the Australian mining industry include what he describes as 'a really focused and determined attempt to honour the relationships and do the right thing'. He tells me that the transformation in the corporations' relationship both to indigenous people and to ideas of reconciliation has produced 'a fantastically different world' compared to several decades ago.

However the programme also remains controversial, and was a focus of discussion in many of my Australian interviews. Jason Glanville agrees that 'there's a much greater role for the corporate sector' in reconciliation efforts than there used to be, pointing to a level of 'corporate interest, engagement and good will' that he did not observe five or six years ago, which on the whole he views as 'a good thing if it's managed properly'. However he also recognizes the limited penetration that this engagement can effect. He points specifically to the resources sector, where he says the corporate head office might be 'brilliant' but a visit to a work site will reveal 'the racist conversation you were having 30 or 40 years ago'. Glanville also acknowledges that the RAP programme has not really asked the corporate sector to engage with questions of redistribution:

> I think we've asked them to have nice events, we've asked them to build relationships and respect, to put blackfellas in jobs and create organizations that are better informed and more culturally safe, and to measure the impact of that. But I don't know that we've actually said to this community of corporate leaders, come and sit with us at the table and talk about redistribution.

He remains optimistic that there is a new generation of corporate CEOs 'who with the right kind of support could do that' but he says that to date 'we haven't asked them to do it and we haven't given them the tools to do it'. RAPs, Glanville says, have 'built a community' but there is more to do to 'activate that community'.

Many others are less optimistic. For example, while Tim Gartrell sees some positives in the RAP programme, and on balance believes that 'it's better to have them than not', he also points out that 'there's always two sides to the master/servant relationship'. Gartrell maintains that corporations setting indigenous job targets 'don't just employ people out of charity. They employ them because there are labour shortages, particularly in remote areas, and they're going to work for [the company, which is] going to make a decent profit out of their effort'. Others agree with this view, and question the programme's transformative potential. One interviewee, who preferred to remain anonymous, sees RAPs as reinforcing a 'colonization mentality' where the 'driving force [is] to lift Aboriginal people out of their mire' rather than to acknowledge the historical circumstances that have led to contemporary indigenous struggles. Leanne Townsend also tells me she is 'not a supporter' of RAPs, which she sees as little more than 'HR equity statements for corporations and businesses'. Townsend sees little in the way of meaningful accountability within the RAP process given that the agreements are 'self-developed and self-evaluated. So of course it's always going to be a great success'. This model, she says, 'suits the government' because it creates an impression of national action on indigenous employment, in particular, but she asks, 'What are the real outcomes?'

Nevertheless the fact that Australian economic elites are at least prepared to engage with questions of reconciliation and socioeconomic redistribution may be seen as a positive contribution to these efforts. Both South Africa and Guatemala face more extreme forms of elite resistance to the kind of redistributive policies that might advance reconciliation efforts.

In South Africa it remains disappointing to many that even after the TRC so few white-owned companies are prepared to acknowledge the ways in which they benefited from apartheid and commit to sharing some of their wealth (Chapman 2002: 277). Even at the time of the TRC this resistance was evident. There were some notable absentees from the three days of institutional hearings, in which representatives from the major social institutions were expected to describe their relationship to apartheid, including the South African Agricultural Union, representing white farmers, and the white Mineworkers Union. Others, including the multinational oil companies, which had been massive investors in apartheid South Africa, simply did not respond to the invitation to attend (Tutu 1999: 218). There remains anger both that the TRC only allowed such a short period in which to attempt to do justice to 'the thousands of victims who suffered at the hands of apartheid's captains of industry', and that white-owned businesses did not take this step towards reconciliation by publicly acknowledging the scope and extent to which they had benefited from apartheid (Barnard-Naudé 2008: 181, 184).

And while white elites and corporations were able to transfer their wealth into the newly democratic regime, there has been little success in motivating the private sector to develop reparations packages (Terreblanche 2012: 124; Doxtader 2004: 31). In 2003, the then president, Thabo Mbeki, announced that the ANC government would not implement the TRC's recommendations on business reparations, leaving victims' organizations such as Khulumani to take action on their own. Even more incredibly, when Khulumani brought claims against multinational corporations in the USA under the 1789 *Alien Tort Claims Act*, the South African government opposed their claims arguing that 'any verdict in favour of the claims would be likely to prejudice investment in the new South Africa'. These struggles, which are deeply painful for those who have already been victimized by the previous regime, underscore the need to shift the focus of reconciliation efforts in the economic domain away from the overwhelming attention on victims and towards a focus on the privileged who, for the most part, have remained untouched by the transition (Muvingi 2009: 179). The private sector still does not regard itself as complicit in colonial and apartheid era crimes. And as Ntsebeza (2010: 88) argues, 'Although part of the problem, they do not see themselves as part of the solution.' This attitude is summed up by Kate Lefko-Everett and her colleagues in their description of the public reaction to Desmond Tutu's revitalisation of the TRC proposal for a 2 per cent wealth tax to be levied on elite South Africans:

> Tutu's comments were met with cries of 'racism' and illegality. These appeared particularly vehement from among segments of the population where such a tax would likely generate the most revenue for anti-poverty measures. The subtext of this debate was one in which acknowledgement, shared responsibility and culpability, and redress for the broad and lasting social and economic consequences of apartheid were treated as completely unpalatable.
>
> (Lefko-Everett *et al.* 2011: 9–10)

The outcry caused by relatively modest proposals such as this indicate the depth of the resistance to more transformative redistribution in South Africa, despite growing evidence that the country's gross inequalities are retarding future development. As Biko (2013: 73–4) suggests, the South African elite needs to decide whether they want to cling on to their wealth while risking the country's long-term socioeconomic stability, or 'embrace the giant progress to be made by reaching for collective gains'. But this will require a reopening of difficult, agonistic conversations about genuine economic transformation, and at present it seems the captains of industry remain steadfastly opposed to any such dialogue.

The struggle to engage economic elites in reconciliation efforts in South Africa pales in comparison to the brute obstruction offered up by Guatemalan elites. The most contested aspects of the Guatemalan Peace Accords related to taxes and fiscal policy, and the commitment—essentially demanded by international participants—that the government must raise the ratio of taxes to GDP by 50 per cent (that is, from under 8 per cent—the lowest tax to GDP ratio in Latin America—to at least 12 per cent) by the year 2000 (Jonas 2000: 80). And while the Accords did not promise to provide land or decent jobs outright, they did indicate a new recognition of governmental responsibility to protect the well-being of the population as a whole (Jonas 2000: 168). Not unsurprisingly given the semi-feudal nature of the Guatemalan economy, these proposals were actively contested during the peace negotiations by the *Comité de Asociaciones Agrícolas, Comerciales, Industriales y Financieras* (CACIF, The Committee of Agricultural, Commercial, Industrial, and Financial Associations), which, according to Jonas (2000: 175) took the view 'We produce the wealth for Guatemala, so why should we have to pay taxes?' Guatemala is a resource-rich country that could conceivably develop policies that would address its astounding levels of poverty, and yet the unbridled self-interest of the elite has obstructed the introduction of a more equitable taxation system. The weak and dysfunctional Guatemalan state has seemingly enabled this position and allowed CACIF to obstruct any reforms that would affect its members' interests. Thus, although achieving more equitable socio-economic redistribution was a central plank of the Peace Accords, the promised reforms have never eventuated.

This resistance from economic elites also had a number of knock-on effects. Without increased revenue from taxation, the Guatemalan state was unable to pay for the hundreds of commitments in the Accords. Combined with the worsening poverty that followed the signing of the Accords, frustration at the lack of any evident peace dividend is thought to have contributed to spiralling violence, which has heightened a general sense of insecurity. This in turn has fuelled the arguments of those who seek to maintain the army's role in internal security (Jonas 2000: 98). All of this has compounded the view that the Guatemalan state's inability to stand up to a tiny minority of greedy elites has made it look 'pretty pathetic', and in the wake of persistent corruption even progressive Guatemalans consider the state so incompetent and corrupt that they too resist paying taxes, 'unwilling to feed the beast' (Nelson 2009: 218). These problems are further exacerbated by the lack of public funding for political parties, which makes them wholly reliant on the private sector, thereby stymieing the political will to tackle the question of fiscal reform. As Raquel Zelaya suggests, the parties ask themselves, 'How can we increase the taxes of those who finance us?'

None of this seems likely to change. The Guatemalan economic elite continue to manipulate politics to their own ends, allowing no space for engagement that would challenge their social and economic dominance. Indeed, in each of the countries in this study, elite self-interest, neoliberal economics, and political compromise have combined to severely limit attempts at redistributive reform that could more effectively support reconciliation efforts. Australia's modest success in terms of land reform and private sector engagement might well be attributed to differences in population scale rather than any more open political engagement. At the same time the power imbalances in relationships between marginalized groups and the political and economic elites have effectively shut down spaces for an agonistic engagement that might reopen these fundamental structural questions. These dynamics do not bode well for other areas of institutional reform that are also important to multi-level conflict transformation.

Note

1 'Closing the Gap' refers to both a campaign (driven by the Australian Human Rights Commission) to 'close the health and life expectancy gap between Aboriginal and Torres Strait Islander peoples and non-Indigenous Australians within a generation', and to a set of agreements by the Council of Australian Governments that is intended to improve opportunities and outcomes for Aboriginal and Torres Strait Islander people in health, education, housing, and life expectancy.

8 Education, policing, and justice

Beyond the economy, transforming key social institutions is a central task in a multi-level approach to conflict transformation. Important institutions might, among others, include education, health, housing, and policing and justice—all of which are essential to the delivery of equity for all groups in the population, and to ensuring that there is an educated, healthy population, enjoying a reasonable level of personal and group security, confident that the key mechanisms for supporting the rule of law will be applied impartially and without discrimination towards any group. Satisfying these conditions, and ensuring that citizens can concern themselves with more than their basic survival, will better enable a population to engage in the agonistic politics of reconciliation.

This chapter considers the challenges and efforts involved in transforming institutions of education and justice. The focus on this narrow set of institutions is merely a reflection of the space limitations in this book—clearly there are other institutions of equal importance. Nonetheless, this relatively brief analysis of two key sets of institutions conveys an understanding of the challenges and complexity involved in institutional transformation more generally. And, not insignificantly, both education and justice and policing are also institutions that have been used as deliberate means of perpetuating and extending oppression in each of the cases in this study. Colonial and conflict-era education systems require a range of reforms, including both structural desegregation and curriculum reform that enables the education of young citizens about a country's historical injustices. Police forces are perhaps even more problematic, requiring a radical transformation from institutions used to maintain the suppression of one or other group, to institutions committed to the rule of law and the security of all citizens. Each of the countries in this study has made efforts in transforming these institutions, with varying degrees of success.

Education

Paulo Freire has famously suggested that, while education 'is not the ultimate lever for social transformation {…} without it transformation cannot occur' (Freire 1998: 37). Yet in deeply divided societies it is the institutions of education themselves that require transformation. Tony Gallagher (2013: 145) advocates what he describes as a 'coexistence approach' to education reform in divided societies, arguing that this framework

> does not provide simple prescriptive answers, but it would imply that schools, whether unitary or separate, encourage processes of inter-action between communities that promote cross-cutting connections; it would encourage the development of curricula that value the rich-ness and intrigue of diversity, while promoting a sense of common good; and it would privilege the principle of social justice, and ensure the rigorous removal of arbitrary barriers to opportunity and progress. An education system working towards these aims would promote the best of democratic practice and encourage intercultural dialogue; and it would recognize that the achievement of this task is a journey rather than a destination.

Clearly these challenges are each considerable, but for the analysis here I will focus on efforts to transform education in two key ways. Firstly, in most cases, including the countries in this study, education has historically been deployed in the marginalization and subjugation of non-dominant popu-lation groups, either by structuring inequalities into the education system, or by denying access to education altogether. Linguistic exclusion of mar-ginalized groups is also common, with indigenous and other oppressed populations forced to learn in the languages of the dominant groups. The legacies of these oppressive education systems are profound, and tackling them requires sustained effort, including through a long-term commit-ment to addressing the systematic underinvestment in education for groups other than social and economic elites. Secondly, education has a role to play in addressing silences about a country's history of violence and injustice, which are typically ignored in school curricula for fear of gener-ating new conflicts and disagreement. Overcoming these fears can support the revision of national narratives in order to reflect critical truths about widespread historical violence (Cole 2007: 20).

In various ways, each country in this study has used education to help sustain an unjust regime. In Australia, Aboriginal and Torres Strait Islander people were either denied access to education altogether, or—as has now been well documented—were removed from their families and forced into assimilationist educational institutions. These institutions were often run by Christian missionaries, which supported the settler state's efforts to 'civilize' the indigenous population, overlaying their mandate of 'protection' with a proselytizing Christianity that denigrated indigenous culture and spirituality. On many missions Aboriginal people were pre-vented from expressing any form of their language or culture. Ceremony was forbidden and even names were replaced with Christian names. The education provided was, with some notable exceptions, intended only to prepare Aboriginal and Torres Strait Islander peoples for work as labourers or domestic staff. Further, where schools were not officially segregated, Aboriginal children could still be excluded 'on demand' if non-indigenous parents requested it.

In these regards, the Australian system resembled a less formalized version of the notorious apartheid system of 'Bantu education' in South Africa. The implementation of the *Bantu Education Act* of 1953 is regarded as a key strategy in the perpetuation of apartheid, and had the explicit intention of ensuring that black South Africans were controlled through racially differentiated access to education. For 40 years the Bantu education system exercised social control over the non-white population by denying them basic skills in critical thinking and problem solving through deliberately substandard education, while also providing the labour market with a pool of unskilled workers (DuPlooy *et al.* 2014). Through the Bantu Education policy South Africa entrenched the structural under-resourcing of African, coloured, and Indian learners and their educators (Biko 2013: 172). As Zackie Achmat (2010: 112) has argued, the apartheid state not only oppressed non-white South Africans through land dispossession and the exploitation of their labour, but also through 'decades of vastly inferior education'. In contrast, its investment in white education allowed most of white society to retain considerable privilege.

The situation in Guatemala was in a sense even more extreme as, after the overthrow of the democratizing Árbenz government in 1954, education in rural areas of the country practically disappeared for four decades until the signing of the Peace Accords in 1996. In light of this, three of the Accords had a direct focus on education, emphasizing its indispensible role, not just in achieving greater socioeconomic equality and reducing social exclusion, but also in creating a multiethnic, multicultural and multilingual society (Reilly 2009: 52). In Northern Ireland, the deep segregation of the education system was not imposed by the state in the same way, but the persistent divisions there have still been a significant focus of reconciliatory efforts in this institutional domain.

Each of these countries has made some limited progress in addressing these legacies of structural division in education. Australia formally ended its policies of indigenous assimilation in the 1960s, moving to policies of integration and, eventually, to a weak form of self-determination. The transformations in the education domain that resulted included the formal end of segregated schooling, although in practice, particularly in rural and remote areas, Aboriginal and Torres Strait Islander children still had limited access to formal education. Today, however, indigenous educational outcomes still trail across several key indicators including rates of numeracy, literacy and school retention and completion. Further, Jacqueline Phillips points out that the terms of these debates in Australia have shifted significantly in recent years, from concerns about addressing historical legacies to a new focus on 'penalizing parents financially for children not attending school regularly', notably through the federal government's 2012 'Stronger Futures' legislation for the Northern Territory, a neopaternalistic approach that threatens to quarantine parents' welfare payments if their children are not attending school. Phillips contends that within this new policy framework, 'We don't hear about the lack of funding to schools in Aboriginal and Torres Strait Islander communities. We don't hear about whether there are teacher shortages. We don't hear about infrastructure in a national sense.'

Further, in most areas of Australia indigenous languages remain at best marginal in schools, and some gains in this area have recently been lost. Thirty years ago there were 21 bilingual education programmes in Australia's Northern Territory, including groundbreaking programmes of 'both ways' education in remote locations such as Yirrkala in northeast Arnhem Land. The Yirrkala approach focused not only on language but on placing indigenous philosophies and ways of learning and being at the centre of the educational experience, with the explicit intention of achieving 'a reconciliation of Yolngu education and Balanda [white] education'. Today, although the Yirrkala school survives, the majority of the bilingual programmes have been decimated, and only three remain. The final blow came in the form of a 2009 policy introduced in the Northern Territory, which mandated that the first four hours of every school day must be taught in English (Stockley 2013).

And the vast majority of non-indigenous students miss out on bilingual education too. For Janet Hunt, among the most exciting things happening in reconciliation in Australia is the small number of schools where non-indigenous children have the opportunity to learn an indigenous language. Initiatives such as these, according to Hunt, 'point the way to what things could look like in the future {…} [towards] {…} a different sense of national identity'. Florence Onus agrees that teaching students the language of the local traditional owners of where the school is located would be significant for the reconciliation process in Australia, and points out that in many parts of Australia schools have these resources 'in their own backyard', with many Aboriginal and Torres Strait Islander people 'quite happy and willing to come and share about the history of the land, the culture and language and the stories'.

In contrast to Australia, the demographics in South Africa provided different motivation for educational reform, and recognition that underdevelopment in education for black, coloured and Indian South Africans was the 'weak underbelly' of the South African economy (Biko 2013: 57–8). Yet despite this awareness only limited transformation has occurred. Achmat (2010: 112) maintains that 'continuing intellectual dispossession of black, working-class and poor children is the 'worst crime of the post-apartheid era'. Parents who are themselves the product of Bantu Education remain ill-equipped to help support their children with the challenges of the new school system (Biko 2013: 178). As a result, Tim Murithi considers education in South Africa to be 'the number one challenge', which he sees 'playing itself out quite tragically'. Transforming the quality of education, particularly in poor, rural areas, will take generations, requiring both structural changes in the way schools are funded and a move away from the 'apartheid psychology' that Murithi observes is still at work in many of the schools themselves.

As a legacy of apartheid, it is clear that the education system is still lagging, both in terms of teacher training and competency and the provision of physical infrastructure. Teacher shortages led to a policy known as 'inferior substitution', which allowed surplus teachers in areas such as the arts and social sciences to be appointed to positions in maths and science for which they were not suitably qualified or experienced, meaning that many struggled or even failed to come to work (Biko 2013: 181–2; Mattes 2012: 140). Persistent disparities in school infrastructure are truly shocking, with some private, almost wholly white schools providing facilities equivalent to the best in the world, while just kilometres away there are students in schools with no desks, or no windows, and extremely primitive, if any, ablution facilities. As Biko (2013: 195–7) points out, of the 24,793 ordinary public schools in South Africa, 3,344 have no electricity, 2,402 have no water supply, while a further 2,611 have an unreliable water supply, 11,450 still use pit-latrine toilets and 913 lack any ablution facilities. To date, there is little evidence that the school-building programmes and increases in government expenditure in education have had any impact on educational attainment, with the Born Frees in fact demonstrating lower levels of high school completion than the immediately preceding generation (Mattes 2012: 141). The transformations that were anticipated from educational reforms have simply not materialized. Biko (2013: 187–9) attributes this to 'a series of glaring policy errors', that together suggest that South Africa has 'failed to comprehend, diagnose and cure its biggest national crisis'.

The language of instruction in South African schools is also considered an area of apartheid legacy in need of significant reform, although this has proven to be another highly contentious area. The Soweto student uprising in 1976 was sparked by a government decision to make Afrikaans the first language of instruction for all South African students, indicating that this issue has been highly politicized for several decades at least. Single-medium education was also one of the final sticking points in negotiating the new South African constitution. The ANC refused to countenance proposals allowing single-medium education, which it recognized as the National Party's efforts to maintain white privilege by refusing to be 'forced' to cater for other languages in formerly white schools. Blade Nzimande, the ANC's chief negotiator on education, insisted that 'to constitutionally entrench single-medium and clearly Afrikaans schools would have entrenched one of the relics of apartheid forever' (quoted in Segal and Cort 2011: 175). The eventual compromise, during a late night negotiating session close to the negotiation deadline, allowed for single-medium institutions to be included as one of the alternatives for the state to consider in upholding people's right to be taught in their home language.

But while Nzimande declared that this deal had 'once and for all closed the chapter on apartheid education in the country' (quoted in Segal and Cort 2011: 182), the reality has been far less transformative. The structural legacy of apartheid has all but overwhelmed the ambitions to offer instruction in multiple languages, and in many schools English or Afrikaans is still the primary medium for instruction. Yet, as Achmat (2010: 113–14) observes, in many communities where English is the primary language in the school, 'the community does not speak English, the family does not speak English, and the teachers themselves do not speak English as a first language', meaning that the majority of African children today remain 'dispossessed of their mother tongue'. The significant impact that this has on young children's ability to develop the capacity for abstract thought, particularly during the first six years of their education, suggests that these legacies will persist for decades to come. Yet as Namhla Mniki-Mangaliso acknowledges, a significant part of the resistance to including African languages in the school system in fact comes from black parents who want their children to be able to work in a white environment where people speak English and Afrikaans. Mniki-Mangaliso believes that these attitudes have taken South Africa 'ten steps backwards'.

In Guatemala, transforming access to education for the dispossessed majority became the 'first test' of the state's commitment to creating institutions capable of serving a multiethnic, multilingual society (del Valle Escalante 2009: 128). In 1995 the government introduced the *Programa Nacional de Autogestión para el Desarrollo Educativo* (PRONADE, the National Programme for Educational Development) with support from international funders. PRONADE devolved responsibility for building schools, hiring teachers, and overseeing curriculum and instruction to local boards made up of parents and community leaders, with the goal of ensuring that at least 70 per cent of elementary-school-age children were attending school. The programme saw new schools open quickly across most of Guatemala, and by 2005 the stated goals had been reached in most areas. This success was matched by the Guatemalan Ministry of Education, which also set about building schools in rural communities, adding Grades 4 to 6 to schools that had previously ended at Grade 3, and providing more middle and high schools in non-urban areas. The department also attempted to improve teacher training in the national school system, including some minimal 'cultural sensitivity training' to address ignorance and stereotyping about Mayan culture. Yet despite these efforts, schools remained under-stocked with critical materials, and teacher discontent remains high. During a 2003 strike, teachers demanded that 'Education reform be put into practice that responded to both the spirit and the letter of the Peace Accords from which it was born' (Maxwell 2009: 86–7).

Moreover, while more children in Guatemala are now beginning school or have access to schools that did not exist before, attainment and completion rates are still dismal. In the decade up until 2009, of students beginning school, 42 per cent failed the first grade and less than 30 per cent reached the sixth grade. Only 10 per cent completed secondary school and a mere 1 per cent went on to graduate from university (Reilly 2009: 52). The figures in rural areas may be worse than this, although the PRONADE schools do perform slightly better due to parental involvement and locally hired teachers (Moore 2007: 4–5). Nevertheless, although PRONADE has clearly increased access to schooling in rural areas, questions have been raised about the quality of education available in these schools (compared to their urban counterparts), in part because the devolved structure sees schools run by community committees without the power to develop the educational system their community needs (Gill 2012). As a result, Irma Alicia Velásquez, one of only eight indigenous Guatemalans with a PhD, believes that the education system in Guatemala remains 'very weak' meaning that 'a big part of the life of this country is missing'. Otilia Lux blames these failures in educational reforms on the associated failure to fully implement the Peace Accords. If this has happened as was intended, Lux maintains, Guatemala would 'have more young people with an education, with jobs, they would have been able to create technological institutions in the north, the south, east, west {…}. We would have well-prepared young people. We wouldn't have violent young people'.

Guatemala also made some efforts to move beyond the traditional single language of instruction (Spanish) to include some of the 22 recognized Mayan languages in classroom teaching. The indigenous accord supported the creation of *Dirección General de Educación Bilingüe Intercultural* (DIGEBI, the General Directorate of Intercultural Bilingual Education), which officially made bilingual education a permanent part of the Ministry of Education and promised Mayan children access to schooling in their heritage languages (Maxwell 2009: 84). However, here too structural problems have intervened to produce a very different reality. DIGEBI has struggled to find native speakers of the 22 languages who are trained as linguists and educators and therefore able to develop teaching materials in all these languages (Maxwell 2009: 89). This is not helped by the continued under-investment in public education (less than 2 per cent of GDP), which has also discouraged continuing international contributions. Thus, despite the ambitions of the Accords, it is evident that a 'major shift' still needs to occur to increase educational capacity and capability.

In contrast to the massive inequalities that have characterized education in Australia, South Africa, and Guatemala, Northern Ireland has faced a different set of structural legacies requiring redress. The history of the conflict in Northern Ireland, and the deep divisions that both structured and perpetuated it, also saw the development of parallel but entirely segregated education systems. Yes, despite some efforts to transform this situation, in fact very little has changed. The first independent integrated school in Northern Ireland was established in 1981, increasing to ten schools by 1989. However it was not until after the Education Reform (Northern Ireland) Order 1989 that integrated education became a distinct 'sector' with state support and clear guidelines for their creation either as new Grant Maintained Integrated (GMI) schools or through the transformation of existing Protestant or Catholic schools (Controlled Integrated (CI) schools).

To be considered integrated, schools must broadly reflect social demographics, although schools transforming to integration may begin with as little as 10 per cent of students from the minority religion, increasing to an overall balance of at least 70:30 within ten years. This policy saw the integrated sector grow to 61 schools by the end of 2008, including 20 CI and 42 GMI schools (Donnelly and Hughes 2009: 148). To further advance this process, in 2010 the Northern Ireland Assembly passed a motion advocating a target of 20 per cent of children in integrated schools by 2020. This goal, however, has met with considerable resistance particularly from the Catholic community, which contests the very idea of 'segregation' as an accurate representation of what they see as parents' preference for Catholic education (Nolan 2012: 156). As a result, only 6 per cent of children in Northern Ireland attend integrated schools—a statistic that raises concerns about the impact of continued educational segregation on the peace process. One view advanced by education experts is that segregated schooling acts as a form of 'social apartheid' in which, regardless of what is taught in the schools, the very fact of segregation 'initiates children into the conflict' by emphasizing differences and hostility, and maintaining mutual ignorance and suspicion (Bell, Hansson and McCaffery 2010: 17).

Others, however, contest the value of integration as a means of contributing to reconciliation and conflict transformation. Donnelly and Hughes (2009: 149) point out that the drive towards greater integration is based on the 'contact hypothesis', which assumes that school-based contact between divided groups can lead to better intergroup relations. This idea is, however, contradicted (or at least questioned) by much empirical research. In their research looking at behavior within integrated schools (in both Northern Ireland and Israel), Donnelly and Hughes (2009: 168–70) found that the attitudes of teachers are key. They point to the complexities that inevitably arise when integration is imposed in a segregated culture in which teachers are mostly drawn from one community and may in fact be quite opposed to the transformation process. In Northern Ireland they found that improving intergroup relations through integrated education was seen as a matter of structure and procedure, with little understanding of the processes by which schools could develop greater tolerance and respect among students. Many teachers also expressed a 'deep-seated fear' about the challenges of engaging with each other (or with pupils) on issues that may lead to confrontation or disagreement. As a result, controversial issues were avoided and relations within the schools were often underpinned by ambiguity and latent tensions.

In light of these various forms of resistance, Wilhelm Verwoerd suspects that the catalyst for greater educational integration in Northern Ireland will be economic. He tells me there is a growing view that 'the levels of segregation are just becoming unaffordable' and suggests that budget strain 'might be the only way to get through this'. Neil Jarman agrees, suggesting that while the Catholic Church is 'reluctant' to move towards greater integration, eventually it will have to succumb to economic pressures, at least with regard to the sharing of resources and facilities. As Jarman says, Northern Ireland 'can't keep all their schools half full'. However Ray Mullan suggests that the 'deep institutional resistance' to integration in education within the Catholic Church and community in Northern Ireland will remain a barrier to further transformation because, 'the Catholic Church believes that if they didn't have their own Catholic schools the children would lose their religion {...} and undermine their sense of Irish identity'. These deep-seated concerns underscore the challenges of further integration. As Mullan explains:

> To have an educational system where both identities were respected, you'd have to have Irish language, you would have to have sport which represented both cultural identities—Gaelic football as well as rugby— you'd have to ensure that history was taught in a way that was respectful of the folk memories and the symbolic events of both communities.

In his view, the small number of integrated schools points to the challenges involved, but also underscore the fact that 'it's not impossible'.

Transforming the curriculum

Concerns about the capacity for structural reforms to address historical legacies in ways that will contribute to reconciliation also animate the second relevant area of educational reform. Central to the issues likely to cause tensions in integrated schooling, or indeed in schooling in divided societies more generally, is the teaching of history. In the wake of violent conflict or historical injustice new history programmes are thought to contribute to establishing a new national narrative—or even multiple narratives—intended to include and 're-humanize' former enemies and marginalized groups in the official history from which they have been previously excluded (Cole 2007: 20–1). Thus, reform of curricula, and especially history curricula, has also been a key area of reconciliation effort in each of the countries in this study.

In Northern Ireland, the Education Reform (Northern Ireland) Order 1989 introduced Education for Mutual Understanding (EMU), which included a focus on cultural heritage, as part of the new curriculum for all grant-aided schools (Bell, Hansson and McCaffery 2010: 17). The EMU curriculum complemented other initiatives such as the development of common programmes and textbooks for teaching history and religion in schools (Gallagher 2013: 136). Some years later, in 2007 the curriculum was changed again, with the introduction of Personal Development and Mutual Understanding (PDMU). The *new* new curriculum included elements on 'Local and Global Citizenship', which were more explicit in asking students to 'Investigate how and why conflict, including prejudice, stereotyping, sectarianism and racism may arise in the community', to 'Investigate ways of managing conflict and promoting community relations and reconciliation', and to 'Investigate the long and short term causes and consequences of the partition of Ireland and how it has influenced Northern Ireland today, including key events and turning points' (Bell, Jarman and Harvey 2010: 19). These changes were intended to counter many schools' aversion to teaching about Northern Ireland's recent past because it was seen to be too controversial for the classroom (Bell, Hansson and McCaffery 2010: 25).

However the impact of these new curricula has relied on the skills and attitudes of teachers, with research suggesting that many schools met the statutory requirements of EMU, but did not deliver the programme in the spirit it was intended (Bell, Hansson, and McCaffery 2010: 18). As is common to many institutions in deeply divided societies, avoiding conflict in education is often prioritized over more agonistic and potentially transformative engagements. Indeed, Derick Wilson sees a form of 'collusion' within the teaching training system in Northern Ireland that maintains a 'culture of silence and politeness'. Kate Turner has also seen evidence of this among recent teaching graduates who are 'terrified' and will say,

> I've learnt history, I've learnt how to be a teacher—but what am I going to do when I talk to a class and little Jimmy's mum turns up at the school the next day and says, 'What the hell are you teaching my son?' Because I'm pretty sure I'm not going to be teaching children what they're taught at home.

South Africa and Guatemala have also attempted to grapple with their recent histories through revised curricula, with varying degrees of success. The South African approach involved the development of what is known as Outcomes Based Education (OBE) and the introduction of Curriculum 2005. The aims of Curriculum 2005, introduced in 1997, were ambitious. They included promoting the values of the new constitution, contributing to rebuilding a divided nation, promoting a sense of national identity, offering equal education for all, inspiring a constituency that had been oppressed by the previous education dispensation and policies, and establishing a socially valued knowledge set to be transmitted to following generations. Yet Biko (2013: 188) contends that the ambitions of OBE and Curriculum 2005 simply could not be met within the significant constraints of South Africa's education infrastructure. Teachers in South Africa have had an inadequate level of training to be able to grapple with the subtleties and complexities of the curriculum through methods such as group participation and problem-solving exercises (Mattes 2012: 150). And research suggests that the 'outcome-based' Curriculum 2005 has failed to effect attitudinal change, in part because democratic values have been too implicit in the curriculum for most students to grasp, but also because the curriculum itself is too 'constructivist' in its approach to knowledge, with the framers perhaps 'embarrassed at the prospect of replacing one official orthodoxy with another' (Mattes 2012: 140).

In Guatemala the problems have been even more complex as, unlike South Africa—where the TRC at least created a public archive able to inform a new curriculum—the country attempted to build a new curriculum from a history of censorship and the manipulation of information. Gustavo Porras declares that the previous school curriculum was 'absurd', forcing pupils to focus on things such as United States geography, which was 'wholly inappropriate as part of a curriculum to respond to students' needs'. In light of the country's history, the Catholic truth commission (Recovery of Historical Memory Project (REMHI) 1999: 315), maintained instead that education officials in Guatemala had an 'obligation to carry out curricular reforms' that would 'provide an accurate account of what happened during the armed conflict in the country', including the findings of both REMHI and the CEH. Indeed, as Emilio del Valle Escalante (2009: 156) has argued, in a society like Guatemala where history is characterized by 'plunder, genocide, foreign capitalist intervention, and four decades of state-sponsored terrorism', transforming the teaching of history by 'rescuing historical memory' should form the most important curricular axis, not just to support intercultural education but in support of 'the national project' as well. Daniel Saquec is critical of the limited extent of reform to the history curriculum. While he agrees that the curriculum should take account of the REMHI and CEH reports, instead he says 'It speaks about colonial history from a Western viewpoint, with little reference to the history of indigenous peoples, let alone what happened in the conflict'.

However, the team of international experts and Mayan scholar-educators who worked to produce a new national curriculum did intend to transform Guatemalan education by creating a total curriculum from kindergarten through to Grade 12 designed to celebrate the diversity of Guatemala's multicultural heritage (Maxwell 2009: 87). Again, however, the results have been disappointing, with the 2003 curriculum still proving 'sadly ethnocentric', presupposing a western European cultural base and reducing Mayan elements of the curriculum to folklore and cultural patrimony rather than a vibrant part of contemporary Guatemalan society (Maxwell 2009: 89–91). As a result, the new curriculum not only fails to address the needs of Mayan communities, it possibly even insults them (Gill 2012), further entrenching the deep social divisions it is intended to address. Rosalina Tuyuc believes the Guatemalan state is 'not interested' in further reforms of the history curriculum because 'it was the state which was responsible for the extermination policy' of Mayan peoples and has no desire for students to learn about it. And Rosenda Camey contrasts state efforts, which she sees an attempt to assimilate Mayan children, with Mayan-led 'community and family strategies to educate our children from our homes based on our cosmovision and our culture as Mayans'. Saquec also praises the efforts of Maya at local and regional levels, such as in the Ixil area, where the Ixil people are 'creating their own educational process' intended to 'strengthen the Ixil language' and ensure that 'children do not abandon their own culture and family and immerse themselves in a completely different culture at school'. He points out that such initiatives have been 'acknowledged positively by the Ministry of Education and by NGOs that work in intercultural bilingual education'.

Australia has a similar history of historical omission or revision, which to date has only been partially addressed. In his 1968 Boyer lectures, the anthropologist W.E.H Stanner spoke of the 'great Australian silence' about the injustices perpetrated against Aboriginal and Torres Strait Islander people. Stanner (2009: 188–9) argued that this silence in Australian history books could not be explained by mere 'absent-mindedness' but had been structured into the Australian identity, creating 'a view from a window which has been carefully placed to exclude a whole quadrant of the landscape'. Over time, this silence began to be addressed, and during the last 30 or so years of the twentieth century Aboriginal and Torres Strait Islander people increasingly demanded that history also be told from their perspectives. Public reports such as the Royal Commission into Aboriginal Deaths in Custody (RCIADIC 1991, discussed further below) and other efforts to foreground Aboriginal and Torres Strait Islander experiences contributed to a new and contested account of the extent of historical injustice, which eventually made its way into school curricula to some limited extent. Linda Burney, who played a central role in developing the first mandatory Aboriginal education policy in Australia, maintains that 'if there was ever an exercise and an effective tool of reconciliation it is making sure that curriculum in schools reflects the truth'. In the 1980s, Burney and her colleagues in the New South Wales Aboriginal Education Unit played a key role incorporating Aboriginal perspectives into the curriculum and producing the first Aboriginal education policy in Australia, which was later implemented in state schools across the country. Today, she points out, 'Aboriginal Australia' is a core component of state education curricula, something she sees as 'one of the key planks of reconciliation'. Indeed, Burney suggests that 'the most powerful, effective, broad way' to introduce this form of 'truth telling' into Australian society 'is through school curriculum, because everybody goes to school'.

Nevertheless, it seems that the impact of these changes has been limited by school-based decision making about what could be taught in some areas of the curriculum, which meant that this critical history does not feature in some schools because some principals do not support its teaching (Council for Aboriginal Reconciliation 2000: 57). Further, a 2014 review recommended that the Australian national history curriculum be revised to 'better recognise the contribution of Western civilization, our Judeo-Christian heritage, the role of economic development and industry and the democratic underpinning of the British system of government to Australia's development' (Donnelly and Wiltshire 2014: 246). Thus, despite decades of work to transform education in Australia in ways that would support broader reconciliation efforts, it seems resistance to addressing the nation's historical legacies is as entrenched as ever.

Policing, justice, and the rule of law

In a very different institutional space, but one no less important for reconciliation efforts, each of the countries in this study has also worked to transform their policing and justice systems. Histories of violence and oppression are almost universally characterized by the subversion or suspension of the rule of law such that public confidence in law and legal institutions is profoundly undermined. Rebuilding these institutions is important to renewing confidence in the state and in the rule of law as a restraint on abuse and injustice (Bell 2013: 249). The failure to address this demand can have the effect of entrenching feelings of powerlessness among those who have been abused by the law, creating significant obstacles to reconciliation efforts (McGregor 2007: 119). Thus, (re)establishing the rule of law is recognized as essential to lasting peace and reconciliation efforts, demonstrating that the state has agreed to reform the institutions responsible for past crimes and provide suitable mechanisms for accountability and oversight (Verdeja 2009: 25). As Ernesto Verdeja (2009: 58) maintains, 'the need for a robust, fair, and transparent legal order is an institutional *sine qua non* of long-term reconciliation'. Indeed, it is not possible to conceive of an agonistic politics in which citizens are able to engage in a vibrant clash of passions without resort to violence unless the principles of the rule of law are accepted and institutionalized, and violence (including state violence) is itself rejected (Verdeja 2009: 61).

One aspect of the restoration of the rule of law involves the investigation and possible prosecution of past human rights abuses—that is, ending the impunity of a previous regime. The rule of law ensures that no one, including government officials, is above the law or can act outside it. Ensuring that such a system has credibility among citizens requires the investigation of violations of civil and political rights to ensure that past and present government officials are held accountable for such violations (Sikkink 2011: 155). This may take the form of prosecutions for past crimes, although prosecutions are not without risk, and the criminalization of political violence is 'potentially destabilizing', transforming actions that may previously have been championed as acts of duty or service into crimes that demand justice and require punishment (Leebaw 2008: 101). Alternatively, a society may pursue various form of truth commission or public enquiry as a means of bringing past wrongs to light, as will be discussed further in Chapter 10. What is important, as Lorna McGregor (2007: 118) argues, is that reconciliation efforts 'adopt a comprehensive and reflective approach connecting the complicity of the past to the role of the legal system as a whole'. McGregor contends that the failure to do this in Northern Ireland has been highly problematic. Contrasted with the high number of prosecutions against paramilitaries and political activists, the lack of prosecutions against state agents, including those involved in high profile 'incidents' like Bloody Sunday (which saw the British military kill 13 civil rights protestors) has perpetuated a perception of bias on the part of the legal system that continues to support the general impunity of state agents (McGregor 2007: 119–20).

These critiques of state impunity suggest that policing reform in deeply divided societies requires going beyond mere professionalization if efforts to restore the legitimacy of police are to have meaning. As Mary O'Rawe (2008: 126) suggests, in these contexts 'what is needed it not merely to reform a state institution but to transform the experiencing of policing for police and policed alike'. In most societies, and most especially in deeply divided societies, the police are viewed as defenders of the status quo, including both government and social and economic elites. As an institution it tends to be 'closed, self-protective and self-perpetuating {…} with high degrees of self-esteem and strong internal cultures', meaning that police officers often resort to violence, remain open to corruption, and can be difficult to hold to account. In divided societies police have a history of exerting the most control over members of non-dominant communities, producing further alienation and antagonism between these communities and the police (Hadden 2013: 74). Transforming policing in divided societies requires that the police force become representative of the whole community; that police operations be carried out by integrated police units wherever this is possible; and that police be trained in understanding and respecting cultural differences. Such changes take time, meaning that divided societies need to plan ahead for a lengthy process of institutional change over the many years it will take to recruit and train a more representative cohort of officers (Hadden 2013: 79).

However, in many divided societies there remains a degree of denial concerning the extent of change necessary to transform policing and police culture (O'Rawe 2008: 126). Australia has certainly been grappling with these challenges for many decades, with some progress but much lingering animosity between indigenous peoples and the justice system. Relations between Aboriginal and Torres Strait Islander peoples and various incarnations of police forces over time have been highly conflictual, reflecting the police role as agents of a colonial state that perpetuated a range of destructive interventions under the regime of 'protection' (Chan 1997: 82). Indeed, Finnane (1994: 111) has argued that

> [i]f any characteristic has distinguished the police in Australia from their original models in England and Ireland, it has been their continually changing role in the government of Aborigines. The police as an institution was not present at the first dispossession in eastern Australia. But the formation of the police forces from the 1830s on added to the colonial state an apparatus of great power and flexibility in completing the process.

The resentment and mistrust that has evolved from this history remains the most notable characteristic of indigenous-police relations in Australia. For many Aboriginal and Torres Strait Islander people it remains impossible to seek redress for crimes committed against them through a system that they understand as an apparatus of state violence.

In the late 1980s, these concerns came to wide public attention through the Royal Commission into Aboriginal Deaths in Custody (RCIADIC), which was established in response to public concern over the deaths in police custody and prisons of 99 Aboriginal people between January 1980 and May 1989. The Commission concluded that the antipathy that many indigenous people held towards the police was the result not only of historical events, but also of their contemporary experiences of contact with the police (Royal Commission into Aboriginal Deaths in Custody 1991: 195). Yet despite significant efforts at reform in the decades since the Commission, Aboriginal and Torres Strait Islander people remain overrepresented in every part of the justice system, including making up over a quarter of the national prisoner population (27 per cent) despite being only around 2.4 per cent of the total population (Australian Bureau of Statistics 2013).

In large part these high rates of incarceration are attributed to a form of racialized over-policing that contributes to high arrest rates and continued poor relations between Aboriginal and Torres Strait Islander people and police. High profile incidents such as the 2008 death of an elderly Aboriginal man, who the coroner described as having 'cooked to death' in the back of a police wagon in Western Australia, only exacerbate these concerns. Leanne Townsend tells me that most Aboriginal and Torres Strait Islander people believe, first, that such a death would never have occurred if the person in custody was non-indigenous, but second, that if this had been a non-indigenous death significant reform of policing would have been an immediate consequence. Townsend contends that 'There's acceptance from blackfellas that that's just how it is. We're treated that way. And an acceptance from white fellas that it's acceptable to treat blackfellas that way.'

Further reform is also resisted. While still in her role at ANTaR, Jacqueline Phillips helped the organization launch a campaign to commemorate the 20-year anniversary of the Royal Commission into Aboriginal Deaths in Custody, with the objective of reducing Aboriginal and Torres Strait Islander imprisonment rates through significant policy reforms. The primary focus of such reform is on the idea of justice reinvestment, which would see the diversion of resources from prisons and corrective services towards local level community prevention initiatives. However, Phillips tells me that it has been very difficult to get 'political traction' on these reforms, in part due to the 'tough-on-crime' rhetoric that infects much Australian politics, combined with resistance from police unions. These attitudes have been influential in limiting the reconciliatory impact of policing reforms, and yet little effort has been made to open up alternative political spaces in which these views could be engaged more effectively.

In Northern Ireland, police reform has been high on the political agenda, and yet the policing deal that was intrinsic to the Belfast Agreement is still not secure (Nolan 2012: 8). Historically, the police force in Northern Ireland, formerly the Royal Ulster Constabulary (RUC), had been drawn almost exclusively from the Protestant/unionist community and, through 'discriminatory and draconian' conduct, has contributed to the deep alienation of the Catholic/nationalist community (Coulter and Murray 2008: 3). Indeed, many in the Catholic/nationalist community have viewed the police as an entirely illegitimate and sectarian force complicit in significant human rights abuses during the Troubles (Hadden 2013: 83) and actively involved in 'shoring up a sectarian state through implementation of its counterinsurgency measures' (Lundy 2009: 330–1). Divergent understandings of the nature of policing in Northern Ireland led to quite different views about whether the service was capable of reform or should be scrapped altogether as an illegitimate institution. Through the negotiation process the parties settled on a compromise between these positions, agreeing on a process of evaluation and re-structuring to make the police force more representative of, and accountable to, both communities (Bell 2013: 254). The resulting Patten Report, with its 175 recommendations for future policing, applied the consociational principles that had structured the Belfast Agreement to the creation of a representative policing structure, including a requirement for 50/50 recruitment from among the two communities (Byrne and Monaghan 2008: 23).

In the wake of the Patten Report, policing reform has remained high on the political agenda in Northern Ireland, although a perception of limited progress has been destabilizing for the peace process overall

(Lundy 2009: 330–1). Certainly many significant reforms have occurred in the renamed Police Service of Northern Ireland (PSNI), but these have been insufficient to overcome the legacies of the past, for two primary reasons. First, the transformation to a more representative service has struggled to maintain momentum. The requirement for 50/50 recruiting was allowed to lapse in 2011 after the PSNI reached the target of 30 per cent Catholic recruits. Since then, both the 'tempo' of Catholic applications has declined and the pattern of Catholics leaving the PSNI after only a few years of service has persisted, meaning that the service remains 'top-heavy' with Protestant officers (Nolan 2012: 58–9). A recent Peace Monitoring Report suggests that any further erosion in the balance between Catholic and Protestant officers 'will put in doubt the representative nature of the service—an essential pillar of the peace settlement' (Nolan 2012: 8). Thus, although the devolution of policing and justice to the Northern Ireland Assembly through the 2010 Hillsborough Agreement is often invoked as the 'last piece of the jigsaw' of the peace process (Nolan 2012: 57) in fact positive experiences of policing remain minimal for both communities. Securing Sinn Féin's endorsement was essential for bringing republicans on board with the reforms, but as a result there is now suspicion in some sections of the Protestant/unionist community that their interests are being left behind. At the same time, the legacy of policing in Northern Ireland remains a 'sensitive and emotive issue' for large sections of the Catholic/nationalist community, who have limited (and usually negative) experiences of policing (Byrne and Monaghan 2008: 5–6).

Second, and related to these historical experiences, there is criticism that the reform of the PSNI did not go far enough in terms of acknowledging the role of policing during the years of the Troubles. Some viewed the Patten Commission as a possible precursor to a formal truth commission, as the process of the review included hearing stories of loss both from the families of police officers who had been killed or injured, and from members of the public who had experienced police brutality or had family members killed by police (O'Rawe 2008: 113). In response to the recommendations arising from these testimonies, the PSNI established the Historical Enquiries Team (HET) as a contribution to dealing with the past and building public confidence in policing, particularly among the Catholic/nationalist community (Lundy 2009: 331). The role of the HET has been to examine all 3,268 deaths attributed to the Northern Ireland conflict, an approach which, while important for the individual families concerned, has failed to deliver an analysis of the 'bigger picture' or the thematic issues related to 'institutions or practices that go to the heart of the causes, context and consequences of the conflict' (Lundy 2009: 339). Transforming policing and justice remains, at least to some extent, constrained by public memories, attitudes and identities that derive from the period of violent conflict and the deep cleavages that continue to divide the society, meaning that each community has found the process of reform extremely difficult (Byrne and Monaghan 2008: 111).

As a result, further transformation in this institutional domain in Northern Ireland will require a deeper engagement with the legacy of the conflict, which may in turn have the effect of 'unblocking' other arenas of social and political resistance to reconciliation efforts (O'Rawe 2008: 126–7). Initiatives addressing such concerns have been developed by organizations such as Intercomm through their Communities and Policing in Transition programme, which brings together community members, statutory organizations and police to develop local plans for improving community–police relations. Kate Wilson from Intercomm tells me that the success of these programmes lie in their relational focus, opening spaces for engagement between police, former RUC, and ex-combatants, and encouraging participants to view police officers as 'a man or a woman with children who is trying to do the best job that they can'. Yet despite the transformations that are evident in these relational efforts, Wilson sees that policing in Northern Ireland still has 'a long journey ahead', and acknowledges that their work is 'only really scratching the surface'. Mistrust still colours relationships with both communities, particularly unionist communities who 'feel that the police is not their police any more' and republicans who still see the PSNI as 'a security force of the Crown'.

Like Northern Ireland, South Africa also decided against scrapping the police and justice systems there, and has similarly attempted a process of root and branch reform. Legal institutions in South Africa were deeply complicit in the apartheid regime yet, despite resistance, there have been some significant transformations of the justice system. Most notable is the establishment of the Constitutional Court, which has in turn influenced the transformation of the wider legal system. Nevertheless, the South African Department of Justice and Constitutional Development (2012: 8–9) has acknowledged that the aspirations laid out in the 1997 five-year national strategy *Justice Vision 2000*, 'largely remain unaccomplished', and recommends further reforms across the judicial system.

Reforming the police force was also a daunting challenge facing the new democratic government. A further compromise required in the negotiated settlement in South Africa was a 'sunset clause' protecting the jobs of apartheid-era civil servants for the following five years. This meant that the new government inherited largely intact state institutions, including the police force and the majority of its existing personnel. Unfortunately, as Graeme Simpson (2000: 7) notes, these officers also brought 'a legacy of popular mistrust and a crisis of legitimacy'. While the settlement effectively dismantled the illegitimate sources of authority that had sustained and policed the apartheid regime, it was considerably less effective in establishing a new and legitimate replacement. Simpson (2000: 8) contends that the impact of these compromises, and the magnitude of the resulting challenges, 'cannot be understated', involving both institutional and cultural transformation along with the establishment of rules and sanctions that support the aims and values of the new constitution. Kindiza Ngubeni echoes this view about the level of public mistrust in the South African police, who historically were seen as 'protecting the system' rather than protecting non-white citizens from the injustices of apartheid. However he also understands the challenges involved in transformation for police, who had to shift from policing political activists to 'dealing with real criminals'. To support this transformation Ngubeni has been working with police in community-police forums that allow the development of shared priorities. As a result of these efforts, Ngubeni sees communities 'starting to trust and starting to own the police'.

Some significant changes in policing in South Africa have taken place. Unlike Northern Ireland, the South African police service was already broadly representative of population demographics at the time of the transition. This was enhanced by the incorporation of former members of the ANC and Pan Africanist Congress armed forces into the South African military and police service, which was negotiated as part of the settlement. More urgent was the need for transformations in the gender balance among serving police, as well as significant change in the racial composition of senior police ranks, which were largely occupied by white Afrikaner men. Symbolic changes were also important, transforming uniforms and insignia, and the name of the institution from a 'force' to the South African Police *Service* (Rauch 2000). Addressing the legitimacy deficit among the South African population has proved far more difficult however, particularly with regard to internal oversight and accountability for police misconduct (Newham 2005).

Transformations have been further compromised by the social panic concerning the rising crime rate in South Africa, which Biko (2013: 210) maintains has produced new abuses and escalating police brutality that receives little oversight, and is accompanied by increasing community vigilantism. Research on civil protest has observed 'heavy-handed and violent' police action that appears to draw on 'the repertoires of apartheid-era repression of protest', further undermining police legitimacy (von Holdt 2011: 30). This observation was underscored by the violence at the Marikana mine in 2012, which resulted in 44 deaths and almost 80 people injured. The images of a largely black police presence turning their weapons on the striking miners was a tragic reminder of the extent of transformation still required in the South African policing and justice system.

Unlike Northern Ireland and South Africa, Guatemala has had to attempt to build a legitimate policing and justice system almost from scratch. During the years of *la violencia* in Guatemala, government forces were able to exercise absolute power without any fear of punishment. For the civilian population, this meant a total sense of powerlessness resulting from their inability to obtain protection or justice (Recovery of Historical

Memory Project (REMHI) 1999: xxxiii). The judiciary was entirely subordinated to the military during the armed conflict, with disputes primarily resolved though extrajudicial mechanisms involving extreme violence. Poor, rural, Mayan communities in particular observed the justice system to be an extension of the forms of oppression and discrimination to which they had been subjected since colonial times (Arriaza and Roht-Arriaza 2010: 214). The lack of effective judicial oversight in fact facilitated the violence and accentuated the arbitrary application of the law. Despite efforts to reform this situation since 1996, today most Guatemalans remain distrustful of the law and the legal system, perceiving it as an institution that benefits only the rich and powerful (Sieder 2008: 71–2). According to José Suasnavar, this lack of trust extends even to the need for community supervision of exhumations, ensuring 'relatives were witnesses to what was happening because nobody trusted the justice system'.

These concerns were addressed to a significant degrees in the Peace Accords, five of which made explicit reference to the justice sector and proposed changes that implied 'root-and-branch transformation' of both legal culture and practice, including a doubling of the budget and a significant expansion of institutional coverage around the country (Sieder 2008: 73). But while some things have improved since 1996, for the most part the justice system remains a poor avenue for Guatemalans seeking justice (Arriaza and Roht-Arriaza 2010: 214). While a number of my interviewees praised the transformation of the office of Attorney-General, which is seen to have become far more thorough, professional, and trustworthy as an arm of justice (a situation that may again change since Claudia Paz y Paz was ousted from the post in 2014), Alvaro Pop maintains that people in Guatemala 'don't go to the courts in search of justice {...} because in reality the laws in Guatemala, in the majority of cases, do not provide justice'. The increasing control of the Guatemalan state by organized crime has dramatically hindered reforms, which, along with resistance among political and business elites and justice-sector employees, means the justice system remains highly ineffective. This is compounded by the vulnerability of judges, lawyers and public prosecutors to intimidation, interference and corruption, to the point that judges are considered at such high risk they are unable to obtain life insurance (Sieder 2008: 79–80) and the investigation of wartime massacres can still led to threats (Arriaza and Roht-Arriaza 2010: 214). And while human rights activists hoped that the limited reestablishment of the rule of law would end impunity for those responsible for human rights violations, many Guatemalan citizens have instead experienced tougher policing of law and order, much as in South Africa (Sieder 2008: 74–5). Julio Balconi maintains that the whole justice system has become a 'vicious circle' where 'the police don't really work well. The courts don't either. The prison system is no good either because that's where the criminal gangs continue to threaten the people, even being in prison'. Overall Balconi feels that there has been 'no substantial improvement' in Guatemala's justice system.

Policing in Guatemala was in particular need of reform at the end of the civil war, and was dealt with in the accord on the Strengthening of Civilian Power and Role of the Armed Forces in a Democratic Society. This accord was seen as central to the peace process as it was aimed at the comprehensive transformation of the counterinsurgency state that had dominated Guatemala through the army's control over internal security. Integral to this accord was the limiting of the army's role to the protection of national security and territorial integrity. In practice, the accord established the National Civilian Police (PNC) as the only body intended to manage public order and internal security, requiring a complete restructuring of all existing police units, which were to be placed under civilian rather than military control (Jonas 2000: 81–2). Shortly after the signing of the accords, however, these reforms were in crisis, centering on the law creating the new PNC, which threatened to leave the country with a militarized police force (Jonas 2000: 141). There were insufficient numbers of trained police available for the new civilian force, and so the reform proposed to 'recycle' up to 90 per cent of the corrupt National Police (PN) and, in violation of the accords, 40 ex-army officers were accepted into the PNC (Jonas 2000: 151), leading to criticism that the reforms were little more that a 'cosmetic reorganization' (Sieder 2003: 223). As new forms of violence escalated in Guatemala's 'post'-conflict society, the 20,000 members of the new PNC proved inadequate to their task, and—under-equipped and poorly trained—lacking appropriate back-up from the justice system (Reilly 2009: 39). Balconi appreciates that the attempt to reform policing in Guatemala was intended to create a force 'with a different philosophy' that could regain the trust of the population. However a lack of long-term investment in developing police training facilities has failed to professionalize policing, leading to a further 'deterioration in its credibility'. In sum, he describes the police in Guatemala as the 'weak part of the chain of justice'.

The public security crisis that resulted from the failed reforms saw the army again employed in police patrols, creating anxiety that the police would be effectively remilitarized before the PNC had become fully operational (Sieder 2003: 223). Catalina Soberanis points out that this arrangement continues through successive government policies of using 'combined forces' of police and military personnel, which she says has not strengthened the police but instead has 'strengthened the idea that the army is the only institution that can really provide security'. This is now reflected in public opinion, which 'does not favour the limitation of the power of the army in relation to citizen security'. In the years since the signing of the Accords these concerns have only grown. As in South Africa, continued lack of confidence in the justice system has seen a rise in vigilantism, including a number of mob lynchings of suspected criminals in rural areas, along with a massive expansion of private security services that reinforce the country's deep socioeconomic inequalities (Sieder 2003: 83, 225).

Taken together, these struggles for institutional transformation underscore the complexity and challenges that typify this domain of reconciliation effort, and the capacity for institutional transformation to support or undermine efforts at the constitutional and institutional levels. In the next chapter I continue this institutional focus, considering the crucial role of domestic, international and religious civil society institutions in furthering reconciliation.

9   Civil society and religion

The institutions of civil society and religious organizations have a crucial role in the work of reconciliation and conflict transformation. Churches and civil society organizations are often more philosophically concerned than others to advance reconciliation, and more practically involved in efforts to transform conflict in their communities. Many aspects of reconciliation require a 'bottom up' approach that emphasizes the role of civil society actors in the determination of peacebuilding priorities. Civil society institutions can play a key role in sustaining moral leadership in conflict transformation work, holding politicians to account and providing important lines of communication between sectors, and between the community and the political leadership. But the work of these actors is complex and often controversial. International organizations have also been important to the work of civil society in conflict transformation work, both as players and as funders. Thus, this chapter also explores the consequences of local reliance on international support, especially when that support begins to dry up.

Core to the concerns in this chapter is the need for the institutions of civil society to act as ballast to the forces of elite resistance to institutional transformation outlined in the preceding two chapters. As Ed Wingenbach (2011: 81) notes, contemporary democratic theory recognizes that politics 'exceeds the institutional forms of the state'. At the same time, however, Wingenbach (2011: 100) also contends that proposing institutions that would produce agonistic democracy may have the effect of domesticating politics 'back into the state apparatus'. Thus, in the face of constant elite resistance, and the power imbalances that this implies, civil society plays a crucial role as social antagonist, constantly provoking conflict and opening space for a political focus on unpopular and marginalized views, articulating dissent as a 'check against the illusion of popular consensus'. There remains an ever-present risk that civil society institutions will become domesticated in the process, a tendency to which they must be constantly alert. Indeed, contrary to the view that the hard work of reconciliation lies in finding consensus, this chapter proposes that the harder—and ultimately more important—task is to maintain political space in which citizens speak truth to power without succumbing to the forces exerted by state-centric political institutions.

Civil society and reconciliation

Since the end of the Cold War, when international actors began to shift their attention towards social transformations that would prevent future conflicts, it has increasingly been recognized that civil society—often seen as representing those groups that had been marginalized in conflict—is essential to reconciliation and democracy (Van Leeuwen and Verkoren 2012: 81). While governments may—through the kind of constitutional transformations outlined earlier in this book—create political space in which diverse communities can engage, it is generally the work of communities that sees these transformations become realities in peoples' daily lives (Daly and Sarkin 2007: 95). Civil society is often conceptualized as a space of un-coerced collective action towards shared goals that ultimately strengthen both democracy and the state (Cubitt 2013: 93). Transforming conflict cannot rely on states and the machinery of government alone, but must also harness the energy of citizens to (re)build their society, pursuing what matters to them through the power of collective action, critiquing or even replacing elite narratives, and ensuring that attention is paid to relational transformation and the underlying cases of fractured social relationships (Sandole 2010: 55; Saunders 2001: 22; Verdeja 2009: 153). NGOs are uniquely placed to understand community priorities, needs and vulnerabilities, often far better than national or international organizations, with the capacity to expand and deepen public discussion about aspects of the past in ways that elites may resist (Daly and Sarkin 2007: 89–90; Verdeja 2009: 78). These ambitions have often been reflected in peace agreements that mandate civil society involvement in reconstruction, in activities designed to build support for the peace agreement in different communities, and in legal and political institutions, underscoring the view that participatory democracy is important to reconciliation (Bell and O'Rourke 2007: 304).

But the work of civil society in reconciliation efforts is not unproblematic, with critiques tending to centre on two primary concerns. The first concerns the nature of civil society itself. Little (2014: 55) cautions against understanding civil society 'merely as the more benevolent counterpart of the state'. He contends that 'eulogizing' more local spaces of community engagement risks ignoring the ways in which violent conflict may be perpetrated and perpetuated *within* civil society. Putting it bluntly, Little suggests 'civil society relations are frequently uncivil'. Indeed, civil society groups may do little more than replicate wider social divisions, providing apologist accounts that simplify or minimize the complexity of past events (Verdeja 2009: 157). Further, the kinds of 'locally grown' projects and initiatives that emerge from civil society may not always reflect peaceful or democratic values (Cubitt 2013: 98). As Patricia Lundy (2009: 327) has argued,

> the idyllic imagery and superficial depictions of homogenous and cooperative "communities" can overlook divisions and conflict {...} [concealing] {...} power struggles and networks, exclusionary tactics by local elites, processes of co-option of ideological conflicts. Indeed, not everyone's voice may be equally heard or everyone's interests addressed, and some may even be silenced or controlled in what appears to be a community-based response {...}. Frequently it is the more visible and vocal and more articulate and educated groups that participate. These are often self-appointed people, and they may not represent or reflect the views and perspectives of the wider community. In such circumstances there is always the danger that decision making becomes entrenched in the hands of a small and self-perpetuating, self-serving clique.

Thus, while civil society initiatives may indeed be 'authentic' and reflect local cultural norms, romanticizing so-called 'peacebuilding from below' may also advance corrupt, patriarchal, or privileged interests that replicate historical abuse and injustice (Ramsbotham *et al.* 2011: 226, 236; Mac Ginty 2013: 5).

A second concern with civil society focuses on its role in entrenching the agenda of the liberal peace, and its capacity to remain energized and politicized in these contexts. As an institution of democracy, civil society may be unintentionally captured by the post-Cold War commitment to liberal democracy as the best model for organizing societies, which in turn may reduce its capacity to contest or resist political elites (Verdeja 2009: 158; Cubitt 2013: 96). Indeed, Dennis Sandole (2010: 78) has suggested that the dominance of the liberal peace model has 'tilted' reconciliation towards 'single-issue efforts, especially by funder-dependent NGOs' with the effect that the 'complex, interconnected causes and conditions of violent conflict' remain unaddressed. The dissipation of dissenting energy that results from a more domesticated public sphere can be a powerful loss for reconciliation efforts (Verdeja 2009: 159). As will be discussed further below, the funding priorities of international actors can shape the efforts and priorities of local civil society, making it crucial to ensure that international agendas and institutions are not privileged over the needs and aspirations of local groups (Mac Ginty 2013: 5). Clearly then, these two critiques—one problematizing the local and the other emphasizing its importance—may also be in tension with one another.

Creativity, competition, and challenge in civil society

Each of the countries in this study has experienced the challenges and complexities of sustaining a space of independent, dissenting civil society able to contribute to wider reconciliation efforts. In Guatemala, for example, in the absence of functioning party systems or political parties free from the influence of economic elites, non-government organizations have played a crucial role both in delivering essential human services, and in channelling community interests and grievances. This has included significant advocacy concerning human rights and justice, often resulting in harassment, intimidation and even the murder of staff in Guatemalan human rights organizations. Despite this, in recent years the NGO sector has created important, constructive spaces for public dialogue aimed at maintaining a 'climate of civility' while exploring alternative public policy solutions (Reilly 2009: 30–1).

During the 1990s, Guatemalan civil society played a unique role in the peace negotiations, through the working of the ASC (discussed in Chapter 5). The ASC had provided Guatemalan NGOs with their first experience of participating in the political process, including drawing in organizations that had previously rejected political participation and prided themselves on their culture of *denuncia* (accusations) as an expression of political resistance (Jonas 2000: 95). After the signing of the Accords, however, the ASC was effectively sidelined as many of its more progressive members directed their energy into electoral campaigns. Particular sectors, notably women's and indigenous organizations, continued to demand participation in order to see the commitments in the Accords implemented and, more broadly, to maintain a place in the arenas of political action (Jonas 2000: 140).

Nevertheless, by the early twenty-first century, political exiles returning to Guatemala began to comment on how difficult it was to organize political activism in the country, following years of 'material and psychological warfare' that reinforced the view that resistance to the elites is futile (Nelson 2009: 223). Diane Nelson (2009: 28) quotes several Guatemalan observers who note that the role of NGOs has been effectively de-politicized since the signing of the Accords, particularly through funding regimes that have become an end in themselves. Organizations are seen to be changing the way they present their causes in order to access funding, and have also become highly competitive with one another. Nelson also points to the 'ambivalent role' that civil society has played in operationalizing the Peace Accords, particularly through the system of *comisiones paritarias* (joint commissions), which brought NGOs, including indigenous and women's organizations, together with the government to work on implementation. While at the time the *comisiones* seemed like another innovative means of institutionalizing political participation, Nelson (2009: 229) notes that in hindsight 'people are now suspicious that they were a distraction' and quotes an anonymous observer, someone who 'participated wholeheartedly' in the *comisiones paritarias* (interviewed in 2005) as saying:

> I'm not sure how it got decided that creating democracy and strengthening institutions would be the job of NGOs, but what it did was to create this whole parallel structure to the state, with the ASC, NGOs, and the 'friendly countries'. The state did not really have much to do with the accords and so now what we have is that peace was never really part of the state's project.

For many in Guatemala this depoliticization of civil society has been devastating. Elena Diez points to the crucial role that Guatemalan civil society must play to 'strengthen institutions' because, she believes 'it's only through a stronger civil society and a more engaged citizenry who are prepared to participate in democracy that the democratic system can change. It can't change itself because self-interest will always win out'.

As in Guatemala, civil society in South Africa played a historic role in ending violence and informing reconciliation efforts. Given the international isolation forced upon the apartheid regime, and thus the impossibility of any significant government-to-government engagement, the international community made considerable investment in support of South African civil society, which led to its sustained influence on the South African transition (Simpson 2000: 2). This role was enhanced by the ANC's desire to ensure that organizations formed by black South Africans were drawn in to the 'ANC family', meaning that after the transition to democracy these organizations retained greater influence than others. Unexpectedly, however, organizations in civil society that were notionally aligned with the ANC were often also its most vigorous opposition, an observation that Steven Friedman and Eusebius McKaiser (2009: 17) suggest contradicts any suggestion that South African civil society has been in decline since the end of apartheid.

However not everyone agrees with this analysis. Kallie Kriel, for example, has also observed the extent to which South African civil society organizations have seen 'their leadership taken up in government', expressing his view that when 'community activists become politicians' they 'lose their goodness'. Rebecca Freeth, a passionate advocate of the importance of civil society, also describes South African civil society as 'a real mess'. She observes that the absorption of the older leadership into government has meant that

> the people who've come up since [1994] have just not been schooled in activism or political engagement {...}. So it's been a quite diluted civil society. It's been a fairly naïve civil society, and it's been a complacent civil society because money did pour in until recently.

Raenette Taljaard also sees that the 'priority list' for South African civil society has become 'very full', with issues like corruption and democratic accountability now 'trumping debates on reconciliation and inequality'.

Yet despite the apparent inevitability of the leadership of NGOs being drawn into the new government, there was also an increase in the range of civil society organizations in the years following the transition to democracy (Muthien *et al.* 2000: 4–5). This has led Friedman and McKaiser (2009: 15) to describe the state of South African civil society as 'vigorous, effective—and shallow'. They note the sector's vigour and effectiveness with regard to its evident influence on political debate and decisions, including the fact that black or predominantly black organizations do not tend to endorse government policy uncritically despite the overwhelming and continuing black support for the ANC as governing party (2009: 15). However, they also suggest that the sector remains shallow in the sense that most do not have deep connections with the poor South African majority, many of whom do not have the means, capacities or contacts to exercise their right to political participation. They note that several studies have found that the poor 'continue to remain outside civil society', meaning that organizations that 'champion the poor have weak roots among them' (Friedman and McKaiser 2009: 17–18). However this is a view that others contest. Despite noting the decline in civil society more broadly, Rebecca Freeth describes the 'growth into the social movement area of civil society' through organizations like the Treatment Action Campaign and Shack Dwellers International. As a result, she sees that 'instead of either white or middle class and educated NGO types speaking on behalf of the poor, the poor are speaking for themselves'.

Yet despite these observations of a diverse and vibrant civil society, there remain concerns that the unusual double status of the ANC has a depoliticizing effect on South African civil society. Its history leading the struggle against apartheid means that the ANC is able to present itself as both the governing authority and as the embodiment of the liberation struggle, enabling it to absorb much of the leadership of dissenting groups and organizations, and leaving little space for more autonomous political engagement and participation (von Holdt 2011: 14). Yet Michael MacDonald (2006: 89) suggests that the sorts of compromises inherent to the negotiated settlement also left the ANC unable to meet some of the central demands made by civil society, particularly those related to more radical economic restructuring and the redistribution of wealth. The resultant criticism has led the ANC to try and curb the independence of South African civil society. Indeed, once we step outside the fairly narrow definition of civil society adopted by Friedman and McKaiser it is evident that they too acknowledge the ways in which grassroots protest activity tends to be 'obliterated' by commentary diminishing angry demonstrations with the misnomer 'service delivery protests'. This rhetoric effectively silences the legitimate voice of the protestors 'by substituting an elite-generated explanation of their actions for an attempt to investigate and listen to their grievances', and reducing the protestors themselves to passive recipients of government services, rather than 'choosing and thinking citizens who demand to be part of the discussion on the way in which government is to serve them' (Friedman and McKaiser 2009: 19).

In Australia, civil society organizations have played a relatively tame role in the reconciliation process. While Australian civil society is replete with indigenous and non-indigenous organizations focused on aspects of indigenous health, education, political representation, and so on (see Maddison 2009 for more), I will focus here on those organizations specifically associated with Australian reconciliation efforts. The Council for Aboriginal Reconciliation actively advanced a 'bottom up' reconciliation process that envisioned social change eventuating once the non-indigenous population was adequately educated about the needs and aspirations of Aboriginal and Torres Strait Islander people. In general terms, both the CAR and its associated groups and organizations adopted very moderate, unthreatening language that would not 'offend the sensibilities of non-indigenous Australians' (Short 2008: 116). As Short (2008: 111) points out, this vision was 'a far cry from the restitution, compensation and acknowledgment demands made by the Treaty campaign from which the reconciliation process eventually emerged'. Nevertheless, the CAR pursued this agenda through the creation of new networks in civil society, particularly following the Australian Reconciliation Convention in 1997. What became known as 'the people's movement for reconciliation' drew in local councils, community groups, service clubs, churches, ethnic groups, conservation, youth, sporting and women's organizations. In its final report, the CAR (2000: 61) described the so-called 'people's movement' as 'one of the most celebrated outcomes of the work of the Council' contending that 'Reconciliation has not ended with the finishing of the Council. The people's movement will take it forward'.

Since the end of the CAR, however, both momentum and cohesion within the movement has dissipated. There is a discernible lack of collaboration among the national and state-based reconciliation organizations in Australia, an issue raised by several of my interviewees. During the period of the CAR, the state councils were contracted to coordinate state level activities, working with trade unions, churches, schools, sports clubs and other community groups, and many expected this model to continue after the end of the Council's term. However, this is not the model that eventuated, with federal government funding supporting only the national body, Reconciliation Australia, while the smaller, state-based organizations have struggled to survive. Those who have been involved with the national body, such as former deputy national director Jason Glanville, acknowledge that during the decade of reconciliation the state councils did their community development work 'incredibly well. They created the people's movement.' However Glanville now sees that while the reconciliation field in Australia has changed dramatically since the end of the CAR, many of the people who had been involved in the state councils 'are still embedded in that same model and are still grieving that they no longer have a contract with the Council and a paid, dedicated piece of work to contribute'.

The view from the other side of this relationship is also frustrated and dissatisfied. Leanne Townsend, at the time of our interview the CEO of a state reconciliation council, clearly finds the relationship between the national body and the states highly disrespectful, suggesting that the state councils are treated as 'just another stakeholder' to the national body, while 'there's no identification that we're actually working in the same space'. Townsend maintains that this structure has functioned because the state organizations work 'at the community level {...} doing the hands on work with local reconciliation groups', but she also finds the relationship quite one-sided, with the more community based work 'put in the too hard basket' by the national body. Indeed, Sharona Torrens from RA describes the national network of organizations as 'more of a communication approach {...} we don't tell them what to do and they aren't involved in our programs'. Torrens points out that the state and national levels are not 'formally linked' and that while they strive for an 'open and engaging relationship' the state councils 'take more of a grassroots approach' while RA 'sits more at the national level'. For former CAR member Linda Burney this approach has seen her 'stepping away from the formal reconciliation process' because it

> didn't support the thing that will make reconciliation in the minds and actions of Australians a reality, and that is the grass roots movement. If you don't have that and if you're not engaging at a local level between Aboriginal and non-Aboriginal Australians, then I'm not quite sure what the point is.

This is not to suggest that Reconciliation Australia does not collaborate. Leah Armstrong emphasizes the way the organization works with other organizations around issues on which it does not have expertise, such as health. But RA's main focus remains on community education and the RAP programme (discussed in Chapter 7), specifically the 'tangible things' that RA can measure as commitments to improving economic participation by Aboriginal and Torres Strait Islander people as contained in many RAPs. Armstrong has chosen to move the organization away from being 'the catchall for reconciliation' to a focus on these more specific areas where 'a small organization can get greater impact'. She acknowledges that the organization has to be 'very careful' about how it communicates on the 'hard issues' such as contentious areas of indigenous policy so as not to 'scare off' the people they are trying to influence. And while she concedes that the organization has been criticized for not taking a more critical stance, she maintains that it is more effective for RA to have the 'quiet conversations {...} behind the scenes to try and influence people' rather than 'being the placard holders out the front'.

In Northern Ireland, civil society has long been recognized as a key institution in the peace process. While not directly involved in the peace negotiations, Northern Irish civil society is thought to have helped create the social conditions in which it was possible for the Belfast Agreement to be accepted and endorsed in a referendum (Nolan 2012: 171). As Bill Shaw tells me, he believes that in Northern Ireland, 'the power sharing executive wouldn't be in place and the peace process wouldn't be in place without the efforts of organizations like our own and others'. In light of this, the decline in influence of civil society organizations after the signing of the Agreement has been described as a 'puzzle' (Acheson *et al.* 2011: 18). On one hand, the sector has in fact expanded considerably since 1998, in large part as a result of funding that has flowed from the European Union, the International Fund for Ireland, and other external funders, rather than as a result of local or regional support (Nolan 2012: 171). In total, domestic and international funding has equalled £2.5 billion, an average of almost £100 million per year, leading Nolan (2012: 172) to observe that 'Nowhere in the world has enjoyed such largesse in relation to population size.' On the other hand, however, it is the development of this so-called 'peace industry', and the resultant 'communalization and professionalization' of reconciliation efforts in the region, which is thought to have stifled creativity and spontaneity in the sector (Power 2011: 11). While some see that the influx of funding has 'invigorated' community organizations in both communities (Etchart 2011: 135), others observe that nationalist organizations in particular have become increasingly drawn into the 'orbit' of the British state (and the European Union) as funding regimes have been allowed to shape their activities and priorities (Bean 2011: 165).

The most significant criticism that has been levelled at civil society in Northern Ireland, however, is that their expression of, and/or support for, sectarian identities may lead NGOs to foster division rather than cross-community integration (Acheson *et al.* 2011: 19). Certainly Northern Irish civil society has been able to draw in diverse participants, including former combatants who now engage in conflict transformation work by employing 'the weaponry of dialogue and legitimate lobbying as a means of communicating their political philosophy to rivals and opponents' (Edwards and Bloomer 2008: 7). The republican ex-prisoner, Gerry Foster, for example, now works with the Prisons to Peace Partnership to engage with a wide range of people, including unionists and those who, in his words, have 'lost loved ones at the hands of Republicans', as well as 'women's groups, youth groups, immigrants, in schools, even Church groups', using these spaces of engagement to encourage groups to 'highlight the class issues' in their communities. But funding has tended to flow to organizations with sectarian identities that engage in what is known as 'single-identity work', which in many cases leaves the deep divisions in society untouched (Nolan 2012: 172). Reinforcing concerns about romanticizing the 'local', Timothy White (2011: 42–3) suggests that civil society organizations in Northern Ireland can in fact cement differences between social groups, where instead they need to be supporting the kinds of programmes and activities that allow relationships to develop *across* community barriers in ways that 'both human-ise and empower the other'.

Such work is certainly in evidence. Roisin McGlone is involved in pre-cisely this kind of effort at interfaces in west and north Belfast, and while she observes that working at the community level is not unlike being 'in the middle of a riot' she also suggests that this is the best place to be: 'if you're in the middle of something, you can influence it. You can talk to the police, you can talk to the activists, and we're there all the time.' Like Gerry Foster's work noted above, this kind of civil society initiative is expli-citly tackling the difficult task of transforming community level relation-ships between former antagonists.

The role of the international community

Alongside these local level efforts is the work of international organiza-tions and donors. International actors have long been influential in the civil society institutional spaces of deeply divided societies. In many cases, such as Guatemala, international interventions have been essential to securing the end of violence. However the role of international actors is also complex and problematic. Since the 1990s, the field of actors working on reconciliation and peacebuilding has grown considerably, including through an increase in the number of large international organizations and the expansion of bilateral donor relationships. Zelizer (2013: 32) now refers to 'the business of peacebuilding' as a field that exists within 'the much greater constellation of the [multi-billion dollar] international aid industry'. While motivated by humanitarian goals, the approach of these actors has tended to focus on statebuilding, specifically the creation of state institutions believed to sustain peace, support the rule of law, enable liberal democracy, and sustain a market-oriented economy (Campbell and Peterson 2013: 336–7). Proponents of this liberal perspective assert the universality of these essentially Western norms and institutions, regarding them as a kind of 'universal template' beneficial for all societies, and investing heavily in the 'good governance' agenda with the assumption that these new institutions will diminish or eliminate discrimination and corruption (Lundy 2009: 325; Mac Ginty 2013: 5). Yet as Little (2014: 55–6) notes, often imported with these views of Western liberal demo-cratic practice are 'assumptions about the inherent negativity of conflict', with these universal models of social and economic development con-sidered helpful to 'smooth troubled political waters'.

This approach to conflict transformation has been criticized on a number of fronts. First, the emphasis on universal models allows inter-national actors considerable power, often at the expense of local actors. These 'foreign generalists' tend to lack in-depth knowledge of specific country contexts and yet wield considerable influence due to their mastery of the universal template, meaning that dissenting domestic voices and local insight are ignored (2012: 7). This leaves international interventions vulnerable to accusations of neocolonialism, compared to former European colonial regimes in which outsiders set the agenda and defined the field of action, cloning their ideas of 'best practice' irrespective of the histories and peculiarities of different cultural and political contexts (Lundy 2009: 326; Cubitt 2013: 97). Second, the institutional focus of liberal interventions seeks to 'avoid politics', but in doing so they act in ways that are far from apolitical, reinforcing existing power structures by default, and leading some to question the relevance of international organizations that fail to engage with political agendas (Van Leeuwen and Verkoren 2012: 86). International organizations and bilateral donors are required to work with (or sometimes around) states, but the institutions they create are often captured by the state and therefore unable to challenge the unequal distribution of power and resources that is perpetuated by the state (Campbell and Peterson 2013: 342). As Van Leeuwen and Verkoren (2012: 85) observe, 'Ignoring politics does not render intervention neutral at all, but instead has the effect of reinforcing the status quo.' Third, the focus on the liberal peacebuilding model tends to render local actors as 'passive recipients' of international aid, whether that aid is understood as beneficial or exploitative, effectively centering the debate on the qualities of the model itself rather than on the complex interactions between domestic and international actors (Zaum 2013: 110).

The funding regimes instituted by international organizations are the subject of particular critical attention. These funding programmes tend to be constrained by shifting priorities and donor fatigue, leading to short-term funding cycles that limit the scope and creativity of interventions, despite the fact that the liberal democratic models they advance would take many years to be realized (Campbell and Peterson 2013: 341; Zelizer 2013: 31). Short-term funding tends to 'atomize' and 'projectify' complex social challenges to create discrete interventions that often miss the mark (Zelizer 2013: 49). International funders also tend to 'cherry pick' among local groups and organizations, supporting those that are more moderate and professional and that focus on questions of democracy, often provoking aggression and competition among organizations (Cubitt 2013: 97–8). In general, donors tend to support service delivery rather than solidarity and political initiatives that might put their relationship with a host government at risk. This has the effect of depoliticizing civil society, particularly with regard to efforts to address issues of power and structural inequality (Van Leeuwen and Verkoren 2012: 85).

But while these criticisms of the 'identikit' nature of Western state/ peacebuilding interventions should be taken seriously, they should not underestimate the capacity of local actors to 'slow, subvert, exploit and avoid' international interventions, effectively 'hybridizing' Western ideas and projects with local cultures and priorities (Mac Ginty 2013: 5). As Cubitt (2013: 108) suggests, 'International partners are not the central players in local politics and local actors are not passive recipients of their largesse. They have genuine objectives of their own.' Nevertheless, as three of the four cases in this study demonstrate (Australian reconciliation efforts have been funded from domestic rather than international sources), international actors *have* shaped domestic reconciliation efforts in important ways.

South Africa typifies the problem of the international community determining the timeframe for reconciliation efforts, with many international donors now moving on to other priorities—an issue raised by many of my interviewees. Kate Lefko-Everett observes South African NGOs 'dropping like flies' as their funding dries up, noting that 'donors are fickle' and 'change with their interest in funding every year'. But Lefko-Everett also observes a degree of donor fatigue, noting an expectation from donor organizations that the South African corporate sector, which she says 'isn't really that supportive' should 'pitch in' more to support the work of NGOs. Hugo Van der Merwe also describes the impact of donor fatigue in South Africa. While his organization and others like it are still funded to do work internationally, particularly elsewhere in Africa, he says there are 'regrets' about the programmes they would like to be doing in South Africa but can no longer get funded; 'things like ex-combatant integration issues are still all largely unaddressed, issues of memorialization, ongoing issues of violence, huge issues like collective violence, service delivery protests. We're scratching for money to continue with that work'. Lucy Holborn points out that because South Africa is now categorized as a 'middle income country', donors in European countries 'view it as a stable democracy' and do not understand that 'our democracy is still very young and there are still things that could potentially threaten it'. Raenette Taljaard agrees, telling me that funding flows have 'dried up' in part because of the global financial crisis in 2008, but also because 'South Africa is seen as a democracy that's done it, box ticked, it's on the road, it doesn't have any profound challenges left' leaving local actors 'up against a wall'.

In Northern Ireland, the European Union's Programmes for Peace and Reconciliation (Peace I, II and III, 1994–2011) have funded literally thousands of projects through local and regional community organizations, development agencies, statutory bodies and a range of other groups. These programmes are considered unique to the specific context of the Troubles in Northern Ireland, and essential to achieving the goals of the Belfast Agreement. The priorities for initiatives funded through the Peace programmes are found in three specific objectives known as the 'distinctiveness (and reconciliation) criteria', which aim to:

- Address the legacy of the conflict: to encourage actions of projects that will address specific problems (legacies) generated by the conflict in order to assist the return to a normal peaceful and stable society;

- Take opportunities arising from peace: to encourage actions which have a stake in peace and which actively help to promote a stable and normal society where opportunities for development can be grasped;
- Pave the way for reconciliation: to build an inclusive process and to promote actions that will pave the way for reconciliation.

(Lynch 2005: 61)

But although these objectives are generally viewed as ideologically quite neutral, Audra Mitchell (2011: 74–7) has pointed to their coercive effects, and argued that in fact 'their logic, ethics and principles have promoted a specific normative project based on transformative models of democracy, governance, development and securitization'. Far from neutral, the programmes seek to transform the entrenched hostilities across the two communities into a participative, inclusive, democratic system, through a re-development of 'the mindsets, values, goals and social structures of the region' in ways that support the constitutional peace process (Mitchell 2011: 75). Over time, this approach has developed into a view of reconciliation that emphasizes a number of specific dimensions: the development of more integrated personal relationships; the integration or inclusion of excluded, deprived or belligerent groups; and the broader European ideal of the integration and equalization of the regions. The final instalment of the programme (Peace III) placed a high priority on projects that adopted cross-community integration as an explicit goal (Mitchell 2011: 77). But while there has been broad participation in the Peace programmes, Mitchell questions whether this can be taken as a sign of public acceptance of these goals. The only options available to civil society organizations in Northern Ireland were participation in, or abstinence from, the EU programmes. Raising objections in other ways could see a group branded as radical, dissident, or as spoilers of the peace process, thereby inviting criticism and exclusion. Where groups did choose to abstain from the programmes, this was generally taken to be an indication that the peace process itself was not yet complete, effectively stifling public contestation or resistance and closing down political space (Mitchell 2011: 88–91).

I certainly found widespread dissatisfaction with this funding regime among my interviewees. Gerry Foster notes widespread skepticism about the use of EU Peace funds, saying

[a]ll sorts of money was pumped in here over the last 15 years {…} but people are literally scratching their heads and going "Where is it?" You know, because it doesn't seem to have come to anything {…} in terms of jobs and stuff like that.

Katy Radford describes the competition for funding in Northern Ireland as creating 'crabs in a bucket—everybody's clipping on each other's heads in order to be able to get the next tiny little slither. It's not a healthy process'. Barry Fennell also notes the intense competition between NGOs in Northern Ireland, where he says 'there's a whole industry running workshops' but a reluctance 'to work with others'. Alan Largey agrees that there is a 'crowded marketplace and all of us doing the same thing' and suggests that 'a good culling of what goes on here would be actually very good for Northern Ireland'. Unfortunately, according to some, the NGOs that have had their funding cut are those that have been critical of the power sharing administration. Michelle Wilson sees this trend as highly problematic for the peace process, which she understands as requiring 'a strong, independent civil society to be in a critical dialogue with the state'. Instead, she says, the power sharing government is 'eroding and neutering the development of independent, critical voices in the NGO sector'.

In Guatemala there can be no doubting that international intervention was essential to securing the end of *la violencia*. The presence of the *Misión de Verificación de las Naciones Unidas de Guatemala* (MINUGUA, the UN Verification Mission in Guatemala) was important in maintaining the impetus towards peace, and represented the international community's commitment to supporting this process. As Susanne Jonas (2000: 47) notes, although the actual human rights situation in Guatemala remained dire, the arrival of MINUGUA 'shifted the balance of forces within the country', and made peace seem possible. MINUGUA was responsible for monitoring the last two years of peace negotiations and then the implementation of the Accords. During the ten years the mission was deployed on the ground in Guatemala, its 400 person advocacy team investigated many forms of human rights violations, produced 9 reports on the progress of peace in the country, and effectively laid the groundwork for institutionalizing effective human rights in the country (Nelson 2009: 297; Carmack 2008: 60). Further, the June 1995 meeting of the Consultative Group of Donor Countries confirmed that they would withhold major funding for Guatemala until the final peace accords were signed and until tax reforms guaranteed that internal funding would become a future reality (Jonas 2000: 46). Indeed, most observers agree that without the international backing of the UN and other international organizations and donors, the peace accords in Guatemala may never have been achieved (Carmack 2008: 62; Sieder 2008: 81).

But the interplay between these international and domestic actors in Guatemala has been highly complex. Jonas (2000: 38) describes 'the endlessly shifting interaction between domestic and international peace efforts', including considerable domestic resistance. While the popular movement and many ordinary Guatemalans felt that the presence of MINUGUA was essential for progressing peace and increasing security, some elites, determined to preserve the status quo, described the mission as a *plaga* (affliction), that was a breach of Guatemalan national sovereignty (Nelson 2009: 297). The Guatemala government engaged in both passive resistance and the active undermining of MINUGUA's efforts, attempting to limit the mission's functions and resist the implementation of MINUGUA's recommendations. Much of this resistance was, in fact, an expression of resistance to the peace process as a whole, with domestic institutions such as the Guatemalan army attempting to 'outlast MINUGUA' and 'survive the peace' (Jonas 2000: 49–50). At the same time, the peace process saw 'increasing convergence' between international actors and local economic elites, specifically though the inclusion of neo-liberal economic frameworks in the peace settlement, which saw rights not conducive to the individualistic framework of the liberal peace (particularly indigenous rights) effectively sidelined (Brett 2013: 223).

Thus, the eventual exit of MINUGUA in 2005 was an ambivalent experience. Many on the right applauded the end of what they saw as interference in Guatemalan domestic sovereignty. But many others also saw MINUGUA's departure as a step towards self-sufficiency, relieving a sense that the UN's presence in the country for such a long period of time had fostered dependency and diminished domestic political capacities (Nelson 2009: 298). And while the departure of MINUGUA and other international actors—strong allies to the indigenous movement—also saw the indigenous movement lose considerable capacity and visibility (Brett 2013: 236–7), in some parts of the country this was a source of relief. For some indigenous groups, the presence of the UN had created a collision between local and global interpretations of human rights, particularly among some evangelical communities, as will be discussed further below (Philpot-Munson 2009: 53).

But along with the UN, Guatemala also saw the exit of most donor nations. As in South Africa, at a certain point the work in Guatemala was thought to be finished. Between 1996 and 2003 Guatemala received US$1.7 billion to support the peace process, but with MINUGUA gone many funders turned their attention to other countries with 'more pressing problems' (Nelson 2009: 306). In the wake of the international organizations, it is evident that the generally weak civil society organizations that existed in Guatemala have been further depoliticized through their dependency on external funding, with many large-scale reconstruction projects collapsing into in-fighting and cynicism (Arriaza and Roht-Arriaza 2010: 220). Other organizations, however managed to survive and even thrive. For example, Carlos Sarti describes the evolution of his organization *Fundación Propaz*, which began life as a programme funded by the Organization of American States (OAS) focused on 'working with government officials, NGOs and indigenous peoples to establish constructive relationships through dialogue'. After the OAS left Guatemala in 2003, *Fundación Propaz* continued its work and 'is now a Guatemalan organization'. But others have not fared so well. Rosenda Camey underscores the frustration many organizations feel when their project funding ends, telling me 'it's like taking the water away from a fish'. Christina Elich observes that the financial crisis has seen the staffing in international organizations in Guatemala change. Instead of the 'very valuable people' she saw at work some years ago, today she sees 'recent graduates that don't have any experience, in charge of millions and millions and millions of dollars from the international community'. She describes this change as 'very dangerous' because she sees these less experienced workers exercising 'an arrogance {...}. They simply say, "If we don't understand it, we can't finance it." That's the slogan of today's international imperialism from the international community {...}. They have no time to learn and they are not listening'.

Faith and religion

Churches and religious institutions are the last group of civil society actors to be considered in this chapter. In many, if not most, deeply divided societies religious actors play multiple roles, including providing essential services, negotiating peace settlements, and contributing to reconciliation efforts. However their roles are not always a positive contribution and religious actors may also incite violence or actively maintain social and political divisions (Huda and Marshall 2013: 153). Outside any instrumental role that religious institutions may play, there is also an assumption that religious identity remains a key factor in many conflict dynamics, and that interfaith dialogue and reconciliation efforts may therefore be key to advancing reconciliation efforts (Abu-Nimer 2013: 69–70). This view suggests that effective reconciliation efforts must be grounded in local institutions and communities, working in partnership with the faith-based organizations that often play a central role in community life (Huda and Marshall 2013: 153). Reconciliation efforts directed through religious organizations may have a heightened legitimacy among faith communities, thereby contributing to breaking down stereotypes, humanizing the other community, and advocating for justice, human rights and nonviolence (Abu-Nimer 2013: 71; Huda and Marshall 2013: 157). But at the same time, however, working with religious actors can also pose complex ethical issues, evoking powerful emotions and drawing on historical memories that may span many centuries (Huda and Marshall 2013: 167). Faith-based reconciliation efforts also tend to be de-politicized, often supported by the dominant political elites while lacking in strategic, in-depth understanding of the political context (Abu-Nimer 2013: 78).

Each of the countries in this study has navigated the role played by religious institutions in reconciliation efforts quite differently. In Australia, by far the most secular country in this study, religious institutions have played a minor role in reconciliation efforts despite their history of complicity in perpetuating historical injustices through their role in administering protection regimes. Christianity has had, at the very least, a conceptual role in Australian reconciliation efforts. While the Australian polity is often assumed to be 'strikingly irreligious', Phillips (2005: 111–12) argues that over the decade of the formal Australian reconciliation process, the debate about what a reconciled Australia might 'look like' and how it might be achieved, 'carried a distinctly Christian tone', exhibiting aspects of what he describes as 'a "secularized" theological politics'. Further, Phillips notes the active role played by Christian churches throughout the decade of the formal reconciliation process. He points out that the text of a parliamentary motion of reconciliation, moved by Prime Minister Hawke in 1988, was taken directly from a pamphlet entitled 'Towards Reconciliation in Australia' produced by 14 Australian Christian Churches. Some churches also made their own efforts to make amends for past injustices. All the major Christian denominational churches have apologized for their role in the child removal practices that created the Stolen Generations, and further measures taken by some churches include improving access to records from missions and other institutions to assist people in tracing their past and finding their families; providing counselling services; and offering to contribute to a national compensation fund for members of the Stolen Generations if such a fund were to be established by the Federal Government (Cornwall 2009: 14).

Nevertheless, as I have argued elsewhere (see Maddison 2014a) there is far more that Australian Christian churches could do. Given that all church property is built on Aboriginal land, a more concrete contribution to the reconciliation process might see Australian churches lead the way in returning land or paying appropriate compensation for loss of land to Aboriginal communities. The *Bringing them Home Report* argued that the return of land would express the churches' recognition that past policies and practices of forcible removal were wrong and, importantly, it would 'indicate their refusal to profit from a practice most have publicly acknowledged was wrong'. But this has not happened to any great extent (Australian Human Rights Commission 1997; Cornwall 2009: 34). Churches could also pay compensation to Aboriginal and Torres Strait Islander people for past harms, in much the same way as they have awarded compensation to non-indigenous people who, as children, were subjected to harm, including sexual abuse, in church-run institutions (Cornwall 2009: 49).

In both South Africa and Northern Ireland religious leaders were more integral to ongoing efforts to end decades of violence and pursue reconciliation (Huda and Marshall 2013: 165). But while in South Africa, reconciliation that drew on religious thinking was a means of opening up transformative space, in Northern Ireland the historical religious divisions between the two communities meant that religious figures had to play quite a different role (Little 2014: 102). Religious organizations in Northern Ireland have tended to reflect, rather than transcend, community sectarianism, a fact acknowledged in a 1993 report by the Irish Interchurch Group on Faith and Politics, which argued that as the churches had had a role in building sectarianism, they must now collaborate in dismantling it

(Smyth 2002: 353). Certainly religion has been integral to the formation of Nationalist, Republican, Unionist and Loyalist identities, and religious and political leaders such as Ian Paisley have deployed religious rhetoric to considerable political gain (Power 2011: 75). As noted in the previous chapter, the Catholic Church actively resisted moves towards integration in education in Northern Ireland. Derick Wilson describes the churches in Northern Ireland as 'often unable to rise to the invitation to speak about all people. They only spoke about their own people {...}. They developed a religion of separation, or of the chosen people, which reinforced one tradition over and against the other'.

But the churches have also provided an institutional space in which religion could challenge the conflict, contributing to reconciliation efforts though internal denominational debate and reflection, ecumenical dialogue between the leadership of the churches, local prayer groups, community development work and public statements intended to inform political debates (Power 2011: 73). This has not always been easy. Maria Power (2011: 86) maintains that the church leaderships in Northern Ireland 'have been stuck between a rock and hard place', on the one hand criticized for not doing enough to support peace and reconciliation efforts, and on the other hand accused of 'betraying their community' when they were critical of violence or encouraged their congregations to become involved in reconciliation efforts involving the other community. Yet these efforts continue. Sara Cook describes the importance of the organization she works with, the East Belfast Mission, in terms of its capacity to work at 'high levels within loyalism':

> Because it is a church, people see it as kind of a neutral space and a place where dialogue can take place, and we have a really interesting pastor who's really used that over the years to try to create some space for movement *within* loyalism {...}. We've done a lot of work between the different loyalist groupings to try to mitigate some of the damage and try to calm things down and essentially save lives.

In South Africa, criticism of religion's role in reconciliation efforts has had a somewhat different focus. In our interview, Michael Lapsley points to the long history of the relationship between religion and politics in South Africa, describing the struggle in South Africa as 'always a theological struggle', and explaining that

> apartheid was a theological reality before it was a political reality. In the 19th century white Christians would not sit at the table of the Lord with black Christians. So the faith issues, the theological issues, are antecedent to modern day political apartheid. It's not accidental that the first few presidents of the ANC were ministers of religion {...}. Black Christians read the Bible and they took it seriously {...} about

justice, about all being made in God's image and likeness {...}. So the struggle in South Africa was {...} a faith issue because, in a way, the truth of the faith was at stake. Either apartheid was true—that the most important thing about us is the colour of our skin—or it was true that we were all God's children made in God's image and likeness; but these ideas couldn't live together.

Lapsley notes the significance of the International Christian Committee eventually condemning apartheid as a 'false doctrine' in 1982. This state-ment came during a long campaign by the South African Council of Churches (SACC) that declared apartheid an unjust political policy that was contrary to biblical messages. From the 1970s, black leaders including Desmond Tutu, Alan Boesak, and Manas Buthelezi had increasingly assumed the leadership of the SACC, which remained one of the few unbanned liberation organizations in the country. These leaders oversaw the rise of black theology, denouncing the Afrikaner theological worldview and promoting 'religious empowerment in the interest of economic, social and political liberation' (Kuperus 2000: 89–90). Hanif Vally believes that one reason the black churches were able to be so involved in the libera-tion struggle was that the oppressors were also 'committed Christians', which created 'a bit of space for the black churches to operate'.

The SACC also became one of the strongest proponents of the South African TRC and its capacity for 'healing' the nation, providing support through community education and pastoral care for both victims and per-petrators (Kuperus 2000: 91). But it is the TRC's focus on forgiveness as a driving idea in reconciliation that has led to the most significant critique of the association between religion and political reconciliation, both in South Africa and elsewhere. The TRC's emphasis on forgiveness fed a concern that particular religious ethics were being endorsed by a state-sponsored body—religious ethics that were not necessarily relevant or suited to a political process (Kiss 2000: 86). The Commission, and particu-larly Desmond Tutu, was criticized for presenting forgiveness as a duty or a moral obligation that good South Africans must accept, an emphasis clearly linked to a Christian worldview (Chapman 2002: 268; Zachar 2006: 69). Critics suggest that the emphasis on forgiveness places an unreason-able burden on victims, undermining their justifiable anger and desire for justice and reparation (Hamber and Kelly 2005; McCaughey 2003: 290). Further, some questioned why the churches, which had played such a crucial role in the struggle against apartheid were not continuing their struggle on behalf of those who remained poor and marginalized in the post-apartheid state (Terreblanche 2012: 14–15).

In Guatemala the churches also played an important role in ending *la violencia* and advancing reconciliation efforts. As in much of Latin America, the emergence of civil society in Guatemala came about largely through the churches, which for the most part have seen themselves as peacemakers in a conflictual context (Reilly 2009: 44). Most remarkable among these efforts was the Catholic Church's leadership of an alternative truth commission in recognition of community fears that the state-sponsored commission would bend to the power of the military and not report the facts of wartime atrocities. The Catholic Church, whose members had been among the primary victims of military violence in the highlands, worked with local human rights NGOS and the UN to secure the mandate for an official truth commission (Sieder 2003: 215). For his efforts, Bishop Juan Gerardi was assassinated the day after the release of the Catholic-led REHMI report (Philpott 2006: 5). Since this time, the Catholic Church in Guatemala has maintained a commitment to documenting atrocity and pursuing social justice, also finding ways to collaborate more effectively with Mayan believers towards more equitable development (Reilly 2009: 44–6).

Historically, the Catholic Church has been the dominant religious institution in Guatemala, but the last three decades have also seen the increasing presence of charismatic Pentecostal Protestant churches—generally referred to as *evangelicals*—which were introduced to Guatemala by North American missionaries. Evangelical churches now include up to 35 per cent of Guatemalans within their congregations (Philpot-Munson 2009: 45). Initially both nationalist intellectuals and some Catholic bishops rejected the evangelicals as Protestant imperialists bringing Cold War ideology from the north. Over time, however, evangelical church leaders have also come to play a role in supporting the Guatemalan peace, and now collaborate with Catholics on a range of reconciliation efforts (Reilly 2009: 46–7). Throughout Guatemala they have created a new sense of community in contexts characterized by postwar fragmentation—driving through the country it is impossible to miss the signs of their influence, in both the innumerable small churches in tiny communities and the enormous, lavish churches in the city. Nevertheless, evangelicals are also seen to work against aspects of the peace process. Philpot-Munson's anthropological study in the Nebaj region observed that while Nebajense Catholics largely support the recommendations of the Peace Accords and the CEH, both Maya and Ladino *evangelical* Nebajenses have been 'more critical':

> They have been clear in their advocacy for a continued military presence in Nebaj, have spread rumours that the proliferation of concepts such as indigenous and human rights will 'bring the wrath of God', have opposed seeking justice for war crimes, and have even obstructed the efforts of forensic anthropologists trying to locate and exhume mass graves {...} in the Ixil area.
>
> (Philpot-Munson 2009: 46)

Philpot-Munson (2009: 51–2) maintains that these controversial perspectives—including describing the international human rights movement as a 'tool of the guerillas' and the CEH and REHMI reports as 'communist' documents—are a strategy for regaining control over their world and a response to their fear of the power of the past.

Amongst these religious complexities in Guatemala are many people working to create spaces of engagement between evangelical views and the more mainstream Catholic perspective on advancing reconciliation in Guatemala. Charles Reilly maintains that, more than in many other countries, Guatemalan churches have 'jointly created space for dialogue and for building a more civil society', helping to 'expand notions of civic responsibility' in a context where elites demonstrate very little (Reilly 2009: 50). And some are trying to make the most of this space. For example Julio Solórzano-Foppa has worked to organize several 'inter-religious gatherings' to support the development of the *Memorial para la Concordia* in Guatemala, focusing on 'Striving to find what's common in their sacred books or their conceptual structures or religions, that deals with memory and concord or reconciliation.' Raquel Zelaya believes such an approach is essential to protecting the gains that have been made to date, pointing out that '90 per cent of the population is Christian' and that 'in Guatemala the evangelical and the Catholic Church are very well trusted'.

Taking opportunities to engage such differences in the spaces that institutions can make available often becomes the task of more relational reconciliation efforts, and it is to these concerns that I turn in the following section.

Part IV
Relational challenges

10 Truth, justice, healing, and forgiveness

The final level of analysis outlined in this multi-level framework is relational; that is, a concern with transforming relationships among people. This level is perhaps closest to popular understanding of reconciliation, pointing to the ways in which reconciliation addresses both historical wounds and their contemporary, relational manifestations. Indeed, the very concept of reconciliation is based on the idea that a stable future order is only possible if the psychological sources of conflict—'the residues of violence and death that linger long after open hostilities have ceased' (Hutchison and Bleiker 2013: 81)—are engaged alongside broader efforts at constitutional and institutional transformation.

Scholars from a range of disciplines have stressed the importance of focusing on the underlying psychological and sociological needs that animate conflictual relations, including the need for recognition, acceptance, respect, security, and justice (Tropp 2012: 4). For some scholars of peacebuilding, such as John Paul Lederach (2005: 34–5) relational concerns are at the centre of reconciliation efforts, with the goal of allowing people in even the most divided societies to imagine themselves in relationship with one another, creating a new social context in which cycles of violence might be broken. Lederach (2005: 85) maintains that relational engagement is key to reconciliation, enabling people to see 'spaces of intersection, both those that exist and those that can be created'. It is in practices of relational engagement that attempt to address these needs that we can most clearly see the requirements for agonistic processes able to support difficult, ongoing conversations about the past: conversations about truth and justice; about forgiveness; about identity; and about learning to live together without violence.

A central challenge in relational reconciliation efforts concerns the way in which the past is addressed or denied. Although many high profile commissions have established themselves with the goal of seeking a singular 'truth', war and violence in fact produce different histories; different understandings of the past that can become the most contested aspect of any reconciliation process. As Brenna Bhandar (2007: 95) argues, many versions of reconciliation maintain a demand for one version of historical truth to be agreed in order for society to agree to restitution and move on. The reality, she contends, is that history is 'a compilation of different threads of memory, threads that are intertwined but also in conflict', meaning that the idea of a single, shared truth about the past is 'nothing more than a fiction'. An agonistic approach suggests that there will never be consensus on the past; there will always be multiple truths, multiple histories, that must somehow coexist.

Facing the past

Questions of how to deal with the past are contested in all societies— stable democracies as well as countries attempting to transform or reconcile—and go beyond the recording of an official history (Forsberg 2003: 67). The particular ambition in post-conflict societies, however, is to democratize history, replacing narratives controlled by elites with narratives that reflect the lives of poor, marginalized, and oppressed groups. History is revealed as another 'territory of injustice' that might be addressed through an agonistic, dialogical engagement between lived experience and official discourse (Sanford 2003: 181, Barkan 2000: xxxiv). Counter-narratives of collective memory may contest hegemonic and institutionalized accounts of a nation's history. These counter-narratives refuse to allow past injustice to be excused as incidental to the nation-building agenda. Indeed without the proper acknowledgment of such injustice it is thought impossible to achieve democratic inclusion (Bashir 2012: 132). The authors of the Catholic truth commission in Guatemala also made this point, arguing that

> the truth cannot remain private. It must be disseminated throughout society, and the authorities must publicly acknowledge the facts. Compiling testimonies is a key component of developing a collective memory that enables people to find meaning in what happened and affirm their dignity; remembrance is a way of acknowledging that it happened, that it was unjust, and that it should never happen again.
> (Recovery of Historical Memory Project (REMHI) 1999: 89)

Coming to terms with the past is particularly important for victims of past atrocities and injustice, for whom the acknowledgment of pain and suffering is also an assertion of identity (Sanford 2003: 12). There is also a political imperative to acknowledging a painful past, most particularly when it is political actors who have perpetrated the pain. For victims in such cases, 'justice to the past is a form of justice in the present and for the future' (Shriver 2002b: 26). Victims of past injustice may never see 'forgetting' as acceptable. As Tony Birch (2007: 112) argues of the Australian case, 'While governments, populist conservatives and some self-proclaimed indigenous "leaders" promote versions of forgetting in order to facilitate "progress," other indigenous people have refused the offer of a future without an identity.'

At the same time, however, there is caution about 'too much remembering', or at least a concern to find a balance between memory and forgetting, between victims 'burying the gruesome past and burying themselves in the memory of it' (Shriver 2002b: 31; Daly and Sarkin 2007: 22). Those who would advocate forgetting suggest that looking backward will not facilitate reconciliation but only 're-traumatize a fragile society' by rekindling anger and animosity and prolonging bitterness (Verdeja 2009: 7). Judith Renner (2012: 58) suggests that it is 'at least as plausible' to suggest that truth telling will exacerbate hate and the desire for revenge as it is to assume it will lead to reconciliation. But as Verdeja (2009: 7) points out, however,

> if forgetting requires burying awful experiences and behaving as if nothing had happened, what kind of reconciliation is this? Who is reconciled? Without some understanding of what happened, it is difficult to see how people could be reconciled with one another—to know whom to reconcile with means knowing who did what and who suffered what. An agreement to forget the past may bring respite from violence and ease a transition, but it is unlikely to remain for long.

This is the premise upon which Verne Harris and his colleagues have been developing the Nelson Mandela Foundation in South Africa, suggesting that

> so much of the dysfunction in our society is a result of us not reckoning with the past or not creating enough space for the past to reckon with us. Until we do that, we'll be banging our heads against the wall.

Problematically, however, many of those who recognize the significance of the past to contemporary reconciliation efforts also pursue a goal of discerning a singular, consensual truth. David Crocker, for example, contends that without 'some agreement about what happened and why' former enemies are unlikely to be reconciled (Crocker 2000: 101). Contesting this view is the recognition that no 'truth' of past atrocity and injustice—indeed, no history at all—will ever be stable or uncontested. To assume otherwise is to misread the way in which political conflicts are (re) produced in public narratives, as Little (2014: 12–13) contends:

> Disparate details and events tend to get brought together into a single narrative to provide a unified story that pushes contradictions and complexities to one side lest they interrupt the flow of the narrative. But the reality {...} is that singular narratives of complex conflicts are never universally consensual and lead us towards an unnecessarily

limited range of potential political strategies for managing conflict situations.

In Guatemala, Julio Solórzano-Foppa makes a similar point, drawing a distinction between 'the recollection of memory', which he associates with 'truth', and 'the construction of memory', which is more concerned with 'how to live with memory {...}. How memory is present, and how it relates to the future {...} what to do with that knowledge'.

Collective memory is rarely held consensually but is more often the product of bitter political debate (Gibson 2004: 70), particularly where a critical history challenges elite hegemony. The 'contested historical terrain' that results from any process of truth telling is likely to involve rigorous debate over both the facts and implications of past actions, as in the case of the 'history wars' in Australia (Muldoon 2008: 128, discussed further below). In this sense, reconciliation efforts should not focus so much on the discovery of one 'truth' but on how accommodation between conflicting historical accounts might be attained in order to 'make a conflict more liveable' (Little 2014: 100). An agonistic approach to reconciliation is most useful here, prescribing only that antagonists acknowledge that they are speaking of the same events, not that they agree on their significance. As Schaap (2005: 84) contends, 'the faith of political reconciliation is that, by engaging in incessant discourse about the world that lies between former enemies, this world might appear more common to them'.

Each of the countries in this study has made choices about how to deal with the past. And these choices influence both what is collectively remembered and what is forgotten (Forsberg 2003: 69). South Africa, Guatemala and Australia have each chosen some version of a truth commission in their approach, as will be discussed further below. Northern Ireland, however, has been unable to contend with the reality of divergent views of the past through any formal process. While the necessity of peace is widely agreed and supported, there is no agreement as to 'the morality (or otherwise) of the use of violence during the Troubles or to who the "real" victims and perpetrators of past violence are' (Aiken 2010: 175). Truth recovery is distrusted as part of a 'republican agenda', ensuring that there is still significant official reluctance to envisage a formal and inclusive mechanism, such as a truth commission, as the appropriate way of dealing with the issue (Lundy and McGovern 2008: 36–7). Indeed, more than any other issue, this anxiety about the past continues to undermine the belief that Northern Ireland has left the Troubles behind (Nolan 2012: 11–12). The failure to communicate about the past, and the lack of a common understanding about the history and causes of past violence, reinforces the sense of isolation and difference between the two communities, underscoring the persistent threat of violence and impeding other reconciliation efforts (McCaughey 2003: 181; Community Relations Council 2011: 27).

The Community Relations Council (2011: 26) suggests that this intransigence about the past in Northern Ireland reflects the 'profound importance' that people in both communities attach to these issues. In a context where ongoing disagreement about the past remains such a volatile issue, Little (2012: 76) shies away from even the language of reconciliation, suggesting that any focus on the history of the conflict is potentially dangerous, a likely way in which 'traditional divisions and conflicts are brought back to the fore of political discussion'. Little contends that despite the years that have passed since the Belfast Agreement, today many people prioritize the relative peace of the present over the risks of reconciliation, with its attendant requirement to face past conflicts and deal with the ways in which they continue to resonate in the present. 'Dealing with the past' is thought of as 'a separate, often mechanistic process' that remains disengaged from wider reconciliation and 'good relations' work in Northern Ireland, maintaining a focus on the needs of victims and survivors rather than considering the impact of the past on the whole society (Kelly 2012: 111). Many still question whether the past should be remembered at all, with local political elites seeming to prioritize damage limitation over truth recovery, advocating the putting aside of a divisive past in favour of an imagined consensus that might support social change (Lundy and McGovern 2008: 29, 43).

However, many others still advocate for the pursuit of a collective truth about the past in Northern Ireland. Despite the 'selective cherishing of traumas and glories' that is evident each marching season, it is also clear that there are many individuals and groups eager to remember more inclusively, to tell history 'against the grain' of their own tradition, and to embrace 'fragments of a common story' in order to pursue reconciliation (Smyth 2002: 337). In this vein, Brendan McAllister emphasizes the need for a truth recovery process that is 'very Northern Irish', one that 'learns from the good things from elsewhere, but fashions something for ourselves'. McAllister advocates a process that is driven by civil society not politicians, and that can enquire into 'people's perspectives and experiences' rather than just 'pure fact'. For the time being, however, a formal 'truth process' such as this seems unlikely.

But this does not mean that truth is not being sought. Rather it means that this work will remain in the domain of civil society, which Ronald Wells maintains 'is strong enough to encourage and enable discourse about forgiveness and reconciliation to go on without an ad hoc commission created for that purpose' (Wells 2006: 190). Eamonn Baker and Trevor Temple exemplify these efforts through their work at Towards Understanding and Healing in Derry. Baker tells me that they each have their stories of the Troubles, but that, like most people in Northern Ireland, they were 'living in compartments, where this compartment is not talking to this compartment'.

> I experienced Bloody Sunday and I saw people shot dead. So I kept telling this story, and over here Trevor kept telling his story. But unless

we're telling each other these stories—and not just telling them, but hearing them—then this disabling social apartheid will be maintained.

Projects such as Towards Understanding and Healing emphasize the 'disparate narratives that comprise the story of Northern Ireland' that together can foster understanding of the complexities of the conflict there (Hetherington 2008: 43). A range of other organizations also contribute to this work, including initiatives such as Healing Through Remembering, which works to open public space in which to address post-conflict truth and collective memory (Lundy and McGovern 2008: 36). Jayme Reaves from Healing Through Remembering points to the effort that the organization has undertaken in order to bring together representative groups to work on various projects, stressing that their work is 'primarily about dialogue and bringing people along'. However she suggests that the effort required to keep these small groups functioning, often taking several years to agree on the content of a working group report, points to how difficult such efforts would be on a larger scale. Yet Kate Turner from Healing Through Remembering also notes that 'no matter how much people say they don't want to, they do actually want to talk about how to deal with the past'. Over time, Turner has observed some significant changes in the wider public discourse. She tells me that when the organization began it would 'get abuse from people saying, "Will you stop it! You're going to destroy the peace process." ' Today, however, Turner says that 'there isn't a day where there isn't somebody on the radio or on in the media who sounds like Healing Through Remembering. People talk about the conflict, they talk about us as a society needing to deal with the past'.

State-sponsored efforts also continue. In 2010 the long-running Saville Inquiry, which examined the deaths and injuries that occurred on Bloody Sunday in Derry/Londonderry in 1972, found that British soldiers were unjustified in shooting unarmed, protesting civilians. The Saville Report prompted an apology from British Prime Minister, David Cameron, but also debate about whether the victims of this event were being privileged over the victims of paramilitary groups during the same period. The work of the PSNI's Historical Enquiries Team (discussed in the previous chapter), which remains the primary investigative mechanism in Northern Ireland, also makes an important contribution to post-conflict truth recovery. Ultimately, however, Terence McCaughey (2003: 296) maintains that it is not enough 'simply to conclude that one side is as bad as the other' in Northern Ireland, in order to avoid 'rocking the boat', or to protect the region's 'painstakingly constructed political accommodation'. He concedes that finding a shared memory of the past in Northern Ireland is an unrealistic expectation, but believes it is possible for people to acknowledge the 'shaming truth' in the views of those with different historical memories, and in so doing gain the right to have their own view respected. McAllister maintains that a divided society like Northern

Ireland must have a rationale about why they would address the past when 'it would involve pain and risk and disturbance'. For McAllister the answer is that these processes would assist in 'deepening the quality of peace, preventing peace from mutating, and promoting the harder work of reconciliation'.

These issues remain far from resolved. In 2009 the Consultative Group on the Past released a report *Dealing with the Past in Northern Ireland* (generally referred to as the Eames Bradley report after its authors) based on two years of consultations across Northern Ireland. The report made several significant recommendations including proposals to establish a Legacy Commission to integrate reconciliation, justice and information recovery processes, to conduct public acts of remembrance, and, most controversially, a recommendation for £12,000 recognition payments to relatives of those killed during the conflict. The report was widely criticized and eventually shelved. For Pádraig Ó Tuama this was a disappointment. The controversy over the proposed reparation payment overshadowed what he saw as some 'amazing suggestions for living subtly with divergent narratives'. More recently still, in 2013, the Northern Irish political parties agreed to a new round of negotiations that they hoped would lead to agreement on parades, flags and dealing with the past, the first time such an initiative had been led by local actors. The negotiations, known formally as the Panel of the Parties of the Northern Ireland Executive, or more colloquially as the Haass-O'Sullivan talks after the negotiation chairs, made progress in some of these areas, particularly on dealing with the past. Ultimately, the parties were unable to reach a compromise agreement on flags and parading by the agreed deadline of 31 December 2013, leaving the future of the negotiations uncertain.

These recent initiatives underscore the importance of dealing with historical issues that continue to frame relationships in deeply divided societies. And while the approach taken in Northern Ireland may indeed be problematic, it needs to be understood in the context of the dominant view of truth-telling as taking place primarily through truth commissions, with other responses to the past condemned as failures to reconcile (Renner 2012: 58). In fact, although truth commissions have indeed become almost mandatory in most reconciliation efforts, these institutions are not always the panacea they are represented to be.

Commissioning the truth

The truth(s) that need to be shared and collectively addressed in conflict transformation work are complex and painful, often requiring a significant policy initiative that can gather the elements of a conflict and create space in which citizens can understand and learn from one another (Daly and Sarkin 2007: 55). As such, truth commissions are an attempt to 'take stock' of the past in a way that may allow divided groups to acknowledge atrocity and injustice and commit to a different future together (Hamber 2012: 335). Truth commissions are thought to combine 'investigative, judicial, political, educational, therapeutic, and even spiritual functions' (Kiss 2000: 70). Their work aspires to develop 'the beginnings of a language of reconciliation (Daly and Sarkin 2007: 76); to 'create a new collective memory' (Hamber 2012: 335); 'establish a historical record of political violence' (Leebaw 2008: 107); 'offer a basis on which to build a shared history' (Chapman 2002: 258); 'establish new norms for breaking the cycle of retaliation and violent conflict' (Gobodo-Madikizela 2010: 134–5); 'generate authoritative historical accounts' and 'issue recommendations for institutional change' (Kiss 2000: 70); and 'foster a more inclusive democratic dialogue by providing official spaces for previously marginalized or silenced populations to share their stories' (Leebaw 2008: 112). If realized, each of these ambitions would certainly make a contribution to wider reconciliation efforts. Their success, however, remains deeply context specific, and always both partial and contingent.

One of the alleged merits of the commission approach—as opposed to more strongly justice-focused approaches such as trial or criminal tribunals—is their contribution to the healing and recovery of victims. Where trials focus on the motivations of perpetrators, commissions are more focused on the feelings of victims (Daly and Sarkin 2007: 61). Victims are supported and enabled to tell their own stories of atrocity and injustice, framed from their own perspectives, and recognized as 'legitimate sources of truth with claims to rights and justice' (du Toit 2000: 136). The focus on victims creates a very different relational experience when compared to a criminal procedure. Commissions allow for the excavation and expression of raw emotions of fear and anger, painful struggle, defeat and survival (Villa-Vicencio 2009: 75). As Martha Minow (2000: 244) suggests, 'Tears in public will not be the last tears, but knowing that one's tears are *seen* may grant a sense of acknowledgment that makes grief less lonely and terrifying.'

It is this emphasis on the public testimony of those who have experienced violence that leads Sonali Chakravarti (2012: 11) to claim that such testimony 'may be one of the best contemporary examples of an agonistic moment in political life'. According to Chakravarti, victim testimony has the capacity to open up political space that is able to challenge normative expectations of consensus and rationality, instead privileging the kind of emotional expression that is rare in formal political institutions (Chakravarti 2012: 14). The effect of these expressions of anger, despair and resentment is to highlight the contested nature of history and memory, and to expand ideas of acceptable political subjectivity, recognizing that a victim's expression of pain and suffering is politically significant (Chakravarti 2012: 15). The effects of these encounters may be profound, not only for victims but in transforming relational reconciliation efforts:

Confronting difficult emotions after war cannot ensure that the emotions will not surface again and permeate politics for years to come, but it is the beginning of a productive conversation about how political expectations have been shaped by violence and the emotions that remain. Those who have experienced the violence of war, from the perspective of perpetrators, victims, family members and bystanders, are all changed in significant ways, especially in relation to the expectations of the state and fellow citizens. Grappling with these effects should not be seen as tangential to the work of politics in the aftermath of war, it is at the core of a process of justice.

(Chakravarti 2012: 20)

Certainly the truth commissions examined in this study have been, to different degrees, transformative. Each of these commissions has opened new spaces for public debate, highlighting existing deep divisions and developing new language in which to discuss future relationships (Daly and Sarkin 2007: 109). More problematic has been the assumption that truth commissions would produce the kind of harmonious reconciliation that was rejected in Chapter 2 as both unrealistic and undesirable. The outcomes of truth commissions are generally far more complex, ambivalent, and ambiguous than the production of a singular narrative of the past, and focusing only on their contribution to community harmony risks overlooking the other, significant contributions they make to reconciliation efforts (Borer 2004: 22; Chapman 2002: 261; Hamber 2012: 336).

Perhaps the most famous truth commission of the past few decades has been South Africa's Truth and Reconciliation Commission (TRC), which has seen many hundreds of thousands of words of text devoted to its analysis. From the outset, the TRC was controversial in its use of conditional amnesty (discussed further below), a process intended to create a 'third way' between the extremes of either Nuremburg-style trials or a blanket amnesty, and agreed as a compromise during the negotiated settlement (Tutu 1999: 30). Although never intended as 'the beginning and the end' of South African reconciliation efforts, it was certainly understood as such by some observers (Mbeki 2010: 2–3). Often the TRC was presented, and at times represented itself, as engaged in a process of 'once and for all' coming to terms with the horrors of apartheid. As has been noted in earlier chapters, however, the narrow definition of violation and abuse adopted by the Commission—generally restricted to those transgressions that were already a crime under apartheid rather than the wider structural crimes of apartheid—in fact contributed quite a limited picture of these injustices (Christodoulidis and Veitch 2008: 15; Barnard-Naudé 2008: 197).

Yet, despite these (and other) evident shortcomings, the *Final Report* of the South African TRC undoubtedly contributed to the emergence of a new, more widely shared collective memory on which the nation has based its ambitions for a stronger human rights culture (Villa-Vicencio and Ver-woerd 2000: 279). As Joan Fairweather (2006: 183–4) suggests, many con-sider that the Commission's most valuable contribution has been to 'hold up a mirror to South Africans showing them a deeply troubled society, a society torn apart and distorted by the obsessive politics of white suprem-acy'. Kenneth Lukoko maintains that the success of the TRC lies in the fact that it was

> the very first time for South Africans of different races, class and other ways of identity, to actually create an understanding of the past together {...}. That was crucial, because it meant that people could see the benefit of placing truth and an interrogation of the past as critical before going forward, to say, 'Even if I want a job, I want a house, I want to become the next business entrepreneur or whatever, it is important for us to pause first and just see how we got here.' {...} We understood that reconciliation would be a stage where people say, 'I may not have agreed with everything you had done in the past {...} but now, for the first time, I'm willing to accept the fact that I need to know your version, because if I don't know then our coexistence in the present is going to hugely compromised.'

The authoritative account that the commission produced laid to rest some of the fictions that each side in the struggle had mobilized to defend their legitimacy, with the effect of moving black and white South Africans closer together in their understandings of the past (Villa-Vicencio and Verwoerd 2000: 279; Gibson 2004: 115). The effect of victim testimony was to 'shake up' the cognitive basis of South African attitudes towards each other, allowing space for dissenting arguments and moral complexity that 'exem-plified the norms of a new democratic society' (Kiss 2000: 90; Gibson 2004: 158). While, as Judith Renner (2012: 57) maintains, there is 'no obvious reason' why the TRC should be seen as 'a universally valid template for reconciliation', it is evident that at the relational level of South Africa's reconciliation efforts it did make a distinct contribution.

In contrast to the singular moral authority exercised by the South African TRC, Guatemala experienced two truth commissions—one state-sponsored and the other driven by the Catholic Church. A specific peace accord created the official *Comisión para el Esclarecimiento Histórico de las Vio-laciones a los Derechos Humanos y los Hechos de Violencia que han Causado Suf-rimientos a la Población Guatemalteca,* (the Commission to Clarify Past Human Rights Violations and Acts of Violence That Have Caused the Guatemalan Population to Suffer, generally shortened to the *Comisión para el Esclarecimiento Histórico* (CEH), the Commission for Historical Clarifica-tion). From the outset this commission seemed likely to satisfy almost no one in Guatemala. The government and army had opposed its creation, and the compromise that made it possible ensured that those responsible for particular acts would not be prosecuted under its mandate (Jonas 2000: 74). The Catholic commission, *Proyecto Interdiocesano Recuperación de la Memoria Histórica* (REMHI, the Recovery of Historical Memory), established in response to civil society skepticism about the merits of the official commission, was more explicitly dedicated to the promotion of reconciliation. Nevertheless, both projects sought to investigate the truth of *la violencia* with the hope of fostering social and political reconstruction in the country. And, perhaps not surprisingly, both reports reached similar conclusions, particularly with regard to apportioning blame for the estimated 200,000 deaths and disappearances, and in accusing the Guatemalan army of perpetuating genocide—REMHI more obliquely, but the CEH report *Guatemala: Nunca Más!* (Guatemala: Never Again!), making the explicit charge based on its analysis of military strategy (Isaacs 2009: 118).

Otilia Lux was one of the CEH commissioners in Guatemala, and describes the Commission's rigorous approach to research, involving over 7,000 testimonies and access to a great deal of unclassified information from the Secretary of State. Yet despite the Commission's finding of genocide in four regions, Lux points out that 'generals in the army and some people in the corporate sector' still deny this, perhaps, according to Lux 'because they might have been involved in the genocide'. Indeed, the strength of the findings in the CEH report shocked many Guatemalans. The Accord that created the Commission had not defined what forms of violence could be investigated, which allowed the CEH to examine the ethnicized nature of the violence (Fullard and Rousseau 2009: 3). When the final report *Guatemala: Memoria del Silencio* (Memory of Silence) was presented to the government, the guerilla, and the UN in February 1999 no one was prepared for the scope of its findings. The presentation of the report to a packed audience was an 'emotionally electrifying experience' particularly for the thousands of victims in attendance who finally heard their experiences publicly vindicated (Jonas 2000: 154).

The political events that followed the publication of the reports of these two commissions were, however, telling. The response to REMHI was 'swift and unequivocal' in the form of the brutal murder of Bishop Juan Gerardi just two days later. But the political chill in response to the CEH report was no less significant. In contrast to the enthusiastic crowds that greeted the public release of the report, the president refused to personally accept it, and its historical veracity was immediately challenged (Isaacs 2009: 118–19). And while the CEH report may be seen by many as 'the authoritative *lectura* (interpretation) of the war' (Jonas 2000: 157–8), the reality was that neither commission secured either official acknowledgment or a commitment to the reparations that both reports had called for (Isaacs 2009: 135–6). Indeed, just nine months after the release of the CEH report, voters elected the *Frente Republicano Guatemalteco* (the Guatemalan Republican Front, FRG), the party founded and led by General Ephrain Ríos Montt, who had been a central architect of the genocidal policy outlined in that report. Ríos

Montt's election prompted a resurgence of violence directed primarily at forensic anthropologists and human rights and indigenous activists—'individuals and groups who sought either to uncover more truth or to bring perpetrators to justice' (Isaacs 2009: 118–19).

Yet despite these significant setbacks, Guatemala's truth commissions are still thought to have delivered a 'serious moral blow' to those who opposed the peace. The finding of genocide left the door open to the future prosecution of responsible individuals (Jonas 2000: 157), eventually pursued through the 2013 trial of Ríos Montt. The commissions are also thought to have made an important difference to the lives of many victims by validating their suffering, providing an opportunity for them to tell their story, and leaving a written record for their children (Isaacs 2009: 138). The involvement of civil society was an important contribution to the development of a new political culture of citizenship (Sieder 2003: 212) and the 'reluctant and limited' acknowledgement of responsibility by the Guatemalan government and army created a new political space in which divergent memories could engage one another (Sanford 2003: 19).

However, it is evident that not all Guatemalans accept the findings of the CEH. Julio Balconi suggests that the reports produced by the Guatemalan commissions are 'not really trustworthy' and 'don't tell the whole truth'. As an example he points to the finding that 400 villages were destroyed in the army's scorched earth strategy, and asks 'How come it's 400 exactly? Shouldn't it have been 405 or 420?' Balconi maintains that the figure has been 'conveniently released to the public by groups condemning the army' without ever having been verified. Gustavo Porras tells me that the reports 'produced part of the truth, but they distorted it'. Porras insists that the representation of the civil war as being 'an ethnic war' is incorrect. Rather it was a war against 'anti-capitalists', which turned many indigenous communities into support bases for the guerrillas and therefore into military targets, meaning that indigenous people were both the intended and unintended victims of the fighting. Porras concedes that the actions of the army were 'disproportionate' and involved 'cruelty that was in many cases worse because of discrimination and prejudice', but differentiates this from an intended ethnic genocide. For these reasons Porras believed that Guatemala still 'lacks a truth that can be accepted by all so that you can achieve peace'. Rosalina Tuyuc, however, sees racism at the root of such denials. She points out that 'the people who have never accepted that there was genocide, were also responsible for these genocides' and maintains that

> denying justice and denying the fact that there was genocide, can only be a proof of the historical racism that has existed. Since it was indigenous peoples who were affected, it doesn't matter that 250,000 people died. That's why they don't accept that there was genocide.

There was also disagreement among my interviewees in Guatemala as to whether the country should still be focusing on the past or looking to the future. Raquel Zelaya maintains that the findings of the two commissions have caused 'great damage to the social fabric', but have primarily affected 'those at a higher economic level' because 'people living in poverty, people who are worried about insecurity' cannot afford to focus on these concerns with the past. But Elena Diez points out that 'the population is divided' because many 'don't accept that there was genocide', which underscores the need for Guatemalan society to 'discuss our past in order to be able to work in a different way in our future'. Doris Cruz also maintains that while some people think the focus in Guatemala needs to be on 'forward looking development', this is 'never going to be possible until people are able to talk safely about the past'. But while Arnoldo Noriega agrees that 'the wounds left by the war {…} have not been healed' he maintains that the stalemate between the army and the guerilla means that 'there is not one winner who can write how history happened. There are too many loose ends {…} and too many conflicts.'

A similar debate has taken place in Australia, although the approach to truth-telling there has been quite different. In Australia there has been no process officially labeled a truth commission, nor did the formal reconciliation process include any such mechanism. Nevertheless there have been three processes that have contributed to Australian efforts to deal with the past—the Royal Commission into Aboriginal Deaths in Custody (RCIADIC), the Inquiry into the Separation of Aboriginal Children from their Families, and the work of the CAR. Although each of these processes followed quite different methodologies, each was commissioned to investigate forms of historic violence against Aboriginal and Torres Strait Islander people and the contemporary impacts of this violence (Read 2010: 186–7). The Inquiry into the Separation of Aboriginal Children from their Families, for example, received written submissions and oral evidence from indigenous organizations, government representatives and former government employees, church representatives, and NGOs, including confidential evidence taken in private from indigenous people affected by the policies and from adoptive and foster parents. The Inquiry report, titled *Bringing them Home* (BTH), included harrowing evidence of the forcible removal of indigenous children that it charged constituted an act of genocide contrary to the UN Convention on Genocide (Short 2008: 93, 98). Tabled in Federal Parliament on 26 May 1997, it concluded that, 'between one in three and one in ten Indigenous children were forcibly removed from their families and communities in the period from approximately 1910 until 1970' (Australian Human Rights Commission 1997: 36–7). Peter Read (2010: 288) describes the accusation of genocide as opening a 'hornet's nest'. The federal government contested the report's findings through arguments that have been described as 'pedantic and tactless in almost equal measure' (Manne 2001: 83), rejecting recommendations that called for an apology or compensation, and those relating to the incorporation of these critical findings into school curricula, arguing that such measures would encourage separatism and guilt (Gunstone 2009: 78).

Yet despite the official government resistance to the *Bringing them Home* findings, it is evident that this inquiry did indeed influence wider reconciliation efforts. Although the issue of child removal had not been seen as significant enough to warrant mention in the preamble to the Australian reconciliation legislation, in subsequent years it became central to the reconciliation process, providing a national forum for indigenous truth-telling and allowing victims' stories of abuse and suffering to enter the public domain (Short 2008: 99). The debates that followed focused on the fundamental question of whether past injustice should be judged by contemporary moral standards, with many Aboriginal and Torres Strait Islander people insisting that coming to terms with the wrongs of Australia's history was a vital prelude to genuine reconciliation (Reynolds 2013: 31). In response, Prime Minister Howard and other participants in what became known as Australia's 'history wars' maintained that Australians needed to end this pointless 'naval gazing' about past injustices and 'move on' (Manne 2001: 3). Indigenous and non-indigenous historians producing a more critical history of colonial violence met considerable resistance, both from a public that had been taught a more 'comforting' history and from historians eager to defend that 'old' history, particularly with regard to the claims of genocide (Reynolds 2013: 27).

Thus, although these debates did open new political space, political intransigence ensured Australia's truth-telling processes did not produce any significant relational transformation. Beyond some symbolic recognition and an eventual apology (discussed below), truth seeking in Australia has not allowed the country to face up to its past, and while the reconciliation process may have brought some people closer together, in the wake of these debates it is evident that indigenous and non-indigenous versions of history remain as far apart as ever (Reynolds 2013: 256; Birch 2007: 112). Tim Gartrell agrees that 'not dealing with the fundamental truth of our history is a real blocker for reconciliation' in Australia. And over the years he sees that 'while fundamental, historical truths such as the dispossession and exclusion of the first Australians from society remain unresolved' public engagement with these foundational concerns has been dissipated 'as a raft of well-meaning, and in many cases worthwhile, initiatives' have been rolled out. This makes it challenging to engage the wider population on issues such as constitutional reform, where Gartrell and his colleagues are trying to 'build a sense of passionate emotion', which is difficult when people do not understand 'the journey the country's been through'. Aside from a grudging acceptance of the narrative concerning Australia's Stolen Generations, it is evident that there is no wider public acceptance of historical wrongdoing towards Aboriginal and Torres Strait Islander people (Read 2010: 288).

What these varying responses to truth-seeking processes suggest is that attaining 'closure' through the determination of a singular, unequivocal truth will always remain elusive. As Martha Minow (2000: 241) has argued, 'the truth can never be full enough, or sufficiently embracing, to overcome intergroup divisions so deep that members see the world differently'. In Guatemala, Carlos Sarti emphasizes the relational nature of 'truth', suggesting that for his country

> what matters is to think about the past, not to find more conflict but to achieve reconciliation. This means that we need to accept that we're interdependent, meaning that the truth for one person is also partly true for somebody else, and the truth of others is related to the rest of the truth of others.

And whatever 'truth' is discovered and debated will likely only raise further questions of relational transformation pertaining to how a society should respond to this history.

Justice, amnesty, and reparation

Overlaying some of the shortcomings with truth commissions as a means of facing the past is the concern that such measures may undermine demands for justice. Jose Serech maintains that while 'the right to truth' is an essential precondition for further reconciliation efforts, 'the right to justice' and 'the right to reparations for damages' must complement a new understanding of truth and history. The 'justice norm' sees human rights violations such as torture, disappearance and summary execution as crimes committed by individuals who should be prosecuted through fair and open trials (Sikkink 2011: 13). From this perspective, ending impunity and holding perpetrators to account, both through trials and through the rejection of past policies is essential to reconciliation, particularly for the victims of past violations (Verdeja 2009: 24; Villa-Vicencio 2004: 3). Human rights advocates in particular have expressed concern that 'truth' may become a substitute for 'justice', threatening the establishment of the rule of law and the principle of respecting the human rights of all citizens (Bashir and Kymlicka 2008: 16). And while it has been argued that trials may impede wider peace processes or block efforts at conflict transformation, to date there is little empirical evidence to support the argument that people must choose peace *or* justice (Sikkink 2011: 133). It is also possible that trials may open agonistic spaces by promoting a reconsideration of previously held truths, redirecting public attention towards victims' claims and stimulating public debate about social and political obligations for reparation well beyond the particulars of a specific case (Verdeja 2009: 104).

But just as truth is complicated and partial, so too is justice. Sikkink (2011: 25) concedes that, like democracy, justice is a powerful concept that 'in practice always falls short of our ideals', leaving victims 'disillusioned with the institutions that can neither heal their broken bodies and minds nor return their loved ones'. Reconciliation may need a more collective approach to justice than is provided by doctrines of individualized universal human rights (Bashir and Kymlicka 2008: 17). Villa-Vicencio (2004: 3) suggests that our understanding of justice needs to become broader and more 'holistic', to include the promotion of a human rights culture, economic transformation, and the building of civic trust. A focus on *restorative* justice prioritizes the reintegration of perpetrators into society, while also restoring the dignity of the victim through an acknowledgement of their suffering (Villa-Vicencio 2003: 240).

Nevertheless, the prosecution of individual perpetrators will retain an important place in some contexts. In Guatemala, for example—as in much of Latin America—trials have been seen as an essential component of conflict transformation, with the REMHI report noting that the demand for 'justice and punishment' of those responsible for violations during *la violencia* was seen as an essential part of the process to 'rebuild the foundations for living together as a society' (Recovery of Historical Memory Project (REMHI) 1999: 50). This was evident in many of my interviewees in Guatemala, which took place shortly after the conviction of Ríos Montt had been set aside.[1] Rosalina Tuyuc, for example, acknowledges the case against Ríos Montt as 'very important' to many Mayan people, because the crime of genocide places him beyond the reach of the amnesty provisions in the Peace Accords. Tuyuc echoes a view I heard many times: 'whatever the result of the trial is, for us the genocide crime has already been tried'. Velásquez underscores this point, telling me that

> [i]n the long history of Guatemala this is the first time that the indigenous people have the opportunity to demand justice for genocide. This is not the first genocide {...}. But this is the first time it has been judged in the national court. So this is symbolic. This is not only against Ríos Montt, this is against the state, which is responsible for the destruction of a people {...}. Right now we are living a historic moment. The process against Ríos Montt is part of this hope to build another country. You know? We can make a change without violence.

Julio Solórzano-Foppa also points to the wider impact of the Ríos Montt trial. Like the South African TRC, the court proceedings were broadcast on television and, as a result, '[f]or the first time this country is talking about the war, because even during the signing of the peace the people were not participating'. The impact of the trial was 'incredible', although it only lasted a few weeks 'it was enough for people to wake up and say "Woah! Something really happened here!"' And Elena Diez disagrees that events like the Ríos Montt trial in Guatemala are 'going to polarize the society', as is often suggested, pointing out that the country '*is* polarized'.

The truth, she says has been 'swept under a carpet' but it is still there and always being 'uncovered a little bit' in ways that continue to cause political discomfort.

In contrast, critics of the trial such as Gustavo Porras contend that the proceedings will only bring 'endless conflict' to Guatemala. Porras maintains that most Guatemalans, including Maya, seek economic and human security over the justice to be found in trials. He tells me that 'it's not true that most of the population of Guatemala or even most of the indigenous population want to punish those who are responsible'. Raquel Zelaya agrees, telling me that in her work with the Peace Secretariat she came to appreciate that the type of justice that many Guatemalans want is 'to bury missing persons. They want there to be a grave. They want the state to recognize that they weren't criminals. They have never told me, "I want these people to be sentenced for genocide."' In light of this Zelaya questions whether a high profile trial will do anything other 'make the army hide more information on where people were buried', effectively keeping justice out of reach.

The demand for retributive justice has also led to criticism of the amnesties offered as a means of securing participation in truth commission processes. Some critics consider that amnesty can never contribute to reconciliation because it implies that the state has the power to pardon those responsible for human rights violation, when in reality this power inheres only in victims, survivors, and their families (Sanford 2003: 261). The amnesty offered by the South African TRC, for example, was conditional upon perpetrators making a full disclosure of their role in human rights violations, and the demonstration that these acts were associated with a political objective. This process has been criticized for amounting to a form of impunity available to perpetrators of torture and murder, and in some senses this is true, creating what has been termed a 'justice deficit' for the new regime that threatened to deprive it of legitimacy in the eyes of many victims (Gibson 2004: 259). While the amnesty hearings in the South African TRC did bring the truth of many appalling atrocities to light, the experience left many South Africans appalled that such violent perpetrators could be granted amnesty for their crimes, a fact often described as among the greatest failings of the TRC process (Gibson 2004: 261). Others, however, counter that the act of making full, public disclosure 'did not constitute simple or crass impunity' and was seen as a remedy to both personal and political amnesia (Villa-Vicencio 2003: 238). In allowing the truth to be aired so fully and so publicly, amnesty became 'a tool of social regeneration' that was a counter to calls for vengeance as, through testifying for immunity, perpetrators 'publicly incriminated themselves and laid bare the evils of apartheid' (Verdeja 2009: 108, 110).

Closely related to these concerns with forms of justice is the demand for reparation as an element of restorative justice. Eric Doxtader (2004: 28) sees reparation as a relational process, 'an exchange that opens and invites opportunities for mutual understanding, reintegration and collective decision-making'. Reparation forms an important component of many reconciliation efforts, whether in the form of monetary payment or through other forms of redress such as exhumations, public acknowledgment, apology, and public mourning (Sanford 2003: 20). Reparation is explicitly concerned with 'the question of how material and symbolic compensation can work to acknowledge the wounds of the past, restore human dignity and create platforms for collective (re)integration and nation-building' (Doxtader 2004: 27–8).

Proposals for financial reparations have been beset with difficulties. In part this stems from the challenges of agreeing on the nature and type of harm that has been done in the context of a contentious and contested history. But often the problem with reparations stems from the tendency to define them in material terms—including monetary payments, health benefits, educational opportunities, and land—which may all contribute to helping those who have been wronged regain their security and plan for the future, but can never provide adequate compensation for what has been lost. In many instances victims of past violations may be more interested in memorials and spaces that explain the truth of the past and enable public debate (Doxtader 2004: 26). Framed in this way, reparations can be seen to create important symbolic benefits for victims and survivors by demonstrating the illegitimacy of past acts (Barnard-Naudé 2008: 200). Suasnavar emphasizes the importance of reparations in this light, in providing 'dignification for victims'. He tells me:

> It's not a question of them having to receive a house or some land, but sometimes just simply the fact of recognizing that they have lost a member of their family and that they are citizens of their country and they are not just individuals but survivors and that they exist.

Suasnavar points to the move in Guatemala to change the name of the national reparations commission to the compensation commission, arguing that 'you cannot repair a life, you can just compensate for some of the damage'. This was a view also expressed by the REHMI report:

> Reparations cannot bring back life nor recover the enormous social and cultural losses. Nonetheless, the government has the obligation to take measures that help to compensate for some of the losses suffered by the victims and survivors of atrocities and crimes against humanity and that enable populations affected by the violence to live with dignity.
>
> (Recovery of Historical Memory Project (REMHI) 1999: 101)

A similar view was expressed by Desmond Tutu in relation to reparations in South Africa, although there the terms were reversed. Tutu (1999: 61) explains that the TRC commissioners tried to avoid the term 'compensation' in recognition of the impossibility of ever compensating for the loss of a family member. However the commission did recommend an amount of money be paid to the recognized victims, an amount that was 'meant to be symbolic rather than substantial':

> It was a way the nation sought to say, in effect, to victims: We acknowledge that you suffered a gross violation of your rights. Nothing can ever replace your loved one. But as a nation we are saying, we are sorry, we have opened the wounds of your suffering and sought to cleanse them; this reparation is as balm, an ointment, being poured over the wounds to assist in their healing.

Disappointingly for these victims, the application of this balm was much delayed, and it was only in 2003 that the South African government authorized a one-off reparation payment of R30,000 (less than US$3,000) to eligible victims (Doxtader 2004: 31). As suggested in Chapter 7, amounts such as this are unlikely to have significant impacts on widespread inequality. As a relational measure, however, such a payment may be important in recognizing the place of victims in a divided society, perhaps contributing to a sense of individual or collective healing.

Apology, forgiveness, and healing

Central to the relational tasks of reconciliation efforts are the projects designed to draw former enemies into relationship with one another through apology, forgiveness and individual and societal healing. Indeed, as discussed in Chapter 2, these ideas often dominate discussion of reconciliation at the expense of more political understandings. Many find the emphasis on apology and forgiveness problematic, both because of the Christian roots of these concepts and because of the burden placed on victims who are asked to forgive the perpetrators of violations against them. Yet despite these concerns, it is evident that these concepts and practices retain an important place in relational reconciliation efforts.

Apologies remain a deeply symbolic means of publicly expressing responsibility and regret for past wrongs, particularly by political elites who are seeking to rebuild damaged relationships and respond to complex social issues (Verdeja 2009: 79, 83). As such, apologies have become 'a liberal marker of national political stability and strength rather than shame', an effort by nations to demonstrate that they have to come to terms with their pasts (Barkan 2000: xxix). Indeed, some consider apology to be the 'defining method of reconciliation politics', transcending rather than satisfying the requirements of 'perfect justice' (Phillips 2005: 119). Verdeja (2009: 85) suggests that elite apologies can perform three key tasks:

First, they promote the restoration of victims' sense of moral value and represent a first step at integrating them as citizens. Second, apologies can generate public reflection and debate about social norms by refocusing public discussion to their violation and requiring a new consideration of desired relations between the state and society. Third, they can make critical reinterpretations of history necessary by reframing the past and consequently undermining apologist historical accounts.

In this view, apologies can perform an agonistic function, opening political space in which citizens may reflect on more critical views of their troubled histories. Importantly, however, an apology should not be interpreted as the end point in a process of conflict resolution. Apologies are not simply an act but a *process* focused on the possibility of a future relationship (Verdeja 2009: 82).

The 2008 Australian apology is an interesting example of much that is effective in apology, and much that remains inadequate. An apology to the Stolen Generations was first recommended in the *Bringing them Home* report, and Prime Minister Howard's persistent rejection of this demand produced an 'unhelpful simplification' of some of the wider issues raised in discussions of reconciliation (Goot and Rowse 2007: 141). On the anniversary of the release of the report the first Sorry Day was held, involving hundreds of community activities and the first signing of Sorry Books that eventually collected hundreds of thousands of signatures in support of a national apology. Although this 'apology movement' continued to grow in subsequent years, it was not until a change of government in November 2007 that there was a firm commitment to proceed with a national apology. On 13 February 2008, during the first sitting of the new parliament, the new prime minister, Kevin Rudd made a moving speech in the House of Representatives that produced an outpouring of emotion around the country. In a moment that had been long anticipated, Rudd acknowledged that:

> The time has now come for the nation to turn a new page in Australia's history by righting the wrongs of the past and so moving forward with confidence to the future. We apologise for the laws and policies of successive Parliaments and governments that have inflicted profound grief, suffering and loss on these our fellow Australians. We apologise especially for the removal of Aboriginal and Torres Strait Islander children from their families, their communities and their country. For the pain, suffering and hurt of these Stolen Generations, their descendants and for their families left behind, we say sorry. To the mothers and the fathers, the brothers and the sisters, for the breaking up of families and communities, we say sorry. And for the indignity and degradation thus inflicted on a proud people and a proud culture, we say sorry.
>
> (Rudd 2008)

Despite the significance of the moment, however, the apology also demonstrated some significant shortcomings familiar to other apology initiatives elsewhere in the world. Firstly, despite significant consultation with indigenous peoples around Australia, the apology seemed designed to contribute to the nation-building agenda that many Aboriginal and Torres Strait Islander people reject, describing them as 'fellow Australians' rather than acknowledging their sovereignty, and omitting any reference to the genocide described in the *Bringing them Home* report, thus failing to adequately recognize the wider injustice perpetrated against them (Muldoon and Schaap 2012: 184, 188). Secondly, this inadequacy was heightened by the government's refusal to even discuss the question of compensation. It has been widely acknowledged that where apologies are not accompanied by 'direct and immediate actions' (Minow 1998: 116), or are otherwise without 'a practical component', which may include paying compensation, they may amount to little more than a 'hollow symbolic statement' that does little to transform the status of victims and survivors (Verdeja 2009: 82). In the Australian case, the failure to offer any kind of material reparations beyond the establishment of the Healing Foundation, reflected a significant failure to acknowledge the political implications of child removal policies as a part of Australia's colonial, nation-building endeavour (Muldoon and Schaap 2012: 188). Indeed, in our interview Florence Onus insists that 'the word sorry is an *action* word. It's not enough to just say sorry. You've got to then take steps and follow it through.'

In light of these shortcomings, it is evident that there are also limits to the type of forgiveness that is possible following the making of an apology. The concept of forgiveness is valued for its restorative capacities and its alleged ability to foster harmony. Without forgiveness, resentment may fuel violence and allow the past to dominate the present and future through a politics driven by vengeance and rage (Potter 2006: 3). One of the world's most prominent advocates of the importance of forgiveness in reconciliation efforts, Desmond Tutu, contends that forgiveness does not require those who have been wronged to condone what has been done, but it does mean that the wrong must be taken seriously, 'drawing out the sting in the memory that threatens to poison our entire existence' (Tutu 1999: 271). Onus also maintains that 'the healing process is about forgiveness'. After apology she believes the 'next step' is 'letting go and forgiveness'. But she acknowledges that many Aboriginal and Torres Strait Islander people are still unable or unwilling to forgive.

Schaap (2005: 109) makes an important argument about the contribution that forgiveness may make to political life. He describes the political undertaking to forgive as 'a struggle to settle the meaning of the wrongful act in the past for the sake of our life in common' (Schaap 2005: 110). Significantly, Schaap suggests that 'a willingness to forgive creates a space for truth telling and the assumption of political responsibility'; a space in which divided societies may struggle over the past and to determine and sustain what is held in common by the society (Schaap 2005: 115).

Nevertheless, the emphasis that has been placed on forgiveness has also been criticized on a number of fronts. First, forgiveness is often criticized for the burden it places on the victims of past wrongs, particularly in the context of official truth commissions and state apologies that may provide victims with little space in which to demand a different type of accountability through which their justifiable anger may be recognized and legitimated (Chapman 2002: 169; Verdeja 2009: 16). Second, it is noted that forgiveness focuses on the societal *symptoms* of past violence and contemporary division, while leaving the *root causes* and existing power inequities intact (Hovland 2003: 15). Hugo Van der Merwe tells me that he can see how the language of forgiveness, so favoured by Desmond Tutu, was 'compelling at that time' for 'a country that was in so much pain'. In retrospect, however, it seems to him that this language has 'created a bit of a cul-de-sac in the discussion on how to move reconciliation forward'. Finally, in contrast to Schaap's view that the capacity to forgive may open political space, Verdeja suggests that a prescribed forgiveness may in fact close it down, overdetermining the shape of reconciliation discourse and defining permissible politics not in terms of the actual content of political claims but in terms of the risk of future conflict and antagonism (Verdeja 2009: 17–18). For Verdeja, this does not mean that forgiveness has no place in political reconciliation, only that it should not be the centerpiece of these efforts (Verdeja 2009: 20).

Much of the significance attached to ideals of forgiveness in reconciliation efforts draws on the belief that the capacity to forgive is linked to both individual and collective healing. At the individual level, victims, survivors, and their families are thought to require both cognitive healing—that is, to understand their experiences in the context of political events—and psychological healing for the injuries that have resulted from trauma, torture, and loss (Daly and Sarkin 2007: 46). Tutu (1999: 105) maintains that many South Africans who testified before the TRC 'had found relief, and experienced healing, just through the process of telling their own story' and the acceptance, affirmation, and acknowledgment that they received in response. Certainly, many of my interviewees emphasized the value of work that focuses on healing. In Australia, Florence Onus reads me a statement, written by Miriam Rose, made by the board of the Healing Foundation that addresses the question of what healing means for their organization:

> What is healing? Healing is a sacred process that strengthens people, families, communities and whole of nations to be restored to wellbeing and wholeness. It is a personal journey that can involve recovery from trauma, addiction and other types of adversity and includes experiences such as cultural renewal, change and reconnection to spirit. Healing is also a collective journey that involves the restoration

of human rights, the process of recognition, building strong community and cultural connections. It is about respect for all members of community including men, women, youth, children and elders and about transcending the harmful legacy of colonisation. In particular, the history of child removal that continues to impact on today's generation. The Healing Foundation recognises that healing is about our journey with non-indigenous Australians and the need to continue to work together to achieve reconciliation and self-determination. Healing must ultimately allow individuals, families and communities to reach their highest potential. Healing can restore lives to strong spirit, strong culture, strong people.

In South Africa, Michael Lapsley remains convinced that 'the healing of memories' allows traumatized people to connect at 'the deepest human level', which he believes is important for national reconciliation. Lapsley pursues this work in what he calls 'safe and sacred spaces' in which people can 'begin to deal with how the past of the nation had affected them as individuals'. Undine Whande has also observed the way in which people who experience 'incredible furious anger' about the wrongs done to them and their communities, can, through processes focused on the healing of memories, 'find a place where [the anger] can sit'. In Northern Ireland, Gerry Foster observes that

> sometimes people just think that they haven't been heard or no one's paying them attention. And if someone from the enemy camp is in the room and hears their story, sometimes that's enough—just that someone's heard how they feel, someone from that side.

In Guatemala, Rosenda Camey believes that the anger and fury that Mayan women are 'carrying inside' is having a range of negative impacts, telling me it has been 'consuming our soul' and making women sick. In response, she has begun working with other women on 'Mayan resilience'. Camey had previously rejected the notion of resilience for its implication that 'indigenous people can withstand everything, we can put up with poverty and earthquakes and war'. Now, however, she is trying to use this idea to connect with cultural ways of healing:

> There's music, we have merriment, we have dance, we have poetry, song, and it's because of this that we're still alive. If it weren't for all of this, if it weren't for all of these methodological tools that exist in our culture, we wouldn't be here anymore.

One individual working in the indigenous healing sector in Australia (who preferred not to be named) tells me that the 'connection to your Aboriginality is the first step to healing'. For this person, the work will continue regardless of what changes at the constitutional and institutional levels of Australian society:

> Even if every non-Aboriginal person in this country packed up and left tomorrow, there's still so much anger in the Aboriginal community that it would do nothing. They could leave all the money and all the buildings and everything behind and go, 'It's yours, sorry about that,' and we'd still be no closer to being healed than we are today. The damage is done.

In this sense, healing processes can be understood as an attempt to negotiate the public emotional life of a divided society, placing anger and fear in context and drawing on other emotions, such as empathy and compassion, in the hope of establishing a more respectful relationship across difference and division (Hutchison and Bleiker 2013: 87). An agonistic approach to reconciliation underscores the open-ended nature of such efforts, allowing that the past can always be revisited and reanalyzed, and countering suggestions that the work of reconciliation is ever complete. Certainly, these relational processes focused on truth, justice, and healing are only one component of reconciliation efforts, not the sole area of endeavor as is often assumed. They are 'a point of departure, rather than a point of closure' (Sieder 2003: 222), often revealing the extent of the effort still required both at other levels and in other relational domains that may enable former enemies to live together without violence.

Note

1 In May 2013 former dictator General Efrain Ríos Montt was found guilty of overseeing the killings by the armed forces of at least 1,771 members of the Maya Ixil population during his 1982–1983 rule. Less than two weeks later, however, Guatemala's Constitutional Court set aside the conviction on a legal technicality. A fresh trial began in January 2015 but was suspended within hours after Ríos Montt's defence team raised doubts about the judge's impartiality.

11 Sharing space

Physical divisions and other forms of segregation between opposing community groups often mark the landscape of deeply divided societies. These may take the form of the 'peace walls' in Northern Ireland, the more subtle spatial and social segregation evident in Australia, or the growing private security architecture of South Africa and Guatemala, all of which have persisted long after the formal end to hostilities. This chapter examines the challenges for societies seeking to find ways to live together again after conflict has kept them apart, exploring both the resistance to physical desegregation and the many ongoing efforts involved in helping communities to share space. The chapter also argues that the persistence of social segregation presents a significant barrier to opportunities for agonistic engagement.

In many divided societies, relational reconciliation efforts have focused on positive contact and prejudice reduction work. Much of this is based on Allport's (1954) contact hypothesis, which suggests that identity barriers can be broken down through the use of controlled contact, focusing on shared concerns (Hancock 2012: 117). Contact theory, which rests on the assumption that inter-group hostility will be reduced if groups are brought into regular contact with each other, has a clear appeal for policy makers seeking to resolve protracted ethnic conflict (Donnelly and Hughes 2009: 150). Practices that have focused on positive contact have tended to prioritize the creation of intergroup harmony and the development of friendships and interpersonal relationships. The belief is that these approaches will contribute to demystifying the unknown 'other' community, thereby fostering reconciliation.

Assessments of the contact hypothesis diverge. On the one hand, especially in urban communities where former enemies rub shoulders on a daily basis, it is thought important to focus less on grand gestures between political elites and more on the development of mundane yet hugely significant nods of respect and recognition among historically segregated citizens in their daily interactions. It is often at this micro level that government-sponsored or community-led interventions can most directly ameliorate antagonisms (Bollens 2013: 375). Developing strategies that will encourage and enable the sharing of space is seen as an important counter to continued segregation, as the latter encourages both 'identity performance' among divided groups and the associated disputes over territory that 'draw sustenance from the need for inter-community separation' (Shirlow 2008: 74–5). On the other hand, critics suggest that positive contact work may avoid some of the more complex relational requirements of multi-level conflict transformation, particularly by promoting false assumptions of equality and muting the drive for more transformative change (Nagda *et al.* 2012: 215). While this is certainly true, moves to increase contact and reduce segregation do have the potential to open political spaces to more challenging agonistic engagement.

Geographies of conflict

In many deeply divided societies, there has been a common historical pattern towards the physical separation of opposing groups. This may have involved the displacement and forced relocation of oppressed groups, the construction of walls and other physical divisions between communities, the building of gated communities, and an increase in security forces. These strategies are often intended to foster perceptions of physical safety, particularly for elites, but invariably also facilitate forms of psychological separation that lead to long-term instability (Bollens 2013: 377). As a result of different combinations of these strategies, each of the countries in this study has been left with a distinctive pattern of division and segregation that reflects the roots of their historical conflicts.

To the outside observer, the Australian case presents a fairly subtle example of segregation, at least in urban areas. Over 70 per cent of all Aboriginal and Torres Strait Islander people today live in cities or regional urban areas (Australian Bureau of Statistics 2008). Like many other social and cultural groups in Australia, indigenous people have not ended up living in cities as a matter of simple choice, but also as a matter of economic necessity. But unlike other population groups, Aboriginal and Torres Strait Islander people have experienced distinctive 'push' factors that flow from Australia's colonial history. As in settler colonies elsewhere in the world, Australian cities are built on land forcibly acquired from Aboriginal people through dispossession and displacement. Many indigenous people were pushed off their land by the encroachment of agriculture and development, and later by growing unemployment in regional areas. In some rural areas of Australia, the places labelled 'towns' were created as 'zones of physical exclusion' for indigenous people, erstwhile 'bastions of colonial privilege' that allowed otherwise white communities to keep Aboriginal and Torres Strait Islander people at arm's length (Rowse 2000: 85). These strategies of exclusion created what were known as 'fringedweller' camps on the edges of many regional towns and urban centres. Today, Gary Highland observes that even though these camps may not exist as they once did, this history has left many indigenous people 'still feeling like fringedwellers in this country'.

In contrast to rural spaces, cities tended to be much more 'absorptive' of Aboriginal people (Rowse 2000: 85), providing a home for the growing diaspora of indigenous peoples displaced by the continuing settler colonial encroachment on their lands. At least until the 1950s, the presence of indigenous people in Australian cities was still understood as a problem (Fredericks *et al.* 2008: 3), and as a potential threat to white safety and civility. Colonial policies insisted that Aboriginal people belonged outside of the city and therefore closely controlled their movement and behavior through curfews, physical containment, and other punitive restrictions. Those who chose to live in ostensibly white cities and towns were also subject to strict controls, but were thought to have signaled their preparedness to abandon their cultural links in order to live 'like respectable middle-class citizens' (Morgan 2006: 48). Today, urban communities still pose difficult questions for the relationships between indigenous and non-indigenous people in Australia, and many non-indigenous people retain the view that the choice to live in an urban area somehow means that Aboriginal and Torres Strait Islander people have relinquished their indigeneity and thus do not form a distinct community. This appearance of physical integration is, however, 'deceptive', with many urban-dwelling indigenous peoples retaining a stronger connection with indigenous people in rural or remote areas than with their non-indigenous urban neighbours (Behrendt 1995: 75–6).

Outside of urban areas, and particularly in the more remote regions of Australia, Aboriginal and Torres Strait Islander groups are often referred to as 'communities' as though each is a homogenous group. Here again, however, Australia's colonial history has created a very different reality. The majority of Aboriginal communities have been created by the forced relocation of multiple kinship groups that, prior to colonization, would have occupied discrete territories—and that in many cases still retain different languages and systems of law, despite their colocation. The dispersal and dispossession that resulted from colonization often threw different groups together, on government reserves and church missions, and in settlements on the fringes of rural towns, where many groups have remained. 'Community' as a term to describe these areas with a predominantly indigenous population only came into common usage in the early 1970s (Peters-Little 2000: 10). Tragically, many of these communities are today experiencing a social crisis, a 'self-perpetuating cycle of poverty and despair' (Stokes 2002: 196), marked by overcrowded housing, alcohol and other substance abuse, high rates of violence, and often extreme poverty. In the latest report on indigenous disadvantage in Australia, the proportion of Aboriginal and Torres Strait Islander households living in houses with access to clean water and functioning sewerage and electricity services had fallen from 83 per cent in 2008 to 78 per cent in 2012–2013 (Steering

Committee for the Review of Government Service Provision 2014). And, despite numerous examples of indigenous success in a range of fields, a view of people living in remote squalor remains the predominant image of Aboriginal and Torres Strait Islander people among a majority of non-indigenous Australians, further exacerbating their experience of social segregation. This stereotype, combined with Australia's population demographics, means that most non-indigenous Australians have little or no contact with indigenous people. Data from the Australia Reconciliation Barometer shows that around six in ten non-indigenous Australians have rare contact (41 per cent) or no contact at all (18 per cent) with Aboriginal and Torres Strait Islander people (Reconciliation Australia 2012: 12).

The Guatemalan and South African cases offer far more extreme examples of continuing segregation, in large part due to the persistence of gross socioeconomic inequality on a mass scale, as has been discussed earlier in the book. But other aspects of these countries' historical conflicts are also contributing to contemporary segregation. Across Guatemala, Judith Maxwell (2009: 91) observes that '[t]he scars of genocide still lie on the land'. The last several decades have seen huge population shifts, with large numbers of Mayan people fleeing to the capital to escape 'napalm, death squads, and civil patrols' during the 1970s and 1980s, and, more recently, to escape poverty, malnutrition, and lack of employment and basic services. The conflict also affected different parts of the country quite differently. The predominantly Ladino eastern region remained relatively untouched by the extremes of violence in the 1980s, while other areas, particularly the rural highlands, were almost obliterated by the scorched earth tactics of the Guatemalan military. This diversity of experience, combined with the existence of over twenty different language groups inhabiting mountainous landscape with limited communication across regions, have combined to maintain the country's deep divisions (Arriaza and Roht-Arriaza 2010: 208). This is also evident in the capital itself, where high crime rates mean that the middle and upper classes rarely go out at night and socialize only among themselves, preferring the security of gated communities and apartment houses where security guards, personal weapons, alarm systems, and razor wire have become the norm. Jose Suasnavar points to the growth in the number of private estates in Guatemala City, suggesting that one instance of robbery or murder will be enough to see a community 'call the security company and close [the community] off with guards':

> Closing our spaces, squares, neighborhoods, gives us the idea that we are safer, but it makes us live in small islands that could lead us to disintegrate as citizens, with little confidence in the external environment.

The growth of these private security estates in Guatemala City is creating an urban landscape that is as divided as the rest of the country. As Reilly (2009: 40) notes, 'The ongoing social casualty is trust.'

A similar pattern of segregation is evident in South Africa. The Institute for Justice and Reconciliation (2006: 11) suggests that South African communities are divided both by their history and by the new socio-political and economic challenges (discussed in Chapter 7) that have led to 'even further division'. As in Australia and Guatemala, many communities in South Africa have been left 'traumatized and dysfunctional' by the ravages of the past, creating a 'double challenge' to both improve the material circumstances of their lives, and 'create functional neighbourhoods where people feel safe and at home' (Institute for Justice and Reconciliation 2006: 4). Undoing the residential segregation through which apartheid-era attitudes and policy were manifested was always going to be an immense task. As Tutu (1999: 274) noted,

> unless houses replace the hovels and shacks in which most blacks live, unless blacks gain access to clean water, electricity, affordable health care, decent education, good jobs, and a safe environment—things which the vast majority of whites have taken for granted for so long—we can just as well kiss reconciliation goodbye.

In 1994 Joe Slovo, the first ANC housing minister, estimated that half the black population lacked secure housing and called for half a million homes to be built in the next five years. As Fairweather (2006: 161–2) notes, however, 'Not only was this target not met, but the RDP houses (labelled "kennels" by the residents) were often even tinier than the "matchbox" houses built for urban Africans in the apartheid era'. Biko (2013: 212) notes the irony of the fact that the current national housing schemes so closely resemble 'apartheid-era town planning and racially segmented development strategies', where today the trade-off for access to a low-quality 'kennel' house is relocation to a distant location in which people must attempt to reconstitute their communities with little social support. Travelling around South Africa today, one is still confronted by the enormous squatter camps, known as 'informal settlements', on the fringes of urban areas. The townships and settlements, often located far from employment opportunities and community amenities, house up to two million people each, in dwellings cobbled together from found materials, generally with limited access to running water, electricity, and ablution facilities, and suffering poor quality state services such as dirt roads, infrequent rubbish collection, and poor storm-water drainage (Saul and Bond 2014: 168). Lucy Holborn agrees that recent housing policy in South Africa has 'recreated the apartheid geography' because the social housing that is built by the government is invariably 'on the outskirts of town all in one group in a desperate place'.

And yet this poverty often exists cheek by jowl with wealthy, predominantly white suburbs. Biko notes the other great irony of post-apartheid South Africa, in the form of higher security gates, more armed response guards patrolling the suburbs and gated communities, and 'a similar tacit complicity to police brutality' to that of the apartheid era (Biko 2013: 210). For the middle-class South Africans locked securely behind electric fencing, razor wire and high walls, life in the 'war zones' of the squatter camps is impossible to imagine (Terreblanche 2012: 104). Haniff Hoosen makes the point that 'the amount of bricks that people use to build a boundary wall on their properties, which are so huge, is sufficient to build two or three houses for the poorer communities'. Oscar Siwali agrees that '[t]he challenge that we still face is that the country is still divided. White people are still living in their separate area and black people are still living in their separate areas'. He describes his own community, where he has lived for nearly 15 years, during which time it has transformed from a primarily Afrikaans-speaking white area to a more mixed area, with an increasing 'exodus' of white residents unhappy with the changing demographics. This was a narrative I heard repeatedly. As Holborn notes, 'Integration is probably only happening in middle class suburbs among people who get to go to mixed race schools and universities.' The difference, as Murithi points out, is that most black South Africans have little mobility. While middle class areas are slowly integrating, townships remain wholly black. Certainly, as Vincent Maphai reminds me, part of the reason for South Africa's continuing segregation is purely demographic given the 90 per cent black population. Maphai tells me 'Black areas will always be largely black. You won't have whites moving into Soweto in droves, so it will always be 90 per cent black residential.' Nevertheless, there are also other forces at play, and the investment priorities of private capital—more focused on developing expensive gated communities than housing in townships—are a clear impediment to the transformation of South Africa's segregated landscape (Muvingi 2009: 180).

Walls of peace

Northern Ireland presents a famous, if somewhat different example of geographic segregation that is worth examining in some depth. Across Northern Ireland, the two main communities predominantly 'live apart', including through very visible forms of residential segregation in which communities are divided by what are known as 'interfaces', which may be either a physical wall or barrier, or a less obvious demarcation in the form of painted kerbstones, graffiti, murals, flags and other emblems (Byrne *et al.* 2006: 13). This way of living has become normalized over generations, meaning that children today are still born into communities effectively divided from their neighbours. As Little (2014: 68) notes, these divisions 'are not just symbols of violence and conflict; in their own way they violently interject in the upbringing of generations of children'. Residential separation remains a central fact of life in Northern Ireland, with geographic areas routinely referred to as either Catholic or Protestant (Nolan

2012: 149). Patterns of living in Northern Ireland are still largely defined by practices of avoidance, with people making choices about where they shop, socialise, work, and educate their children based on proximity to members of the other major community (Acheson *et al.* 2011: 32). Brendan McAllister emphasizes the significance of these dynamics of segregation:

> You know, violence is no longer the defining feature of our conflict here. Division is. Most of the division is polite and civil. The international media will feature the riots that occasionally happen, and the peace walls, but they're not typical. There aren't any peace walls where I live, but I can show you the dividing lines.

According to the Northern Ireland Housing Executive (NIHE), 90 per cent of social housing in Northern Ireland is still segregated (although only 16 per cent of housing falls into this category) despite over 80 per cent of respondents to the Northern Ireland Life and Times Survey expressing a preference for living in a mixed-religion neighbourhood (Nolan 2012: 10, 151). Further, socially deprived communities continue to carry the heaviest socio-spatial burdens created by fear and residential segregation (Shirlow 2008: 86). Many of the most segregated communities—those divided by the so-called 'peace walls' that carve up many areas of Belfast—are also amongst the poorest and most traumatized, and the existence of barriers and interfaces continues to limit economic opportunities by keeping employers and investment at bay (Community Relations Council 2008: 3, 5).

Of course the divisions between communities are never absolute. Neil Jarman points out that the definition of segregation in Northern Ireland is an area where 80 per cent of residents come from one community, meaning that even in these situations there is 'a nucleus of sharing', although he acknowledges that the minority community 'doesn't get a chance to express its collective identity' through the display of flags or cultural symbols, or in other community celebrations. Nevertheless, for the majority in Northern Ireland, the 'default position' continues to be an expectation that there will be parallel provision of services for divided communities, and where parallel services are not available there are evident 'chill factors' that continue to shape people's choices and behaviour (Community Relations Council 2011: 73). Jarman describes to me the two bus routes traversing the area around where we are meeting as an example of public policies that 'support and sustain segregation and reduce the opportunities to share and integrate':

> One bus works its way entirely through Protestant areas and the other one works its way entirely through Catholic areas. They only meet at those crossroads. One comes along and turns this way and the other one comes down and turns that way. So there's a point there where

the buses actually meet but they immediately go off in different directions again.

And this situation is not improving. Indeed, there is evidence to suggest that Northern Ireland has become *more* segregated since 1998, including through the construction of additional interfaces and barriers (Power 2011: 5). The construction of a new peace wall in Belfast was in fact commissioned as late as 2007, close to a decade after the signing of the Belfast Agreement, creating a 25-foot high barrier within the grounds of an integrated primary school in an effort to quell inter-communal violence and disorder (Byrne 2012: 12).

Research for the Belfast Interface Project in 2012 found 99 security barriers and other forms of 'defensive architecture' across Belfast (Byrne 2012: 11). Certainly the peace walls remain the most visible reminder of both the violence of the Troubles, and the continuing segregation between communities, 'a tangible as well as a symbolic manifestation of division' (Byrne 2012: 5, 10). These structures, first built by the British Army in 1969 in response to sectarian violence, were originally constructed from rolls of barbed wire, metal fencing, or low gates, and were intended as temporary barriers to keep the peace. Over time, however, they have evolved into ever more elaborate brick structures, topped with steel fencing and incorporating designs and landscaping intended to disguise their harshness. These structures are clearly no longer seen as temporary but are considered a permanent intervention into the urban landscape (Community Relations Council 2008: 27). Some of them are simply extraordinary to an outsider's eye. Alexandra Park in north Belfast for example, has a peace wall running right through it, dividing the park itself into a Protestant section and a Catholic section. As the Community Relations Council (2008: 3) reminds us, interface barriers do more than provide for physical separation, they also remind the community

> that the hostility, fear and anger of the past remain alive and continue to threaten the peace of people and communities {...}. They freeze the geography and demography of single-identity communities and prevent all sorts of normal freedom of movement {...}. Their continued existence is the greatest single piece of evidence that relationships are not yet 'normal' or equal, but continue to be characterised by insecurity, threat and anxiety.

The Council also points out that the security policy that has led to the erection of these barriers has not been accompanied by thinking and policy-making about when and how they might be removed. It argues that Northern Ireland 'cannot seriously speak of a 'peace process' if people are obliged to live in fear of what might happen to them if they were not physically divided from the neighbouring community' (Community Relations Council 2008: 4).

Community attitudes to the peace walls and other interfaces vary. Research by the University of Ulster (Byrne *et al.* 2012: 27–8) shows that 76 per cent of the general population would like to see peace walls come down now or in the near future, and 38 per cent believe peace walls are still necessary because of the potential for violence. This compares with residents living in close proximity to a peace wall, 69 per cent of whom maintain that the walls are still necessary because of the potential for violence, with 58 per cent remaining worried about police ability to preserve peace and maintain order if the walls were removed. This suggests that while the wider population consider the issue of peace walls in relation to community segregation, local residents remain concerned with questions of physical security. In the face of criticism that walls and barriers reflect failed policy for dealing with security and community difference, advocates of partition maintain that the barriers are both cost effective and able to address inter-communal violence quickly compared with regular policing responses (Byrne 2012: 7). Derick Wilson tells me that, for the middle class, the construction of peace walls and interfaces had the effect of allowing many of them to 'live normally, as if the problem was not theirs':

> The interface areas brought a form of order to this society. Because until the interfaces were created, every time there was an incident, the whole society shook. But once we corralled people behind and within interfaces and walls, then many of the middle classes were able to continue to have the illusion of 'a good life.'

Owen Donnelly emphasizes the value people place on the walls, telling me 'After thirty years of killing and bombing and then an uneasy peace, it's still a very valuable uneasy peace {...}. [People don't want to] {...} do anything that would threaten that'. This certainly chimes with my own observations—the not uncommon sight of properties adjoining a peace wall also having completely caged in backyards suggests that even a wall does not provide an adequate sense of security for these residents, who remain fearful of rocks and other projectiles. Martin McMullan echoes this view, pointing out that it is easy for outsiders to call for the walls to come down, '[b]ut to live there, safety is paramount', and the walls allow people living in these communities to feel that they are in a 'little safe bubble'. At the same time, this can also mean that young people 'won't venture outside of that community for a job, even if they're unemployed and there's a job across the street, because of safety'. As the Community Relations Council (2011: 9) puts it:

> Segregation is not 'choice' but the result of threat, violence, exclusion and hatred, and the fact that it carries on, even 17 years after

the paramilitary ceasefires, is evidence that we have not yet put these monsters to bed. And for as long as they are around what we have is a fragile truce not a real peace.

It is certainly the case that paramilitarism remains a factor in many, mostly working-class, communities, which as Jarman points out, 'has an impact on things like levels of intimidation, of threat, active or incipient, that people might feel in terms of moving into shared areas, mixed housing'. But Michael Culbert questions the extent of genuine danger, asking, 'What exactly is the danger, bar a perception of something or other nebulous?' The challenge, he says, 'is convincing the people at the local level that the dangers really have gone'.

But regardless of the rationale, it seems that in the absence of an alternative policy response to inter-communal violence, the construction of barriers and walls continues to instil a sense of safety and confidence within communities (Byrne 2012: 7,13). Ray Mullan comments on the 'catch 22' of the peace walls in Belfast, noting that 'the wall is a barrier to developing relationships and yet it's the weakness in the relationship that requires a wall in the first place'. Some research also reflects this community ambivalence, showing that residents believe the walls both reduce violence and increase security, and maintain 'tensions and antagonisms between communities' (Community Relations Council 2008: 37). Nevertheless, Mullan believes that the community relations work that his organization and others have been undertaking has seen the walls 'become porous', with more communities opting to open gates in walls at certain times of the day, a development he sees as very positive. But, as Alan Largey suggests, pointing to his head, 'it's the walls in here you need to knock down first'.

This is also an issue that goes beyond the urban areas. While most towns and villages in Northern Ireland tend not to have the physical barriers evident in Belfast and Derry/Londonderry, similar patterns of avoidance persist. Contested spaces in these communities may still give rise to tension and division, and many people's behaviour, movement and sense of safety remain dominated by knowledge of land ownership and patterns of residence, with real effects on the behaviour and attitudes of both individuals and communities (Bell, Jarman and Harvey 2010: 4). Martin McMullan points to the different ways in which this culture of segregation has become normalized among young people in Northern Ireland. He points to a nearby small town, which he describes as 'a Protestant town', which is close to 'a little Catholic town'. In this area, McMullan tells me, 'The Catholics know that they can go to the cinema on a Thursday night. The Protestants know that that's the Catholic night. Young people just accept that {...} but yet they think the conflict hasn't impacted on them'.

Often these less obviously divided communities exist quite peacefully in parallel to each other, with little interaction and very few incidents of violence unless there are 'trigger events' such as disputes over parades or the marking of space with flags and other emblems (Bell, Jarman and Harvey 2010: 10). But in some ways it is the persistence of this kind of self-imposed segregation, without the existence of walls and barriers, which really underscores the relational demands of reconciliation efforts. The competing narratives of the past, discussed in Chapter 3, are evident in the political symbols, flags, and parades that mark the physical and social geography of Northern Ireland, and are a constant reminder of the division between the two main communities (Bell, Hansson and McCaffery 2010: 13). The challenge of undoing these accepted patterns of psychological and physical division is immense.

Changing the landscape

Efforts to transform the landscape of deeply divided societies are taking place across several fronts. Urban planning and other aspects of public policy remain important tools for desegregation. In the wake of violent, historical conflicts, debates about the use of space can become 'potent proxies' for dialogue on other contentious socio-political issues that may still be too difficult to address directly. As Scott Bollens (2013: 375) contends:

> Debates over proposed projects and discussion of physical space provide opportunities to anchor and negotiate dissonant meanings in a post-conflict society; indeed, there are few opportunities other than debates about urban life where these antagonistic impulses take such concrete forms in need of pragmatic negotiation.

According to Bollens, the very act of negotiating over building and development can create opportunities to engage in inclusive processes able to 'provide a laboratory and incubator for cross-ethnic inter-group dialogue, negotiations, and joint production of outcomes', thereby allowing members of divided communities to get to know one another as 'pragmatic partners', even while their more profound differences remain (Bollens 2013: 379).

Public policy in areas such as housing also provides opportunities for transforming geography. Ray Mullan emphasizes the possibilities for more integrated housing, but stresses the need for the Housing Executive to support these initiatives through careful planning:

> We have managed to persuade the Housing Executive to run pilot schemes of integrated housing to show that it is possible, that you can actually have a real residential system based on people of different political and religious backgrounds living together. It needs to be managed {...}. It's not something where you can just put a poster up and say right this is now an integrated housing area {...}. What's

important is that there's a big space in it, that there's a community centre of some sort where people can meet, because if people don't have the opportunity to meet other than across their garden fence, you don't create a community.

Good planning can allow for the creation of an 'everyman's land' within communities, supporting the mutual use of contested spaces and allowing porosity to replace borders without losing the feeling of protection provided by interfaces and other barriers (Bollens 2013: 381).

Generally however, urban planning continues to struggle in the face of the kinds of historical legacies of inequality discussed in Chapter 7. In South Africa, for example, Kindiza Ngubeni maintains that the ANC 'messed up when it comes to the issue of housing'. People are moved from squatter camps to formal housing, and the empty shacks are flattened in an effort to diminish the squalor, but with a massive shortfall in available housing new shacks 'keep on mushrooming'. Relocating people to far-off housing developments has also been ineffective, with many returning to live in squatter camps nearer to the cities in order to access employment opportunities. Later, as people retire and return to the RDP housing they were allocated, they rent out their urban shack as an additional source of income, creating an informal market in poor quality real estate that is driven by persistent poverty. Oscar Siwali acknowledges this, telling me that

until services are fully available to the poorest of the poor, we cannot talk reconciliation. Until the poor communities receive services as the richer or better off communities receive services, until the garbage is picked up as often as it is picked up on the other side. When those things are able to happen, then you can talk about a country where people are able to live together.

Other approaches to geographic transformation, based on the contact hypothesis, draw on ideas of 'indirect reconciliation', which invert standard conceptions of reconciliation—as progressing from acknowledgment to trust to reconciliation—to finally enable communities to work together cooperatively. In contrast, the indirect approach begins with the idea that joint practical activity, involving tasks on which people need to cooperate, will in and of itself create trust and reconciliation, without the need to discuss the rights and wrongs of the past (Govier 2009: 48). In many instances, this type of indirect reconciliation is thought to be happening informally. For example, Namhla Mniki-Mangaliso suggests the importance of South Africans 'just getting on with it' by interacting in the workplace. Her research on the experiences of young executives in South Africa reveals that although many of them are still dealing with issues of prejudice or powerlessness, they are 'making it work, in one way or another, just simply because they have to. Because you have to wake up and go to work and deal with whatever issues you're facing.' Mniki-Mangaliso believes that these workplace relationships are creating other relational breakthroughs in an otherwise segregated society, stating, for example,

> My white colleague in my office might come to my kid's birthday party and start learning about what the party means for me and my culture. Then I might visit them during whatever celebration they have. That convergence is starting to happen. There's not enough of it, but I think it's starting to happen, and I think that's taking us somewhere.

In other instances, however, more formalized efforts are being made to break down patterns of segregation and avoidance. Sometimes these are centred around sport, or art, music or theatre projects, based on the view that the creative and expressive field of human activity 'both nourishes and defines the emergence of a culture of peace' (Ramsbotham *et al.* 2011: 347). In Guatemala, Julio Solórzano-Foppa tells me of several such initiatives that recognize Guatemala as 'a country that has a huge amount of real cultural life in communities', and are using cultural practice as 'the bridges between the different communities'. In Northern Ireland, Jim O'Neill describes a project that brings young people in Derry/Londonderry together with visual artists to develop murals that commemorate important issues and incidents in their communities, giving the young people a sense of ownership over public space and stimulating public dialogue. In South Africa, Shirley Gunn and her colleagues at the Human Rights Media Centre work to bring a wide range of stories to public attention, producing multimedia works that showcase voices not being heard in the mainstream. Gunn highlights the capacity of these narratives to initiate wider dialogue, telling me she is always focused on 'creatively taking opportunities, seizing opportunities, creating opportunities to reach as many people as possible' because she believes that 'the power of narrative can make a difference'. Other efforts at breaking down segregation focus on social interaction around shared concerns such as the environment. For example, Janet Hunt describes a programme developed by ANTaR groups in the Australian Capital Territory in Australia involving public walks guided by indigenous rangers, during which non-indigenous participants can learn about indigenous techniques for managing the environment, an initiative Hunt describes as a strategy for 'breaking down barriers'.

Ways of marking public space are also being contested. Efforts to change the names of streets, sporting grounds, airports and even whole cities have been a feature of desegregation efforts in South Africa and, to a lesser extent, Australia. In Australia, colonial and settler placenames were superimposed over the top of indigenous ways of referring to places, and in recent years there has been an effort to reclaim indigenous naming practices (Hercus and Simpson 2002). One famous example involves the spiritually significant rock site in Central Australia that had been dubbed 'Ayers Rock' by European explorers in the 1870s, with the reclaiming of the Pitjantjatjara and Yankunytjatjara name 'Uluru' reflecting the indigenous ownership of the area following the handing back of the surrounding national park in the 1980s. In South Africa, however, Achille Mbembe (2008: 6–7) suggests that debates over renaming public spaces have often had the effect of 'breaking wide open' the country's 'dirty little secret of prejudice'. Undine Whande points to the 'long battles over street names' that indicate the challenges still remaining in this domain. One South African blogger (Duggan 2012) points out that these processes of renaming are really about 'history and memory and the way in which what we (or others) remember illuminates what we (or they) choose to forget'. This same blog quotes a 2007 press release from the Inkatha Freedom Party, which underscores the significance of these debates in reconciliation efforts:

> We have always contended, since the early days of the struggle against apartheid, that the names of buildings and places directly associated with the worst excesses of our colonial and apartheid past would have to change to allow for a process of healing and reconciliation. We have always maintained that the symbols of our past oppressive regime will have to give way to appropriate symbols of democracy.

Indeed, these processes of (re)naming, and their implications for memory and memorialization, remain potent forces in the marking of segregated communities, particularly with regard to the commemoration of past struggles and lives lost. In Australia, for example, it remains a source of considerable anger for many Aboriginal and Torres Strait Islander people that there is no monument or remembrance shrine recognizing the indigenous lives lost in the frontier wars that marked invasion and colonization (Watson 2007: 29). Despite ongoing campaigns, the Australian War Memorial has rejected all calls to recognize frontier warfare, a stance that as Henry Reynolds (2013: 46–7) contends, would not stand out as such stark hypocrisy 'had modern Australia not decided that war was the transcendent national experience, that the Australian War Memorial could pre-eminently instruct the young in what it meant to be Australian'. And in contrast, the installation known as Reconciliation Place in Canberra, Australia's capital—intended as a monument to reconciliation itself—is completely silent on the issue of frontier conflict, an example of what Peter Read describes as 'reconciliation-without-history' that characterized the years of the Howard government during which Reconciliation Place was constructed. The site is described officially as 'a place which recognizes the importance of understanding the shared history of Indigenous and non-Indigenous Australians', and yet it carefully avoids any confrontational aspects of this history in favour of rock engravings and platitudes. The only exception is the memorial to the Stolen Generations, which also happens to be the only memorial planned by the victims of past government policies and created without government monitoring and interference (Read 2010: 290).

Larger museums have also proved to be problematic. Peace museums, now developing around the world as part of an international movement, are intended to provide spaces in which art and other media can engage attendees in reflection on the past and the significance of peace. South Africa has certainly embraced the museum movement enthusiastically, turning the former prison on Robben Island off Cape Town into a museum and building both the Apartheid Museum and, more recently, Freedom Park. Smaller museums and memorials abound, marking many of the significant events during South Africa's struggle history. And yet there remain some significant problems with a great deal of curatorial practice in South Africa. As Verne Harris suggests, 'The mode is not one of engagement'. At the Apartheid Museum, for example, Harris says 'you can see school kids going through in huge numbers {...}. But there's no actual serious attempt to engage them.' Harris maintains that this approach is primarily 'about reinforcing a small number of dominant narratives {...}. We're not actually interested in fleshing out some of the counter narratives, creating space for new interpretations'. Narratives of reconciliation seem particularly problematic. On my visit to the Apartheid Museum the exhibition on reconciliation had been dismantled, reflecting dissatisfaction with its contents. And at Freedom Park, the final room reflecting the contemporary moment in South Africa's journey over many hundreds of years, pointed only to the new South African flag as an example of its reconciled status, before instead highlighting a display on the Gacaca community courts in Rwanda as an example of reconciliation in action.

It will be interesting to observe how these practices of memory and memorialization develop and mark the landscape in Guatemala. At present, it is possible to observe several dozen small memorials to the conflict, each of which reflects community efforts to commemorate local deaths. These vary greatly around Guatemala, from a mural, to a small monument in a cemetery, to a small museum of four or five rooms. Diane Nelson (2009: 80) describes these memorials as 'brave co- and counter-memorations' that are 'doing vital memorializing work' to help 'create a public, shared, and fixed rendering of the mass experience of violence'. It is disappointing, Nelson says, that more attention is not paid to these efforts, 'that they have not had more resonance', although it is evident that this apparent lack of interest can be at least partly ascribed to the fact that 'most people's energies are devoted to barely surviving'. Nevertheless, there is certainly no national memorial or museum acknowledging the period of civil war and the damage it left behind.

Several Guatemalans are working to rectify this situation. Dissatisfied with small-scale, local memorialization, Julio Solórzano-Foppa and his colleagues have embarked on the creation of a national museum and memorial, the proposed *Memorial para la Concordia*, which aims to 'speak about all the victims' and seeks 'the dignification of all victims, caused by either side'. The project will both gather together information on the victims and provide what Solórzano-Foppa calls a 'shrine space' that will allow people to mourn Guatemala's 45,000 disappeared (including Solórzano-Foppa's own mother) who do not have a grave that can be visited on *Dia de los Muertos*. These memorial spaces are to be complemented by a museum for human rights, which will place the war in Guatemala in the context of other Latin American Cold War counterinsurgency wars, and also in the wider historical context of other genocides such as the holocaust in World War II. The location of the proposed memorial is also significant. The selected site is the location of the former secret police archives—in themselves a treasure trove of information about deaths and disappearances during *la violencia* that was only discovered in 2005—which also housed a clandestine jail known as *La Isla*. Solórzano-Foppa thinks it is fitting to carry on the tradition of building memorials 'in places where violations of human rights occurred', and to locate it in a grim section of Guatemala City that is 'very populated' but 'has no contemporary development whatsoever and has a lot of violence and crime and youth gangs and drugs'. Solórzano-Foppa hopes that building the memorial there will open up that part of the city to a wider range of people, potentially transforming the cityscape.

Histories of conflict are marked on the landscape in other ways as well. For example, there are approximately 2,000 murals marking different territories in Northern Ireland, often representing a threatening militarism that sends a clear warning for others to stay away. To address this legacy, the Arts Council of Northern Ireland has been working with a consortium of other organizations on a project called 'Re-Imaging Communities', which aims to 'replace paramilitary murals and insignia with less threatening expressions of identity', for example in new murals of the football player George Best, or in representations of Celtic mythology. Indeed, while I was in Belfast I witnessed one of the more famous paramilitary murals, on Sandy Row, being painted over. The image of a balaclava-wearing armed militant, accompanied by the text 'YOU ARE NOW ENTERING LOYALIST SANDY ROW HEARTLAND OF SOUTH BELFAST ULSTER FREEDOM FIGHTERS', was replaced with a traditional rendering of King William III, the Prince of Orange. The new image still clearly marked the area as staunchly Protestant and loyalist, but the image itself was far less threatening. Overall, however, these efforts have met with only mixed success. While over 150 new artworks have been created since the Re-Imaging Communities project began, new murals depicting balaclava-wearing loyalist paramilitaries have also appeared on walls in east Belfast, 'an assertion by the paramilitary groups in that area that it was still in business' (Nolan 2012: 75–6).

Considerable public funding and effort is still directed towards managing these issues in Northern Ireland, including through the Northern Ireland Housing Executive's Community Cohesion Unit, which has particular responsibilities for managing issues relating to flags and sectional symbols; segregation and integration; race relations; interface areas and communities in transition (Byrne *et al.* 2006: 27). Local organizations have also formed what are known as Interface Working Groups, or Interface Monitoring Groups, which bring together representatives from the PSNI with youth and community organizations to discuss activity at local interfaces and plan interventions where required. Often the focus is on working towards the taking down of a barrier, although as Ray Mullan reminds me, this is a 'slow process' that requires a consideration of 'how confidence might be developed within local communities'. In Derry/Londonderry, the post-conflict architecture of the city is also having an impact on the way the two communities relate to one another. In 2011 the Peace Bridge was constructed across the River Firth, making Saint Columb's Park into a shared space that is now easily accessible from the city side of the river. The park is now an area of greater inter-community interaction, which is also the source of some considerable anxiety within the local Interface Monitoring Committee. I sat in on one of these meetings and heard thoughtful discussion about whether groups of young men drinking beer and playing football in the park constituted a security concern, as had been reported in local media. During this discussion a police officer responded to these media reports quite forcefully, saying 'We're learning how to share this space together, and there are people out there who don't want us to succeed.'

Parades also continue to hold particular significance in the management of divided and contested spaces in Northern Ireland. In Belfast I was shown houses built on parade routes that had been constructed without any downstairs windows that could be broken during an outbreak of violence. Although very few parades each year do become violent, they all remain significant markers of the deep division between the two communities. The political response has also been significant, including the creation of the Parades Commission in 1997 as a means of managing disputes about parade routes. The Commission has, however, never been accepted by the Orange Order and sections of the unionist community as a legitimate adjudicator of these disputes (Jarman *et al.* 2009: 17). The approach of finding 'local accommodation' to parading disputes has also proven problematic, especially given the policy of the Grand Lodge of the Orange Order not to meet with 'Sinn Féin controlled residents groups', or with the Parades Commission itself, which clearly limits the potential for achieving local accommodation through face-to-face discussion (Jarman *et al.* 2009: 18). Brendan McAllister finds the administration of parading disputes disappointing. The task, he says, is not to 'Balkanise' Belfast by maintaining segregation based on community affiliation:

> Because if we're really to make this society healthy, we must challenge communities by saying, 'If you want to be a healthy community, show how you look after your minorities, whoever they are.' Instead, we have an attempt to administer cultural expression around parades, by saying, 'There's Protestant ends of this city, and there's Catholic ends, and the Protestants should walk only in the Protestant areas.' {...} They would never say it that way, but that's what they're doing.

Regardless of such shortcomings, however, it would seem that privileging the local in these efforts is crucial. It is, as Leon Wessels (2010: 15) notes, 'at the local level that most people experience conflict' suggesting that this is also where 'the chances of reconciliation are greatest, because people know both each other and the issues at hand'. Much of the effort involved in remaking the landscape of divided societies is also the work of rebuilding communities (Gobodo-Madikizela 2010: 138–9). And while national-level policies and initiatives will remain important, they cannot on their own respond to the needs and experiences of people living in geographically diverse local spaces, and they can ignore both the diverse ways in which people in different localities experienced the conflict, and the importance of local power dynamics that are central to people's lives (Arriaza and Roht-Arriaza 2010: 206). Indeed, as we drill further into practices of relational reconciliation in the next chapter, the significance of micro level, local initiatives will become more evident, not least in terms of their capacity for enabling local communities to engage with concerns that traverse all the levels of a multi-level conflict transformation framework.

12 The need for ongoing dialogue

Beneath the relational demands of dealing with the past, and underlying efforts to break down physical segregation and support divided societies to live together without violence—indeed, underlying *all* the constitutional, institutional and relational challenges outlined in this book—is the need for micro-level efforts that will actually facilitate relationships among people.

Dialogical engagement can, and does, take many forms including community relations work, storytelling, elite dialogue and so on. This type of engagement is a form of political intervention designed to draw opposing groups into a process of listening to one another that can of itself function to expand political space. Many scholars note the importance of these micro-level engagements to wider processes of conflict transformation as they create space for 'the voices of the oppressed' to be heard, in all their anger and pain, which is considered necessary 'if the politics of reconciliation is to avoid prejudging the very issues in dispute' (Bashir 2012: 139). Through what Schaap (2005: 84) describes as 'engaging in incessant discourse about the world that lies between former enemies', it is hoped that the capacity to share understanding about this world might become possible. Designed within an agonistic framework, the goal of such processes is to expand understanding of other perspectives, increasing the social and political capacity for difference to coexist and inform a non-violent democracy. In the majority of post-conflict situations it is only at this micro level of engagement that the deepest, toughest issues are addressed. This chapter explores different models and contexts for relational work, and considers how this work can help build wider 'structures of reconciliation' across the society.

This chapter also draws together many of the other threads in this book. It again emphasizes the need for an agonistic approach to reconciliation work. It stresses the need to draw diverse groups of citizens into processes that confront the very terms of their belonging. And it underscores the crucial interrelationships between constitutional, institutional and relational efforts at reconciliation, highlighting the fact that this work requires patience and persistence across all socio-political domains.

Why dialogue?

Transforming the ways in which people in deeply divided societies can talk with one another is an essential aspect of multi-level conflict transformation. Reconciliation efforts that enable divided societies to live together democratically and without violence rest on the ability of even the most ideologically steadfast individuals and groups to transform their view of themselves, of others, and of themselves in relationship with others. They can foster these abilities by making space for dialogue, which in turn may contribute to cooperation and coexistence (Smithey 2011: 10). Indeed, a willingness to engage in dialogue with former enemies can be seen as a thread that runs through most reconciliation efforts, developing among participants the crucial capacity to understand and respond to the aspirations of others (Villa-Vicencio 2009: 49–50, 64). Writing of the Australian context, Michelle Grattan contends that 'Talking is the tool of reconciliation. At the political level, even when big differences over history and politics remain, face-to-face dialogue can be a clearing house for tension' (Grattan 2000: 8). And while the '*purpose of participation* (what gets done)' is certainly important, it is often the '*experience of participating* (what gets made)' that is most critical in terms of developing 'cultures of public engagement' (Escobar 2011: 13).

Elsewhere I have defined dialogue as 'a political intervention focused on creating and holding open the political space in which people in divided and post-violent conflict societies can engage across difference with a view to transforming their relationships' (see Maddison 2014b). Dialogue is

> more structured than good conversation; it is less structured than formal mediation or negotiation. It has purpose, destination and product. As a microcosm of their bodies politic, participants absorb events in the communities around them and together learn to design ways to change the relationships that cause conflict.
>
> (Saunders 2001: 12)

Unlike monological communication, in which people, ideas, and arguments remain in disconnected spaces, dialogue creates a communicative relationship that opens an in-between space in which relationships and ideas can be engaged, worldviews can be broadened, and perspectives can be reshaped (Escobar 2011: 15–16). Participants in dialogue can be supported to engage '*about* and *across* differences', engaging in critical reflection on how their own experiences connect to the lives of others as a way of understanding different perspectives on the historical and contemporary conflicts that divide them and that continue to shape the structures of power in their societies (Nagda *et al.* 2012: 213–14). Dialogical engagement seeks to bridge the gap between individual and collective experience, providing a safe and structured opportunity for divided groups to explore attitudes about the issues that continue to polarize them (Dessel and Rogge 2008: 201). These processes are concerned with improving the quality of political discourse in divided societies, creating what Harold Saunders (2001: 6, 9) has described as a 'public peace process' through which groups of citizens, functioning as 'a microcosm of their communities', can design and participate in programmes intended to transform conflictual relationships. Jim O'Neill describes this work as comprising 'little micro-processes, little bits in the jigsaw that get put together'. In this work, he says, 'We're not creating a volcano, we're just creating little fires. But every little fire helps towards building something bigger.'

Ganesh and Zoller (2012: 67) have described three orientations towards dialogue: collaborative, co-optive, and agonistic. They draw distinctions between these orientations based on the underlying assumptions about conflict, power, and the role of difference that are hidden in each, arguing that orientations towards consensus in dialogue have the effect of 'delegitimizing' certain forms of 'activist communication'. In contrast, they argue in favour of an agonistic approach, which enables a broader range of communication styles by 'acknowledging issues of power and conflict as a central feature of dialogue'. Agonism suggests the possibility for conflict in dialogue to become 'an opportunity for constructive rather than destructive intergroup relationships' (Nagda *et al.* 2012: 213). Indeed, rather than bracketing or avoiding conflict, the aim in agonistic dialogue is to 'transform actually or potentially violent conflict into non-violent forms of social struggle and social change' (Ramsbotham 2010: 53). This is a pragmatic approach to conflict that highlights changing power relationships and the mobilization of identities, while remaining alive to concerns with justice and material needs (Ganesh and Zoller 2012: 77). Oliver Escobar (2011: 14) insists that dialogue practitioners should aim 'to frame conflictive issues not as stumbling blocks or no-go zones, but as areas that require further exploration through collaborative investigation'. In Northern Ireland, Jim O'Neill agrees, maintaining that dialogue processes should not 'run away' from extreme views among members of a group, but instead must have ground rules in place to ensure that those views can be expressed and that people can listen without injury.

An important dynamic that may allow agonistic dialogue to contribute to relational reconciliation efforts is its capacity to include emotional or non-rational forms of expression. As Lederach (2005: 149) contends:

> The repetitive, too often destructive, and violent energy that explodes around immediate crises in settings of protracted conflicts attests to the idea that much is at stake for those involved. It is not a matter of talking them into rationality, bringing them to pragmatic solutions, or finding a way to let go of the past that they hold dear. Our challenge

is to engage the source that generates the energy while creating processes that move it towards constructive expression and interaction.

Yet the emotional and explosive nature of identities and histories of conflict often lead the designers of dialogue processes to avoid engaging these concerns in favour of a more 'rational' engagement (Eisikovits 2010: 144). Rational debate requires that participants neutralize or contain their emotions in ways that often also mean suppressing aspects of their identities. This both neglects the importance of emotions for engaging citizens in public, political exchanges, and—more significantly—reinforces existing power relationships by excluding those who for various reasons have not mastered the skills of rational debate (Escobar 2011: 38). Calls for 'civility' can alienate and exclude those citizens whose strong emotions transgress what is an arbitrary behavioural boundary (Walsh 2007: 43). Dialogue can allow citizens to deal with the emotional dimensions of reconciliation work that 'linger underneath and beyond' the constitutional and institutional levels of transformation (Hutchison and Bleiker 2013: 85). A genuine contribution to political reconciliation requires an engagement with others as a 'complete, full-bodied entity' (Eisikovits 2010: 144), which involves bringing emotions such as fear and anger into the public sphere and allowing them a place in dialogue processes (Hutchison and Bleiker 2013: 84–5). In Guatemala, Carlos Sarti suggests that without this attention to emotional expression, dialogue is 'no use' as it merely means that 'people meet, they smile at each other and pretend that everything's fine, but then they leave and nothing changes'. Instead, he says, Guatemalans 'need to sit down and talk about what is dividing us {…}. We need to speak from our heart and from our heads'.

Engaging with emotions in this way also allows a more direct engagement with power in processes focused on relational transformation. James Tully (2008: 240) argues that justice 'demands a democratic dialogue in which partners listen to and speak with, rather than for, each other', where participants can speak in their own languages and on an equal footing with one another. These principles are now understood as 'the first step in a just dialogue'. Dialogue processes can allow for a direct focus on imbalances of power and do away with the pretense that relational processes can somehow achieve an elusive freedom from power (Walsh 2007: 45). Understanding relationship as a site of change and focusing dialogue processes on relational dynamics requires 'an intentional communication process' that engages explicitly with conflict, difference and power (Nagda *et al.* 2012: 213). Well-conceived dialogue may incorporate the recognition of systemic power imbalances into the process (Dessel and Rogge 2008: 213–14).

Nevertheless, Oliver Ramsbotham suggests that the approach of 'fostering relational empathy' through dialogue excludes what he describes as 'radical disagreement', in which the conceptual and emotional space for mutual respect does not exist. While he agrees that the potential for divided societies to 'live with paradox' is inspiring, he maintains that the most intense, protracted political conflicts may be held so rigidly that they are simply not amenable to this type of transformative approach. Further, Ramsbotham contends that the belief that increasing understanding of one's enemies will lead to greater trust neglects the possibility that instead 'more understanding will make it even clearer to participants why they hate each other' (Ramsbotham 2010: 75, 80, 83). And in contrast to the kind of agonistic pluralism outlined by scholars such as Chantal Mouffe, which fundamentally informs the conceptual framework of this book, Ramsbotham proposes a different kind of agonistic dialogue: one that is not 'domestic-ated' within the democratic *agon*, but characterized by a more brutal verbal exchange between enemies, 'a fierce, but often experienced, discontinuity in day-to-day conversational practice' (Ramsbotham 2010: 94–5).

I agree with Ramsbotham that there are intractable political conflicts that are not easily amenable to transformative relational efforts. However, I think there is little distance between his understanding of agonistic dialogue and the mode of dialogue outlined here. Rather, the type of engagement between enemies that Ramsbotham outlines may be another step on the continuum of agonistic relational engagement that is an essential contribu-tion to wider reconciliation and conflict transformation efforts. Certainly the challenge of learning to engage with former—or current—enemies, fol-lowing generations of violence, hostility, oppression, confrontation, stereo-typing, and derision is not easy. And yet without such efforts it is unclear how progress will be made in any of the constitutional, institutional or rela-tional spaces that require transformation if deeply divided societies are to develop less violent, more democratic politics. In this sense, dialogue is the bedrock of reconciliation.

Relational dialogue

As a political practice that brings enemies and adversaries into engage-ment with one another, all dialogue can be understood as relational. The increasing focus on dialogue as a tool for conflict transformation has high-lighted the significance of relationships as a site for analysis and change:

> To address identity-based conflicts, relationship building is valued over immediate resolution; recognition of the human impact of con-flict is valued over managing solutions; and retooling with new ways of thinking and relating in the context of justice is valued over existing conflict resolution methods that maintain the power hierarchy.
>
> (Nagda *et al.* 2012: 226)

Indeed, relational dialogue makes several significant contributions to wider reconciliation efforts. Dialogue *assumes* a focus on relationships, 'a relation between self and other that explores both similarities and differences of experiences and perspectives' (Nagda *et al.* 2012: 214). Where political elites may focus on negotiating agreements or developing policies intended to support conflict transformation efforts, citizens focus on relationships. The capacity to build and change relationships is an opportunity for citizens to realize their democratic power. For many, other positive changes associated with conflict transformation will be meaningless if there has not been a corresponding transformation in the human conflicts that shape their daily lives (Saunders 2001: 32). Indeed, in countries where division 'tears at the soul of a nation' it is not clear that there are meaningful alternatives to 'honest encounters, talking long and hard into the night, listening carefully to stories that give expression to the needs and aspirations of one's opponents' (Villa-Vicencio 2009: 71).

Undine Whande sees the potential of dialogue to have 'a healing, transformative dimension', creating unique opportunities for engagement between people who are 'unlikely to have that kind of conversation' in any other circumstance. For Pumla Gobodo-Madikizela (2010: 133) even public forums such a truth commissions present an opportunity to bring victims, perpetrators, and beneficiaries of oppressive regimes together for sustained dialogue about the past, which, she suggests may be 'the only action that holds out promise for lasting peace in post-conflict societies'. Verne Harris agrees that dialogue and memory 'go hand in hand', suggesting that '[t]here is no remembering without dialogue'. Participants in the Rural Communities Network in Northern Ireland also describe dialogue as the 'essence' of their work, 'creating that space to have difficult conversations—conversations that we would ordinarily avoid'. Indeed, as Geraldine Smyth (2002: 338) suggests, 'It is in coming together to name the brokenness that people recover the capacity to see more widely and deeply than before.'

The countries in this study have each approached relational dialogue processes in different ways. In Northern Ireland there has been a strong emphasis on the idea of 'storytelling'. This mode of dialogical engagement is intended to counter past exclusions based on alleged 'irrationality', unmasking the inequalities that protect more 'reasonable' modes of engagement and instead creating room for the voices of oppressed and marginalized people to narrate their experiences on their own terms, reconstructing their own narratives (Hetherington 2008: 50; Bashir 2012: 139). Stories are a widely understood medium for remembering and making sense of the past, as well as expressing hopes for the future, expressing human frailty and vulnerability as well as strength and resilience (Villa-Vicencio 2009: 76). Oliver Escobar (2011: 24) considers storytelling one of the key dynamics in dialogue, 'one of the most egalitarian means of communication', that allows those who may not feel sufficiently articulate to participate in argument and debate to share what is important to them.

In Northern Ireland, storytelling processes are seen as a means of placing personal experiences of the Troubles 'on record' in order to create a richer, shared narrative of the past as a means of 'truth' recovery that counters the resistance to an official truth commission discussed in Chapter 10 (Lundy and McGovern 2008: 37–8). Examples include the Towards Understanding and Healing Project, which has focused on story-telling in an effort to 'bring together all of the disparate narratives that comprise the story of Northern Ireland in order to better understand the complexities of a conflict that informs how we relate to one another' (Hetherington 2008: 43). In her own work, Sara Cook has observed that 'story-telling and dialogue work very slowly and gradually towards societal change' and are 'virtually impossible to measure'. But she maintains that making these processes available to divided groups 'eventually moves a society towards a much more peaceful situation'. She recalls many parti-cipants in dialogue or storytelling processes reporting that they will 'never be able to look at the other community the same way again [without] real-izing that it's comprised of mothers and children and fathers and brothers'. For Cook, this process of 'humanizing' the enemy 'eventually yields political and societal dividends'.

Storytelling is often used as a method within 'community healing' efforts that are also a central focus of many relational dialogue initiatives. Com-munity healing requires strategies to enable divided groups to come together to communicate about their past grievances and reflect upon the ways in which their emotions about historical conflict 'force the past into the politics of the present' (Hutchison and Bleiker 2013: 86). In South Africa, the Insti-tute for Justice and Reconciliation undertakes a range of community healing initiatives that focus on the 'interrelated goals' of memory, dialogue, recon-ciliation and development. Community healing processes support com-munities to speak about the deep-rooted legacies of apartheid, and the trauma and violence that persist in their collective memory, in the belief that communicating these memories will enable communities to build a shared understanding of their past. These processes are approached with the under-standing that suspicion, fear, and the divisions of the past make dialogue dif-ficult. Thus the IJR programmes support communities to engage in sustained dialogue intended to deepen conversations, explore issues in depth, and effectively build relationships. The approach strives towards communities finding new ways of working together that both confront the past and enable a more creative approach to contemporary challenges (Institute for Justice and Reconciliation 2006: 8–10). The women in the organization South African Women in Dialogue also spoke passionately about the relational aspects of their work, which is underscored by what they described as 'a bold approach' in which they can speak openly with one another

> irrespective of our skin, we are sisters {...}. We experience the same pain with children, we experience the same pain with husbands? {...}

We dialogue with one another so we can undo our burden instead of carrying it all {...}. If I don't, how would you know I'm suffering?

Australia and Guatemala have also valued such approaches. The formal Australian reconciliation process took a similar approach to intra-community dialogue, although focused more on education than healing. During its term the CAR produced Study Circle kits intended to enable small, self-managing groups to undertake an eight-week programme exploring reconciliation and a range of Aboriginal and Torres Strait Islander issues (Gunstone 2009: 96). These study circles went on to form the nuclei of the 'people's movement for reconciliation' discussed in Chapter 9, and facilitated some important self-reflection among the non-indigenous participants. Aboriginal and Torres Strait Islander people have also developed their own dialogue processes focusing on violence and trauma, undertaking what Judy Atkinson (2002: 259) describes as 'the hard work to change, to name with courage and hope, the possibility of healing'. Mayan communities in Guatemala too have created 'safe collective spaces' in which communities use dialogue to facilitate the 'collective recovery of psycho-social community identity', which also 'establishes the community as the conduit from the individual to the nation' (Sanford 2003: 244–5).

In several instances, interviewees spoke of the need to build 'confidence' among single groups or communities before attempting to bring them into dialogue with another group or community. In South Africa, Sello Hatang maintains the importance of designing dialogue processes that fit the needs of different communities, 'not one size fits all', and questions whether the methodologies developed by international actors such as the UNDP should be applied 'across the board'. Kindiza Ngubeni speaks of first engaging in dialogue with 'the angry people in the community' before bringing in other groups, in an effort to 'create an environment' that is conducive to 'combined dialogue'. In Northern Ireland, Jim O'Neill describes a process of working with a men's group in the loyalist Tigers Bay area of North Belfast. This process started by 'just talking about what it's like growing up in their community and what the issues are for them in that community'. The next step was taking the group to Derry/Londonderry to visit the Free Derry Museum and meet with some of families of the Bloody Sunday victims. O'Neill says this meeting produced 'an amazing discussion because it really opened their eyes'. The Bloody Sunday families also found the visit 'opened their eyes' about 'so-called hard-nosed loyalists' who turned out to be 'really interested in listening to what they were saying'. But the key to this successful engagement was the slow process that took them there, with O'Neill maintaining that it is a 'big mistake' to assume that 'everybody's ready to engage with the other side'.

Dialogue between communities in this mode has perhaps been the most common approach to relational reconciliation, as has been well documented in Northern Ireland. Where dialogue is absent, it is understood that resentments are likely to fester, undermining wider efforts at conflict transformation (Community Relations Council 2011: 26). In recognition of this, organizations across Northern Ireland have been engaged in community relations work over several decades, both before and since the Belfast Agreement, with the specific aim of transforming their society's historical, social and political divisions. The Community Relations Council, for example, has engaged in or funded a range of inter-communal engagement strategies including:

- Mutual understanding work ('to increase dialogue and reduce ignorance, suspicion and prejudice');
- Anti-sectarian and anti-intimidation work ('to transfer improved understanding into structural changes');
- Cultural traditions work ('to affirm and develop cultural confidence that is not exclusive');
- Political options work ('to facilitate political discussion within and between communities, including developing agreed principles of justice and rights');
- Conflict resolution work ('to develop skills and knowledge which will increase possibilities for greater social and political cooperation').

(Fitzduff 1989 quoted in Ramsbotham 2010: 75)

These approaches have often been criticized for being too 'safe', perpetuating the 'whatever you say, say nothing' approach to inter-communal relations in Northern Ireland that avoids dialogue about contentious issues in favour of silence or politeness (Power 2011: 11). Nevertheless, there is evidence to suggest that this work has had some impact. A 2008 study carried out by researchers from the University of Ulster and Queen's University Belfast suggests that the integrated 'community relations' approach has indeed promoted inter-community tolerance, trust, friendship, and understanding in Northern Ireland, while also reducing anxiety, bias, prejudice, and perceptions of threat (Aiken 2010: 184–5). Neil Jarman describes the kind of lengthy, 'fractured' processes that have been undertaken to advance community relations and bring divided communities in Belfast into dialogue with one another, which in one case involved

a fifteen year process of building dialogue between people, which started off with very tentative, mediated engagement. People weren't prepared to be in the same room with each other to try and reduce tensions {…}. Sometimes people were encouraging and sometimes people were antagonistic to it. It depended very much on what the wider macro political environment was like.

Initially, while people were not prepared to be in a room together, dialogue took place over the phone and was focused on 'managing tensions' that were fuelling recurrent cycles of violence, gradually building trust. Jarman observes that:

> Over a period of time you started to move from that occasional dialogue in the summer months, to sustaining that afterwards, to moving from just talking on the phone to actually saying, 'Okay, well we can sit round a table and talk.' Gradually, that range of conversations increased, as people got to know each other, relationships built and trust built, and dialogue was developed.

Over time, Jarman observed that the people participating in these dialogue processes developed their own commitment to maintaining them, even when their communities were trying to 'break' these networks. When outbreaks of violence did disrupt the process, 'the time before they could start again would be shorter'. Now, Jarman says, 'The shit can hit the fan but people don't walk out of the room anymore {…}. They'll explain to each other why they couldn't stop the shit hitting the fan that particular time and what they did to try and stop it'.

There are certainly many challenges to this work, key among these being the difficulty of getting members of the dominant communities into the room. Many of my interviewees emphasized the importance of ensuring a diverse range of participants in dialogue processes. In South Africa, for example, Rebecca Freeth suggests that in convening a dialogue process 'the first challenge is to get people into the same room who wouldn't normally sit in the same room because they are so locked into relationship of blaming the other'. The key, according to Freeth, is helping participants to see that their 'own perspectives and experience don't hold the whole picture, or the whole truth of that picture' but that 'together they are able to see more of the system that they're in than they can see on their own'. Michael Lapsley also stresses the need to include 'African people, coloured people, white people' in dialogue processes. He tells me that, 'If you just have African and coloured, or African and white, you haven't got the whole equation.' However this diversity is not always easy to achieve. Lapsley recalls that his organization employed a white member of staff for several years just to try and bring white participants into their processes. Eventually they accepted that these efforts 'weren't going to move forward in any kind of way'. Tim Murithi also points to the challenges of engaging white South Africans in dialogue work. The IJR has 'to a large extent just tended to work with black and coloured people [because] the white people would never turn up'.

In Australia it remains the case that it is predominantly white people who participate in community reconciliation events. Jacqueline Phillips describes these participants as 'well-meaning people trying to do good things, who have good hearts and want to see positive change', but notes that 'there's often not a single Aboriginal person in the room'. In this sense, she points out, these efforts are 'not relational'. Phillips also sees what she describes as 'wonderful initiatives at the community level', but notes that these events tend to be attended by 'a group of people who are already committed to these issues, who already have relationships with the Aboriginal people in the room, meeting together with the Aboriginal people who already know what the issues are'. While she suggests that people probably leave these events 'with a really nice feeling' she questions their impact. As Irene Watson (2007: 31) has argued, Australia needs to

> hear more Aboriginal voices, particularly those Aboriginal voices that go beyond the representations of the popularly perceived 'leaders'. Aboriginal peoples are diverse, and so are our situations, interests, desires and dreams. To create the space that will hear that diversity will require patience and the making of time to listen beyond the one minute grab.

Indeed, Australia has generally been less successful in developing processes of inter-community dialogue than the other countries in this study. Mick Gooda points to a common dynamic between indigenous and non-indigenous people in Australia, where a lack of trust leaves non-indigenous people 'scared to come into the space', concerned that they are going to 'stuff up' (that is, say something offensive to indigenous people) and then be abused. And while Leah Armstrong sees that there is a 'hunger' for the more difficult conversations in Australia, she suggests it is challenging for people and organizations to 'actually open up and make the safe space for those conversations'. She suggests the organizations that have strong governance structures associated with their Reconciliation Action Plans, particularly where they have indigenous advisory boards, are more open to 'just laying the conversation out' when issues of race and racism come up, and confronting what this means for their organization.

Australian attempts at intercultural dialogue have certainly been restricted by the tendency to control the types of indigenous voices that participate, and a preference to hear only the more moderate perspectives, while continuing to silence those who call for more radical constitutional transformation. The range of issues that has been open to dialogue has also been limited, particularly since the 1980s. For example the CAR Study Circle kits mentioned above did not include material on indigenous sovereignty or other aspects of constitutional transformation that might have challenged the nationalist underpinnings of the formal reconciliation process (Gunstone 2009: 96). This tendency to control the conversation before it has even begun remains a stumbling block to dialogue in Australia. Where non-indigenous people have been interested to focus on their *relationships* with indigenous people, Aboriginal and Torres Strait Islander peoples have been far more concerned to ensure that issues associated with the *constitutional and institutional* levels of conflict transformation are at the centre of the conversation, as has been the case elsewhere.

Constitutional and institutional dialogue

The relational dialogue processes discussed above undoubtedly play a crucial role in reconciliation efforts in and of themselves. In many contexts, however, there have also been important efforts to employ dialogue processes at the national level to engage political elites in questions of constitutional and institutional transformation. These efforts recognize that merely inviting previously excluded and marginalized groups to participate in existing institutions is highly problematic when those institutions themselves require transformation (Bashir 2012: 139). Often these processes are referred to as 'elite dialogues', and, rather than working with citizens at the community level, they aim to bring polarized political elites into dialogue and engagement with one another.

In Guatemala dialogue has played an important role at the constitutional and institutional levels since before the signing of the Peace Accords. In 1989 the National Reconciliation Commission (CNR) (created by the 1987 Central American Peace Accords) sponsored a National Dialogue to consider ending the violent conflict. Despite the fact that the army, the government, and the business elites boycotted the process, the dialogue brought together the other organized sectors of Guatemalan society, who together argued in support of a political settlement to the war. And beyond this formal outcome, the National Dialogue played a role in beginning to democratize Guatemala, opening new spaces for public debate within what was still an extremely repressive environment, making it possible to discuss issues that had been 'undiscussable for decades' (Jonas 2000: 39–40).

Since this time, formalized dialogue processes have become institutionalized within Guatemalan politics, with mixed results. Arnoldo Noriega recalls the founding of the National Permanent Dialogue System in 2008, created as a presidential commission under President Álvaro Colom. Noriega contends that the programme was labeled a 'system' because its architects 'wanted to give it a systemic approach' rather than adopt an ad hoc process of 'one commission for each demonstration or each protest'. In 2012, however, incoming president Otto Pérez Molina downgraded the importance of the dialogue system, with Noriega suggesting that today '[i]t's not important among the government, and its members are now just marginal members of the government. There's no longer leadership and overall we lost the systemic approach.' Mariel Aguilar also describes her experience of national dialogue in Guatemala, emphasizing the importance of the diversity of participants, 'people from the armed forces, guerrilla, and people from the government institutions, from the government, and the civil society'. Among this diverse group focusing on 'the concept of peacebuilding', Aguilar observed the participants 'learning how to listen to each other and how to try to put on the other shoes and understand different points of view'. For Aguilar, 'the benefit of this space was that nobody had to make compromises, so everybody could talk and say what they think {…} people could talk about things that they never talked about before'. However Aguilar believes that the national mood was more conducive to such dialogue in the immediate wake of the signing of the Peace Accords. Today, she says, 'if we tried to make the same experience it wouldn't work'.

Noriega believes the system has also lost its capacity to be proactive in anticipating situations in which dialogue could help to facilitate discussion in an institutional space. In the case of planned mining projects, for example, (a highly contentious area of economic activity in Guatemala, as discussed in Chapter 7) Noriega maintains that 'the most intelligent thing' would be to 'create a dialogue {…} with all the stakeholders' including the mining company, the community, and the government, with benefits that would potentially include both peaceful development and sustainable investment. Instead the government now tends to favour a security approach to managing conflict, involving the police and the army. As a result, Noriega says, 'there have been deaths, the investments are in danger [and] mining projects have been paralyzed or stopped because communities have blocked the entrances to these projects'.

The other side of this coin, however, is that the institutionalization of dialogue in Guatemala has also undermined the legitimacy of the process. Catalina Soberanis suggests that, up until recently, institutionalization has been a strength 'because every time we feel as though we're right to the edge and we're going to fall off, everybody gets scared and says, "Okay, dialogue! We need to find a solution to this, we need to talk to each other." People have been prepared to 'trust in the process and the rules of the game' whether or not they trusted those involved. Now, however, people tend to turn to government for these initiatives, where 'the people who really have the power are going to impose their agenda' from above. Adrian Zapata suggests that Guatemala has seen 'an excess and saturation of dialogue' since the signing of the peace accords. He also contends that most dialogue processes have maintained existing patterns of exclusion, such that 'you will find the same people in all dialogue processes'. Somewhat sarcastically he suggests that, '[t]he only doubt you might have when you go to a dialogue process is that you'll wonder what hat people will be wearing'. Dialogue in Guatemala, he suggests, has 'turned into a way of life' and he questions whether it has achieved anything more than 'neutralizing certain levels of conflict'.

Carlos Sarti also believes that the approach to dialogue in Guatemala 'has failed'. Although there has been an increase in what he describes as 'the culture of dialogue', this is 'not strong enough to overcome the conflict culture'. Sarti agrees that the creation of the national dialogue system in Guatemala reduced the impact of the process, as 'people believe that it is not independent of government, not autonomous or impartial'. Daniel Saquec also suggests that what was once a genuine commitment to dialogue in Guatemala has become little more than a form of consultation, where 'very often people speak about dialogue, but what they're doing is just informing [communities] about a certain position and are very inflexible'. Such an approach rules out 'a collective development of solutions': 'It's like saying, "Well, we're going to sit down, but this is our position. Either you agree or you don't agree." Before the dialogue, it's as if the direction of the dialogue has already been determined.' Elena Diez agrees, suggesting that too much of the activity labeled 'dialogue' in Guatemala has been 'public policy dialogue', which she suggests is 'not transformational'. In contrast she believes that the more transformational work on which she has focused has 'changed the way that people see each other and created a different sort of relations with one another'. Yet as someone who has been involved in supporting, convening and participating in national dialogues in Guatemala over many years, Diez now says that in her 'most depressing moments' she wonders 'What have we done all these years? {...} What did these dialogues produce? I mean they didn't change the country.'

South Africa has also made considerable use of dialogue processes in progressing aspects of its constitutional and institutional transformation. Beyond the negotiations that enabled the 1994 transition and the development of the new constitution, South Africa has also engaged in pioneering work with a process known as 'scenario planning' dialogue. Scenarios, which have a strongly narrative quality, are intended to be 'internally logical stories' that spell out how political, economic, social, and technological forces (or anything else considered relevant) might play out in a given situation. Participants use narrative and metaphor, telling stories that reflect their own perspectives and experiences, as a way of learning about each other, accommodating differences in order to generate a shared understanding of the problem and, ultimately, a shared view of how the future might unfold (Segal 2007: 8).

One of the most famous examples of elite, transformative dialogue of this type was the Mont Fleur Scenarios, held in 1991–1992. The Mont Fleur team included 22 people in politics, business, academia, and trade unions who were thought to be on a trajectory to senior leadership positions, an unofficial collection of both 'the existing establishment and the establishment-to-be—a microcosm of the future South Africa' who saw the project as an opportunity to 'participate in giving birth to the "New South Africa"' (Kahane 2004: 20). The group's facilitator, Adam Kahane (2012: 6) recalls that the subtle shift in orientation brought about by the scenario approach, which asks people to think about what *could* happen rather than what *will* or *should* happen, 'opened up dramatically new conversations'. The team eventually produced a set of four scenarios, which, through extensive dissemination in the media, had a significant impact on public discourse at a crucial time in South Africa's transition.

Beyond the scenarios themselves however, what was remarkable about Mont Fleur was that a group of former enemies had found a respectful and productive way to work together. This accomplishment sent an important message to the wider population. According to Kahane (2004: 26), the 'essence' of the Mont Fleur process

> was that a small group of deeply committed leaders, representing a cross-section of a society that the whole world considered irretrievably stuck, had sat down together to talk broadly and profoundly about what was going on and what should be done. More than that, they had not talked about what other people—some faceless authorities or decision makers—should do to advance some parochial agenda, but what they and their colleagues and fellow citizens had to do in order to create a better future for everybody. They saw themselves as part of—not apart from—the problem they were trying to solve. The scenarios were a novel means to this engaged problem-solving end.

In the years since, the Mont Fleur project has come to have almost 'iconic status' around the world as a project that made a significant contribution to South Africa's peaceful transition, and which pioneered a new way of working in divided societies (Segal 2007: 55). The model has been replicated in many post conflict societies, including in extensive work by the Democratic Dialogue project of the UNDP in Latin America.

There was also an attempt to replicate the Mont Fleur process in South Africa in the Dinokeng scenarios, undertaken between 2008 and 2009. The Dinokeng project focused on the fact that in the 15 years since the transition to democracy, the task of post-conflict transformation had revealed itself as 'entirely grittier and more complex' than anyone had anticipated (Dinokeng Scenarios 2009: 1). The project brought together a group of 'citizen-leaders' from across South Africa with the goal to 'create a space and language for open, reflective and reasoned strategic conversation among South Africans, about possible futures for the country, and the opportunities, risks and choices these futures present'. But although the participants produced three important scenarios, these have had little impact on wider transformation efforts in South Africa, causing some to question the value of the process. Haniff Hoosen, for example, suggests that Dinokeng was a 'wasted opportunity'. Hoosen felt that the scenarios produced in the Dinokeng process were 'not a surprise to most South Africans', who understand that 'promoting hatred amongst people {...} is not a successful road to walk'. Still he felt that in a context where political leaders are 'pulling South Africans in different directions', the scenarios should have provided an opportunity for South African leaders to say, 'This is the road that we now need to walk, for these reasons.' One of the convenors of the Dinokeng process, businessman Rick Menell, does contend that the process made a 'fundamental contribution to the language of vision setting and leadership in the country'. As the participants worked to disseminate the scenarios after the workshops they carried with them their experiences and an ability to articulate new stories about the possible future of South Africa. But it was perhaps a failure to fully appreciate the socio-political context in South Africa that ultimately diminished the impact of the Dinokeng scenarios, according to another convenor, Mamphela Ramphele:

> The failure of South Africans to embrace the Dinokeng Scenarios in 2009 was a source of great frustration for me. But it was largely due to the fact that we didn't understand, as the convenors of those scenarios, just how deeply wounded South Africans were. We expected disengaged South Africans to simply realise the error of their ways and choose to walk together {...}. Unless we confront this woundedness, we cannot make progress.
>
> (Ramphele quoted in Kahane 2012: 72)

Yet even these less influential processes are thought by some to have changed the tone of the debate. Vincent Maphai, a committed supporter of dialogue processes (having convened both the Mont Fleur and Dinokeng processes), points to the 'power of dialogue':

> There's something about talking that keeps the options open. You may not be listening with your ears but you are listening with your bloodstream, something gets in. We started with nothing, so for me what was remarkable was that we met in the first place, and what was even more remarkable was that, given the positions we initially had, eventually we came up with four scenarios endorsed by everyone {...}. And that was 1992! There were killings outside when we were going through all of that.

Maphai suggests that some of the common ground in these processes is encountered not in the discussion of political content, but in recognizing a shared humanity. He recalls a moment in the Dinokeng dialogues where a participant he described as 'from the real Afrikaner right wing' spoke about his dead father, who would have been furious to see his son speaking English instead of Afrikaans in such a forum. While Maphai points out that he is 'not familiar with that world', he could relate to the anxiety of disappointing a deceased parent, drawing a parallel with his own late mother, a conservative Catholic woman, who would have been horrified to hear her son discussing the need for young people to use condoms. For Maphai, moments like these allow participants in dialogue to 'move from listening to actually wearing somebody's shoes'. Namhla Mniki-Mangaliso, also a participant in the Dinokeng process, found the relational aspects of that process the most transformative, telling me

> [a] process like that forces you to come into contact with people who are unlike you {...}. Then even though you thought they were from the other side of life, because you have trust in the same space you actually have to discover each other. It was the discovery of each other for me that was the most beautiful in Dinokeng—because you could not avoid discovery of other people's humanity.

She also relates a moment of engagement with another participant, someone with whom she imagined she had nothing in common, only to find that they were both newlyweds with small children and lived in the same area. For Mniki-Mangaliso, this was a moment when she 'could see him beyond his white Afrikaans maleness' and 'could see his humanity'. She found these moments especially significant because 'there are very few places in South Africa where you have an opportunity like that'.

Today South Africa is pondering the need for some new form of national dialogue. Villa Vicencio and Soko (2012: 31) contend that:

> The scope and magnitude of the challenge that faced South Africa at the time of [the] 1994 elections and that again confronts the nation, requires 'time-out' in which to ask—who are we, what now, and where to next? In 1994 it evoked a political revolution and promised a far-reaching ethical, if not spiritual or deeply inward, reorientation of society. The present demand involves a similar need to turn away from a habitual preoccupation with self-centred privilege and greed. It indicates a need to turn toward the wider community with whom we are connected and a form of behavior that recognizes the interests of others alongside our own.

They further suggest that this need for 'a second national conversation' should focus on the kinds of institutional transformation discussed earlier in this book (Villa-Vicencio and Soko 2012: 35). Wessels (2010: 11) also contends that South Africa needs to 'agree to dialogue' about the 'smouldering issues' of racism, poverty, and crime, otherwise they will remain 'strangers to one another'. Kate Lefko-Everett agrees that there is not enough 'strong, open, frank space for good progressive dialogue on issues about race' in South Africa. Instead, these discussions are governed by 'huge eruptions in the media'. However, Steven Friedman remains concerned that politics will get in the way of future dialogue efforts. While he agrees that South Africa 'desperately needs' a new national dialogue he has

> no belief at all that we'll get the national dialogue that we need, because the national dialogue that we need is not one in which [political elites]

sit around a table, trying to find common ground. It's one in which they're honest with each other. But the default position in the society is so much to look for phony consensus.

Indeed, Ananda Nyoka sees that the capacity for effective national dialogue in South Africa has actually declined in recent years:

There's a sense that the discourse right now is one of anger; that we've moved away from the kind of dialogue that got us to where we were in 1994, you know, [processes like] CODESA where people were willing to put aside their own interests. There was a sense that people wanted to compromise. There was a sense that people cared about the future of South Africa, where we were going. What's happened over the years, post '94, is a lot of polarization {...}. The discourse is very much that of anger.

Jody Kollapen (2010: 25) points to the 'fear and uncertainty, the creation of unrealistic expectations, the reopening of wounds long thought healed' all of which create a sense of 'lethargy' about the need for national dialogue on these issues. For this reason Kollapen suggests that a new dialogue should 'start in small and familiar places within communities rather than in the glare of a major national event'. His hope is that if such a project were 'managed with integrity, people may trust the process, engage it with sincerity, and consider the possibilities and opportunities of what a shared citizenship and a shared humanity could mean for all'.

Certainly, there were many among my interviewees who questioned the value and impact of dialogue, both in South Africa and elsewhere. Hugo Van der Merwe is skeptical about the transformative possibilities in many dialogue processes. While he agrees that 'people can come into new insights, can shift the boundaries of their thinking', he has also seen too many instances where at the end of a weekend-long dialogue process, where people have done 'fantastic work':

A white person coming out of it says, 'Wow! I really feel connected to you and let's maybe have another weekend like this in a couple of months?' The black person that comes out of it says, 'It's really nice that we're now connected! Can I come to talk to you tomorrow about where I can find a job for myself or my brother?' The white person says, 'Oh my God, no! That's not what I was trying to get into. This isn't about a change in how we live, it's a change in how we think.'

Lucy Holborn has also observed many disappointing dialogue processes that predominantly engage an elite group 'who are already thinking critically about the whole process' and 'inadvertently exclude the sorts of people that they really should be including, who have day-to-day experience of prejudice or resentment'. And Undine Whande observes resistance to the more challenging conversations in South Africa, suggesting that these efforts are 'very quickly dominated by white liberals {...} [and] {...} we are only moving in the spaces that are familiar, that are middle-class spaces'. Effective dialogue also requires a modicum of trust—whether in the process or in the other participants—and in deeply divided societies where a history of oppression of one group by another has characterized relationships, as discussed in Chapter 4, trust and openness are often absent (James 1999: 590).

Dialogue can also sit in tension with people's desire for the types of observable, institutional transformation discussed in Chapters 7 and 8. It is for this reason that dialogue is at once both popular and controversial, often criticized as unproductive, with effects that are neither generalizable to any wider constituencies nor durable in terms of lasting change among participants (Eisikovits 2010: 140). Dialogue is difficult, slow, time-consuming, and expensive. Processes may 'collapse into an illusion of peace' or become a deceptive comfort zone in which former enemies are seduced by good feelings that substitute for transformative action and material transformation (Villa-Vicencio 2009: 49–50, 82). In Guatemala, Arnoldo Noriega argues that

> if dialogues and negotiations aren't transformed into public policies and concrete actions which can be measured, then dialogue will be weakened {...} it loses its value and it loses credibility. The risk is that we'll end up going back to a violent situation.

Julio Balconi also contends that dialogue must translate into action. Too often, he says, 'Documents are produced and that's it {...} nothing happens afterwards, absolutely nothing.' In South Africa, Ananda Nyoka has observed what she describes as 'dialogue fatigue' where '[p]eople are tired of talking, they're tired of dialogue. Precisely because there's no action coming out of that, but also because all these dialogues that are happening are not connected.' Certainly it is the case that dialogue processes can look like they are contributing little to wider reconciliation efforts, and often require that participants commit to a long term engagement with no guarantee of any material outcome. This is another indicator of the kind of patience that reconciliation efforts require. Rebecca Freeth contends that 'in the middle of it, it may look like nothing good is happening at all. In fact there's lots of conflict and people are upset {...}. It's not going to look great all the way through this process'.

What is evident here—and indeed across all the complexities mapped in this book—is that the constitutional, institutional and relational levels of conflict transformation cannot, and should not, be disentangled. Kenneth Lukoko makes the sobering observation that the challenge for

South Africa is that 'the enormity of the social damage, of the trauma, is bigger than the capacity of the country to deal with it'. He suggests that

> every community would have to pause almost for a year to talk about this, to perhaps do justice to it. So in the face of that tension then we sometimes make the mistake of thinking {…} let's move on. It's too difficult. There's just too much to deal with in the past.

And while Lukoko appreciates the significance of some of the constitutional and institutional level transformations in South Africa, he maintains that such progress 'doesn't take away the need to talk, because the need to talk is about creating a common sense of belonging, so that we see things from the same angle'.

The need for patience and persistence

In the wake of historical violence, societies must confront a plethora of demands, across multiple levels of society, some of which risk reopening old wounds or disrupting a fragile peace. The challenges involved in these processes are immense, but in most societies emerging from violent conflict there is also considerable energy and enthusiasm being directed towards these efforts. In the countries in this study, and indeed in deeply divided societies around the globe, it is possible to observe political actors of all kinds prepared to engage in a politics of reconciliation across the multiple socio-political levels outlined here, with all the risks and complexities that this implies. I was fortunate enough to speak to many of them, and I hold a deep admiration for their persistence, their resilience, and their unshakeable belief that their efforts, at all levels, will make a difference over time. Many of them also instinctively understood the concept of reconciliation as I have outlined it in this book; that is, as a complex, multi-level, process of constitutional, institutional and relational transformation, in which conflict will always be present and has potential to be both creative and democratic. The framework that this book has mapped out makes clear that the process of transforming conflict is indeed challenging. None of the relational work discussed in the last three chapters will be effective without concurrent efforts at the constitutional and institutional levels. At the same time, efforts towards constitutional and institutional transformation will have far less impact if they are not underpinned by efforts to transform relationships shaped by violence and division. The immensity of these combined levels of effort suggests that this work is not just multi-level it is likely also multi-generational. As Wessels contends, in deeply divided societies, 'the past has no finish line: it is always there', meaning that 'those who are serious about reconciliation should never lose patience' (Wessels 2010: 11, 15).

Multi-level conflict transformation is rarely linear, and the levels themselves are porous and overlapping. Reconciliation efforts require that, as citizens struggle to know and understand one another, they must question what they thought they already knew. This is a deeply unsettling process. Reconciliation is also unlikely to meet all the transformational demands that citizens make, either in the short or the long term; there may be no end to human efforts to right past wrongs. These limitations should not, however, 'excuse inaction, naïve idealism, or undue delay' (Villa-Vicencio and Doxtader 2004: ix). Crucially, reconciliation efforts will not, and should not, do away with conflict, but must instead focus on harnessing conflict's powerful, democratic potential. As Villa-Vicencio (2009: 155) argues

> Never easy, reconciliation does not presuppose agreement on all solutions to all such issues. It does presuppose a willingness to address these concerns politically rather than in blood. This requires a willingness to think new thoughts and imagine new solutions.

If one thing can be taken away as a certainty from this book it is that reconciliation efforts, across all the complexities of all the levels outlined here, cannot be undertaken by individuals, by government departments, or even by communities in isolation from one another. The approach to reconciliation proposed here acknowledges that meaningful conflict transformation requires from *whole societies* a degree of patience, persistence, creativity, risk, tolerance of conflict, and substantial investment over a long period of time. As a process, reconciliation will not 'end with a flourish', but it may be hoped that, over time, a political emphasis on reconciliation may give way to 'the day-to-day stuff of normal politics' (Daly and Sarkin 2007: 254). Caution is needed however. Even a country like Australia, where it might be said that day-to-day politics now takes precedence over the politics of reconciliation, cannot be said to 'be reconciled'. As Schaap reminds us, political reconciliation is forever confronted by the risk of politics, as 'the will to forgive is confronted by the prospect of the unforgiveable', such that the new beginning we believe we have created does not come to pass, and old hurts and division come back to the fore (Schaap 2005: 151). These contests, this ever-conflictual reconciliation, is the stuff of politics, and a nation's best efforts are required to ensure that space is always retained for the political contestation required to transform society in order that citizens might live together without violence.

Bibliography

Aboriginal and Torres Strait Islander Commission (1995) *Recognition, rights and reform: A report to government on native title social justice measures*, Canberra: Aboriginal and Torres Strait Islander Commission.

Abu-Nimer, M. (2013) 'Religion and peacebuilding', in R. Mac Ginty (ed.) *The Routledge handbook of peacebuilding*, Abingdon: Routledge.

Acheson, N., Milofsky, C., and Stringer, M. (2011) 'Understanding the role of non-aligned civil society in peacebuilding in Northern Ireland: Towards a fresh approach', in M. Power (ed.) *Building peace in Northern Ireland*, Liverpool: Liverpool University Press.

Achmat, Z. (2010) 'No reconciliation without social justice', in F. du Toit and E. Doxtader (eds) *In the balance: South Africans debate reconciliation*. Johannesburg: Jacana Media.

African National Congress (2012) *The second transition? Building a national democratic society and the balance of forces in 2012*. Version 6.0 as amended by the Special NEC, 27 February edition, Johannesburg: ANC.

Aiken, N.T. (2010) 'Learning to live together: Transitional Justice and intergroup reconciliation in Northern Ireland', *The International Journal of Transitional Justice*, 4(2): 166–88.

Alexander, A. and Mngxitama, A. (2011) 'Race and resistance in post-apartheid South Africa', in S. Essof and D. Moshenberg (eds) *Searching for South Africa: The new calculus of dignity*, Pretoria: Unisa Press.

Alexander, N. (2013) *Thoughts on the new South Africa*, Johannesburg: Jacana Media.

Allport, G.W. (1954). *The nature of prejudice*. Cambridge, MA/Reading: Addison-Wesley.

Altman, J., Linkhorn, C., and Clarke, J. (2005) *Land rights and development reform in remote Australia*, Working Paper no. 276/2005, Canberra: Australian National University.

Arbour, L. (2007) 'Economic and social justice for societies in transition', *International Law and Politics*, 40(1): 1–26.

Arriaza, L.J. and Roht-Arriaza, N. (2010) 'Weaving a braid of histories: Local post-armed conflict initiatives in Guatemala', in R. Shaw and L. Waldorf (eds) *Localizing transitional justice: Interventions and priorities after mass violence*, Stanford: Stanford University Press.

Arthur, P. (2011) 'Introduction: Identities in transition', in P. Arthur (ed.) *Identities in transition: Challenges for transitional justice in divided societies*, New York: Cambridge University Press.

Atkinson, J. (2002) *Trauma trails, recreating song lines: The transgenerational effects of trauma in Indigenous Australia*, Melbourne: Spinifex Press.

Auspoll (2012) *Evaluating the effectiveness of Reconciliation Action Plans*, Canberra: Reconciliation Australia.

Australian Broadcasting Corporation (2014) *Q&A: Live from Garma Festival, Arnhem Land*, 4 August, available online at www.abc.net.au/tv/qanda/txt/s4040700.htm

Australian Bureau of Statistics (2008) *Population distribution, Aboriginal and Torres Strait Islander Australians*, Canberra: Australian Bureau of Statistics.

Australian Bureau of Statistics (2013) *Prisoners in Australia*, Sydney: Australian Bureau of Statistics.

Australian Human Rights Commission (1997) *Bringing them Home: Report of the National Inquiry into the Separation of Aboriginal and Torres Strait Islander Children from Their Families*, Sydney: Human Rights and Equal Opportunity Commission.

Barkan, E. (2000) *The guilt of nations: Restitution and negotiating historical injustices*, Baltimore: The Johns Hopkins University Press.

Barnard-Naudé, J. (2008) 'For justice and reconciliation to come: The TRC archive, big business and the demand for material reparations', in F. du Bois and A. du Bois-Pedain (eds) *Justice and reconciliation in post-apartheid South Africa*, New York: Cambridge University Press.

Bashir, B. (2012) 'Reconciling historical injustices: Deliberative democracy and the politics of reconciliation', *Res Publica*, 18(2): 127–43.

Bashir, B. and Kymlicka, W. (2008) 'Introduction: Struggles for inclusion and reconciliation in modern democracies', in B. Bashir and W. Kymilicka (eds) *The politics of reconciliation in multicultural societies*. Oxford: Oxford University Press.

Bean, K. (2011) 'Civil society, the state and conflict transformation in the nationalist community', in M. Power (ed.) *Building peace in Northern Ireland*, Liverpool: Liverpool University Press.

Behrendt, L. (1995) *Aboriginal dispute resolution*, Sydney: Federation Press.

Behrendt, L. (2003) *Achieving social justice: Indigenous rights and Australia's future*, Sydney: Federation Press.

Bell, C. (2009) 'Transitional justice, interdisciplinarity and the state of the "field" or "non-field"', *The International Journal of Transitional Justice*, 3: 5–27.

Bell, C. (2013) 'Peacebuilding, law and human rights', in R. Mac Ginty (ed.) *The Routledge handbook of peacebuilding*, Abingdon: Routledge.

Bell, C. and O'Rourke, C. (2007) 'The people's peace? Peace agreements, civil society, and participatory democracy', *International Political Science Review*, 28(3): 293–324.

Bell, J., Hansson, U., and McCaffery, N. (2010) *The Troubles aren't history yet: Young people's understanding of the past*, Belfast: Community Relations Council.

Bell, J., Jarman, N., and Harvey, B. (2010) *Beyond Belfast: Contested spaces in urban, rural and cross border settings*, Belfast: Community Relations Council and Rural Community Networks.

Benson, P. and Fischer, E.F. (2009) 'Neoliberal violence: Social suffering in Guatemala's postwar era', in W.E. Little and T.J. Smith (eds) *Mayas in postwar Guatemala: 'Harvest of Violence' revisited*, Tuscaloosa: The University of Alabama Press.

Beyers, M. (2009) 'Pandora's Box? Engaging with our pasts: Initial explorations from the victims sector and republican community', *Shared Space*, 8: 49–65.

Bhandar, B. (2007) '"Spatializing history" and opening time: Resisting the reproduction of the proper subject', in S. Veitch (ed.) *Law and the Politics of Reconciliation* Aldershot: Ashgate Publishing.

Biko, H. (2013) *The great African society: A plan for a nation gone astray*. Johannesburg: Jonathan Ball Publishers.

Birch, T. (2007) ' "The invisible fire": Indigenous sovereignty, history and responsibility', in A. Moreton-Robinson (ed.) *Sovereign subjects: Indigenous sovereignty matters*, Crows Nest: Allen and Unwin.

Bollens, S.A. (2013) 'Urban planning and policy', in R. Mac Ginty (ed.) *The Routledge handbook of peacebuilding*, Abingdon: Routledge.

Bond, P. (2005) *Elite transition: From apartheid to neoliberalism in South Africa*. 2nd edition. Scottsville: University of KwaZulu-Natal Press.

Boraine, A. (2000) 'Truth and reconciliation in South Africa: The third way', in R.I. Rotberg and D. Thompson (eds) *Truth v. justice: The morality of truth commissions*, Princeton: Princeton University Press.

Borer, T.A. (2004) 'Reconciling South Africa or South Africans? Cautionary notes from the TRC', *African Studies Quarterly*, 8(1): 19–38.

Bradfield, S. (2004) 'Citizenship, history and Indigenous status in Australia: Back to the future, or toward treaty?' *Journal of Australian Studies*, 80: 165–76.

Bradfield, S. (2006) 'Separation or status-quo? Indigenous affairs from the birth of land rights to the death of ATSIC', *Australian Journal of Political History*, 52(1): 80–97.

Brahm, E. (2003) 'Conflict stages', in G. Burgess and H. Burgess (eds) *Beyond Intractability*, Boulder: Conflict Research Consortium, University of Colorado.

Brett, R. (2013) 'Peace stillborn? Guatemala's liberal peace and the indigenous movement', *Peacebuilding*, 1(2): 222–38.

Brewer, J. (2013) 'Sociology and peacebuilding', in R. Mac Ginty (ed.) *The Routledge handbook of peacebuilding*, Abingdon: Routledge.

Brown, S. and Magilindane, F. (2004) 'Economic transformation', in C. Villa-Vicencio and E. Doxtader (eds) *Pieces of the puzzle: Keywords on reconciliation and transitional justice*, Cape Town: Institute for Justice & Reconciliation.

Burrell, J.L. (2009) 'Intergenerational conflict in the postwar era', in W.E. Little and T.J. Smith (eds) *Mayas in postwar Guatemala: 'Harvest of Violence' revisited*, Tuscaloosa: The University of Alabama Press.

Byers, S. (2013) 'Republican youth and generational change in Northern Ireland', *Open Democracy*, available online at www.opendemocracy.net/ourkingdom/sean-byers/republican-youth-and-generational-change-in-northern-ireland

Byrne, J. (2012) 'Belfast and beyond: Local and international narratives of physical segregation', *Shared Space*, 12: 5–22.

Byrne, J., Gormley-Heenan, C. and Robinson, G. (2012) *Attitudes to peace walls: Research report to the Office of the First Minister and Deputy First Minister*, Belfast: Office of the First Minister and Deputy Frist Minister.

Byrne, J., Hansson, U., and Bell, J. (2006). *Shared living: Mixed residential communities in Northern Ireland*, Belfast: Institute for Conflict Research.

Byrne, J. and Monaghan, L. (2008) *Policing Loyalist and Republican communities: Understanding key issues for local communities and the PSNI*, Belfast: Institute for Conflict Research.

Campbell, S. and Peterson, J.H. (2013) 'Statebuilding' in R. Mac Ginty (ed.) *The Routledge handbook of peacebuilding*, Abingdon: Routledge.

Carmack, R. (2008) 'Perspectives on the politics of human rights in Guatemala', in P. Pitarch, S. Speed, and X.L. Solanoe (eds) *Human rights in the Maya region: Global politics, cultural contentions, and moral engagements*, Durham: Duke University Press.

Castan, M. (2000) 'Reconciliation, law and the Constitution', in M. Grattan (ed.) *Reconciliation: Essays on Australian reconciliation*, Melbourne: Black Inc.

Chakravarti, S. (2012) 'Agonism and the power of victim testimony', in A.K. Hirsch (ed.) *Theorizing post-conflict reconciliation*, London: Routledge.

Chan, J. (1997) *Changing police culture: Policing in a multicultural society*, Cambridge: Cambridge University Press.

Chapman, A.R. (2002) 'Truth commissions as instruments of forgiveness and reconciliation', in R.G. Helmick and R.L. Petersen (eds) *Forgiveness and reconciliation: Religion, public policy, and conflict transformation*, Conshohocken, PA: Templeton Foundation Press.

Christodoulidis, E. and Veitch, S. (2007) 'Introduction', in S. Veitch (ed.) *Law and the Politics of Reconciliation*, Aldershot: Ashgate Publishing.

Christodoulidis, E. and Veitch, S. (2008) 'Reconciliation as surrender: Configurations of responsibility and memory', in F. du Bois and A. du Bois-Pedain (eds) *Justice and reconciliation in post-apartheid South Africa*, New York: Cambridge University Press.

Clark, P. and Palmer, N. (2012) 'Challenging transitional justice', in N. Palmer, P. Clark, and D. Granville (eds) *Critical perspectives in transitional justice*, Cambridge: Intersentia Publishing.

Cole, E.A. (2007) 'Introduction: Reconciliation and history education', in E.A. Cole (ed.) *Teaching the violent past: History education and reconciliation*, New York: Rowman and Littlefield.

Community Relations Council (2008) *Towards sustainable security: Interface barriers and the legacy of segregation in Belfast*, Belfast: Community Relations Council.

Community Relations Council (2011) *Towards a shared society? Response to the consultation on the Programme for Cohesion, Sharing and Intergration*, Belfast: Community Relations Council.

Connolly, W.E. (1991) *Identity/Difference: Democratic negotiations of political paradox*, Minneapolis: University of Minnesota Press.

Cooper, D. (2005) 'Escaping from the shadowland: Campaigning for indigenous justice in Australia', *Indigenous Law Bulletin*, 6(10): 15–17.

Cornwall, A. (2009) *Restoring identity: The final report of the Moving Forward consultation project*. Revised edition. Sydney: Public Interest Advocacy Centre.

Coulter, C. and Murray, M. (2008) 'Introduction', in C. Coulter and M. Murray (eds) *Northern Ireland after the troubles: A society in transition*, Manchester: Manchester University Press.

Council for Aboriginal Reconciliation (2000) *Reconciliation – Australia's challenge*, Final Report of the Council for Aboriginal Reconciliation to the Prime Minister and the Commonwealth Parliament, Canberra, December: Commonwealth of Australia.

Crocker, D.A. (2000) 'Truth commissions, transitional justice, and civil society', in R.I. Rotberg and D. Thompson (eds) *Truth v. justice: The morality of truth commissions,* Princeton: Princeton University Press.

Crosby, A. and Lykes, M.B. (2011) 'Mayan women survivors speak: The gendered relations of truth telling in postwar Guatemala', *The International Journal of Transitional Justice*, 5(3): 456–76.

Cubitt, C. (2013) 'Constructing civil society: An intervention for building peace?' *Peacebuilding*, 1(1): 91–108.

Daly, E. and Sarkin, J. (2007) *Reconciliation in divided societies: Finding common ground*. Philadelphia: University of Pennsylvania Press.

del Valle Escalante, E. (2009) *Maya nationalisms and postcolonial challenges in Guatemala*, Sante Fe: School for Advanced Research Press.

Deloitte (2007) *Research into the financial cost of the Northern Ireland divide*, Belfast: Deloitte.

Department of Justice And Constitutional Development (2012) *Discussion document on the transformation of the judicial system and the role of the judiciary in the developmental South African state*, Johannesburg: Department of Justice and Constitutional Development.

Dessel, A. and Rogge, M.E. (2008) 'Evaluation of intergroup dialogue: A review of the empirical literature', *Conflict Resolution Quarterly*, 26(2): 199–238.

Dodson, M. (2003) 'The end in the beginning: Re(de)finding Aboriginality', in M. Grossman (ed.) *Blacklines: Contemporary Critical Writing by Indigenous Australians*, Carlton: Melbourne University Press.

Dodson, P. (1997) 'Reconciliation in crisis', in G. Yunupingu (ed.) *Our land is our life: Land rights—past present and future*, St Lucia: University of Queensland Press.

Dodson, P. (2000) *Beyond the Mourning Gate: Dealing with Unfinished Business*. The Wentworth Lecture 12 May 2000, National Gallery of Australia: AIATSIS.

Dodson, P. (2008) 'Reconciliation', in R. Manne (ed.) *Dear Mr Rudd: Ideas for a better Australia*, Melbourne: Black Inc.

Donnelly, C. and Hughes, J. (2009) 'Contact and culture: Mechanisms of reconciliation in schools in Northern Ireland and Israel', in J.R. Quinn (ed.) *Reconciliation(s): Transnational justice in postconflict societies*, Montreal: McGill-Queen's University Press.

Donnelly, K. and Wiltshire, K. (2014) *Review of the Australian curriculum: Final report*, Canberra: Australian Government Department of Education.

Doxtader, E. (2004) 'Reparation', in C. Villa-Vicencio and E. Doxtader (eds) *Pieces of the puzzle: Keywords on reconciliation and transitional justice*, Cape Town: Institute for Justice & Reconciliation.

Doxtader, E. (2012) 'A critique of law's violence yet (never) to come: United Nations' transitional justice policy and the (fore)closure of reconciliatio', in A.K. Hirsch (ed.) *Theorizing post-conflict reconciliation*, London: Routledge.

Doxtader, E. and du Toit, F. (2010) 'Introduction', in F. du Toit and E. Doxtader (eds) *In the balance: South Africans debate reconciliation*, Johannesburg: Jacana Media.

du Toit, A. (2000) 'The moral foundations of the South African TRC: Truth as acknowledgment and justice as recognition', in R.I. Rotberg and D. Thompson (eds) *Truth v. justice: The morality of truth commissions*, Princeton: Princeton University Press.

du Toit, S.F. (2009) 'Tensions between human rights and the politics of reconciliation: A South African case study', in J.R. Quinn (ed.) *Reconciliation(s): Transnational justice in postconflict societies*, Montreal: McGill-Queen's University Press.

Duggan, J. (2012) 'What's in a (street) name?' *The Archival Platform*, 24 February, available online at www.archivalplatform.org/blog/entry/whats_in_a_street_name/

Duplooy, E., Henkeman, S., and Nyoka, A. (2014) 'Reconciliation for South Africa's education system', *Lifelong Learning in Europe*, (2), available online at www.lline.fi/en/article/policy/622014/reconciliation-for-south-africa-s-education-system#title1

Edwards, A. and Bloomer, S. (eds) (2008) *Transforming the peace process in Northern Ireland: From terrorism to democratic politics*, Dublin: Irish Academic Press.

Eisikovits, N. (2010) *Sympathizing with the enemy: Reconciliation, transitional justice, negotiation*, Dordrecht: Martinus Nijhoff Publishers.

Escobar, O. (2011) *Public dialogue and deliberation: A communication perspective for public engagement practitioners*, Edinburgh: Edinburgh Beltane.

Essof, S. and Moshenberg, D. (2011) 'Introduction: Searching for South Africa', in S. Essof and D. Moshenberg (eds) *Searching for South Africa: The new calculus of dignity*, Pretoria: Unisa Press.

Etchart, J. (2011) 'Loyalism and peacebuilding in the 2000s', in M. Power (ed.) *Building peace in Northern Ireland*, Liverpool: Liverpool University Press.

Expert Panel on Constitutional Recognition of Indigenous Australians (2012) *Recognising Aboriginal and Torres Strait Islander Peoples in the Constitution: Report of the Expert Panel*, Canberra: Department of Families, Housing, Community Services and Indigenous Affairs.

Fairweather, J.G. (2006) *A common hunger: Land rights in Canada and South Africa*, Calgary: University of Calgary Press.

Finnane, M. (1994) *Police and government: Histories of policing in Australia*, Melbourne: Oxford University Press.

Forde, F. (2014) *Still an inconvenient youth: Julius Malema carries on*, Johannesburg: Picador Africa.

Forsberg, T. (2003) 'The philosophy and practice of dealing with the past: Some conceptual and normative issues', in N. Biggar (ed.) *Burying the past: Making peace and doing justice after civil conflict*, Washington DC: Georgetown University Press.

Frayling, N. (2009) 'Towards the healing of history: An exploration of the relationship between pardon and peace', in J.R. Quinn (ed.) *Reconciliation(s): Transnational justice in postconflict societies*, Montreal: McGill-Queen's University Press.

Fredericks, B., Leitch, A., and Barty, R. (2008) ' "Big mobs in the city now": The increasing number of Aboriginal and Torres Strait Islander people living in urban areas', paper presented at the World Indigenous Peoples' Conference on Education, Melbourne.

Freire, P. (1998) *Teachers as cultural workers: Letters to those who dare teach*, Boulder: Westview Press.

Friedman, S. and McKaiser, E. (2009) *Civil society and the post-Polokwane South African state: Assessing civil society's prospects of improved policy engagement*, Johannesburg: Centre for the Study of Democracy, Rhodes University/University of Johannesburg.

Fullard, M. and Rousseau, N. (2009) *Truth-telling, identities and power in South Africa and Guatemala*, New York: International Center for Transitional Justice.

Gallagher, T. (2013) 'Education for shared societies', in M. Fitzduff (ed.) *Public policies in shared societies: A comparative approach*, Basingstoke: Palgrave Macmillan.

Galtung, J. (1969) 'Violence, peace, and peace research', *Journal of Peace Research*, 6(3): 167–91.

Galtung, J. (1990) 'Cultural violence', *Journal of Peace Research*, 27(3): 291–305.

Ganesh, S. and Zoller, H.M. (2012) 'Dialogue, activism, and democratic social change', *Communication Theory*, 22: 66–91.

Gibson, J.L. (2004) *Overcoming apartheid: Can truth reconcile a divided nation?* Cape Town: HSRC Press.

Gilbert, K. (1988) *Aboriginal sovereignty: Justice, the law and the land*, Canberra: Self-published.

Gilbert, K. (2002 [1973]) *Because a white man'll never do it*, Sydney: A+R Classics, Harper Collins Publishers.

Gill, H. (2012) 'More isn't always better: The controversy of increased access to education in Guatemala', *Prospect Journal*, 9 April, available online at http://prospectjournal.org/2012/04/09/more-isnt-always-better-the-controversy-of-increased-access-to-education-in-guatemala/

Gobodo-Madikizela, P. (2010) 'Reconciliation: A call to reparative humanism', in F. du Toit and E. Doxtader (eds) *In the balance: South Africans debate reconciliation*, Johannesburg: Jacana Media.

Goot, M. and Rowse, T. (2007) *Divided nation? Indigenous affairs and the imagined public*, Melbourne: Melbourne University Publishing.

Govier, T. (2009) 'A dialectic of acknowledgment', in J.R. Quinn (ed.) *Reconciliation(s): Transnational justice in postconflict societies*, Montreal: McGill-Queen's University Press.

Grattan, M. (2000) 'Introduction', *Reconciliation: Essays on Australian reconciliation*, Melbourne: Black Inc.

Guelke, A. (2012) *Politics in deeply divided societies*, Cambridge: Polity Press.

Gunstone, A. (2009) *Unfinished business: The Australian formal reconciliation process*. 2nd edition. Melbourne: Australian Scholarly Publishing.

Gutman, A. and Thompson, D. (2000) 'The moral foundations of truth commissions', in R.I. Rotberg and D. Thompson (eds) *Truth v. justice: The morality of truth commissions*, Princeton: Princeton University Press.

Hadden, T. (2013) 'Policing for shared societies: An institutional approach to reform', in M. Fitzduff (ed.) *Public policies in shared societies: A comparative approach*, Basingstoke: Palgrave Macmillan.

Hamber, B. (2010) 'Masculinity and transition: Crisis or confusion in South Africa?' *Journal of Peacebuilding and Development*, 5(3): 75–88.

Hamber, B. (2012) 'Transitional justice and intergroup conflict', in L.R. Tropp (ed.) *The Oxford handbook of intergroup conflict*, New York: Oxford University Press.

Hamber, B. and Kelly, G. (2005) *A place for reconciliation? Conflict and locality in Northern Ireland*, Belfast: Democratic Dialogue.

Hamber, B. and Kelly, G. (2009) 'Beyond coexistence: Towards a working definition of reconciliation', in J.R. Quinn (ed.) *Reconciliation(s): Transnational justice in postconflict societies*. Montreal: McGill-Queen's University Press.

Hammet, D. (2010) 'Ongoing contestations: The use of racial signifiers in post-apartheid South Africa', *Social Identities*, 16(2): 247–60.

Hammond-Callaghan, M. (2011) ' "Peace Women", gender and peacebuilding in Northern Ireland: From reconciliation and political inclusion to human rights and human security', in M. Power (ed.) *Building peace in Northern Ireland*, Liverpool: Liverpool University Press.

Hancock, L.E. (2012) 'Belfast's interfaces, zones of conflict or zones of peace', in C.R. Mitchell and L.E. Hancock (eds) *Local peacebuilding and national peace: Interaction between grassroots and elite processes*, London: Continuum.

Hayes, B.C. and McAllister, I. (2013) 'Gender and consociational power-sharing in Northern Ireland', *International Political Science Review*, 34(2): 123–39.

Hercus, L. and Simpson, J. (2002) 'Indigenous placenames: An introduction', in L. Hercus, F. Hodges and J. Simpson (eds) *The land is a map: Placenames of indigenous origin in Australia*, Canberra: Pandanus Books for Pacific Linguistics.

Hetherington, M. (2008) 'The role of Towards Understanding and Healing', in L. O'Hagan (ed.) *Stories in conflict: Towards understanding and healing*, Derry: Yes! Publications.

Hinton, A.L. (2010) 'Introduction: Towards an anthropology of transitional justice', in A.L. Hinton (ed.) *Transitional justice: Global mechanisms and local realities after genocide and mass violence*, New Brunswick: Rutgers University Press.

Hirsch, A.K. (2012) 'Fugitive reconciliation', in A.K. Hirsch (ed.) *Theorizing post-conflict reconciliation*, London: Routledge.

Hirsch, A.K. (2012) 'Introduction: The Agon of reconciliation', in A.K. Hirsch (ed.) *Theorizing post-conflict reconciliation*, London: Routledge.

Holkeboer, M. and Villa-Vicencio, C. (2004) 'Rights and reconciliation', in C. Villa-Vicencio and E. Doxtader (eds) *Pieces of the puzzle: Keywords on reconciliation and transitional justice*, Cape Town: Institute for Justice & Reconciliation.

Houston, K. (2012) 'A shared future or a civic future? Speaking truth to power-sharing', *Shared Space*, 12: 23–40.

Hovland, I. (2003) 'Macro/micro dynamics in South Africa: Why the reconciliation process will not reduce violence', *Journal of Peacebuilding and Development*, 1(2): 6–20.

Huda, Q. and Marshall, K. (2013) 'Religion and peacebuilding', in C. Zelizer (ed.) *Integrated peacebuilding: Innovative approaches to transforming conflict*, Boulder: Westview Press.

Hutchison, E. and Bleiker, R. (2013) 'Reconciliation', in R. Mac Ginty (ed.) *The Routledge handbook of peacebuilding*, Abington: Routledge.

Institute for Justice and Reconciliation (2006) *Community healing: A resource guide*, Cape Town: Institute for Justice and Reconciliation.

International Center for Transitional Justice (2012) *Strengthening Indigenous rights through truth commissions: A practitioner's resource*, New York: International Center for Transitional Justice.

Irlam, S. (2004) 'Unraveling the rainbow: The remission of nation in post-apartheid literature', *South Atlantic Quarterly*, 103(4): 695–718.

Isaacs, A. (2009) 'Truth and the challenge of reconciliation in Guatemala', in J.R. Quinn (ed.) *Reconciliation(s): Transnational justice in postconflict societies*, Montreal: McGill-Queen's University Press.

James, M.R. (1999) 'Critical intercultural dialogue', *Polity*, 31(4): 587–607.

Jarman, N., Bell, J., and Rallings, M. (2009) 'Dialogue or disengagement? Responding to disputes over parades', *Shared Space*, 8: 17–29.

Jonas, S. (2000) *Of centaurs and doves: Guatemala's peace process*, Boulder: Westview Press.

Jung, C. (2011) 'Canada and the legacy of the Indian residential schools: Transitional justice for indigenous people in a nontransitional society', in P. Arthur (ed.) *Identities in transition: Challenges for transitional justice in divided societies*, New York: Cambridge University Press.

Kelly, G. (2012) *Progressing good relations and reconciliation in post-agreement Northern Ireland*, Derry: University of Ulster.

Kiss, E. (2000) 'Moral ambitions with and beyond political constraints: Reflections on restorative justice', in: R.I. Rotberg and D. Thompson (eds) *Truth v. justice: The moraility of truth commissions*, Princeton: Princeton University Press.

Knox, C. (2011) 'Tackling racism in Northern Ireland: "The race hate capital of Europe"', *Journal of Political Science*, 40(2): 387–412.

Knox, C. (2014) 'Northern Ireland: where is the peace dividend?' *Policy and Politics*, fast track article, available online at www.ingentaconnect.com/content/tpp/pap/pre-prints/content-PP_052

Kollapen, J. (2010) 'Reconciliation: Engaging with our fears and expectations', in F. du Toit and E. Doxtader (eds) *In the balance: South Africans debate reconciliation*, Johannesburg: Jacana Media.

Krog, A. (1998) *Country of my skull: Guilt, sorrow, and the limits of forgiveness in the new South Africa*, New York: Three Rivers Press.

Krüger, C. (2006) 'Spiral of growth: A social psychiatric perspective on conflict resolution, reconciliation, and relationship development', in N.N. Potter (ed.) *Trauma, truth and reconciliation: Healing damaged relationships*, Oxford: Oxford University Press.

Kuperus, T. (2000) 'Building a pluralist democracy: An examination of religious associations in South Africa and Zimbabwe', in W.E. Van Vugt and G.D. Cloete (eds) *Race and reconciliation in South Africa: A multicultural dialogue in comparative perspective*, Lanham: Lexington Books.

Kwenda, C.V. (2003) 'Cultural justice: The pathway to reconciliation and social cohesion' in D. Chidester, P. Dexter, and W. James (eds) *What holds us together: Social cohesion in South Africa*, Cape Town: Human Sciences Research Council Press.

Lederach, J.P. (2005) *The moral imagination: The art and soul of building peace*, New York: Oxford University Press.

Leebaw, B.A. (2008) 'The irreconcilable goals of transitional justice', *Human Rights Quarterly*, 30(1): 95–118.

Lefko-Everett K., Nyoka, A., and Tiscornia, L. (2011) *SA Reconciliation Barometer Survey: 2011 Report*, Cape Town: Institute for Justice and Reconciliation.

Lijphart, A. (1969) 'Consociational democracy', *World Politics*, 21(2): 207–25.

Little, A. (2007) 'Between disagreement and consensus: Unravelling the democratic paradox', *Australian Journal of Political Science*, 42(1): 143–59.

Little, A. (2009) 'The Northern Ireland paradox', in A. Little and M. Lloyd (eds) *The politics of radical democracy*, Edinburgh: Edinburgh University Press.

Little, A. (2012a) 'Disjunctured narratives: Rethinking reconciliation and conflict transformation', *International Political Science Review*, 33(1): 82–98.

Little, A. (2012b) 'Rhetorics of reconciliation: Shifting conflict paradigms in Northern Ireland', in A.K. Hirsch (ed.) *Theorizing post-conflict reconciliation*, London: Routledge.

Little, A. (2014) *Enduring conflict: Challenging the signature of peace and democracy*, New York: Bloomsbury Publishing.

Little, W.E. (2009) 'Introduction', in W.E. Little and T.J. Smith (eds) *Mayas in postwar Guatemala: 'Harvest of Violence' revisited*, Tuscaloosa: The University of Alabama Press.

Lundy, P. (2009) 'Exploring home-grown transitional justice and its dilemmas: A case study of the Historical Enquiries Team, Northern Ireland', *International Journal of Transitional Justice*, 3(3): 321–40.

Lundy, P. and McGovern, M. (2008) 'Telling stories, facing truths: Memory, justice and post-conflict transition', in C. Coulter and M. Murray (eds) *Northern Ireland after the troubles: A society in transition*, Manchester: Manchester University Press.

Lynch, C. (2005) 'The Peace II programme in Northern Ireland and the border counties: A 'distinctive' development programme?' *Journal of Peacebuilding and Development*, 2(2): 59–76.

Mac Ginty, R. (2013) 'Introduction', in R. Mac Ginty (ed.) *The Routledge handbook of peacebuilding*, Abingdon: Routledge.

Mac Ginty, R., Muldoon, O.T., and Ferguson, N. (2007) 'No war, no peace: Northern Ireland after the Agreement', *Political Psychology*, 28(1): 1–11.

MacDonald, M. (2006) *Why race matters in South Africa*. Scottsville: University of KwaZulu-Natal Press.

Mack, H. (2011) 'What is reconciliation?' in G. Grandin, D.T. Levenson, and E. Oglesby (eds) *The Guatemala reader: History, culture, politics*, Durham: Duke University Press.

Maddison, S. (2009) *Black politics: Inside the complexity of Aboriginal political culture*, Sydney: Allen & Unwin.

Maddison, S. (2011) *Beyond white guilt: The real challenge to black-white relations in Australia*, Sydney: Allen and Unwin.

Maddison, S. (2013) 'Indigenous identity, "authenticity" and the structural violence of settler colonialism', *Identities: Global Studies in Culture and Power*, 20(3): 288–303.

Maddison, S. (2014a) 'Missionary genocide: Moral illegitimacy and the churches in Australia', in J. Havea (ed.) *Indigenous Australia and the unfinished business of theology: Cross-cultural engagement*, available online at www.palgraveconnect.com/pc/doifinder/10.1057/9781137426673.0007

Maddison, S. (2014b) 'Relational transformation and agonistic dialogue in divided societies. *Political Studies*, early view online at http://onlinelibrary.wiley.com/doi/10.1111/1467-9248.12149/abstract

Maddison, S. and Shepherd, L.J. (2014) 'Peacebuilding and the postcolonial politics of transitional justice', *Peacebuilding*, 2(3): 253–69.

Magubane, B. (2000) 'Race and democratisation in South Africa: Some reflections', in Y. Muthien, M. Khosa and B. Magubane (eds) *Democracy and governance review: Mandela's legacy 1994–1999*, Pretoria: Human Sciences Research Council.

Manne, R. (2001) 'In denial: The stolen generations and the right', *Quarterly Essay*, 1.

Mansell, M. (2003) 'Citizenship, assimilation and a treaty', in H. McGlade (ed.) *Treaty – let's get it right!* Canberra: Aboriginal Studies Press.

Mansell, M. (2005) 'Why Norfolk Island but not Aborigines', in B.A. Hocking (ed.) *Unfinished Constitutional Business*, Canberra: Aboriginal Studies Press.

Mattes, R. (2012) 'The "Born Frees": The prospects for generational change in post-apartheid South Africa', *Australian Journal of Political Science*, 47(1): 133–53.

Maxwell, J.M. (2009) 'Bilingual bicultural education: Best intentions across a cultural divide', in W.E. Little and T.J. Smith (eds) *Mayas in postwar Guatemala: 'Harvest of Violence' revisited*, Tuscaloosa: The University of Alabama Press.

Maybury-Lewis, D. (2003) 'From elimination to an uncertain future: changing policies towards Indigenous peoples', in B. Dean and J.M. Levi (eds) *At the risk of being heard: identity, rights and postcolonial states*, Ann Arbor: University of Michigan Press.

Mbeki, T. (2010) 'Reconciliation in South Africa', in: F. du Toit and E. Doxtader (eds) *In the balance: South Africans debate reconciliation*, Johannesburg: Jacana Media.

Mbembe, A. (2008) 'Passages to freedom: The politics of racial reconciliation in South Africa', *Public Culture*, 20(1): 5–18.

McCaughey, T. (2003) 'Northern Ireland: Burying the hatchet, not the past', in N. Biggar (ed.) *Burying the past: Making peace and doing justice after civil conflict*, Washington DC: Georgetown University Press.

McGregor, L. (2007) 'Reconciliation: Where is the law?' in S. Veitch (ed.) *Law and the Politics of Reconciliation*, Aldershot: Ashgate Publishing Ltd.

McGregor, R. (2011) *Indifferent inclusion: Aboriginal people and the Australian nation*, Canberra: Aboriginal Studies Press.

Meiring, P. (2000) 'Truth and reconciliation: The South African experience', in W.E. Van Vugt and G.D. Cloete (eds) *Race and reconciliation in South Africa: A multicultural dialogue in comparative perspective*, Lanham: Lexington Books.

Miller, Z. (2008) 'Effects of invisibility: In search of the "economic" in transitional justice', *The International Journal of Transitional Justice*, 2: 266–91.

Minow, M. (1998) *Between vengeance and forgiveness: Facing history after genocide and mass violence*, Boston: Beacon Press.

Minow, M. (2000) 'The hope for healing: What can truth commissions do?' in R.I. Rotberg and D. Thompson (eds) *Truth v. justice: The morality of truth commissions*, Princeton: Princeton University Press.

Mitchell, A. (2011) *Lost in transformation: Violent peace and peaceful conflict in Northern Ireland*, Basingstoke: Palgrave Macmillan.

Moore, A.S. (2007) *Meeting EFA: Guatemala PRONADE*, Washington DC: EQUIP2 USAID.

Morgan, G. (2006) *Unsettled places: Aboriginal people and urbanisation in New South Wales*, Kent Town: Wakefield Press.

Mouffe, C. (2000) *The democratic paradox*, London: Verso.

Mouffe, C. (2005) *On the political*, London: Routledge.

Mouffe, C. (2007) 'Democracy as agonistic pluralism', in E.D. Ermath (ed.) *Rewriting democracy: Cultural politics in postmodernity*, Aldershot: Ashgate.

Mudrooroo (1995) *Us mob: history, culture, struggle. An introduction to Indigenous Australia*, Sydney: Harper Collins Publishers.

Muldoon, P. (2008) '"The very basis of civility": On agonism, conquest and reconciliation', in W. Kymlicka (ed.) *The politics of reconciliation in multicultural societies*, Oxford; New York: Oxford University Press.

Muldoon, P. and Schaap, A. (2012) 'Confounded by recognition: The apology, the High Court and the Aboriginal Embassy in Australia', in A.K. Hirsch (ed.) *Theorizing post-conflict reconciliation*, London: Routledge.

Mulgan, R. (1998) 'Citizenship and legitimacy in post-colonial Australia', in N. Peterson and W. Sanders (eds) *Citizenship and Indigenous Australians: Changing Conceptions and Possibilities*, Melbourne: Cambridge University Press.

Muthien, Y., Khosa, M., and Magubane, B. (2000) 'Consolidating democracy and governance in South Africa', in Y. Muthien, M. Khosa, and B. Magubane (eds) *Democracy and governance review: Mandela's legacy 1994–1999*, Pretoria: Human Sciences Research Council.

Muvingi, I. (2009) 'Sitting on powder kegs: Socioeconomic rights in transitional societies', *The International Journal of Transitional Justice*, 3(2): 163–82.

Nadler, A. (2012) 'Intergroup reconciliation: Definitions, processes, and future directions' in L.R. Tropp (ed.) *The Oxford handbook of intergroup conflict*, New York: Oxford University Press.

Nagda, B.A., Yeakley, A., Gurin, P., and Sorenson, N. (2012) 'Intergroup dialogue: A critical-dialogic model for conflict engagement', in L.R. Tropp (ed.) *The Oxford handbook of intergroup conflict*, New York: Oxford University Press.

Nelson, D.M. (2009) *Reckoning: The ends of war in Guatemala*, Durham: Duke University Press.

No

Newham, G. (2005) 'Strengthening democratic policing in South Africa through internal systems for officer control', *South African Review of Sociology*, 36(2): 160–177.

Newspoll, Saulwick and Muller, and Mackay, H. (2000) 'Public opinion on reconciliation: Snap shot, close focus, long lens', in M. Grattan (ed.) *Reconciliation: Essays on Australian reconciliation*, Melbourne: Black Inc.

Nolan, P. (2012) *Northern Ireland peace monitoring report. 1.* Belfast: Community Relations Council.

Nolan, P. (2014) *Northern Ireland peace monitoring report. 3.* Belfast: Community Relations Council.

Noma, E., Aker, D., and Freeman, J. (2012) 'Heeding women's voices: Breaking cycles of conflict and deepening the concept of peacebuilding', *Journal of Peacebuilding and Development*, 7(1): 7–23.

Ntsebeza, L. (2010) 'Reconciliation and the land question', in F. du Toit and E. Doxtader (eds) *In the balance: South Africans debate reconciliation*, Johannesburg: Jacana Media.

Ntsebeza, L. (2011) 'The land question: Exploring obstacles to land redistribution in South Africa', in I. Shapiro and K. Tebeau (eds) *After apartheid: Reinventing South Africa*, Charlottesville: University of Virginia Press.

O'Rawe, M. (2008) 'Policing change: To reform or not to transform?' in C. Coulter and M. Murray (eds) *Northern Ireland after the troubles: A society in transition*, Manchester: Manchester University Press.

O'Reilly, M. (2013) 'Gender and peacebuilding' in R. Mac Ginty (ed.) *The Routledge handbook of peacebuilding*, Abingdon: Routledge.

Peters-Little, F. (2000) *The community game: Aboriginal self definition at the local level*, Canberra: Australian Institute for Aboriginal and Torres Strait Islander Studies.

Peterson, N. and Sanders, W. (1998) 'Introduction', in N. Peterson and W. Sanders (eds) *Citizenship and Indigenous Australians: Changing Conceptions and Possibilities*. Melbourne: Cambridge University Press.

Phillips, M. (2005) 'Aboriginal reconciliation as religious politics: Secularisation in Australia', *Australian Journal of Political Science*, 40(1): 111–24.

Philpot-Munson, J.J. (2009) 'Peace under fire: Understanding evangelical resistance to the peace process in a postwar Guatemalan town', in W.E. Little and T.J. Smith (eds) *Mayas in postwar Guatemala: 'Harvest of Violence' revisited*, Tuscaloosa: The University of Alabama Press.

Philpott, D. (ed.) (2006) *The politics of past evil: Religion, reconciliation, and the dilemmas of transitional justice*, Notre Dame: University of Notre Dame Press.

Potter, N.N. (2006) 'Introduction', in N.N. Potter (ed.) *Trauma, truth and reconciliation: Healing damaged relationships*, Oxford: Oxford University Press.

Powell, D. (2010) 'The role of constitution making and institution building in furthering peace, justice and development: South Africa's democratic transition', *The International Journal of Transitional Justice*, 4: 230–50.

Power, M. (ed.) (2011) *Building peace in Northern Ireland*, Liverpool: Liverpool University Press.

Prandi, M. (2013) 'Economics for shared societies' in M. Fitduff (ed.) *Public policies in shared societies: A comparative approach*, Basingstoke: Palgrave Macmillan.

Pratt, A. (2005) *Practising reconciliation? The politics of reconciliation in the Australian Parliament, 1991–2000*, Canberra: Parliament of Australia Parliamentary Library.

Quinn, J.R. (2009) 'Introduction', in J.R. Quinn (ed.) *Reconciliation(s): Transnational justice in postconflict societies*, Montreal: McGill-Queen's University Press.

Ramphele, M. (2008) *Laying ghosts to rest: Dilemmas of the transformation in South Africa*, Cape Town: Tafelberg.

Ramsbotham, O. (2010) *Transforming violent conflict: Radical disagreement, dialogue and survival*, London: Routledge.

Ramsbotham, O., Woodhouse, T., and Miall, H. (2011) *Contemporary conflict resolution*. 3rd edition. Cambridge: Polity Press.

Rauch, J. (2000) *Police reform and South Africa's transition*, Cape Town: Centre for the Study of Violence and Reconciliation, available online at http://csvr.org.za/docs/policing/policereformandsouth.pdf

Read, P. (2010) 'Reconciliation without history: State crime and state punishment in Chile and Australia', in F. Peters-Little, A. Curthoys, and J. Docker (eds) *Passionate histories: Myth, memory and Indigenous Australia, Aboriginal History Monograph 21*, Canberra: ANU E Press.

Reconciliation Australia (2012) *Australian Reconciliation Barometer 2012*. Canberra: Reconciliation Australia.

Recovery of Historical Memory Project (REMHI) (1999) *Guatemala: Never Again! The official report of the Human Rights Office, Archdiocese of Guatemala*, Maryknoll: Orbis Books.

Reilly, C.A. (2009) *Peace-building and development in Guatemala and Northern Ireland*, New York: Palgrave Macmillan.

Renner, J. (2012) 'A discourse theoretical approach to transitional justice ideals: Conceptualising "reconciliation" as an empty universal in times of political transition', in N. Palmer, P. Clark, and D. Granville (eds) *Critical perspectives in transitional justice*, Cambridge: Intersentia Publishing.

Reynolds, H. (1998) 'Sovereignty', in N. Peterson and W. Sanders (eds) *Citizenship and Indigenous Australians: Changing Conceptions and Possibilities*, Melbourne: Cambridge University Press.

Reynolds, H. (2013) *Forgotten war*, Sydney: New South Publishing.

Ridgeway, A. (2004) 'The underlying causes of the Redfern riots run throughout Australia', *Online Opinion*, 23 February, available online at www.onlineopinion.com.au/view.asp?article=1989

Rooney, E. (2006) 'Women's equality in Northern Ireland's transition: Intersectionality in theory and place', *Feminist Legal Studies*, 14(3): 353–75.

Roux, T. (2008) 'Land restitution and reconciliation in South Africa', in F. du Bois and A. du Bois-Pedain (eds) *Justice and reconciliation in post-apartheid South Africa*, New York: Cambridge University Press.

Rowse, T. (2000) 'Housing and colonial patronage, Alice Springs, 1920–65', in P. Read (ed.) *Settlement: A history of Australian Aboriginal housing*, Canberra: Aboriginal Studies Press.

Royal Commission into Aboriginal Deaths in Custody (1991) *National report. 1*, Canberra: Australian Government Publishing Service.

Rudd, K. (2008) *Apology to Australia's Indigenous peoples*, House of Representatives, Parliament House, Canberra, 13 February.

Ryan, S. (2013) 'The evolution of peacebuilding', in R. Mac Ginty (ed.) *The Routledge handbook of peacebuilding*, Abingdon: Routledge.

Sanders, W. (2005) 'Never even adequate: Reconciliation and Indigenous affairs', in C. Aulich and R. Wettenhall (eds) *Howard's second and third governments: Australian Commonwealth Administration 1998–2004*, Sydney: UNSW Press.

Sandole, D.J.D. (2010) *Peacebuilding*, Cambridge: Polity Press.

Sanford, V. (2003) *Buried secrets: Truth and human rights in Guatemala,* New York: Palgrave Macmillan.

Saul, J.S. and Bond, P. (2014) *South Africa, the present as history: From Mrs Ples to Mandela and Marikana,* Johannesburg: Jacana.

Saunders, H.H. (2001) *A public peace process: Sustained dialogue to transform racial and ethnic conflict,* New York: Palgrave.

Schaap, A. (2004) 'Political reconciliation through a struggle for recognition?' *Social and Legal Studies,* 13(4): 523–40.

Schaap, A. (2005) *Political reconciliation,* London: Routledge.

Schaap, A. (2006) 'Agonism in divided societies', *Philosophy & Social Criticism,* 32(2): 255–277.

Schaap, A. (2007) 'The time of reconciliation and the space of politics', in S. Veitch (ed.) *Law and the politics of reconciliation,* Aldershot: Ashgate Publishing Ltd.

Schaap, A. (2009) 'The absurd proposition of Aboriginal sovereignty', in A. Schaap (ed.) *Law and agonistic politics,* Farnham: Ashgate.

Schirch, L. (2008) 'Strategic peacebuilding: State of the field', *Peace Prints: South Asian Journal of Peacebuilding,* 1(1): 1–17.

Schuld, M. (2013) 'The prevalence of violence in post-conflict societies: A case study of Kwazulu-Natal, South Africa', *Journal of Peacebuilding and Development,* 8(1): 60–73.

Segal, L. and Cort, S. (2011) *One law, one nation: The making of the South African Constitution,* Johannesburg: Jacana Media.

Selim, Y. and Murithi, T. (2011) 'Transitional justice and development: Partners for sustainable peace in Africa?' *Journal of Peacebuilding and Development,* 6(2): 58–72.

Shirlow, P. (2008) 'Belfast: A segregated city', in C. Coulter and M. Murray (eds) *Northern Ireland after the troubles: A society in transition,* Manchester: Manchester University Press.

Short, D. (2005) 'Reconciliation and the problem of internal colonization', *Journal of Intercultural studies,* 26(3): 267–82.

Short, D. (2008) *Reconciliation and colonial power: Indigenous rights in Australia,* Aldershot: Ashgate.

Shriver, D.W. (2002a) 'Forgiveness: A bridge across abysses of revenge', in R.G. Helmick and R.L. Petersen (eds) *Forgiveness and reconciliation: Religion, public policy, and conflict transformation,* Conshohocken, PA: Templeton Foundation Press.

Shriver, D.W. (2002b) 'Where and when in political life is justice served by forgiveness?' in N. Biggar (ed.) *Burying the past: Making peace and doing justice after civil conflict,* Washington D.C.: Georgetown University Press.

Sieder, R. (2003) 'War, peace, and the politics of memory in Guatemala', in N. Biggar (ed.) *Burying the past: Making peace and doing justice after civil conflict,* Washington DC: Georgetown University Press.

Sieder, R. (2008) 'Legal globalization and human rights: Constructing the rule of law in postconflict Guatemala?' in P. Pitarch, S. Speed, and X.L. Solano (eds) *Human rights in the Maya region: Global politics, cultural contentions, and moral engagements,* Durham: Duke University Press.

Sieder, R. (2011) '"Emancipation" or "regulation"? Law, globalization and indigenous peoples' rights in post-war Guatemala', *Economy and Society,* 40(2): 239–65.

Sikkink, K. (2011) *The justice cascade: How human rights prosecutions are changing world politics*, New York: W.W. Norton and Company.

Simpson, G. (2000) *Rebuilding fractured societies: Reconstruction, reconciliation and the changing nature of violence- Some self-critical insights from post-apartheid South Africa*, Cape Town: Centre for the Study of Violence and Reconciliation.

Smithey, L.A. (2011) *Unionists, loyalists and conflict transformation in Northern Ireland*, New York: Oxford University Press.

Smyth, G. (2002) 'Brokenness, forgiveness, healing, and peace in Ireland', in R.G. Helmick and R.L. Petersen (eds) *Forgiveness and reconciliation: Religion, public policy, and conflict transformation*, Conshohocken, PA: Templeton Foundation Press.

South African National Planning Commission (2011) *Diagnostic overview*. Johannesburg: National Planning Commission.

Stanner, W.E.H. (2009) *The Dreaming and other essays*, Melbourne: Black Inc.

Staub, E. and Pearlman, L.A. (2002) 'Healing, reconciliation, and forgiveness', in R.G. Helmick and R.L. Petersen (eds) *Forgiveness and reconciliation: Religion, public policy, and conflict transformation*, Conshohocken, PA: Templeton Foundation Press.

Steering Committee for the Review of Government Service Provision (2014) *Overcoming Indigenous disadvantage: Key indicators 2014*, Canberra: Australian Government Productivity Commission.

Steyn, M. (2001) *Whiteness just isn't what it used to be: White identity in a changing South Africa*, Albany: State University of New York Press.

Stockley, T, (2013) 'Yirrkala celebrates 40 years of bilingual education', *Reconciliation Australia News*, available online at www.reconciliation.org.au/news/yirrkala-celebrates-40-years-of-bilingual-education/

Stokes, G. (2002) 'Australian democracy and Indigenous self-determination, 1901–2001', in G. Brennan and F.G. Castles (eds) *Australia reshaped: 200 years of institutional transformation*, Cambridge: Cambridge University Press.

Stolper, D. and Hammond, J. (2010) *2010 Reconciliation Barometer*, Sydney: Reconciliation Australia.

Suarez, J. and Jordan, M. (2007) *Three thousand and counting: A report on violence against women in Guatemala*, Washington D.C.: Guatemalan Human Rights Commission USA.

Terreblanche, S. (2012) *Lost in transformation: South Africa's search for a new future since 1986*, Johannesburg: KMM Review Publishing Company.

Thompson, L. (2001) *A history of South Africa*. 3rd edition. New Haven: Yale University Press.

Thornton, E. and Whitman, T. (2013) 'Gender and peacebuilding', in C. Zelizer (ed.) *Integrated peacebuilding: Innovative approaches to transforming conflict*, Boulder: Westview Press.

Tickner, R. (2001) *Taking a stand: Land rights to reconciliation*, Sydney: Allen & Unwin.

Tropp, L.R. (2012) 'Understanding and responding to intergroup conflict: Toward an integrated analysis', in L.R. Tropp (ed.) *The Oxford handbook of intergroup conflict*, New York: Oxford University Press.

Tully, J. (2000) 'The struggles of Indigenous peoples for and of freedom', in D. Ivison, P. Patton, and W. Sanders (eds) *Political theory and the rights of Indigenous peoples*, Cambridge: Cambridge University Press.

Tully, J. (2008) *Public Philosophy in a new key, Volume I, Democracy and Civic Freedom*, Cambridge: Cambridge University Press.

Tutu, D.M. (1999) *No future without forgiveness*, New York: Image Books.

UN Women (2012) *Women's participation in peace negotiations: Connections between presence and influence*, New York: United Nations Entity for Gender Equality and Empowerment of Women.

Van Der Westhuizen, C. (2010) 'Reconciliation in the shadow of "100% Zulu boy"', in F. du Toit and E. Doxtader (eds) *In the balance: South Africans debate reconciliation*, Johannesburg: Jacana Media.

Van Leeuwen, M. and Verkoren, W. (2012) 'Complexities and challenges for civil society building in post-conflict settings', *Journal of Peacebuilding and Development*, 7(1): 81–94.

Van Marle, K. (2007) 'Constitution as archive', in S. Veitch (ed.) *Law and the Politics of Reconciliation*, Aldershot: Ashgate Publishing Ltd.

Van Wyk, C. (2014) 'How fear compromises meaningful transformation', *IJR News*, 3 September, available online at http://ijr.org.za/news-and-events.php?nid=193&type=news

Venema, D. (2012) 'Transitions as states of exception: Towards a more general theory of transitional justice', in N. Palmer, P. Clark, and D. Granville (eds) *Critical perspectives in transitional justice*, Cambridge: Intersentia Publishing.

Verdeja, E. (2009) *Unchopping a tree: Reconciliation in the aftermath of political violence*, Philadelphia: Temple University Press.

Villa-Vicencio, C. (2003) 'Restorative justice in social context: The South African Truth and Reconciliation Commission', in N. Biggar (ed.) *Burying the past: Making peace and doing justice after civil conflict*, Washington DC: Georgetown University Press.

Villa-Vicencio, C. (2004) 'Reconciliation', in C. Villa-Vicencio and E. Doxtader (eds) *Pieces of the puzzle: Keywords on reconciliation and transitional justice*, Cape Town: Institute for Justice & Reconciliation.

Villa-Vicencio, C. (2009) *Walk with us and listen: Political reconciliation in Africa*, Washington DC: Georgetown University Press.

Villa-Vicencio, C. (2010) 'Reconciliation: A thing that won't go away', in F. du Toit and E. Doxtader (eds) *In the balance: South Africans debate reconciliation*, Auckland Park: Jacana Media.

Villa-Vicencio, C. and Doxtader, E., (eds) (2004) *Pieces of the puzzle: Keywords on reconciliation and transitional justice*. Cape Town: Institute for Justice & Reconciliation.

Villa-Vicencio, C. and Ngesi, S. (2003) 'South Africa: Beyond the "miracle"', in E. Doxtader and C. Villa-Vicencio (eds) *Through fire with water: The roots of division and the potential for reconciliation in Africa*, Cape Town: Institute for Justice and Reconciliation.

Villa-Vicencio, C. and Soko, M. (2012) *Conversations in transition: Leading South African voices*, Cape Town: New Africa Books.

Villa-Vicencio, C. and Verwoerd, W. (2000) 'Constructing a report: Writing up the "truth"', in R.I. Rotberg and D. Thompson (eds) *Truth v. justice: The morality of truth commissions*, Princeton: Princeton University Press.

Von Holdt, K. (2011) 'Overview – Insurgent citizenship and collective violence: Analysis of case studies', in K. Von Holdt, M. Langa, S. Molapo, N. Mogapi, K. Ngubeni, J. Dlamini, and A. Kirsten, (eds) *The smoke that calls: Insurgent citizenship*, *collective violence and the struggle for a place in the new South Africa*, Cape Town: Centre for the Study of Violence and Reconciliation.

Wale, K. (2013) *Confronting exclusion: Time for radical reconciliation. SA Reconciliation Barometer Survey: 2013 report*, Cape Town: Institute for Justice and Reconciliation.

Walsh, K.C. (2007) *Talking about race: Community dialogues and the politics of difference*, Chicago: The University of Chicago Press.

Watson, I. (2007) 'Settled and unsettled spaces: Are we free to roam?' in A. Moreton-Robinson, (ed.) *Sovereign subjects: Indigenous sovereignty matters*, Crows Nest: Allen and Unwin.

Wells, R.A. (2006) 'Northern Ireland: A study of friendship, forgiveness, and reconciliation' in D. Philpott (ed.) *The politics of past evil: Religion, reconciliation, and the dilemmas of transitional justice*, Notre Dame: University of Notre Dame Press.

Wessels, L. (2010) 'Good faith is not enough: We have to dialogue', in F. du Toit and E. Doxtader (eds) *In the balance: South Africans debate reconciliation*, Johannesburg: Jacana Media.

White, T.J. (2011) 'The role of civil society in promoting peace in Northern Ireland', in M. Power (ed.) *Building peace in Northern Ireland*, Liverpool: Liverpool University Press.

Wingenbach, E. (2011) *Institutionalizing agonistic democracy: Post-foundationalism and political liberalism*, Farnham: Ashgate.

Woolford, A. (2010) 'Genocide, affirmative repair, and the British Columbia Treaty Process', in A.L. Hinton (ed.) *Transitional justice: Global mechanisms and local realities after genocide and mass violence*, New Brunswick: Rutgers University Press.

Zachar, P. (2006) 'Reconciliation as compromise and the management of rage', in N.N. Potter (ed.) *Trauma, truth and reconciliation: Healing damaged relationships*, Oxford: Oxford University Press.

Zaum, D. (2013) 'International relations theory and peacebuilding' in R. Mac Ginty (ed.) *The Routledge handbook of peacebuilding*, Abingdon: Routledge.

Zelizer, C. (2013) 'The business of peacebuilding', in C. Zelizer (ed.) *Integrated peacebuilding: Innovative approaches to transforming conflict*, Boulder: Westview Press.

Zelizer, C. and Oliphant, V. (2013) 'Introduction to integrated peacebuilding', in C. Zelizer (ed.) *Integrated peacebuilding: Innovative approaches to transforming conflict*, Boulder: Westview Press.

Index